The evolution of group analysis

Edited by
Malcolm Pines

*Institute of Group Analysis (London)
and the Tavistock Clinic, London*

Routledge & Kegan Paul
London, Boston, Melbourne and Henley

First published in 1983
by Routledge & Kegan Paul plc
39 Store Street, London WC1E 7DD,
9 Park Street, Boston, Mass. 02108, USA,
296 Beaconsfield Parade, Middle Park,
Melbourne, 3206, Australia, and
Broadway House, Newtown Road,
Henley-on-Thames, Oxon RG9 1EN
Set in 10/12 Press Roman by
Columns, Reading, Berks
and printed in Great Britain by
The Thetford Press, Thetford, Norfolk

Library of Congress Cataloging in Publication Data

The evolution of group analysis.
(International library of group psychotherapy and
group process)
Bibliography: p.
Includes index.
1. Group psychoanalysis – Addresses, essays, lectures.
I. Pines, Malcolm. II. Series. [DNLM: 1. Psycho-
analytic therapy. 2. Psychotherapy, Group.
WM 460.6 E93]
RC 510.E93 1983   616.89'152   82-21561

ISBN 0-7100-9290-3

Contents

Contributors

M. L. J. Abercrombie, BSc, PhD
Biologist by training, worked on perception and reasoning with medical students at University College, London (*The Anatomy of Judgement*, 1960). Founder member of the Group Analytic Society, London, of which she is currently President. Other publications include (1970) *Aims and Techniques of Group Teaching*, Guildford, Society for Research into Higher Education. Co-editor of Penguin New Biology Series, co-author *Penguin Dictionary of Biology*.

Professor Wilfred Abse, BSc, MD, FAPA, FRC Psych, DPM, FBPSS
University of Virginia, Director of Psychiatric Education, St Albans Hospital, Radford, Virginia 24143. Professor Abse is a psychoanalyst and group analyst and his publications include *Speech and Reason* (1971) and *Hysteria and Related Mental Disorders* (1966).

Professor E. James Anthony, MD, FRCPsych, DPM, AGPA
Psychoanalyst and group analyst, author of numerous publications in the field of adult, adolescent and child analysis. Co-author with S. H. Foulkes of *Group Psychotherapy: The Psychoanalytic Approach* (1957). Honorary and Founder Member of the Group Analytic Society, London.

Barbara Dick, MB, CHB, DPM
Former Consultant Psychiatrist with special interest in psychotherapy in the National Health Service, now in private practice as an analyst. Member of the Group Analytic Society, London.

Helen E. Durkin, PhD
Faculty and Senior Supervisor and Training Analyst at the Post Graduate

viii   *Contributors*

Center for Mental Health, New York. Honorary Member of the Group Analytic Society (London). Honorary Fellow AGPA and member of the Board of Directors. Permanent Fellow of the American Ortho-Psychiatric Association. Member of the New York Academy of Science. Publications include *The Group in Depth* (1974).

Dr John Evans, BSc, MB, BCH, MRCP, FRC Psych
Director of the Young Peoples Unit, Royal Edinburgh Hospital, Edinburgh. Chairman of the Analytical Psychotherapy Training Committee, Scottish Institute of Human Relations. Editor of the journal *Adolescence* 1975 onwards, author of *Adolescent and Pre-Adolescent Psychiatry* (1982).

Professor Romano Fiumara
Associate Professor of Medical Psychology, University of Rome. Member of the International Association of Analytical Psychology. Member of the Group Analytic Society (London). Founder Member of the Italian Society of Biological Psychiatry.

Professor David R. Hawkins
Director, Consultant-Liaison Service, Michael Reese Hospital and Medical Center, Chicago, Illinois. Professor of Psychiatry, Pritzker School of Medicine, University of Chicago. Former Professor of Psychiatry, University of North Carolina. Former Professor and Chairman, Department of Psychiatry, University of Virginia.

H. J. Home, MA
Psychoanalyst and group analyst. Founder Member of the Institute of Group Analysis (London). Honorary Member of Group Analytic Society (London).

Professor Ernest H. Hutten, PhD, FRSA
Emeritus Professor of Theoretical Physics, University of London. A former pupil of Albert Einstein. Professor Hutten had a close personal relationship with S. H. Foulkes and has a keen interest in the theory of psychoanalysis and group analysis. Among his publications are *The Origins of Science* (1956), *Creative Science: Einstein and Freud* (1976) and *Psychoanalysis as Science* (to be published).

Professor Michel Laxenaire
Professor at the Faculty of Medicine, University of Nancy; Chief of the Medical Psychological Service of the Hospital Jeanne d'Arc.

Professor M. Rita M. Leal, MA, PhD
Professor of Clinical Psychology, University of Lisbon. Member of the
Group Analytic Society (London).

Dr T. F. Main, MD, FRCPsych, FRANZCP, DPM
Member of British Psychoanalytical Society; President Institute of
Psychosexual Medicine. Former Medical Director at the Cassel Hospital.
Honorary Member of Group Analytic Society (London).

Dr P. B. de Mare, MRCPsych, DPM
Former Consultant Psychotherapist, St Georges Hospital, London,
Halliwick Hospital. Founder Member of Group Analytic Society
(London); Member of the Institute of Group Analysis (London). Dr de
Mare was one of the S. H. Foulkes's earliest collaborators and is the
author of *Perspectives in Group Psychotherapy* (1972). Dr de Mare is a
former President and Honorary Member of the Group Analytic Society.

Helle Munro, CANDPsych
University of Copenhagen. Diploma of Psychology, London ABPSS.
Member of the Group Analytic Society (London).

Dr Malcolm Pines, MB, CHB, FRCP, FRCPsych, DPM
Consultant Psychotherapist, Tavistock Clinic, London. Former Consult-
ant Psychotherapist Maudsley and Cassel Hospitals, London. President
of the International Association of Group Psychotherapy (1980-83).
A psychoanalyst and group analyst, Dr Pines was a collaborator with
S. H. Foulkes and is a former President of the Group Analytic Society
(London), Chairman of the Training Committee of the Institute of
Group Analysis, London.

Dr F. Rof Carballo
Member Real Academia Nationale de Medicina, Spain. Honorary
Member of Real Academia Medicina Valladolid; Founder Institute of
Psychosomatic Medicine, Madrid, Institutio de Ciencias del Hombre,
Madrid. Author of many books on medicine, psychosomatic medicine
and psychoanalysis.

Professor Max Rosenbaum, PhD
Clinical Professor Adelphi University. Co-Director American Short
Term Therapy Center; Consultant Harlem Valley, Manhattan State,
South Beach Psychiatric Centers. Former Clinical Professor, Department

of Psychiatry, New York University. Amongst his publications are
Group Psychotherapy. Theory and Practice and *Group Psychotherapy
and Group Function* (1975).

Professor Saul Scheidlinger, PhD

Professor of Psychiatry (Psychology) Albert Einstein College of
Medicine, New York. Former Editor, *International Journal of Group
Psychotherapy*. Currently President of the American Group Psycho-
therapy Association. His most recent book is *Focus on Group
Psychotherapy* (1982).

A. C. Robin Skynner, MB, FRCPsych, DPM

Member of the Institute of Group Analysis (London), Member of
Group Analytic Society (London). Founder Member and first Chairman
of the Institute of Family Therapy (London). Amongst his publications
is *One Flesh: Separate Persons* (1976).

Sheila Thompson, AAPCW

Former Principal Mental Health Social Worker, London Borough
Newham. Co-author with Dr J. H. Kahn *The Group Process as a Helping
Technique* (1970).

George A. Vassiliou, MD, FAGPA

Director of the Athenian Institute of Anthropos, President World
Association of Social Psychiatry. Founder and President (1972-1980)
of the Mediterranean Socio-Psychiatric Association.

Vasso G. Vassiliou, PhD

Associate Director of the Athenian Institute of Anthropos. Co-Author
with George Vassiliou of many works in the field of group psychotherapy and general systems theory.

Siegmund Heinrich Foulkes

Biographical notes

1898   Born 3 September 1898 in Karlsruhe (Baden), the son of Gustav Fuchs, timber merchant, and Sarah née Durlacher. He had three elder brothers and an elder sister.

1916   Matriculated from Gymnasium.

1917-19   Served as telephonist and telegraphist in German army.

1919   Began medical studies at Heidelberg. Later studied at Munich (1921) and Frankfurt (1921-23).

1923   MD Frankfurt. First marriage to Erna Stavenhagen.

1923-24   'Practical' half year in Berlin at the Charité II.

1924   Spent year at family firm in Karlsruhe, as German runaway inflation made economic outlook for doctors doubtful. Birth of son Thomas.

1925   Returned to postgraduate studies at Frankfurt, and did a year and a half of clinical medicine under Professor Strassburger, and two years of neurology under Professor Kurt Goldstein. Daughter Lisa born in 1927.

1928   Began psychoanalytic and psychiatric studies in Vienna. Psychoanalyst: Dr Helene Deutsch. Psychiatric training under Professors Wagner-Jauregg and Pötzl. Worked with Heinz Hartmann, Hans Hoff, Erwin Stengel and others.

1930   Returned to Frankfurt to join recently founded Frankfurt Psychoanalytic Institute where he was in charge of clinic. Private practice as specialist psychiatrist and psychoanalyst. Birth of second daughter Vera in 1931.

1933   Left Germany and settled in London on the invitation of Dr Ernest Jones. Attended Westminster Medical School.

1936   British medical qualification: LRCP LRCS Edinburgh,

LRFPS Glasgow. Private practice as psychoanalyst in London. Divorced 1937.

1938   Naturalised British subject. Married, secondly, Kilmeny Graham. Changed name to Foulkes.

1940   While expecting call-up for war service practised psychotherapy and group psychotherapy at Exeter. First groups conducted both privately and at Exeter Child Guidance Clinic.

1942   Wrote first article on group analysis (published in 1944). Joined Royal Army Medical Corps. Appointed Major (Specialist in Psychiatry) and posted to Northfield Military Hospital near Birmingham. There introduced group methods on large scale and later took leading part in transforming hospital into therapeutic community, the first of its kind.

1946   Returned to London after army service. Took consulting room at 58 Portland Place. Held regular meetings with colleagues interested in group psychotherapy.

1947-50   Associate chief assistant, Department of Psychological Medicine, St Bartholomew's Hospital.

1948   Publication of *Introduction to Group-Analytic Psychotherapy*. Convened group to present study of communication in a group at International Congress of Mental Health, London.
Visited USA (Lectured in New York, visited Boston, Washington and Baltimore).

1950   Appointed Consultant Physician to the Bethlem Royal and Maudsley Hospitals (postgraduate teaching hospital attached to Institute of Psychiatry).

1951   Took consulting rooms at 22 Upper Wimpole Street to allow development of a centre for group analysis. Training seminars in group analysis.

1952   Founded the Group-Analytic Society (London) whose President he was from 1952 to 1970.

1954   As a member of the International Committee for Group Psychotherapy attended first International Congress in Toronto. Member of Council of British Psycho-Analytical Society.

1958   Second visit to USA. Lectured in New York. Visiting Professor at University of North Carolina Medical School.

1959   Death of Kilmeny Foulkes in USA.

1960   Married Elizabeth Marx.

1961-62   Chairman of Medical Section of British Psychological
          Society.
1963   Retired from Bethlem Royal and Maudsley Hospitals.
          Appointed Hon. Physician to Joint Hospitals for one year to
          do research into the networks of patients.
1964   Appointed Physician Emeritus to Joint Hospitals.
1964-65   Chairman of Psychotherapy and Social Psychiatry Section
          of Royal Medico-Psychological Association (which became
          Royal College of Psychiatrists).
1965   Consultant for UNESCO in Israel (mainly to advise on school
          psychological services).
1967   Founded Group Analysis (International Panel and Correspon-
          dence). Editor 1967-75.
1970   Retired from practice. Continued with teaching, writing and
          editing.
1971   Appointed Foundation Fellow of Royal College of Psychia-
          trists.
1974   Gave a month's intensive course in group analysis in Austria.
1976   Died 8 July.

Bibliography of S. H. Foulkes
compiled by Elizabeth T. Foulkes

(Note: Papers dated before 1938 were published under the author's
original name, S. H. Fuchs.)

Books

*Introduction to Group-Analytic Psychotherapy. Studies in the social
integration of individuals and groups.* London, Heinemann, 1948;
New York, Grune & Stratton, 1949. Reprinted, Karnac, 1983.
(and Anthony, E. J.) *Group Psychotherapy: The Psychoanalytic
Approach.* Harmondsworth, Penguin, 1957, revised 1965, 1973.
Translations:
Psicoterapia psicoanalítica de grupo. Buenos Aires, Paidos, 1964.
Groepstherapie. Utrecht, Aula, 1966.
Psicoterapia de grupo. Rio de Janeiro, Biblioteca Univ. Popular, 1967.
Psychothérapie de groupe: approche 'psychanalytique. Paris, EPI,
1969.

(and Kadis, A. L., Krasner, J. D., Winick, C.) *A practicum of group psychotherapy*. New York, Harper & Row, 1963, revised edn 1974.
Translations:
Italian edition: Milan, Feltrinelli, 1967.
Spanish edition: Mexico, Fondo de Cultura Económica, 1969, 1974.
French edition: Paris, EPI, 1971.
German edition: *Praktikum der Gruppenpsychotherapie*, ed. P. Kutter, Stuttgart-Bad Camstatt: Frommann Holzboog, 1982.
Therapeutic Group Analysis. London, Allen & Unwin, 1964; New York, International Universities Press, 1965.
Translations:
Analisi terapeutica di grupo. Turin, Boringhieri, 1967; 1974.
Psychothérapie et analyse de groupe. Paris, Payot, 1970.
Grupo-analise terapeutica. Lousä, Publ. Europa-America, 1970.
Gruppenanalytische Psychotherapie. München, Kindler Verlag, 1974.
(and Prince, G. S., eds) *Psychiatry in a Changing Society*. London, Tavistock, 1969 (2 chapters by SHF).
Group-analytic Psychotherapy: Method and Principles. London, Gordon & Breach (Interface), 1975.
Translations:
Italian: *La Psicoterapia gruppoanalitica: metodo e principi*, Rome, Astrolabio, 1977.
German: *Praxis der gruppenanalytischen Psychotherapie*. München & Basel, E. Reinhardt Verlag, 1978.
Swedish: *Gruppenanalytisk psykoterapi*. Stockholm, AWE/Gebers, 1979.
Spanish: *Psicoterapia Grupo-Analítica: método y principios*. With posthumous prologue by Juan Campos Avillar, Barcelona, Gedisa, 1981.

Audio cassettes

Group-analytic psychotherapy. Behavioral Science Tape Library, New Jersey, 1972. Three 60-minute cassettes: six half-hour talks.

Articles

Über die determinierende Kraft des Namens bei einem Schizophrenen.

Int. Z. Psycho-Anal. 16: 495-501, 1930.

Zum Stand der heutigen Biologie. Dargestellt an Kurt Goldstein: *Der Aufbau des Organismus.* Imago 22: 210-41, 1936.

On Introjection. *Int. J. Psycho-Anal.* 18: 269-93, 1937.

Über Introjektion. *Imago,* 23: 420-46, 1937 (translation of preceding paper).

Some remarks on a chapter of Helen Keller's book *The World I Live in. Psychoanal. Rev.* 28: 512-19, 1941.

The idea of a change of sex in women. *Int. J. Psycho-Anal.* 24: 53-6, 1943.

Psycho-analysis and crime. *Canadian Bar Rev.* 22: 30-61, 1943. *Also in: English Studies in criminal science* (Cambridge University) Toronto, Canadian Bar Assoc., 1944.

Group-analysis: studies in the treatment of groups on psycho-analytical lines (with E. Lewis). *B. J. med. psychol.* 20: 175-84, 1944.

A memorandum on group psychotherapy. AMD 11 BM (for army use), 1945.

Group analysis in a military neurosis centre. Lancet, vol. 1, 1946; 303-13. *Also in:* M. Rosenbaum and M. Berger (eds), *Group psychotherapy and group function,* New York, Basic Books, 469-76, 1963. *Spanish translation* in *Revista de la Sanidad Militar Argentina* 47: 319-25, 1948.

On group analysis. *Int. J. Psycho-Anal.* 27: 46-51, 1946,

Principles and practice of group therapy. *Bull Menninger clinic* 10: 85-9, 1946.

Crime begins and ends within the community: it's you and me. *Horizon* 14: 260-72, 1946.

Group therapy: a short survey and orientation with particular reference to group analysis. *B. J. med. psychol.* 23: 199-205, 1950.

Remarks on group-analytic psychotherapy. *Group psychother.* 4: 56-9, 1951.

Concerning leadership in group-analytic psychotherapy. *Int. J. group psychother.* 1: 319-29, 1951.

Contribution to a symposium on group therapy. *B. J. med. psychol.* 25: 229-34, 1952.

Some similarities and differences between psychoanalytic principles and group-analytic principles. *B. J. med. psychol.* 26: 30-35, 1953.

Recording group-analytic sessions: a chart of attendances and other significant data. London, Group-Analytic Society (11 pages and 3 tables). 1953.

Group-analytic observation as indicator for psychoanalytic treatment. *Int. J. Psycho-Anal.* 35: 263-6, 1954.

Group-analytic psychotherapy: a short account. *Acta psychother.* 3: 313-19, 1955.

Progress in psychotherapy, 1956: Comments. *Group psychother.* 9: 305-10, 1956.

Group-analytic dynamics with specific reference to psychoanalytic concepts. *Int. J. group psychother.* 7: 40-52, 1957. *Also in:* Kissen, M. (ed.), *From group dynamics to group psychoanalysis.* Washington DC, Hemisphere, 1976.

Comments on Fairbairn's paper. *B. J. philos. science.* 7: 324-9, 1957.

Out-patient psychotherapy: a contribution towards a new approach (with A. Parkin). *Int. J. soc. psychiatry* 3: 44-8, 1957.

Discussion of Dr L. S. Kubie's paper 'Some theoretical concepts underlying the relationship between individual and group psychotherapies'. *Int. J. group psychother.* 8: 20-25, 1958.

Psycho-analysis, group psychotherapy, group analysis. *Acta psychother.* 7: 119-31, 1959.

The application of group concepts to the treatment of the individual in the group. *In: Topical problems of psychotherapy*, vol. 2, 1-15, and ('Afterthoughts') 51-6. Basel, Karger, 1960.

Some observations on teaching psychotherapy. *In: Topical problems of psychotherapy*, vol. 3, 206-9. Basel, Karger, 1960.

Spanish translation: Revista de psiquiatria y psicologia medica 4: 80-2, 1960.

Theoretische and praktische Grundlagen der analytischen Gruppenpsychotherapie. *Z. f. Psychother. & med. psychol.* 10: 229-37, 1960.

Group processes and the individual in the therapeutic group. *B. J. med. psychol.* 34: 23-31, 1961.

Psychotherapy 1961. *B. J. med. psychol.* 34: 91-102, 1961.

Psychotherapy and group psychotherapy. *In:* Kadis, Krasner, Winick and Foulkes: *A Practicum of group psychotherapy.* New York, Harper & Row, 1963, 1-10. 2nd edn, 1974, 1-7. *Also in* (abbreviated): Ehrenwald, J. (ed.): *The history of psychotherapy.* New York, Aronson, 1976.

Group psychotherapy: the group-analytic view. *In: Proceedings of VIth Internat. Congress of Psychotherapy* (London, 1964). Basel, Karger (vol. I, 150-54), 1965.

Some basic concepts in group psychotherapy. *In:* J. L. Moreno (ed.), *International handbook on group psychotherapy*, New York, Philosophical Library: 167-72, 1966.

German translation: Z. f. Psychother. & med. Psychol. 15: 125-30, 1965.

Illness as a social process. *Psychother. & psychosom.* 14: 217-25, 1966.

Discussion of Ivanov, N. V.: *A Soviet view of group therapy. Int. J. of psychiatr.* 2: 214-17, 1966.

On group-analytic psychotherapy. *In: Proceedings, IVth Intern. Congress of group psychotherapy* (Vienna 1968). Vienna, Verlag, d. Wiener mediz. Akademie, 2: 123-130, 1968.

On interpretation in group analysis. *Int. J. group psychother.* 18: 432-44, 1968.

De l'interprétation en analyse de groupe. *In:* P.-B. Schneider (ed.), *Pratique de la psychothérapie de groupe.* Florence, Giunti/editrice universitaria, 2: 61-84, 1968 (translation of preceding paper, incl. extra material).

Über die Interpretation in der analytischen Gruppentherapie. *In:* G. Ammon (ed.), *Gruppenpsychotherapie.* Hamburg, Hoffman & Campe, 1973 (translation of preceding paper).

Some autobiographical notes. *Group analysis* 1: 117-22, 202-5, 1968.

Group-dynamic processes and group analysis: a transatlantic view. *Group psychoanal. and group process* 1: 47-73, 1968.

Dynamische Prozesse in der gruppenanalytischen Situation. *Gruppenpsychother. & Gruppendynamik* 4: 70-81, 1970 (translation of preceding paper). *Also in: Psychoanalyse und Gruppe.* Ed. A. Heigl-Evers. Göttingen, Vandenhoeck & Ruprecht, 1971.

Access to unconscious processes in the group-analytic group. *Group analysis* 4: 4-14, 1971.

L'accés aux processus inconscients dans le groupe d'analyse de groupe. *In: Groupes: psychologie sociale clinique et psychanalyse. Bulletin de psychologie.* Univ. de Paris, numéro spécial, 1974 (translation of preceding paper).

Oedipus conflict and regression. *Int. J. group psychother.* 22: 3-15, 1972.

L'Oedipe et la regression en psychothérapie de groupe. *In:* P.-B. Schneider (ed.), *Pratique de la psychothérapie de groupe,* vol. 3. Florence, Giunti/editrice Universitaria, 57-75, 1972 (translation of preceding paper with additional material).

Preface to P. B. de Maré: *Perspectives in Group Psychotherapy.* London, Allen & Unwin, 1972.

The group as matrix of the individual's mental life. *In:* L. R. Wolberg and E. K. Schwartz (eds), *Group therapy 1973.* New York, Intercontin. med. book corp. 211-20, 1973.

My philosophy in psychotherapy. *J. Contemp. psychother.* 6: 109-14, 1974.

A short outline of the therapeutic processes in group-analytic psycho-therapy. *Group analysis* 8: 59-63, 1975.

Some personal observations (in celebration of the Journal's 25th anniversary). *Int. J. group psychother.* 25: 169-72, 1975.

Problems of the large group from a group-analytic point of view. *In*: L. Kreeger (ed.), *The large group: dynamics and therapy*. London, Constable, 35-56, 1975.

Italian translation: *Archivo de psicnol. neurol. e psichiatr.* 35, 423-45, 1974.

German translation: *Die Grossgruppe*. Stuttgart, Klett, 1977.

Preface to: D. W. Abse. *Clinical Notes on Group-Analytic Psychotherapy*. Bristol, Wright, 1974.

On group-analytic psychotherapy (1949). *In*: M. Rosenbaum and M. Berger (eds): *Group Psychotherapy and Group Function*. 2nd edn, New York, Basic Books, 336-46, 1975.

The leader in the group. *In*: Z. A. Liff (ed.), *The Leader in the Group*. New York, Aronson, 83-94, 1975.

Qualification as a psychoanalyst as an asset and as a hindrance for the future group analyst. *Group Analysis*. 8: 180-2, 1975.

Group psychotherapy. *In*: *Encyclopaedic Handbook of Medical Psychology*. S. Krauss (ed). London, Butterworth, 216-17, 1976.

Notes on the concept of transference. *In*: L. R. Wolberg, M. L. Aronson and A. R. Wolberg (eds): *Group Therapy 1976*. Stratton Intercont. med. book corp. New York. 52-8, 1977.

Book reviews, abstracts and ephemeral writings not included.

Introduction

The original idea for this volume was for it to be a *Festschrift* for Michael Foulkes. Dr V. Varma proposed it, and consulted with Dr Foulkes, who guided him in his choice of contributors. The diversity of the topics here presented indicates the broad encompassing sweep of Dr Foulkes's professional and cultural interests. Dr Foulkes' sudden death, however, forced a change of plan: the *Festschrift* had now to be a commemorative volume. Dr Varma gracefully invited me to take over the editorship and we owe our thanks to him for initiating this work. I endeavoured, on the basis of what had been already started, to produce a work with a broad perspective on the evolution and range of group-analytic theory and practice.

Amongst the contributions are the first three annual S. H. Foulkes lectures, which are sponsored by the Group-Analytic Society and which are printed as chapters. The speakers are all collaborators of Dr Foulkes from his earlier days in military psychiatry and the immediate post-war period. Dr Main and Professor Anthony bring vividly to life the portrait of the man and the significance of his work in the historical context. Professor Abse relates the work of group analysis to recent advances in psychoanalytic theory, particularly in the realm of narcissism.

Dr de Maré, a longstanding and close collaborator, evokes for those who knew Foulkes well vivid memories of his style of thought and of work. Others who had a long personal association with Dr Foulkes are Mrs Abercrombie, Dr Hutten and Mrs Sheila Thompson; these three articles from areas outside clinical psychotherapy illustrate the fertile effect of group-analytic ideas. Helen Durkin, Saul Scheidlinger and Max Rosenbaum are transatlantic colleagues who shared with Dr Foulkes the historic days of the development of group-analytic psychotherapy. It is particularly interesting to see how Foulkes's ideas contributed to Helen Durkin's work on general systems theory. George and Vasso

1

Vassiliou, world travellers and system theorists, had a long and fruitful friendship with Dr Foulkes and when in London always called on him to discuss and to exchange ideas. James Home, Robin Skynner and myself had long collaborated with Michael Foulkes in the Group Analytic Society and Practice and were, together with him, co-founders of the Institute of Group Analysis. Rita Leal represents the flourishing Portuguese analytic movement founded by Professor E. Cortesão. The influence of Foulkes's ideas in Europe are ably represented by Professor Laxenaire and Professor Fiumara, who show how the systems of Lacan and Jung respectively can be integrated with group analysis. The article by Professor Rof-Carballo, who also shared ideas with Foulkes many years ago, introduces us to a European and psychosomatic perspective. Professor Hawkins worked with Dr Foulkes both at the Maudsley Hospital, London, and at the University of North Carolina where Foulkes spent a happy and productive period as a visiting professor. The work of Dr Barbara Dick and Dr John Evans illustrates the value of the group-analytic approach in clinical work with adults and adolescents, and, finally, Helle Munro has shared with us the evolutionary perspective that she and Foulkes used to enjoy discussing together. My own article will, I hope, serve as an outline to the rich mine of Foulkes's writings, which still remain to be sifted, refined, expanded and commented on, aims which will be realised in future volumes.

I wish to express my thanks to Dr Lionel Kreeger who was to have been my co-editor until circumstances forced him to withdraw; our discussions were helpful in planning this work.

Malcolm Pines

Chapter 1

The application of some principles of group analytic psychotherapy to higher education

M.L.J. Abercrombie

Except for five years of work on perceptual disorders of brain-injured children my professional life has been concerned with the education of zoologists, doctors, architects, and university teachers. Its latter two-thirds have been profoundly influenced by Dr Foulkes's ideas about group analytic psychotherapy, and especially by personal experience of his way of behaving as a conductor. In the context of the recent enormous expansion and intensification of interest in small-group teaching in higher education (Abercrombie, 1970), the relationship of teaching and psychotherapy is of more than personal importance, and the autobiographical tone of this chapter may be more acceptable now than it might have been thirty years ago. Abse (1974) and his colleagues, now in the USA, have also been strongly influenced by Foulkes's ideas in their teaching of psychiatry (see especially his chapter 8, 'The Learning Group'). Examples of teachers in the UK whose work in groups has been influenced by group psychotherapy (in these cases, of the Tavistock orientation) are Ottaway (1966) (social workers), Richardson (1967) (teachers), Balint (1957) (doctors) and Gosling et al. (1967) (doctors, social workers).

There is a basic similarity between teaching and psychotherapy, namely that both are concerned in helping people to learn to behave in the future in certain prescribed situations in ways they would not do otherwise. An important difference between them is in the extent to which unlearning is necessary. In teaching it is supposed that the recipients (pupils) have not yet learned how to behave in the required way because of youth or ignorance – they are as empty vessels waiting to be filled. In psychotherapy it is supposed that the recipient (patient) has already learned bad habits and must unlearn these and develop different reactions to the same situations.

But even so academic a skill as learning to read, for instance, may

3

involve quite different processes for different people: one child may learn without being taught, apparently spontaneously; another with a teacher's help, another only if so-called emotional barriers are broken down by therapeutic methods. The same piece of information can, in some circumstances, be taught didactically while in others psychotherapy is necessary. A modern schoolchild has no difficulty in learning that the earth is a sphere and moves around the sun, but there was a time when the idea was rejected by quite clever adults. They had very good reasons for being unable to learn it − because it ran counter to strongly held religious beliefs. Learning anything new must involve some unlearning, because our knowledge and understanding forms a consistent whole which must undergo some modification, however slight, when incorporating something new.

There were three main phases in my work on teaching in groups, each a response made possible to a contemporary fashionable interest by the availability of research funds. I hope that as I briefly review them it will become clear how much these developments owe to my contact with Dr Foulkes, which has extended over some thirty years. My debt is not only to his theoretical formulations in writing and teaching (as in discussion in the Group Analytic Society, London) but above all to the experience of being in his therapeutic groups as a patient, and later as a co-therapist.

Training in scientific method

As a teacher of zoology at Birmingham University I began to realise some of the difficulties of training students in scientific method − how to observe accurately and comprehensively and draw reasonable conclusions from what one sees; how to see differences and similarities between things, to classify, judge, test, predict and extrapolate validly, how to analyse and synthesise usefully. It was in those early days commonly assumed that these skills followed automatically from the absorption of the current body of scientific knowledge. But it became clear that it was much easier to teach a student the facts than to help him to think about them; it was easier to demonstrate to a student what you could see in a specimen than to help him to discover anything else, or to distinguish what he thought was there from what was really there. Teaching the content of the premedical biology course to medical students, whether it was the insides of earthworms, evidence for belief in the theory of evolution, or the life cycle of the malaria parasite, did not seem to be preparing them for the practice of diagnosis – for using knowledge to behave effectively towards something that was only partly familiar or perhaps quite new and unexpected. It seemed difficult to make use of other people's experience without being confined by it. The difficulties seemed to be connected with the student's perception of his own relationship to knowledge, through his relationship to his teachers. It was the authority-dependency situation that needed to be modified. (At that time I was impressed with the inhibiting effect on education of the too uncritical absorption of a body of knowledge, but as I later learned from Dr Foulkes (1975, p. 168), there are also resistances to the simple taking in of information – in his experience particularly strong when men were being taught by a man.)

So I started to teach less didactically in small discussion groups in which students were encouraged to learn by interaction with each other rather than by passive absorption of the teacher's knowledge. But this was not easy either. In the post-war years in the Anatomy Department at University College London, some of our preclinical medical students were ex-service men who wanted to be taught as quickly and effortlessly as possible in the old-fashioned way. I complained to a colleague about the belligerent behaviour of an aggressive group of students, comparing it jokingly to what I had read of group psychotherapy, and he gave me an introduction to a friend who was conducting therapeutic groups of skin patients at the Middlesex Hospital. I dropped in on one of his sessions and realised that if I could produce for students the kind of social climate he had established for his patients, half of my troubles would be over. The doctor was a colleague of Dr Foulkes, and through him I joined one of Dr Foulkes's groups.

I want to stress that it was the social climate, the 'group situation' that seemed important, and for an activity, learning to behave scientifically, that is usually regarded as rational, objective, emotion-free.

The 'situation' which finally evolved (the project, financed partly by the Rockefeller Foundation, covered ten years) for training preclinical medical students in scientific ways of behaving was as follows. The students met with me in groups of twelve for one and a half hours at weekly intervals, for a course of eight sessions. The theme of the course was introduced with a demonstration of the projective nature of perception, which leaned heavily on the transactional approach of Ames (see Ittelson and Cantril, 1954; Kilpatrick, 1952). This served to emphasise personal involvement in any act of perception, the importance of the observer's basic unrecognised assumptions (expectations, attitudes or schemata) and the influence of contextual factors. The similarity of these processes in everyday life and in science was stressed. The meetings were firmly structured in time and place. For twenty minutes or so the students worked individually at a scientific task, such as comparing and contrasting two radiographs, evaluating a published report or an experiment, or defining the word 'normal'. There followed free discussion about the individual responses to the task, in which the egocentric nature of perception became clear. Each person had responded idiosyncratically to the same stimulus pattern, according to his personal basic assumptions and reactions to contextual factors. By comparing and contrasting his own judgments and those of his peers he could become conscious of some of the multitude of interacting factors that had profoundly influenced him but of which he had been unaware. Whereas in the didactic situation he is offered the teacher's judgment, the authoritative correct one, with which to compare his own, in the group he is confronted with eleven others, made by his peers, which he must evaluate on their own merits.

Students who had taken the course behaved more scientifically in a test than those who had not taken it, in that they tended to distinguish better between descriptive statements ('facts') and inferences, to make fewer false inferences, to consider alternative hypotheses more frequently, and to be less set in reaction to a stimulus pattern by previous experience of a similar one (James *et al.*, 1956).

In Foulkes's terminology, the groups could be described as short-term (8 weeks), closed (12 students) and monosymptomatic (deficiency in scientific objectivity). They were quite different from therapeutic groups in two ways: first, in that attention was focused on a particular topic by the initial exercise done individually. Second, the members were colleagues, not strangers to each other and there could be no insistence on 'abstinence', no attempt to prevent meeting outside the group; on the contrary, discussion often continued both between members of the same, and of other groups. I felt this was an advantage, in encouraging the transfer of training beyond the group situation, and disseminating the ideas talked about within it into the rest of their learning. They resembled therapeutic groups in that discussion was free in the sense that there was no directive chairmanship; it was *associative* in that the perception of the relationship of seemingly irrelevant topics was encouraged, and *analytic* in that the attempt was made to clarify and specify the meanings of statements.

In conducting the group I tried to avoid being didactic, and to weaken the authority-dependency relation and encourage the strengthening of peer relationships. Undoubtedly I was perceived as an authority figure, as a professional scientist, as representing the department and the college, and as administrator of the course. I convened the groups, stated their purpose, fixed the time and place of meeting, arranged the programme of exercises, and opened and closed each session. I had the advantage, however, of not being an examiner; the course was optional, though there were few absentees. For the rest, I tried to establish a group situation conducive to learning through the sharing of experiences of the initial individual task. This involved making a supportive, non-threatening climate in which constant challenge to habitual ways of thinking was tolerable. I made few statements, and kept them very short; avoided breaking silences; listened hard and made use of what I had heard; encouraged contemplation and questioning. The project is reported in some detail in *The Anatomy of Judgement*.

Improving the education of architects

The second project, at the Bartlett School of Architecture at University College London and suppported by the Leverhulme Trust Fund, took place in a very different setting from the first one. There had been widespread rethinking about architectural education and a thoroughly revised course was being implemented. Whereas with the medical project I focused effort on a small part of the course, and in some isolation from the rest of it, with the architects I was involved with the whole course as a kind of educational consultant, sitting in on classes and taking part in the many departmental discussions on curriculum and general teaching and examining problems. If the work in medical education had analogies with therapeutic groups, that with architectural education had analogies with therapeutic communities (another of Dr Foulkes's interests). Keeping in mind that students learn a great deal that is not deliberately taught, picking up habits and attitudes from the general climate or culture of the School, we aimed to make this as favourable as possible, trying to ensure that the symbols worked with us and not against us.

A major problem, as in any period of rapid change, was communication, and we attempted to improve this by many and various meetings for discussion. Discomfort and confusion followed the need for students and staff to accommodate to the continuing changes in courses and examinations. This was exacerbated by changes in role. The non-architectural teachers who came to teach subjects formerly covered by the studio staff brought the different attitudes and work methods of their own disciplines. It was not clear how these could usefully be integrated into design training. Practising architects found themselves teaching students whose knowledge in the new areas exceeded their own.

There was great scope for many different kinds of group work. The notion that an architect's work involves human relationships was firmly adopted, and we tried to make professional education the medium for good personal development. Task oriented group work was organised in structures of varying sizes and constitutions — within the same year (sibling groups), and in a cross-section of the school (over 5 years), to give experience of working with different levels of expertise, and for different aims — for collecting information, or for designing.

Free group discussion of current experiences of working in groups was encouraged. There were several cases of conflicting attitudes or ideas that it was necessary to come to terms with. For instance, the old conception of the architect as a 'prima donna' artist, and the belief that an aesthetically good design could not be made by a group, conflicted with the realistic need for team work in the design of complicated buildings like schools and hospitals. There is a need to identify with a master architect, and at the same time a need to be weaned away from authorities. There is a conflict between the effectiveness of competition in stimulating effort, and the need for co-operation. Interchange of personal reactions to experiences was used to sharpen students' sensitivity to the physical and social environment, so that they could better appreciate peoples' needs, and understand how the things architects do to the environment will fulfil or frustrate the consumers' needs. For instance, students who were designing an outpatient clinic visited a hospital to see what went on in the waiting room. In discussing their designs, the question arose about the need for one large waiting room, or small ones for each clinic, and should patients be filtered off to wait alone to see the doctor, their friends staying downstairs in the public waiting room? Personal reactions to this were varied, and in discussion of fears of going to hospital, one thought that, though children might be afraid, grownups would not be. But examples were brought up of patients being unable to listen to the doctor's instructions, or understand or remember them, and the advantage of having a more objective friend there was accepted, even when the emotional impact of visiting hospital was denied.

Towards the end of this generalised project a more intensive involvement with a particular class was undertaken, financed by the Social

Science Research Council. This was with a new one-year postgraduate course leading to a Diploma in Architecture. The intention was to make a special attempt to educate for change and for autonomy in learning – to encourage students to take responsibility for their current education and to prepare to continue to learn throughout life. This involved a change in the authority-dependency relationship that characterises our educational system, with far-reaching implications for changes in personal interaction between students and teachers. In order to facilitate the changes in attitude required we (Paul Terry and I) ran weekly groups with students and their tutors in which topics of current interest in the class work were spontaneously discussed. The problems of becoming less dependent on authoritative teachers were closely associated with those of becoming responsible designers and of adopting the professional status for which the Diploma qualified them. Among the themes that emerged were: the wish to remain dependent which conflicted with the wish and need to become self-reliant; feelings of impotence; discomfort due to the lack of perceived structure in the course; realistic fears of failure as a result of being independent and fantasy fears of reprisals from rejected authorities; resentment at feeling manipulated and timidity in taking the initiative to manipulate; depression at feeling abandoned by tutors; exhilaration at feeling emancipated; recognition that one could have and use internalised as distinct from imposed values. These are closely interrelated with two other major themes we have studied, professionalism and the design process.

While the students' most clearly expressed fear was that of failing to learn and to qualify, the tutors' was that of becoming redundant in the new learning situation. It is not without significance that the course took place during the intense and world-wide phase of student revolt (1968-9). The course and some aspects of the group discussions have been reported in some detail (Abercrombie *et al*, 1970-78).

Improving small-group teaching

The third project, also undertaken at University College London, was sponsored by the University Grants Committee. It resulted from the great increase in small-group teaching that followed the expansion of tertiary education in the 1960s, and the widespread dissatisfaction with didactic teaching methods. The difficulties that many teachers felt in conducting small-group classes successfully resulted from the fact that their own educational experience did not include group work, so they had no model to rely on, and behaved in seminars that were intended to encourage student interaction, as they did in lectures, tutorials, and practical classes where more didactic methods are appropriate. We therefore organised – my colleague Paul Terry and I – small groups for teachers to discuss their current work in small-group teaching. These were of the usual pattern, one and a half hours long at weekly intervals. Teachers from many disciplines and from different institutions came. As is to be expected in the relatively unstructured situation discussion ranged widely, but could always be seen to be relevant to the academic situation. The set-up was intended to simulate in some respects the situation the teachers might wish to use with their student groups. As conductors we strove to encourage interaction among the teachers, and to weaken dependence on ourselves as authority figures. In reporting their own experiences in group teaching and comparing and contrasting themselves with the others, each could get heightened awareness of his own behaviour as a teacher. Between meetings they could try out new ways of behaving in their classes, and report back for further discussion. Four functions of group discussion can be differentiated which can help participants to manage their classes more effectively: the group can offer mutual support; can provide opportunities for increased self-awareness; can help to develop greater empathy with students; and can serve as a model for one kind of small-group teaching.

Discussion in the group was reassuring at the personal level in the usual way – it soon became clear that no one person's difficulties are peculiar to himself. In these groups it was reassuring in another way also – at the professional level, because it also became clear that the problems were not trivial, but related to very general and fundamental aspects of higher education which warrant intense and scholarly examination.

As one member spoke of a recent happening and the others questioned and commented, it became clear that the incident described is only to be understood within a complicated situation: the relation of the particular class to the rest of the institution, the personalities of the participants – students and teacher alike – their past and present educational experiences, their various immediate and long-term objectives. Slowly, the network of assumptions that each of us has relative to education and to personal relations in it begins to become manifest, whereas usually we are quite unaware of them. Confronted with a wide range of alternative ideas and of ways of behaving to a specific event, one can recognise some parts of one's own idiosyncratic complex of assumptions and question their usefulness. The following examples, taken from replies to a questionnaire given at the end of the project to evaluate it, illustrate the reactions of some participants:

R55: The discovery that to develop new feelings about one's occupation is different from and more difficult than, accepting new ideas — theories — about it, is going to be very important to me I know, and I feel a corresponding gratitude to those group meetings for this discovery. I suppose it is strange that someone engaged with literature, which demonstrates continually just that difference and relationship between ideas and feelings, should make that discovery relatively late; but then that very lateness confirms the difference between assenting to ideas and having an attitude from within one.

R46: In seminar groups I used always to feel that I was a failure if I failed to show myself in charge, and I tended to dominate any group (probably to reinforce my own confidence) without any idea that this expression of confidence and competence might in any way be disruptive to the discussion. I feel I have now more hope of being able to encourage the less confident in a group to talk and the more confident not to dominate.

R32: At times I was helped to understand my confusion in relationship to the students, to understand my needs of the students. As a result I have gained more tolerance of my difficulties and there-fore, more tolerance of students' difficulties and anxieties.

R49: I know it's no longer so important to me to be constantly reas-sured that students like me. Nor for that matter is it so impor-tant for me to like them personally.

The wish to be liked was often expressed; in a discussion one said 'I wonder if part of the problem . . . is that you want them to like you, and that's even more important than that they should feel you are competent.' In another discussion when excessive teaching loads were talked about, one said 'Yeah, it is exhausting, but I find that I'm now aware that I do it to satisfy myself, because I want to be needed, to be indispensable.' Confiding in each other in this way they learn to recog-nise their own needs which lie behind their motivation for teaching, and can direct these feelings into more effective channels.

Empathy with students

While the teachers are talking about their own behaviour as teachers, their position as learners in this group of peers meeting with a conductor is analogous with that of their students. An important part of the group work is in taking advantage of this duality to help to get more empathy with students. Examples of questionnaire replies which illustrate this are:

R45: I have become much more sensitive to what students are feeling in many group situations, and also their 'latent' as well as 'manifest' interpretations of things I might say . . .

R51: I'm freer to assess what sort of encouragement or guidance a student needs at a given moment, because I'm more at ease in my own role. Previously, there was some degree of anxiety in my relations with students which hindered my perception – and even caused *me*, I suppose, to be hoping for *their* encouragement.

The switching of viewpoints is illustrated in a discussion when a participant said 'because we've met for so long and we see how important the interplay of people in the group is we realise that this interplay will directly reflect how freely or in what broad fields the students feel able to discuss a fairly narrow set exercise'. Later another reported a conversation he had had with two students about whether teachers and students could ever be friends, and recalled his own feelings as a student towards his teachers.

Learning from the conductor's behaviour

Perhaps the most significant thing to be learnt from the conductor's behaviour is the habit of evoking conversation by saying little and listening a lot, which will be useful in almost any kind of teaching by discussion.

The conductor's withdrawal from the dominant authoritarian teaching role, designed to encourage interaction among the other participants, illustrates to the teacher how he can liberate his own students. Two participants reported as follows:

R49: Instead of viewing a group as an opportunity for students to understand clearly *my* thinking on some topic, I now regard them as opportunities for students to clarify, communicate and to understand their own ideas about a topic. I am, therefore, much more silent in groups of students, and try, with varying degrees of success, to behave less didactically than I used to.

R33: Previously I probably tended to 'tell' students what I thought they should think. My first reaction to the discussion was the opposite: to try and be a permissive receiver of their ideas. I hope I have now developed some capacity for 'finding out where the students are at and showing them how to take the next step'. I have also at the same time become aware that there are many emotional problems to be overcome in communication between students and staff.

However, this comparatively non-dominating behaviour of the conductor is so alien to the image of the teacher that many on first experiencing it were disappointed and resentfully demanded to be taught. By contrast a very few have been disappointed that we did not go further into psychotherapy, or use sensitivity training methods. However one participant wrote:

I have learned to value highly the non-emotive atmosphere of the teachers' discussion group: through this I have been learning to behave unemotionally in professional situations; or where some emotion seems desirable, I have the freedom to express as much as is desirable. The peaceful discussion of potentially intense situations seems to have given me greater control in work situations.

The project is reported in 'Talking to Learn'.

Comparison with psychotherapy

Though in these three projects the focus of attention was on behaviour in academic work, undoubtedly some participants were affected in wider areas of social interchange. One of the medical students, for instance, said after the course that he could talk with the vicar now, and several teachers reported improvements in communication with colleagues as well as with students. It may be noted that some changes in the teachers' behaviour reflected changes in their self-image. It was not, however, the main intention to effect personality changes of a psychotherapeutic kind, and the method of conducting the groups accordingly differed from those of psychotherapy and techniques such as 'sensitivity training'. The conversation remained within a socially acceptable framework, and relevant to the professional task. Participants might refer occasionally to past educational experiences, but we were not so concerned (as psychotherapy often is) to explore the *genesis* of basic assumptions, of habitual idiosyncratic ways of thinking, but rather to study their *effects* in present behaviour with the object of considering whether it would be more effective to change them. Nor were we much concerned with personal emotional intragroup reactions, as 'sensitivity training' sometimes seems to be. We relied mostly on the use of something analogous to the 'mirror reaction' described by Foulkes (1964, p. 110):

A person sees himself, or part of himself — often a repressed part of himself — reflected in the interactions of other group members. He sees them reacting in the way he does himself, or in contrast to his own behaviour. He also gets to know himself — and this is a fundamental process in ego development — by the effect he has upon others and the picture they form of him.

The participant was moved to maintain or modify his behaviour by comparing and contrasting his own reactions with those of several peers rather than by measuring himself against an authority as in the conventional teaching situation, or against an external ideal or cultural norm, as in the therapeutic situation.

As remarked above, I think it was the way Dr Foulkes behaved in a group (Foulkes, 1975, ch. 6) that I found most helpful in establishing a climate conducive to learning about one's own mental processes and how to monitor them. The climate must be supportive, so that members are encouraged to talk freely and to listen to each other. Everything that happens in the group is regarded as meaningful and relevant — nothing that is said is silly, stupid or beside the point. The conductor avoids dominating the conversation with frequent and long speeches, speaks tentatively, not dogmatically, tolerates silences for contemplation, and leaves it to others to break a silence unless anxiety builds up too strongly. One learns to accept the hostility that often results from members' discomfort at the conductor's non-directive non-authoritarian role.

The content of discussion, focused on academic affairs, is of course very different from that in psychotherapy.

A central recurrent theme in these educational groups is that of the relationship between teacher and pupil, authority and ignorance, autonomy and dependence, i.e. matters relating to the transference situation in psychotherapy. The phenomenon of 'resonance' described by Foulkes (1975, pp. 122, 132) probably plays a part in the resolutions of conflict in this area.

Most of the conductor's comments are concerned with analysis, i.e. making meanings more precise and specific by separating things that are better kept apart and bringing others together that are helpful. Deep interpretations are avoided (Foulkes, 1975, p. 112: 'Interpretation is a verbal communication by the conductor to the group, or to members of the group, in order to draw their attention to a certain meaning of which he thinks they are unaware').

The unconscious material which must be uncovered and made conscious in psychotherapy concerns 'the internalised results of painful, traumatic, undigested and unintegrated childhood experiences and constellations', (Foulkes, 1964, p. 171). By contrast, the assumptions (schemata, expectations or attitudes) that are brought to light in the educational discussions so that their usefulness can be examined, are conceived of as mental structures, organisations of past experiences, of a less threatening, much more rational kind, which subserve skilled perceptual behaviour and have dropped out of consciousness for convenience' sake. They come automatically and effortlessly into action, usually in a beneficial way, increasing the speed and ease of recognition and classification of stimulus patterns, and enabling us to predict and extrapolate validly if the new experience is sufficiently like the old. It is in new or changing conditions that the unconscious use of these natural psychological processes leads us astray (see Abercrombie, 1960).

In summary, I think it is justifable to apply the term 'ego-training in action' to this work in education, as Foulkes applies it to group analytic psychotherapy (e.g. 1964, p. 82). Further, it may be perhaps recognised as an example, in a limited field, of psychopedagogy for which Bettelheim (1972) has made penetrating and eloquent pleas.

Acknowledgment

Aspects of the work reported here were supported by the Rockefeller Foundation, the Leverhulme Trust Fund, the Social Science Research Council, and the University Grants Committee.

References

Abercrombie, M. L. J. (1960), *The Anatomy of Judgement*, London, Hutchinson; (1969) Harmondsworth, Penguin.

Abercrombie, M. L. J. (1970), *Aims and Techniques of Group Teaching*, 4th edn 1979, Guildford, Society for Research into Higher Education.

Abercrombie, M. L. J., Forest, A. J., and Terry, P. M. (1970), 'Diploma project 1968-69', *Architectural Research and Teaching*, I, pp. 6-12.

Abercrombie, M. L. J., and Terry, P. M. (1973), 'Students' attitudes to professionalism', *Universities Quarterly*, pp. 465-74.

Abercrombie, M. L. J. and Terry, P. M. (1977), 'A contribution to the psychology of designing', *Journal of Architectural Education*, 30, 4, pp. 151-8.

Abercrombie, M. L. J. and Terry, P. M. (1978), 'Reactions to change in the authority-dependency relationship', *British Journal of Guidance and Counselling*, 6, pp. 82-94.

Abercrombie, M. L. J. and Terry, P. M. (1978), *Talking to learn*, Guildford, Society for Research into Higher Education.

Abse, W. (1974), *Clinical notes on group analytic psychotherapy*, Bristol, Wright.

Balint, M. (1957), *The Doctor, his Patient and the Illness*, London, Pitman.

Bettelheim, B. (1972), 'Psychotherapy and psychopedagogy', *Psychotherapy and Psychosomatics*, 20, pp. 44-55.

Foulkes, S. H. (1964), *Therapeutic Group Analysis*, London, Allen & Unwin.

Foulkes, S. H. (1975), *Group-analytic psychotherapy*, London, Gordon and Breach.

Gosling, R., Miller, D. H., Woodhouse, D., and Turquet, P. M. (1967), *The Use of Small Groups in Training*, Hitchin, Codicote Press.

Ittelson, W. H., and Cantril, H. (1954), *Perception, a Transactional Approach*, New York, Doubleday.

James, D. W., Johnson, M. L., and Venning, P. (1956), 'Testing for learnt skill in observation and evaluation of evidence', *Lancet*, ii, pp. 379-83.

Kilpatrick, F. P. (1952), *Human Behaviour from the Transactional Point of View*, Hanover, NH, Hanover Institute for Assoc. Res.

Ottaway, A. K. C. (1966), *Learning through Group Experience*, London, Routledge & Kegan Paul.

Richardson, E. (1967), *Group Study for Teachers*, London, Routledge & Kegan Paul.

Chapter 2

Some complementary functions of group-analytic psychotherapy and individual psychoanalysis

Wilfred Abse

Introduction

Writing in 1961, Leo Stone usefully defines the 'basic practically universal' longing of mankind for an omnipotent parent figure as a force that 'permeates our whole social organisation, is obvious in religious attitudes, in attitudes toward rulers and other powerful political figures, or indeed toward charismatic ideologists of any type'. He then goes on to ascribe to such 'primal transference' the tendency of man to dedicate his energies not only, on occasion, to leaders and causes that ultimately prove false, but also to the regrettably uncritical commitment (or antagonism) to systems – even in the field of hard science – that are congruent with man's unconsciously prejudiced hope of relating to an omnipotent source.[1] He goes so far as to suggest that 'our own field has been a conspicuous example of this tendency'.

To move from the phylogenetic experiences in the horde to the ontogenetic experiences in the family we discern another kind of transference that relates the individual infant to his mother by early libidinal bonds that replaces primary narcissism and provides the foundation for the infant to become aware of the dramatis personae of his unfolding life. It is this second kind of 'primal transference', also so called by Freud, which replays the events and relationships of the individual story on which psychoanalysis focuses and which becomes a tool in psychoanalytic resolution of disturbance. In discriminating between two types of primal transference Stone implies that although the second facilitates the advance and successful conclusion of psychoanalytic treatment, the first may be largely inaccessible to dyadic exploration and resolution; it 'underlies and is anterior to' the clinical phenomena with which psychoanalysis deals. His suggestion is that if the 'clinically significant' portion of the primal transference can be

expunged, the remainder, if not too severely distorted, can be freed to
flower in appropriate common social experiences that, no longer
impeding, may actually enhance the individual's grasp of environmental reality. The psychoanalyst is aware that the phylogenetically
based primal transference is likely to surface from time to time in the
individual's interaction with his family and the larger social group
and is obliged to heed the comment of Aristotle that he who remains
uninvolved in the society around him must be either god or beast.

Stone's statement offers at least two possibilities: the primal horde
transference may be so severely distorted as to prevent the individual's
participation in what is socially acceptable; or the latent craving for an
omnipotent parent may be such that it actually facilitates his bonding
with others in common 'constructive' enthusiasms and activities. We
can also posit the existence of that rare spirit whose involvement with
others is so discriminating as to reject from consideration those widely
supported attitudes, ideologies, and prejudices that by keeping bar-
barism alive introduce so much tragedy into the human scene.

Freud (1937) held in 'Analysis Terminable and Interminable' that
three interacting factors determine whether or not an analytic treatment will succeed. These include any traumatic circumstance or event
the patient may have suffered; the constitutional strength of his instinctual strivings as compared with his ego strength; and any alterations his ego may have undergone. The neurosis arising chiefly from
traumatic experience is the condition most readily amenable to psychoanalysis. It is the patient who has constitutionally strong instincts along
with an ego unfavourably altered by his defensive struggles who
presents problems for his analyst and whose psychoanalysis may be
virtually interminable. In the case of such an analysand one must
consider whether group-analytic psychotherapy may hold a key to
further progress. Involvement in group-analytic psychotherapy may
offer access to the unconscious cravings and fantasies that are part of
the archaic heritage of all human beings, and 'alterations' of the ego
that resist individual analysis may become accessible to the influence
of the group.

The formulation of Heinz Kohut (1971) concerning the dynamics
of narcissism shed considerable light on some aspects of the primal
transference and related alterations of the ego. He points to the evolution of a 'grandiose self' from feelings of incapacity, helplessness, and
worthlessness experienced after early separation-individuation experiences (ego processes), and he emphasises also projective identification
with idealised parents. Such concepts not only contribute to our

understanding of the narcissistic resistance often encountered in individual analysis, but they sharpen our awareness of its existence. It remains true, however, that severe ego-syntonic character disorders are often much more readily amenable to group-analytic psychotherapy in a well-composed and conducted group than in individual analysis.

The social field and analytic psychotherapy

It sometimes happens that a patient in individual analysis is incidentally involved simultaneously in crucial social events from which come revelations that increase the therapeutic leverage.[2] There are instances in which the course of treatment would have been stalemated, considerably retarded, or concluded unsuccessfully had not such extra-analytic events occurred. Three examples will serve as a basis for discussion of such events and their relationship to therapeutic experiences in group-analytic groups.

1. A middle-aged woman was in treatment for symptoms that included colitis. Although she was ordinarily affectively expressive, she wore a mask of imperturbability whenever she came face to face with her divorced husband in social situations in which she could not avoid the confrontation, and was impassive whenever she spoke in treatment of current interaction with him. She carefully nursed an image of herself as a poised and gracious woman, which she was in truth, and she rejected any possibility that she entertained any hostile jealous impulses and feelings. Her narcissistic adherence to this picture of herself and to a posture of perfect behaviour was maintained until her ex-husband's new wife left him; her colitis abruptly disappeared when she heard of this. The temporal connection, and the relationship of her colitis to her hostile jealousy, became gradually apparent to her during further interpretative work of the kind that had been quite ineffective previously. Moreover, she was able to explore her feelings about her reference group, which, she felt, would appreciate from his second wife's defection how 'impossibly difficult' her ex-husband was to live with. In this way she became able to approach guilt feelings and the self-punishing aspects of some of her symptoms, including the colitis, all of which were internal reactions to death-wishes.

2. A young man in analysis stopped addressing his analyst as 'Sir', and seemed in many other ways to show that repeated interpretations had enabled him to work through his excessively submissive and ingratiating traits which defended against severe castration anxiety and

unconscious homosexual problems. Then, in applying for a new position, he had to appear before a selection committee, and was interviewed by its members individually after the joint session. During the individual interviews he was asked to explain his excessively ingratiating behaviour to the committee. When he reported this event to his analyst and discussed it with him, it became clear how he had heeded the analyst's interpretations. When the group experience betrayed the persistence of his need to placate others, it became evident that the changes he had made vis-à-vis his therapist reflected partly his compliance with the analyst's altered expectations of him and also left him too compelled to be compliant to others! The group experience thus provided needed leverage that had not been available in dyadic interaction.[3]

3. A middle-aged man suffered from severe periodic migraine attacks. It became apparent that although he was able to deal with many irritations and frustrations during the workday without impatience or immediate appearance of any symptoms, an attack would come at home during the evening of a day in which some major frustration had been experienced, often being triggered then by any mild criticism from his wife. The cumulative arousal of hostile feelings was examined and clarified, along with the defences he used against such feelings; their relevance to the problems he was having with his migraine attacks was interpreted during the first ten months of his treatment, which was interrupted by a summer holiday for both patient and therapist. When the sessions with his therapist resumed in the autumn the patient announced that he had made a great discovery during the summer; while attending group sessions at the National Training Laboratories in Bethel, Maine, he had been confronted in the group with the nature of his problem of unexpressed hostility!

In each of these cases the impact of extra-analytic events loosened narcissistic resistance and made the analytic work more productive. In the first case, an abrupt change in bodily function, obviously connected with the patient's feeling of being socially vindicated, was eloquent enough. In the second, the questioning of the selection committee members was decisive. In the third, investigative work accomplished within a group pointed out decisively to the patient the origin of his problems. In the ambience of analytic work bodily changes and the challenges and sanctions of a group outside the dyadic interaction can make a marked impact on consolidated narcissistic resistance against enlightenment.

Clinical experience indicates that, in general, the symptom neuroses, i.e., hysterical neurosis of the conversion type, obsessive-compulsive neurosis; phobic neurosis; and any combination of these, usually respond adequately in individual psychoanalysis. However, character disorders, including some that are severe, respond at a perceptibly more rapid rate when dealt with by group analytic psychotherapy in a properly composed group. Although the regression that takes place in the more obvious transference is likely to be less deep in group than in individual psychoanalysis, the group's impact is powerful. Its power reflects the way in which the primal transference is rooted in the phylogenetic struggle for survival, and its effect is enhanced by the approximation of the therapy group to social reality. On the other hand, very early and very complex problems of pairing in a dependent role with another – to such a high degree the business of individual psychoanalysis – are brought only inadequately into group analytic psychotherapy. The conductor of the group cannot, because of the nature of the situation, give time and attention to scrutinise and interpret in detail the idiosyncratic early experience of each group member. We are thus facing a paradox: the situation of the analytic group makes it easier to challenge narcissistic resistances, but it is often only in prolonged psychoanalysis that narcissistic developments and defences can be understood in detail, and overcome.

Narcissism and group psychology

Freud (1921) emphasised the attachment of group members to their common leader, and the consequent bonding with one another. The libidinal tie to the leader becomes an intense identification with him which is internalised until the group member unconsciously replaces his ego-ideal with his image of the leader – or modifies his ego-ideal to accord more nearly with such an image. The introjection causes a moulding of the ego itself to accord with an inner model of which the leader continues to represent the outer form. The secondary identification with other group members produces aim-inhibited object-ties to each of them along with an identification with the group as a whole. These libidinal ties, formed of intense identifications and strongly dependent mutual attachments, make a psychic cement that, although operating outside of awareness, often leads to the adoption of a common ideology. This ideology may have but a thin façade of rationality, since when selected drive derivatives and affects are intensified intellectual processes are often inhibited. A group is usually more emotionally labile and less intellectually fastidious than the individuals who compose it. Freud (1921) suggested that these two commonly manifested characteristics of group life relate to the group's ability to transcend individual narcissism. It is certainly evident that strongly cohesive groups are often founded on archaic types of object relationships; the individual member approaches and shares a narcissistically satisfying, purified group pleasure-ego and entertains the belief that all things felt to be bad or unpleasant exist only beyond the group's domain.[4] The pervasive contemporary experience of being lonely, uprooted, and superfluous, of occupying no recognised or esteemed place among other men in a common world, has given rise to all kinds of movements that loudly betray the archaic device of elevating the individual ego to the grandiose proportions that the ego of the group and its leader seem to have.

Such regressive group dynamics, outlined in terms of a narcissistic dimension, can come to full fruition in inspirational religious and political groups, especially under the aegis of a personally charismatic leader. These dynamics are present also in healing groups of whatever sort, but in group-analytic psychotherapy these strong regressive tendencies are soon impeded and frustrated by the discriminative activity of the conductor, and by a climate developed for the enhancement of psychodynamic insight. Interpretations and other interventions – including comments designed to foster attitudes of self- and group-observation – lead to an established ideal of reflection and contemplation. This ideal goal takes into account the 'material' displayed in expressive verbal interaction and thus allows for the bringing into consciousness of unconscious themes, wishes, and fantasies – as well as the defences used to avoid acknowledging and elucidating them. Interpretations can then be offered concerning denial, minimisation and any other distortions of social reality, including many generally accepted contemporary fads and fashions. The ego-ideal is placed firmly at the service of group observation and self-analysis.

Paradox and complement

The small group-analytic situation provides the matrix for powerful support as well as pressures to enable a productive challenge of the group's and each member's narcissistic defences, although the situation limits the possibilities of reaching into idiosyncratic details adequately. Moreover, as part of this process as outlined above, the small group-analytic situation necessarily provokes the common regressive primal transference which then emerges for conscious appraisal in terms of the omnipotent group-object individual-self merger. Thus group analysis becomes empowered to explore the narcissistic dimensions of individual psychology and psychopathology in some ways that are superior to those available in dyadic analysis. It should also be noted that the primal transference of any one member is inextricably conflated with his own early experiences in life and the conflicts generated within his family of origin. Freud (1909) discussed this matter sixty-eight years ago in his account of Little Hans.

The paradox of greater access to the problems of pathological narcissism but of lesser possibilities for detailed individual exploration of it is paralleled by the fate of the separation anxiety that the termination phase of group-analytic psychotherapy arouses. Whatever it has previously offered to mitigate the separation-anxiety and griefs of each member, all the members share, as their joint experience draws near its close, distress over the impending loss of group support and the readiness of their fellows to enter into understanding verbal exchange. They may bring strong defences to bear against this expected loss; these may sometimes include an exaggerated glorification of the group and contempt for those outside it. Such developments provide an opportunity for group-analytic work. However, as I have previously pointed out (Abse, 1974), it is the end-phase of group therapy that displays its limitations most conspicuously. Each group member who exhibits separation-anxiety, depressive emotions, and multiform idiosyncratic fantasies because of the momentous impact of the group's impending dissolution will have much less time for consideration of termination than would be his lot in prolonged individual analysis.

It thus becomes apparent that analysis in a group can profitably complement individual psychoanalysis, and that the opposite is true also. The integration of the two techniques requires careful consideration of the sequential or simultaneous involvement of the two modalities, and also of the possibility that no general conclusion in this respect will fit each and every case.

The superego and group psychology

In recent years the discussion of pathological forms of narcissism has overshadowed that of the neurotic ramifications of unconscious sources of guilt feelings. Inasmuch as the constraints and demands of the archaic aspects of the internal superego are inextricably involved with degradation of self-esteem, and, as Strachey (1934) emphasised, the therapeutic action of psychoanalysis is largely concerned with weakening the power of the archaic aspects of the superego, it sometimes seems as if recent discussions of narcissism, however valuable, are too far removed from the basic clinical problem of unconscious sources of guilt. The necessary therapeutic modification of the superego is brought about in individual psychoanalysis through the transference to the analyst of both positive and negative attitudes toward the parents. While the more hostile part of the transference is unavoidable and is, indeed, necessary, it is only by projecting and enjoying the support of the more positive aspects of the superego (originally the helpful, loving parents) that the patient can face his repressed impulses and inner conflict.

In those other forms of psychotherapy in which suggestion is more prominent than in analytic exploration, the physician immediately puts himself in a position of command as a superego representative. Ernest Jones (1923) pointed out that the peculiarly high degree of suggestibility that is characteristic of hypnosis comes from the full projection of the superego on the person of the hypnotist. When the subject feels his hypnotist's suggestion to be an immoral one, however, the latter is apt to lose his role as superego representative and lose at the same time his subject's uncritical obedience. The projection is usually withdrawn in such a case, and the subject 'awakens' as his core superego reasserts its power. On the other hand, in the group the projection of the superego is apt to be more thoroughgoing and enduring; even when he is subjected to suggestions, previously held to be immoral, from the group of which he is a member the individual all too seldom 'awakes'.

Freud (1921) made it abundantly clear that the character of a group is highly dependent on the character of its leader, who is *par excellence* the figure onto which the superegos of group members are projected. The individual is also faced in the group with the impressive power of numbers. In the analytic therapy group positive dependent transference is amplified by primal transferences engendered by the experience of relating to one's fellows and the common leader; through the leader's (conductor's) utilisation of the group (by means of these powerful combined transferences) the therapeutic task of reducing the baleful effects of neurotic guilt feelings is considerably eased. An enduring impact can be made, even on stubbornly or chronically depressive characters.

The point about the group's ability to reduce the power of the archaic superego is not to be misunderstood as endorsement of 'immorality'. After all, analytic therapy, whether offered in groups or to the individual, is a kind of technique designed to cure and prevent neuroses. Besides, group-analytic groups develop an awareness of adult moral values, including consideration of others, in respect to sexual and other matters. A climate for this kind of exploration is created by an emphasis on the values of understanding and of liberation from narrow dogmatism. Freud (1933) insisted that 'the very nature of reason is a guarantee that it would not fail to concede to human emotions and to all that is determined by them, the position to which they are entitled'.

Conclusion

The considerations we have raised bear upon the strengths and weaknesses of group-analytic psychotherapy as a means of treatment compared with psychoanalysis. We have mentioned that the arousal of the primal transference may advance analytic work in the group on a magic craving for an omnipotent leader, and that this work may help solve some otherwise very refractory narcissistic problems. Moreover, narcissistic defences are often more easily challenged within the group, and more enduring and far-reaching modifications of the superego are more quickly achieved. Lastly, the attachments formed within and to the group in an atmosphere of acceptance permit a reworking of ambivalent past attachments and rejections in a way that modifies the swing from narcissistic omnipotence to convictions of being inferior and helpless. All such aspects of superior potential leverage in a group are to be contrasted with the higher therapeutic potentials psychoanalysis offers for the working-through of transferences in individual detail, especially those concerned with the early relationship with the mother.

Many analytically oriented psychiatrists have come in recent years to combine a weekly individual session with once-a-week or twice-a-week group sessions, and some of them claim more effective therapeutic leverage by the use of this schedule with otherwise refractory cases of character disorder. Such mixed treatment, of course, gives the patient more total time and attention from the therapist, in addition to benefits provided by the mobilisation of the primal transference in the group. However, this combined procedure raises the level of the primal father transference in a way that increases the difficulties of analysis, at least in my experience. No doubt the power of suggestion is greatly enhanced in group psychotherapy as in hypnosis, and this enhancement is conducive to symptom relief in patients with symptom neuroses refractory in individual therapy. We want, of course, to secure as much therapeutic cooperation on the adult level as we can in order that the parentifying and primitive magical transference is raised to awareness. From the point of view of analytic work, patients simultaneously engaged in individual and group therapy may be too heavily engulfed in a highly charged primitive transference, yet in the heat of such transference symptoms may melt away — and the patient become disinclined to accept further analytic help. When the group therapist is not the same individual as the psychoanalyst, the combined treatment encounters other difficulties; the group may be used as a forum in which to discuss the personality of the individual therapist. Such a topic is more appropriate and useful in the dyadic situation. Or the discussion of group events and personalities in the group may be used as resistance in the individual sessions. Such a double-crossed leakage can become a formidable obstacle to individual progress in treatment, especially when there is inadequate communication about a patient between the two therapists.

It has been my experience that psychoanalysis and group-analytic psychotherapy should not be provided simultaneously; either one may come first. Experience in group-analysis vastly enlarges the ego-consciousness of the person who has undergone individual analysis; Hans Sachs is reputed to have said that 'a successful psychoanalysis only scratches the surface of the unconscious', and there is little doubt that subsequent experience in a group does extend both the area and depth of this abrasion. On the other hand, there are individuals whose psychological-mindedness, in terms of depth psychology, is so deficient that only an experience in a group that breaches their armour can ready them for psychoanalysis. In any event, experience in a group-analytic process is sure to provide a new perspective — one that includes Trigant Burrow's (1953) realisation that man is characteristically uneasy with his own kind much of the time, sometimes desperately so, and that, confronted by others, he is usually defensively concerned with his own identity. Perhaps, ideally, the sequence might well be: psychoanalysis followed by group-analytic psychotherapy followed by further psychoanalysis.

In the study of patients in analytic group treatment at the Tavistock Clinic by Malan *et al.* (1976), a strong positive correlation between favourable outcome and previous individual psychotherapy was evident. Of course, this study concerned itself with but one kind of analytically oriented group therapy, but even among the many cases of unsatisfactory outcome there were some patients who described benefits gained from their involvement in group treatment. One such patient found himself able to get along better with others, and thus better able to cope with increased responsibilities and difficult situations in his work. Another felt that the group had enabled him to cope better with his symptoms; finding out that so many others had problems had helped him cope better with his own. Malan *et al.* (1976) raise the question whether it is appropriate to apply to the group the strictly psychoanalytic approach used with individuals.

In Foulkes's view (1948), which he maintained over the years, the group-analytic situation stands between 'self-analysis' and 'the free ocean of life', so it is inappropriate to apply unmodified concepts of psychoanalysis to treatment in the group. The value of group-analytic therapy as a complement to individual psychoanalysis is fully realised only when the group itself is used as a therapeutic instrument whenever possible, and concepts founded on group dynamics are applied.

Notes

1 C.f. Wilfred Trotter, *Instincts of the Herd in Peace and War*, London, 1916; New York, 1916.
2 The term 'special event' is often used to allude to anything that alters or intrudes upon the basic psychoanalytic situation. Group events are among such 'special events'. See S. S. Weiss, 'Effect on transference of "Special Events" occurring during psychoanalysis'.
3 I am grateful to Dr Vamik Volkan for this example from his analytic practice.
4 Splitting mechanisms include simultaneous disavowal and acknowledgement existing as an 'alteration of the ego', as well as the split between 'all good objects', 'all bad objects'. C.f. Vamik Volkan (1976).

References

Abse, D. Wilfred (1974), *Clinical Notes on Group-Analytic Psychotherapy*, Bristol, Wright; Charlottesville, University Press of Virginia.
Burrow, Trigant (1953), *Science and Man's Behavior: The Contribution of Phylobiology*, New York, Philosophical Library.
Foulkes, S. H. (1948), *Introduction to Group-Analytic Psychotherapy, Studies in the Social Integration of Individuals and Groups*, London, Heinemann Medical Books.
Freud, Sigmund (1909), *Analysis of a Phobia in a Five-Year-Old Boy*, vol. 10 of Standard Edition, ed. James Strachey, London, Hogarth Press, 1964.

Freud, Sigmund (1921), *Group Psychology and the Analysis of the Ego*, vol. 18 of Standard Edition, ed. James Strachey, London, Hogarth Press, 1964.

Freud, Sigmund (1933), *The Question of a Weltanschauung*, New Introductory Lectures, Lecture 35 in vol. 22 of Standard Edition, ed. James Strachey, London, Hogarth Press, 1964.

Freud, Sigmund (1937), 'Analysis Terminable and Interminable' in *The Standard Edition of the Complete Psychological Works of Sigmund Freud*, vol. 23, ed. James Strachey, London, Hogarth Press, 1964.

Jones, Ernest (1923), 'The nature of auto-suggestion', *International Journal of Psychoanalysis*, 4, p. 293.

Kohut, Heinz (1971), *The Analysis of the Self: A Systematic Approach to the Psychoanalytic Treatment of Narcissistic Personality Disorders*, New York, International Universities Press.

Malan, David H., F. H. G. Balfour, V. G. Hood, A. M. N. Shooter (1976), 'Group psychotherapy. A long-term follow-up study', *Archives of General Psychiatry*, vol. 33, No. 11, pp. 1303-15.

Stone, Leo (1961), *The Psychoanalytic Situation*, The Freud Anniversary Lecture Series, New York, International Universities Press (quotations from pp. 70, 71).

Strachey, James (1934), 'The nature of the therapeutic action of psycho-analysis', *International Journal of Psychoanalysis*, 15, pp. 127-59.

Volkan, Vamik (1976), *Primitive Internalized Object Relationships*, New York, International Universities Press.

Weiss, S. S. (1975), 'Effect on transference of "Special Events" occuring during psychoanalysis', *International Journal of Psychoanalysis*, 56, pp. 69-75.

Chapter 3

The group-analytic circle and its ambient network

E. James Anthony

Preamble: thoughts on a summer's day

Almost every year I would visit London in the summer and spend a
day at Hampstead with Michael Foulkes. We would pass as much time
as possible in the back garden, if the sun was out, talking of topics that
interested us both — the future of group-analytic psychotherapy and
its relation to psychoanalysis, the frenetic therapeutic movements that
periodically swept the United States like epidemics of affective disorder, and the sometimes convoluted and obscure politics of the
American Group Psychotherapy Association. Sometimes we became a
'group of two' and the transactions between us would grow animated,
amusing and even a little acidulated; and sometimes, unpredictably, we
would drop into an older type of psychoanalytic coupling as our
thoughts drifted silently between us. We said nothing but seemed to be
in close contact. This pattern of interchange was not surprising since I
had undergone a psychological birth or 'hatching' (as Mahler has put
it although I do not like the farmyard context) on the couch in analysis
with him and had later graduated to a group-analytic circle and on the
the ambient professional network beyond.

We frequently recalled the period at Northfield where I was for a
year a somewhat bemused and bewildered participant in the so-called
'Northfield Experiment'. I remembered the first tentative salute that I
offered as most unlikely Captain, RAMC, to Foulkes, a most unmilitary
Major, RAMC, receiving in exchange a somewhat bizarre manual
gesture that could have meant anything from 'stand at ease' to 'come
and have a cup of coffee'. At this army hospital I gained my first
experience as a group and community psychiatrist under his tutelage
(with a little Adlerianism thrown in by Major Bierer plus a touch of
Bionism, Rickmanism, and several other 'isms' that from time to

time were incorporated into the Experiment. However, my main loyalty was to Foulkes.) In those days my naïvety was such that North-field was only a neurosis centre as far as I was concerned and it was only later, after the war, that I learned to my surprise and pleasure that I had been unknowingly a part of a group psychotherapeutic history — a fact upon which I dined out frequently in the United States during my early residence there before Northfield receded into obscurity. Nevertheless, the ideas that were generated there are vividly alive to this day.

During this quasi-military phase, I found myself very much drawn towards Foulkes as a person. At first I found it difficult to understand his groping habit of speech, the inexplicable hesitations, the mental detours, the sudden truncation of sentences, the often entangled syntax and the tapering of the thought processes that left you floating un-accountably in the air. It was only many years later, after intensive couch and circle experiences, that I began to develop the same com-municative style myself although never with the same numinous nebul-ousness that was altogether his special trait. Unconscious identifications can only go so far but as I gradually came to learn how effective it was as a therapeutic tool, I began to make more conscious use of it. The inconclusiveness compels the patients to tease things out for them-selves and to strive towards making sense out of dimly perceived internal ideas, Each hesitation acted like a small psychological prod that set the associations going. Perhaps the most valuable lesson I received from Foulkes was on the value of unobtrusiveness on the part of the therapist and on the limitations of explicitness. This fitted very well into my developing approach to children, picked up in part from Piaget, in which one feels one's way into the mind almost surreptitiously, forgetting the rules of grammar and any attention to punctuation. Not only did I begin to communicate like Foulkes but over the many years of contact I also caught myself at times behaving like him, for instance, running my hand through my hair when perplexed but, again, less effectively because of increasing baldness. As I said before, unconscious identification can only go so far! At Northfield we had worked and played together. I found that his tennis, like his therapy, was un-expected, often surprising and allowed his opponents to do most of the work. (I have become increasingly impressed, while observing patients in groups, how often the style is the man, invading his whole personality and presentation of himself.)

When the war ended, I was certain of only two things: I wanted to become a psychiatrist-psychoanalyst and I wanted to work with children.

At this point life chose to place me on a Foulkesian conveyor belt that carried me steadily along as his analysand in a training analysis, as an analyst sharing an office with him, as his student in group dynamics and group psychotherapy, as a co-therapist in an analytically-orientated group, as a fellow consultant at the Maudsley Hospital, as a co-author of a book on group therapy from the psychoanalytic point of view, and, finally, as joint visiting professors at the University of North Carolina in the United States. On immigrating to America, I was regarded by many of the group therapists there as his junior representative or *alter ego* and treated with much undeserved respect as a consequence. For instance, on the 25th Anniversary of the American Group Psychotherapy Association I was invited to give the address mainly out of respect for him and his work. (I ought to mention in passing, that I do talk a great deal in America for a very simple reason: if you speak English there in the peculiar way in which it is spoken on this island and are given to pronouncing tomato as to-mah-to rather than to-may-to, invitations to lecture tend to pour in!)

On those lovely summer days that I continued to spend with him on my visits to the delectable isle, I was struck, as always, by his sustained enthusiasm for his life work and interests. He would outline plans for future projects that would have taken decades to accomplish. It was not the energy so much as the hopefulness that I found infectious and that I respond to whenever and wherever I meet it. For instance, I recall my dear co-author, Dr Therese Benedek, starting a monumental work on Female Sexuality in her eightieth year and almost completing the job before she died: I recall Rene Spitz taking me round his apartment and showing me a huge library of infant films that had still to be analysed. He told me with pride that there was at least twenty years of work ahead, and at that time he was in his eighties. During the later years with Foulkes, the *momentum mori* was never very far away. As we sat in the garden in the lukewarm light that often passes for sunshine in Britain, he would sometimes start to shiver because his thermal homeostasis was poorly regulated and would complain of peculiar sensations. For some reason that I could never quite understand, he regarded me as a dependable physician and would often interrupt our analytic and group conversations for a mini-consultation on his heart, his thyroid, his erratic temperature and his insomnia. Having been in succession analysand, pupil, colleague and son, I was ready to accept the new role and research the medical textbooks on his behalf. The insightful part of me regarded all this lightly as the inevitable touch of hypochondriasis that accompanies existence in the 70-year-olds when health becomes more precarious. I remember on one occasion when he took me for a visit to the neighbouring cemetery and showed me the area where his ashes would be scattered. We also looked at the psychoanalytic circle of ashes around us – the great figures of our profession reduced to small urns of inorganic material that was immobile, insensitive, mindless, affectless and uncommunicative, bringing up the ancient morbid speculation in a new form: was it better to be Freud dead than a live pig? Yet, for neither of us did it occasion any undue existential anxiety as we continued our vivid discussions in the unresponsive company of the dead, and I was reminded so much of Goethe's expression (often quoted by Freud) of 'the dear, lovely habit of living' and, for the life of me, as I stared at the urns and the grass plots, I saw images not of ashes but of books, recordings, articles, teaching seminars and therapeutic sessions.

As you will have noted from this ragbag of memories, I am nostalgic for so many different portions of my life with Foulkes. Thirty-three years is a large part of a lifetime and for a certain portion of this period he was the most important person in my life. Before I come to talk about his work and its impact on me and my work, I do want to quote from a short review that he wrote on the book by Max Schur, *Freud: Living and Dying* (1973), because it says something about his way of looking at the human scene and perhaps something about what he thought that we, his followers, should do about his work:

> That Freud emerges as a human person (he said) will not surprise anyone. What is more surprising is that he seems to have been more disturbed than would have been obvious from his work. It becomes apparent that his compulsive working was partly a flight from anxious restlessness and depressive moods. His work appears altogether more in the nature of a self-cure from personal suffering, as in the case of great creative writers and artists. Actually this corresponds to an impression I had long formed from Freud's work itself. Namely, that it should be treated as a creative imaginative piece of writing, although it stresses a scientific attitude and is undoubtedly written in a scientific spirit. In other words one should understand Freud's work in the light of his own time and his own personal language and thinking. One cannot build too much on it that is new without being in danger of losing its essence. *We should rather, after having taken it in fully, build afresh, if further essential advances are intended.*

It will be easily perceived that an unresolved, idealising and transmuting transference is still at work in this interrupted relationship.
About half way through our lives together, he became Michael to me
and I James to him, but he could never be just Michael because he had
been so much else besides and so much more. When I walked into his
presence, I walked partly into my own past history and into many years
of intimate revelations and feelings. He knew me both from the outside
and from the inside, from the couch and from the group analytic
circle, and from our shared ambient network. These represented different levels of knowing, of understanding and of interacting. I, in turn,
got to know him better than one usually gets to know one's analyst
and that was an unexpected 'growth experience': we became a working
pair in place of a working through pair! (I am reminded here of Winnicott's belief that at the termination of analytic treatment the self-to-self
relationship should be established.)

It is because I came to know him so well that I am more than confident that he would say the same thing about his own work as he said
of Freud's — that one cannot build too much on it that is new without
being in danger of losing its essence and that after having taken it in
fully, we should rather build afresh, if further essential advances are
intended. I saw in him later, as I never saw in him from the tilted
perspective of the couch or from within the magic circle of the group,
some of the same elements that he detected in Freud — restlessness,
somatic anxieties, doubts and depressions and a push towards new
psychological horizons. I think that all of us, Freudians, have this touch
of Freudian neurosis about us enhancing our sensitivity and empathy
to the hurts of others. The Freudian malaise was also, as Freud himself
recognised, a prelude to creativity. In many ways, Foulkes was as
much a Freudian as anyone else that I have known, but this in no way
barred him from exploring areas largely left untouched by Freud. He
saw no dissonance at all in being both a psychoanalyst and a group
analyst.

Before proceeding to my main task, let me say something about
Freud as a social theorist, an aspect of him that has largely been overlooked, especially by psychoanalysts.

Psychoanalysis and group analysis

Freud has sometimes been accused of being 'intrapsychically fixated'
with only a modicum of interest in the world about him or people

inhabiting it. It has also been alleged, in spite of much evidence to the contrary, that his followers trailed submissively behind him along the inward path and developed repugnances to multipersonal and transpersonal situations that made them reluctant to accept group psychotherapy as a related and alternative mode of treatment. It is true that psychoanalysts who have undertaken group analysis have been treated with some antagonism by many 'classical' psychoanalysts, and it is true that Freud candidly admitted on one occasion that his preoccupation with developing psychoanalysis gave him little time to explore neighbouring areas of the biological and social sciences without leaving a large number of loose ends up in the air. It was Hartmann, with his thrust towards a general psychoanalytic psychology, who first pointed to Freud's many contributions to social psychology. For example, in his paper on *Civilization and Modern Nervous Illness* (1908), Freud had presented explicitly and systematically the influence of cultural factors on instinctual life and the genesis of neurosis. In his early theory of neurosis, he postulated the sexual abuse of the child as a critical factor of aetiology. His fascination with the theme of *Totem and Taboo* (1913) led him to apply analytic knowledge to anthropological problems and introduced his speculation on primitive parricide. However, it was in his work on Group Formation (1921) that he first tried to explain group-psychological phenomena and constructed an elegant working model depicting the libidinal constitution of groups (with a leader and not too much organisation) in which the group members erected the same object in the place of their ego ideal and thus identified themselves with one another in their ego. The graphic representation used by Freud could fit very well into any modern textbook of analytic group dynamics although understandably it does not present the whole theoretical picture. This 'simple idea' for explaining group psychology occurred to him during the spring of 1919 and he brought the idea to fruition two years later. On the one side, he attempted to explain the psychology of groups on the basis of changes in the psychology of the individual, and on the other side, he used the psychology of the group to formulate a structure of the individual's mind that initiated his structural theory. He realised, he said, that he was only touching on the very fringe of a very large subject that was still in its infancy and if one could think oneself into his outlook at the time, there was obviously present an implicit hope that someone else in his following might cultivate this promising soil further.

The phenomenology with which he chose to deal would be familiar to all present-day group-analytic psychotherapists: the aggressions and counter-aggressions, the cross-identifications, the powerful suggestions operating between group members, the disinhibitions that develop gradually over time, and the pervasive presence of love and hate, envy and jealousy and narcissism and narcissistic idealisation. He also touched on the subtle and still mysterious working of empathy, on problems of leadership, deputy leadership and groups that are leaderless. He recognised the emergence of the personal myth through which the individual made his way out of the group matrix.

Perhaps his most significant contribution to group dynamics was to stress the antagonism between neurosis and group formations, entailing a marvellous piece of clinical deduction. When the individual was removed from his usual group formation, he became a prey to neurosis, or, to quote Freud directly, 'where a powerful impetus has been given to group formation, neuroses may diminish and, at all events temporarily, disappear'. He goes on to say that 'justifiable attempts have also been made to turn this antagonism between neurosis and group formation to therapeutic account'. We know that in this discussion he is talking mainly of the large group but the same argument could be used with respect to the small group. Furthermore, the therapeutic potential of the small group would not be offset by some of the disadvantages attributed by Freud to the large group, that is, more controls, incompetent functioning, and a proclivity to immature primary process thinking. If, as Freud says, the neurotic, deprived of group experience, creates his own world of imagination, his own religion, his own set of symptoms, his own system of delusions, then why did not this first great group-analytic psychologist not take the next important logical step and insist that for certain types of cases immersion in a therapeutic group could be curative and should be tried? Had he taken this initiative, he would have created two interrelated therapies – psychoanalysis and group analysis – sharing a basic metapsychology, a common language and a theoretical and clinical cross-fertilisation of each other. There would have been no splitting of psychologies necessitating later struggles toward resynthesis.

Ostow (1977) has made some interesting speculations on the development of Freud's very significant social theory based on the relationship of the group to its leader. According to him, the three main works in this context – *Totem and Taboo, Group Psychology* and *Moses and Monotheism* – represent three stages in the emergence of the primal leader as an irreplaceable hero who is ultimately responsible for the group's cultural development. All three throw an interesting light on the mechanism of maintaining leadership following the death of the leader and the account can be looked upon as an intriguing allegorical account of the early history of the psychoanalytic movement as understood by Freud as well as an expression of his fears and fancies for its future. At the age of 56, he had to deal with the defection of his most promising disciples and so he wrote of the death wishes underlying the rebelliousness. At 65 he appeared more concerned with the problem of finding a suitable though necessarily lesser replacement for the leader after his death. The new leader would hold the group together, purging internal threats, cultivating a loyal cadre and exploiting the libidinal needs of the group members. (At this point, he had Otto Rank in mind as his successor.) Shortly before his death he once more returned to developments following the death of the old leader but the fate of the group is now separated from the fate of its doctrine. Although a continuity of leadership is still taken for granted, the leadership role is viewed more sceptically. In the absence of a leader, a group of elders could assume the guardianship of the system. The presentation of valuable theory and memory of the old leader was handed to a trained élite (who would presumably be responsible for setting up the needed institutes and societies). Inevitable within this evolution was the phenomenon of splitting since there were always good and bad sons (and daughters) who would tend to go their separate ways.

Although he spoke of conservation of 'valuable theory' Freud wanted no embalming of psychoanalysis. He refrained from speaking of it as a system but accentuated instead its unfinished character, its flexibility, and the tentative nature of a considerable part of it. He himself made many adjustments and reformulations and expected subsequent practitioners to do the same. As Foulkes said of him in the comment quoted earlier, his followers should rather, after having taken in the theory fully, build afresh if further essential advances were to be made.

In Britain the antagonism between psychoanalysis and group analysis has been less striking than in America since more of the leading psychoanalysts in this country have shown a profound interest in group-dynamics. To those of us who are amphibian (in the sense of Sir Thomas Browne), it is quite difficult to understand why once again we should be confronted with a dilemma of two cultures – the individual therapeutic culture and the small and large group culture. It almost seemed as if the 'pure' psychoanalysts equated an interest in group psychotherapy with heresy and regarded practitioners who mixed their therapeutic cultures with suspicion and sometimes downright hostility. Foulkes experienced some of this and many creative psychoanalysts in the United States also suffered from what James Joyce once referred to as being nailed to a 'cruelfiction', and it is indeed a cruel fiction with very little bearing on the realities of group analysis. The mischievous and mistaken segregation of two-body and many-body therapies has led to prejudice and demeaning attitudes: the individual approach was looked upon as 'deeper', intrapsychic, metapsychologically based and technically tied to the extraordinary phenomenon of transference and the transference neurosis during which an artificial illness was generated and 'cured' during the treatment. The group approach, by comparison, was seen as somewhat shallow, interpersonal or transpersonal, lacking in metapsychological underpinning, relatively ahistorical and diluting all its therapeutic efforts by concentrating on too many individuals at one and the same time. It also attempted to handle the complexities of transference within a setting that was quite unsuitable for it and even laid false claims to the production of a group transference neurosis. This automatically received the opprobrious accusation of 'wild analysis', than which there is no worse indictment in psychoanalysis.

Foulkes was quite clear in his autobiographical notes (1969) that the 'two cultures' represented a false dilemma. As he put it:

> I myself have not ever maintained that the interest in group analysis goes at the expense of that in psychoanalysis; as I have so often explained, group analysis is both less than psychoanalysis as well as more. Looking at it solely from a psychoanalytical point of view it is not more than application of psychoanalytic insight, thinking and attitude to the psychotherapy in the group. From the point of view of psychotherapy as a whole and of the study of human beings, it has contributions to make which exceed those of psychoanalysis although in no way replaces them.

This was a very balanced statement that did not detract or subtract from one or the other and it is regrettable that the antagonisms exist and continue to exist. The most striking and yet predictable fact is that the greatest opposition comes from psychoanalysts who have no experience whatsoever of a therapeutic group, have not understood the implications of Freud's *Group Psychology* or why he felt a need to write it and often react to group treatment more with rivalry than understanding, whereas it is clear to the unbiased that the two modes of therapy could be, both therapeutically and scientifically, synergistic in their relationship. Having said this, it should also be added that not every psychoanalyst is psychologically equipped to become a group analyst and vice versa, although every psychoanalyst who is thoughtful in this area should undertake to have a group therapeutic experience so that he might better understand the conflicts that plague his institutions and societies and perhaps deal with them more effectively. This statement, however, must be tempered with the further knowledge that an understanding of group dynamics does not by any means prevent group associations from suffering from similar 'group diseases' or internecine strife. Like war, such group divisiveness as Freud pointed out, is built into human constitutions and institutions and often the best one can do is to develop mitigating tactics. There is no doubt that the paranoid vision is growing in intensity with our psychological sophistication that leads to everybody becoming, in Freud's words, 'continuously engaged in a psychological analysis of his fellow beings'.

The group-analytic circle

The group-analytic approach to group psychotherapy, incorporating as it did much of the thinking of psychoanalysis, was not built in a day, since it set out to deal with certain problems that had immediately engaged the attention of Freud seventy years ago when he postulated a reciprocal influence between individual and group in which the individual's psychology altered the psychology of the group and the group psychology restructured the mind of the individual. Clearly these subtle reciprocating mechanisms required a bifocal mode of observation with eyes equally focused on the individual and the group. If this mutual influence existed then a multivariate condition required to be investigated. Group analysis set out to do just this.

It was evident from the beginning that psychoanalysis and group analysis made uncomfortable bedfellows since both individual and group attempted to make themselves heard at the same time, creating for the uninitiated the veritable babel that demanded both the skills of a psychoanalyst as well as the skills of a group analyst to integrate the infantile neurosis, infantile sexuality, the original family conflict, the powerful mechanisms of repression and the internalised conflict between instinct, immature ego and internalised authority with the here-and-now transactions, communications, interactions and group conflicts. Foulkes was aware of the difficulties from the start and gradually forged his method through trial and error using the group as a laboratory situation in which his evolving ideas were continuously put to the test of observation, reformulated and revised. (What is most disturbing and dismaying about the deluge of new group techniques that have inundated us in recent years is the fact that they arise like mushrooms overnight, are greedily consumed with sometimes poisonous consequences and then, within a short space of time that marketeers refer to as a fad period, or financially as a fat period, they sicken and disappear leaving a host of disorientated and disorganised patients behind them like iatrogenic monuments.)

In the psychoanalytic situation, Freud openly declared that he disliked being stared at by patients and retreated behind the couch while the unconscious groups belonging to the patient's life (to quote the amusing title of Fritz Redl's paper) retreated 'under the couch'. What Redl was implying here was that the analytic situation that appeared visibly so bare was in fact haunted by groups from the primary family organisation onward and that the air was clamorous with the voices, supporting and persecuting, of friends, relatives and enemies who made up the social orbit of the patient. The 'group under the couch' continued to exercise its unseen effects throughout the treatment and the patient had to learn how to deal with them as well as with himself and his analyst. Hartmann had made reference to 'the entire complexity of an individual's relationships to his fellow men as objects of love, hate, fear and rivalry'. Like Freud, he did not take the further step of suggesting a confronting circle – a psychosocial interface where internal and external could meet. One cannot help suspecting that the psychoanalytic situation (and Freud would be the first to admit this) caters to the psychological comfort of the analyst – his invisible location, his free-floating attention (sometimes unfortunately conducive to dozing), the 'tilted relationship' with the patient, the short 45- or 50-minute hour, the focus on a single patient. The group-analytic therapist incarnates the 'group under the couch', settles them down in a circle of chairs, transforms each of them into a patient and not a projection and joins the circle himself for an hour and a half to two hours in a face-to-face encounter. There is no concealment, no diplomatic immunity, no 'tiltedness' and total body exposure so that a scratch of the nose or a stifled yawn cannot pass unnoticed and all the narcissistic investments of charisma – omnipotence, omniscience, optimal mental health, god-like serenity and even deeper archetypal attributes – can be put to savage test. The magic circle, with its multiple layers of communication, of consciousness and of control; its channels of influence and its eye-to-eye contact can prove a trial by fire for the therapist who has spent his lifetime in hiding behind the couch.

Foulkes was ambivalent about the use of the term leader since the leadership qualities of the group analyst are antithetical to the leadership described in Freud's *Group Psychology*. He is a leader who does not lead, a leader who does not impose his views, a leader who does not plan the strategy for the group, a leader who often follows where the group leads and a leader who gradually abrogates much of the leadership credited to him by the group to the group itself. Neither Foulkes not I, as we left the security behind the couch to join the marketplace of the circle, ever felt that we altered our analytic posture. We remained psychoanalysts within the group but added a group analytic perspective — a vision of the total group as a functioning entity. The strain was in us and not in the patients. It was our perspective that flitted between individual and group, between past and present, between intrapsychic and transpersonal and between the understanding of individual psychopathology and group psychopathology.

The psychoanalytic situation creates its own peculiar phenomenology within the frame that demarcates it from the reality of the outside world. At the core of the situation is a peculiar illusion of encapsulation and inwardness that gradually fosters a regressive transference that culminates in an artificial illness. The general transference that occurs between people in everyday life for the most part passes unnoticed, although every now and then one will hear an angry wife saying to her husband: 'Please don't treat me like your mother; I am *not* your mother.' Unfortunately this does not constitute a mutative interpretation in Strachey's sense and generally does little more than provoke a high degree of indignation on the part of the husband. Transferences may also occur between children and their parents, especially when parents take up a therapeutic attitude to their young which they sometimes feel compelled to do to make amends for maltreatment or emotional neglect. Parents who are trained psychotherapists tend to be special offenders in this respect.

Foulkes distinguished between T and t, regarding the group-analytic group as *essentially* a transference group that facilitated the transfer of unconscious fantasies between the membership. Thus t and T both played an integral part in group proceedings as conducted by group-analytic psychotherapists but a special question then arose: how big was T? Was it as big only as a floating transference manifestation or was it big enough to be considered a transference neurosis crystallising in a certain member or was it even bigger than that to involve the whole group in a transference neurosis? (Such professional ruminations are familiar to me as a child analyst since, from the time of the first analyses in Vienna, we have been debating what size of *t* the immature apparatus of the child can handle.)

There is no doubt that the dynamics of the group are usually more lively than one meets with in individual psychotherapy or psychoanalysis. In both situations, individual and group, the level of communication fluctuates with the level of transference, the stage of treatment and the degree of resistance. However, because of the greater body exposure, the body itself in the group tends to take a very active role. I am also sure that Foulkes is right in his shrewd observation that the ego gets more of a workout in the group than it does in the individual situation since it has to keep pace with a kaleidoscopic set of transactions. The self is more prone to narcissistic injury and insult than in the more considerate dyadic setting.

Although the conductor's perspective is bifocal, his interpretations are invariably directed to the group as a whole and this was the first and most enduring group lesson that I learned from Foulkes and that he learned from Freud. It has often been said that a transference neurosis in psychoanalysis is to some extent cultivated by the analyst, although most would regard it as self-generating. The reverse of this may have a certain modicum of truth: the failure of the transference neurosis to appear may often be traced to certain characteristic types of counter-transference in the therapist. Group interpretations, systematically practised by the group analyst, can have a remarkable effect in 'groupifying' (I must apologise for the cross-Atlantic verbal concoction) the group.

One cannot claim, I think, although many of my colleagues in America would do so without reserve, that the group provides the patient with two therapies for the price of one! From time to time, he gets individual psychotherapy or even a touch of psychoanalysis and, at the same time, he obtains the large bonus of group treatment. Here I must make something of a disclaimer. Foulkes, like Freud, was forever fighting the good fight for his own created form of therapy, but, unlike Freud, he tended to overestimate what the group could do. As Freud became older, his interest in psychoanalysis as providing an incomparable instrument for the investigation of the individual mind grew stronger and his belief in its therapeutic power became gradually weaker. I will quote what Foulkes had to say about this (*Therapeutic Group Analysis*, 1965):

By and large, the group situation would appear to be the most powerful therapeutic agency known to us. I imagine it will become more and more the usual psychotherapeutic approach out of which individual treatment emerges for special conditions, personalities or aims. Psychoanalysis, for instance, will always remain the method of choice for the intimate and detailed working through of the infantile neurosis, of the personal transference neurosis under conditions of regression. On the other hand, group analysis is not less intensive than psychoanalysis, given comparable circumstances, but in certain respects is more intensive.

The claim is large but the evidence is by no means as large and depends more on personal conviction. I remember, when people thought that child analysis was little more than applied psychoanalysis, Mrs Klein would reiterate that not only was child analysis as psychoanalytic as adult analysis; not only was it as capable of generating a transference neurosis; but, it was also deeper. From my own experience, I would say that I have not found, even though swayed in that direction by strong loyalties, that child analysis is deeper than adult analysis or that group analysis is more intensive than psychoanalysis. What I would say is that group analytic psychotherapy offers us an incomparable instrument for the understanding of the group mind or the psychology of the individual in the group situation. The phenomenology it stirs up is as exciting as anything one finds in psychoanalysis — the mirror reactions, the personifications, the impersonations, the resonances, the role playing and the dramatisations. It is much weaker at the present time than psychoanalysis in theory and will need to build a more substantial theoretical superstructure out of the process of communication, of mirroring, of configuration and of translation (the group equivalent, as Foulkes puts it, of 'making the unconscious conscious'.)

For my own part, I again feel more in touch with the unconscious and with the unconscious fantasy in the psychoanalytic situation than I do in the group situation and my experience has been that it is harder to get at unconscious fantasies, especially deep, destructive, paranoid and depressive varieties within the circle of the group to the point when one can deal with them therapeutically. We must also constantly bear in mind that anti-therapeutic processes are even more inclined to operate in groups than in individual therapy since the counter-transference of the therapist is greater and the sadism and envy of the group members are not restricted by any analytic considerations. It is claimed that these antitherapeutic measures can eventually become therapeutic if the patients survive them and become 'realistically hardened' but one must remember that the group circle contains many vulnerable members whose self-esteem is precariously regulated and whose sensitivities are almost raw.

I really do not feel that at any time, even in seven to eight years of analysing the same group, have I succeeded in carrying out a 'psycho-analysis of the group' *à la* Wolf. The idea has always seemed bizarre to me and a contradiction in terms. I have a strong repugnance to such facile extrapolations especially when they contain inherent contradictions. It is so important for us in group-analytic psychotherapy to keep creating our own metatheory and not borrow indiscriminately from neighbouring therapies that do not fit the context at all.

Let me say something about the future of the group-analytic circle as it might develop over time. Every now and then in the history of the therapeutic sciences, certain key words suddenly appear and illuminate the intellectual landscape. Two of these words that are highly pertinent and have become the basis of metapsychology are process, structure or frame. Both process and structure have temporal meanings and are encompassed within a field that has special boundaries. The temporo-spatial aspects of the field have certain qualities that make it peculiarly different from the rest of the world. Process and structure together generate content and content can be described as the stories that patients tell within the individual and group situation or the non-verbal messages that they convey.

Process is a dynamic phenomenon that exists in a state of flux and it is characterised by spontaneity, freedom, experience, conflict and movement. Process conveys the sense of life so that when one reads the process notes from a group session one almost has the feeling that one is participating in it. It is vivid, exciting and interesting and many therapists are predominantly processists, thinking in process terms and speaking in process language. From time to time they segment the process and create events, and the event system is generically referred to as content.

Structure, on the other hand, is now a worldwide movement involving psycholinguistics, psychoanalysis, literature, anthropology and politics. Structure is relatively static but its great advantage is that it allows the formulation of theory, for the development of epistemology, for the acquisition of insight and understanding and for the evolution of a scientific language. Many psychoanalysts are predominantly structuralists and think in terms of inter- and intra-systemic conflicts within a special apparatus. Structuralists have a need to know where they are at any point of time and the conditions of their surroundings. Many therapists, like Freud, start off as processists and gradually evolve into structuralists or sometimes keep a balance between the two. As one gets older and more experienced and more skilled, one finds a need for structure, whereas the young therapist floats along comfortably on the wings of process. It is a moot point whether processists are better therapists and structuralists better theorists.

Again we have a sense of two cultures because the extreme processists often find themselves alienated from the structuralists and look upon them as less dynamic and less in touch with the essence of existence. Therapists with an obsessional turn tend towards structure, whereas hysterics are happier with process. Freud felt the need to create a structure of the individual mind using group psychology as a medium. Group psychotherapists have to create a structural model that fits both the intrapsychic and extrapsychic needs of the group. It is not sufficient for us to talk of a 'group mind' or a 'group ego' or a 'group superego' since these are all filched from the younger psychology. We do have a pressing need to develop our own metapsychology and to buttress it with good theory. We further need to look developmentally at the group observing how its history unfolds and the stages become delineated, but I would concede that this may be a professional bias on my part. Foulkes and I spoke of the group historian, the member who kept the archives of the group and reminded us of anniversaries, earlier events, developments and traumata. The group analyst, like the psychoanalyst, must carry the history of his patients inside him and from time to time it may be necessary for him to reconstruct the early group experience of the members – primary family groups, latency groups, early heterosexual groups, homosexual groups, adolescent groups, etc.

One speaks of restructuring in psychoanalysis: to what extent can the same term apply to group analysis; do we see restructuring of the individual members as individuals or do we see a restructuring of their group behaviour or of the behaviour of the group? Many psychoanalysts with whom I have discussed this question are extremely doubtful that any restructuring can take place in the personality without the help of a regressive transference neurosis which they are convinced cannot occur in the group. Both Foulkes and I have seen and described what amounts to a transference neurosis developing spontaneously in a group member. In my own case, I found myself unable to make use of it without neglecting the rest of the group. In any case, such restructuring refers to the individual psychoanalytic structure and not to the structure that we hope to see eventually emerging in group analytic psychotherapy.

One can perhaps take a cue from the work of Lévi-Strauss and his elegant development of a structural system around kinship and one might perhaps be capable, taking a cue from Chomsky, of evolving structure around the manifest and latent communications that occur in groups.

Let me say something about advances in therapeutic method within group-analytic groups. Having arranged an environment that is 'between brackets' (to use Husserl's term) as it were, an intermediate area between the workaday world and the insubstantial state of dreams and fantasies, and having instituted an atmosphere that was non-threatening, non-judgmental, non-consequential but above all therapeutically creative, what can we say about the curative factors that begin to work within the group matrix?

First of all, I'd like to think of the group as a creative matrix with unconscious and preconscious components, intermingling primary processes, visual stimulations, admixtures of rationality and irrationality, realism and irrealism, and regressions following on progressions. The therapists in this setting may often feel that the answers to his many clinical questions are there lying somewhere within the group but difficult to get at without first working through the questions. (This is reminiscent of the remark by Gauss: 'I have had my solutions for a long time but I don't know how to arrive at them.') For the patient in therapy, as for the individual in life, travelling is more often the problem than the arrival.

What seems to spark off the creative process in the group-analytic circle is its loose-endedness and its climate of non-expectation, rather like a Becket drama in which there is no plot, no beginning, no end and no sense or some sort of supersense. I have often thought of it as the aprogrammatic challenge of the blank white sheet. In the early nineteenth century Ludwig Borne offered some astonishing advice to those wishing to be original writers: They should sit for three days in front of a few sheets of paper and set down without falsification or hypocrisy anything that came into their minds − women, war, literature, crime or resentment at authority − and they would be surprised at what novel and startling things would bubble up. Seventy years later Freud offered the same suggestion to his patients and things certainly began to bubble up. It was not surprising that Foulkes as a psychoanalyst let out the same blank sheet of paper metaphorically within the group circle and gave implicit permission to the members to play freely and regressively their spontaneous ideas. The space within the circle becomes a projective screen, a practising ground for rudimentary interactions, an intermediate transititonal and play area in Winnicott's sense and a place for everyday creativity.

Once the group begins, a whole host of reactions and interactions, mechanisms and strategies, feelings and fantasies and mysterious communicating silences make their appearance. It is hard to catalogue the numerous identifications that begin to occur that can be labelled as transmuting, empathic, projective, suggestible, counter-transferential, imitative, etc. There are identifications with aggressors, with the attacked, with the vulnerable, with the sadistic and with the masochistic members of the group who are currently functioning in this mode.

As in individual psychotherapy, the understanding of the group process can be enhanced by following the circulation of affects as they resonate within the circle. Familiar cycles are those in which digressions are followed by fears of retaliation, guilt, attempts at reparation, depression, rage and then once again attack: erotic approaches are followed by rebuffs, shame, withdrawal, erotic fantasy, excitement and further declarations of passion.

The analysis of defences is not a standard or systematic procedure in groups but the therapist deals with initial resistances and conscious propositions very much as he does in the individual case. Because of the number of persons involved, the method of dealing with transference or characterological resistances is more or less on an *ad hoc* basis and may need to be, as in the individual case, interpreted over and over again, but mainly to the group as a whole rather than to any particular member. One of the most striking resistances, as in all treatment, is the resistance to change and one may detect this not only in the individual member, but in the group as a whole and even in the therapist himself. The therapist, in fact, needs to carry out his 'analytic toilet' (Glover) even more than he does in the psychoanalytic situation.

The other transactions that I myself have observed in which I have taken a specialised interest relate to certain complementary interactions between members in which one responds to another in such a way as to generate a total response. After a few such occurrences, group consciousness as a whole becomes sensitised to their appearance and reappearance and the group may intervene to break the cycle. Such complementary transactions include voyeurism and exhibitionism, sadism and masochism, dominance and submissiveness, depression and elation, progression and regression and heterosexuality and homosexuality.

The major burden of therapy lies on the shoulders of the therapists during the initial phase of the group before the group establishes itself as an efficient therapeutic instrument. In this beginning period, the task of the therapist is to 'encapsulate' the group psychologically within the circle so that their therapeutic lives are contained within it, to increase the psychological sensitivity of the group to inner experiences, thoughts, feelings, fantasies and dreams and to provide them with a model of the therapeutic posture with its essential ingredients of tolerance to new and disturbing material, attentiveness to what is being said, preoccupation with the life of the group, lack of anxiety in dealing with sexual and aggressive approaches, spontaneity in interactions and above all the capacity to maintain an even keel even when the group is floundering badly or is in a state of ferment. Every now and then, at the start, he may touch on the deeper reservoirs of feeling and fantasy to make manifest to the group its own hidden qualities and resources. My own tendency in the group is to remain as much as possible in a free-floating preconscious state, hovering as it were over the group and ready to empathise with emerging elements. In this state, I am keeping a watchful eye on myself, on the individuals and on the group as a whole. When the group is moving well and I am in attunement with it, I must confess to a certain enthralment with the creative process at work. Attentiveness to the group process allows the therapist to seize upon the appropriate moments for intervention. To paraphrase Pasteur, 'Therapeutic opportunity comes to the prepared mind.'

In America a great deal has been made of the counter-transference responses of therapists and co-therapists as useful instruments in group therapy and in certain instances there is no doubt that these counter-transference techniques become little better than opportunities for acting out on the part of the therapists. Yet, used discriminately and under the aegis of empathy, this method can enhance the interrelationship between therapist and group and intensify transference reactions.

The self has almost displaced the ego in certain psychoanalytic circles in America and some psychoanalysts, like Gedo, have made the psychology of the self the mainspring of the psychoanalytic process. Group therapists, in turn, are beginning to lay special emphasis on narcissism as it occurs in the group, on the regulation of self-esteem, on the emergence of the individual as an identity, on idealising and mirroring transferences as described by Kohut. Sad to say, in all this, the group therapists have not blazed their own trail but have followed where psychoanalysis has led.

My own special therapeutic interest within the group-analytic circle is the way in which the members play, not in the context of Berne but of Winnicott (I have noticed from Dr Pines' paper (Group Analysis, 10.1.1977) that Winnicottian ideas have been invading the Institute of Group Analysis and I am very glad of this). I would agree with him very much that we need to have the notion of space, of transitional phenomena and of play to illuminate the process in the group. I always feel the group situation, when I first enter it, as a potential space between the group and myself, and sometimes I feel the space as wide open and threatening (in an ocnophilic way as Balint would say) and sometimes as a very friendly space full of the goodnesses that the members at certain times pour into it. My own image at such times is more maternal than paternal and I can sense in myself the need to feed the group and I can sometimes be narcissistically hurt when the group vomits this good food back. Sometimes, as in child analysis, I find myself enjoying the play of the group especially when it is creative, relaxed and articulate. Again, in the guise of the maternal imago, I like to think of the group-analytic circle as a good place to come to especially if the outside world is tiring, conflicting, provoking, irritating and disturbing. As one would expect, the group members often try to convert this good place into a bad place where they can spit and vomit and excrete to their full regressive satisfactions. I like the circle to be a place where one can feel at home and where the good and the bad are equally acceptable for therapeutic consideration.

From all these points of view, the group has a tremendous task ahead of it when it first begins: the members need to take each other in and create internal representations or the unconscious group that is further shaped by work in the group; the group needs to develop its history, its therapeutic skills, its mirroring capacities and its matrix, the term coined by Foulkes.

Lastly, as I sit within the circle, I am often astonished by the variegation that appears cognitively: unless the group is very carefully selected, it may be quite heterogeneous or the imaginations may work in quite different ways, either divergently or convergently, either predominantly intuitively, concretely or very abstractly. All these modes of thinking make transactions at times confused and the group members may fail to get through to one another without a great deal of mutual help. There is no doubt that a great deal of incomprehensibility takes place during the initial phase of the group treatment. The vocabulary itself may set limits to understanding for different members until they begin to realise that language within the group is intended for communication. On the psychosexual scale, the members may be fixated at different levels — the oral, the anal, the phallic or the genital stages – and since these organise their nuclear unconscious fantasies, the members may have basic difficulties in empathising with one another. On a more advanced psychosocial scale, some may be trying to deal with the problem of autonomy, others with obtaining serious and satisfying work, others with carving out clear-cut roles and identities for themselves, others with developing intimacies and closenesses that previously have not been possible. All in all, for a child-orientated individual like myself, the group-analytic circle offers a marvellous picture of a developmental-transactional world in action. One has only to add class and ethnic factors to make the totality even more complicated.

The ambient network

Of all Foulkes's ideas that have enchanted, intrigued and preoccupied me, his theory of network, even though incompletely developed and not too well thought through, has had a major impact on my own investigative work. I can remember the time when the idea first began to interest him and we talked about the possibility of developing a project (funded from American sources we thought hopefully) which would allow us to explore the salient and undeniable fact that every individual is part of a psychosocial network, hierarchically ordered and channelled in particular ways for communication and contact. Like Foulkes, I have, over the past two decades, become convinced (and this is so true of the child) that how the patient represents himself to us is the symptom of a disturbance that involves a whole network of circumstances and people. As Foulkes put it: 'It is this network of interacting circumstances and persons which is the real operational field for effective and radical therapy.'

The problem that confronted us was how to trace the network into all its ramifications therapeutically. (Networks have been explored sociologically and the amount of psychopathology within a given social orbit has been quantified so that we know, from the work of Post and others, that 'birds of a feather flock together' especially with regard to psychopathology.) In order to get at the complete network, we would need to institute degrees of therapy that fanned out from an individual source; for example, a child attending a therapist at a child guidance clinic; his parents being seen by a social worker; the family as a whole being treated by a family therapist; a relatives group being conducted by a group therapist, with younger members being allocated to one group and older members to the other; the parents and their more intimate friends would also be seen in a group so that there would be an interdigitating set of multipersonal therapies.

When I was in London I used to visit the residential unit as a consultant. It was at a time when my group-analytic curiosities were at their highest, when my therapeutic zeal was at its keenest, when my youthful inexperience was at its greatest and when my belief in 'talking cures' was absolute. Not only did I believe that I could establish a workable, cross-communicative group-analytic group situation with children but also with their networks. For me, at that time, the institution was not an institution but a set of interlocking group-analytic circles made up of teachers, therapists, administrators, maids, cooks, cleaners and gardeners and I observed that the children passed comfortably or uncomfortably from one part of the network to another as they were served their meals, received their laundry, gossiped in the kitchen, learned in the classroom, were disciplined in the office, had their chests sounded with a stethoscope or received their formal group-analytic therapy.

My reason for organising the institution as a group-analytic circle within an ambient network was to render the latent life of the community more manifest, make the collective unconscious more conscious, localise disturbances before they erupted unexpectedly and unmanageably and in general, give myself the opportunity to keep an overall eye on the psychosocial environment. Had I been in the position to explore thoroughly my own unconscious fantasies at the time, I might have come up with various versions of the God Complex (Jones) with all its built-in narcissism, omnipotence and omniscience. In my relative state of innocence, however, the situation worked very well. Because of the interlocking nature of the groups – the staff groups, the children's groups, the staff-children's groups, the parents' groups and the administrative groups, I found that when the community was disturbed by interpersonal difficulties, the micro-analysis of the group and the macro-analysis of the network soon allowed me to focus on the location of the disturbance, its level, its content, its size, its intensity and its pattern (by pattern I meant the dynamic interpersonal figuration of interlocking personnel).

There were two procedures at work: a configurational analysis that helped to determine the nature and extent of the disturbing interaction, the communications that fed into it and the localisation of the epicentre. The second procedure had to do with an early version of what Dr Rene Thom, the French mathematician, has now developed into a 'catastrophe theory' that attempts to show how a series of continuous events such as the regular complaints inside an institution gradually increases the tension of the occupants as reflected in such simple things as minor illnesses, little delinquencies, unexpected runaways, episodes of 'mass hysteria', as these symptoms of stress and strain followed along some well-defined fault. As a result, there might be a sudden eruption of mass rebelliousness (or in the case of the rumblings of continental movements, into earthquakes). If careful records are kept of the group proceedings, one is able to distinguish sharp changes in the atmosphere.

In my institution, one of the male staff smacked a child. There was an administrative outcry and the man was immediately shifted from the unit. In the mixed group of children, the instance occupied a whole session. The children were indignant about the matter. They wanted me to take sides and express an opinion. Did I agree with the children being smacked? I said I personally did not smack children, but many parents did and felt they were doing the right thing. I asked them what they felt about this, and, to a child, they were against it. Children should never be smacked because it hurt them. I pointed out that this was what the parents intended; but then one of the children remarked that it was often worse to be scolded. 'That', said another child, 'is only because there is something the matter with our minds: it makes us sensitive.' What she objected to was that the smack had been on the bottom; that was very undignified. 'They think you can treat a child any way you like. Mr P. only beat John, because he was teasing him about kissing Mrs X.' This was the first hint that the children knew something more than they had previously let out. When asked about the kissing they had supported John because they did not like Mr P. In the staff group that followed, the members were also highly indignant about the situation, especially because Mr P. had been removed. The boy had been asking for it for a long time, they said; he was a real troublemaker; he was not maladjusted; he was just a malingerer. They also tried to induce me to take sides: did I think it was fair that a member of the staff should be removed unheard just because he struck a bad boy for using a very dirty word with regard to Mrs X? When I asked what the word was, Mrs X blushed and said she would rather the matter was forgotten. (The word, I discovered later, was prostitute.) In a mother's group shortly after, the mother of the boy said to me: 'I hear he got hit by one of the staff; I can quite understand why; he is really a most provocative boy. Just before he was admitted, I gave him a smack and he said he would tell his father that he caught me kissing the milkman. I had to give him half a crown even though it was quite untrue. I knew what a suspicious man my husband was!' So far it appeared, therefore, that the child used the same threat with the nurse when he got smacked as he did with his mother when he got half a crown; that without seeing any smoke, he had diagnosed a fire and then fabricated the smoke (was this also true in the case of his mother?); and the children had known it to be untrue but wanted to get an unpopular member of the staff into trouble. In a final mixed group of staff and children some time after this, the boy admitted to the staff members that he had made up the story and when they asked him why he had done it, he replied 'It's what I imagined they were doing. When I first came in here I imagined all the men and women were having sex together and couldn't get it out of my mind. I thought Mrs X shouldn't do that sort of thing because she had children.' The vignette illustrates the amount of unconscious and preconscious knowledge that people within the network accumulate about one another.

In passing, it is clear that at that time and equally now, I ran the group-analytic groups with children from latency onward as I did the groups of adults. The children react, show interest in one another, make contact, interact, communicate, form relationships, become mutually interdependent and construct, as Foulkes, a 'feedback system'. In the groups we are concerned with the basics of interpersonal caring, of contact and of communication and of the modification of these within the gambit of the group. My tendency is to treat the group of children as a whole and to assume that the individuals are also being treated and I detect as much transference, both T and t, in operation and displacements of old reactions into the treatment situation as with the adult group.

It would seem that the same theoretical battles are often in progress: is child analysis the equivalent of adult analysis? Is group analysis with children the equivalent of group analysis with adults? As I have grown up, grown older and become more experienced, I tend to distinguish less between individuals at different parts of the human life cycle: old people remind me in their greeds and frustrations of infants; adolescents tend to be as negativistic as toddlers and grown-up men and women behave at times very much like adolescents (at least in America where the enthusiasm for youth must be seen to be believed).

Within the network, one often sees how improvements in one section lead to setbacks in another; how dependencies that are being resolved stimulate authoritarianism; how rumour and suspiciousness emanating from the circle invades the network and vice versa; how group-analytic transferences reactivate all the ambivalences, the depressions and the dependencies of the pre-oedipal period as well as at times parts of the repressed oedipal conflict; how the network will effect as its repercussions in the group and how the group influences the network.

Conclusion

I started this talk with recollections of many a summer's day spent with Michael Foulkes. I am now, in my conclusions, reminded of one of the best-loved essays by Freud, 'On Transcience'. As you will remember, it involved a conversation that he had with a young poet, presumably Rilke, on the beauty of the summer countryside that filled the poet with joylessness although he could appreciate the beauty. Freud, notoriously regarded as an arch-pessimist, disputed the need for pessimism; for him beauty stimulated enjoyment. Being Freud, however, he was not by any means going to let the matter rest there and after some analytic consideration, he concluded that the poet was defending against the process and pain of mourning.

I, too, have had to come to terms with the fact that there will be no more group-analytic and network discussions on summer days in Hampstead, no more anticipations of the future of the movement, its theory and its technique, by its founder. At first, I sensed, like Rilke, the ugliness underlying the smiling face of existence. But mourning comes to an end as life goes on, as group institutions and societies grow and the young are always coming along to take their share of the load. The death of the leader is a time for grief, for reconsideration, for reorganisation but not for catastrophe. As Freud put it:

> When once the mourning is over, it will be found that our high opinion of the riches of civilisation has lost nothing from our discovery of their fragility. *We shall build up again and more lastingly than before.*

This would also have been the message that Michael Foulkes would have given to his successors.

Chapter 4
Out-patient analytic group psychotherapy: A ten-year study of the outcome
Barbara Dick

This study is based on eleven therapy groups conducted from 1963 to 1973 in the psychiatric clinics of two District General Hospitals. It began with the need to explore 'the revolving door phenomenon' and the apparently hopeless prognosis for many neurotic patients. My senior colleague, Franz Greenbaum, became interested in group psychotherapy as a possible development from the individual psychotherapy sessions which, being within the NHS setting, were inevitably limited. He led a weekly group and I was his observer and recorder. Although Foulkes and Anthony's *Group Psychotherapy* (1957), was our bench book, this first group involved little of the group-analytic approach and was basically leader-centred. Patients brought individual dreams for group discussion and these were explored with his help. Both therapist and members enjoyed these sessions of explanations and patients were seldom absent. My colleague died after two years, and it was depressing to note that yet again the group members were faced with a further reinforcement of their familiar pattern of attachment and loss, and without opportunity to work this through. I was myself too inexperienced to recognise that there was an urgent need to embark on this task with the group, partly due to the fact that I was also involved in a mourning process, as my colleague had been my analyst. Those two years of group experience were, however, invaluable for me as a learning process, for it became clear how much is invested by both therapist and patient in a therapy group. The needs of both are intermeshed and any attempt to change the revolving door pattern must involve the mutual desire of both therapist and members to achieve the same goal. The conductor of a therapy group is in a powerful position, and his unconscious attitude to the dependency and passivity of his patients will inevitably be reflected in the group process and its outcome.

The task of all the groups reported here was to offer members the possibility of changing from their chronic patienthood status to that of an on-going, coping person.

In view of this, the objects of the study were:

1 To test the assumption that a closed analytic therapy group has potential as an agent of positive change for its members, from the status of chronic patienthood to that of an on-going and coping person, independent of the psychiatric services.

2 To (a) define factors which are relevant to patients' suitability for analytic group therapy; and (b) to define group structure suitable for patients conditioned to expect failure of therapy.

3 To attempt to formulate change of stance and attitude and to observe whether it is maintained after termination of the group.

Outline of study

Ninety-three neurotic or borderline syndrome out-patients, 52 female, 41 male, aged between 19 and 45 years and with a history of from one to ten years of unsuccessful psychiatric therapies, were involved in the study (Tables 4.1 and 4.2). Fifteen patients had at one time been in-patients and fifteen had made one or more serious suicide attempts.

There were eleven groups held over the two-year period. All patients were initially referred by consultant colleagues or by GPs. I was myself the therapist in all these groups, working as a psychiatrist and psychotherapist with a Jungian analytic training within the NHS. Each group had a regular recorder/observer with whom I was in close contact. These were social workers or junior doctors interested in psychotherapy.

After referral, each patient was involved in five or more individual psychotherapy sessions with me, with a view to assessment of suitability.

Task of therapy group

The primary task was that of facilitating change of stance and attitude. As group psychotherapy was frequently seen to be the end of the therapeutic road by those making the referrals and those referred, it was of considerable importance to avoid a reinforcement of previous therapeutic failure. The medical model had proved itself inappropriate

Table 4.1 Treatment prior to group therapy

Treatment	Number of patients
Pharmacological only	38
Pharmacological plus	
8-25 individual psychotherapy sessions*	38
ECT outpatient 8	12
inpatient 4	
Behaviour therapy	4
Hypnosis	2
Leucotomy	1
Total treatments	95

(One patient had previously had ECT, behaviour therapy and leucotomy.)

* All patients had 5-8 sessions of individual psychotherapy for assessment purposes prior to group therapy.
Individual psychotherapy session were for 30 minutes fortnightly.

Table 4.2 Length of duration of symptoms prior to group therapy

	Under 1 yr	1-2 yrs	2-5 yrs	5-10 yrs	10+ yrs	Total
Number of patients	1	15	38	27	12	93

for these patients, and there seemed a need for the therapist to change stance and attitude in relation to selection and preparation of patients. This selection procedure, therefore, included the attempt to make a therapeutic alliance with the patient, his family, his GP and helping agencies already involved, as change for the patient would inevitably concern them. Selection was, therefore, based on assessment of patients' suitability for analytic group therapy.

Selection

Therapist's selection criteria

(a) All patients had a minimum of five preliminary individual sessions. Selection was made where the symptoms appeared to be both the cause and the effect of the long-standing dependency patient role, both maintaining the past child/parent relationship in the here-and-now situation, and continually reinforcing this. Such patients describe stress in the whole range of relationships with parent/authority figures and in situations where they themselves are involved in the exercise of authority and responsibility. In relationships with bosses, senior colleagues or workmates, and at home in the role of spouse or parents, they appear to be compelled to fail to fulfil their potential as adults and continue to present themselves as dependent children. Their symptoms cry out 'Keep me safe and parent me'. They live inappropriately and stressfully as children in an adult world.

The five individual sessions provided a basis of relationship between the patient and therapist. It is always a psycho-shock for the patient to be asked to bring along a dream. Tranquillisers and ECT have been the previous basis of therapy for many years and we start here the process of facilitating for each patient the relating of their conscious to their unconscious self. I eliminated here those whom Wordsworth (1819) epitomised in Peter Bell:

> A primrose by a river's brim
> A yellow primrose was to him
> And it was nothing more.

Such patients seemed likely to be defending against a psychotic breakdown in their concretism.

(b) An additional therapist requirement was that members should be currently working, either as housewives or outside the home. This ensured a reality-basis for analytic group therapy in an out-patient setting, where no other therapy was offered, except medication already assessed by the patient to be only marginally effective.

(c) Reasonable expectation that a patient would be locally domiciled for the eighteen months of group therapy was also sought by the therapist.

(d) The upper age limit was 45 in order to give optimum potential for change.

Patient's self-selection

This was based on motivational strength towards change. It needed to be sufficiently strong to cope with the considerable and necessary tension involved in analytic group therapy and the processes of change. All potential members were informed that therapy offered no easy option and that during the eighteen months they would frequently feel worse rather than better.

Motivation was also assessed by the patient's acceptance of the 'group contract'. This outlined:

1. Regular attendance at weekly sessions for eighteen months.
2 Total confidentiality concerning all group transactions.
3 The requirement to bring painful material, feelings and current life events to the group.
4 A ban on socialisation between members outside of group sessions.
5 The cessation of individual contact with the therapist.

This last requirement had particular relevance in that 38 of the 93 patients had previously had 8 to 25 individual therapy sessions while awaiting a group place.

The graduation from the one-to-one relationship to a shared one is challenging to a patient and a further test of motivational strength (Wolff and Solomon, 1973). Those who opted for group therapy were encouraged to feel highly privileged and the majority came into the group with considerable hope, which in itself is significantly correlated with positive therapy outcome (Goldstein, 1962). Some patients were stimulated to find a job in order to qualify for group therapy.

GPs and social workers had frequently become enmeshed with their patients over the years. They were specifically briefed concerning the eighteen months of the group life and its storms and stresses, and urged to avoid increase of medication or pressure to refer elsewhere, but in spite of this preparation there were early terminators whose GPs were faint-hearted under pressure.

Family involvement in selection

The collusion of a key relative of the family nexus in preserving the status quo of patients is of crucial importance in the failure to maintain therapy, as Foulkes (1975) has indicated. While spouse and key others may assert their support for therapy, they frequently manipulate or unconsciously prevent its action. An attempt was made prior to final selection to explore the strength of this collusion with key relatives and to enlist their positive support. In spite of this, owing to the unconscious nature of the collusion, family stress was common during and after group therapy. My hope, however, was that the excessively vulnerable and those too enmeshed in collusively restrictive outside relationships would be daunted either by the forecast of storm and stress or by the opposition of the collusive partner and no persuasion was offered to any patients in order to avoid further experience of failed therapy.

It will be seen that the patient's suitability for therapy was based on self-selection, which in turn was based on the therapist's selection of appropriate criteria hypothesised as being conducive to positive outcome. The assumption was made that the matching of a patient to appropriate therapy is as important as the matching of pharmacological or other therapies to diagnostic criteria.

Prior to the starting of the group, a questionnaire was completed by therapist and patient in joint consultation, with a view to establishing a starting base line for the 'measurement' of change through the group experience. This questionnaire used eight parameters of the patient's life experience and of their acceptability of them to him. Further description of this questionnaire will be given when referring to its completion at termination of the group and at regular follow-up.

Symptoms of patients accepted for group therapy

Patients in this study suffered from the full range of symptoms listed in the Hamilton Anxiety Rating Scale. In addition, some were included with obsessional compulsive symptoms, sexual difficulties and deviations, uncontrollable antisocial or aggressive behaviour and alcoholism. Thirteen borderline syndrome patients were included some of whom described paranoid ideas, delusions and hallucinations, both auditory and visual, of variable duration, but who fulfilled criteria for selection (Table 4.3). The symptom most stressed by the patient on referral was accepted as the predominant one. Symptom removal was not seen as the primary task of therapy, however, as symptoms were regarded as an integral part of the constellation of failure to achieve full adult potential, and the primary task that of basic change of status. Overall management of symptoms was explicitly handed over to the patient's GP with emphasis on the importance of maintenance of attendance at the group sessions and the maintenance of medication at a minimum.

Table 4.3 Predominating presenting symptoms

	Depression	Phobic anxiety	Psycho-somatic	Sexual	Obsessive compulsive	Anxiety	Aggressive antisocial	Paranoid delusional hallucinating	Alcoholism	Total
Number of patients	40	9	8	9	6	10	4	5	2	93

Group composition

Foulkes and Anthony (1957), Whitaker and Lieberman (1964), Yalom (1970) and others share the clinical sentiment that the heterogeneity of patients' symptoms and conflict areas and patterns of coping, facilitates the process of change in interpersonal transactions. Whitaker and Lieberman stress in addition the importance of the homogeneity of patients' vulnerability to anxiety, 'The greater the span between the polar types (diagnoses and disturbances), the higher the therapeutic potential, if the group can stand it', as Foulkes sums up. This approach to group composition was used with all the groups reported here. In addition, in this series the attempt was made to include in each group a range of educational, social and occupational backgrounds, in order to facilitate an exchange of thinking, feeling, intuition and sensation transactions. My training as a Jungian analyst led me to regard all four aspects as facilitating to each other (Jung, 1923). Each group also included some borderline syndrome patients who fulfilled other criteria for selection.

The eleven groups had an average of nine members, with a balance of the sexes as far as possible.

The average number of sessions per group was sixty-three, held over a period of eighteen months. (Four patients in the first three groups started late and continued with the next group. This was not repeated and the remaining groups were closed.)

It was seldom possible to realise our theoretically conceptualised model of group composition, as in the psychiatric department of a district general hospital the pool of suitable patients at the start of a group is limited in size. This, however, in my opinion in no way invalidates the importance of a facilitating group composition and the reverse of this can be damaging to a group.

Group setting and structure

These groups met weekly in the evening to avoid disruption of working life. Two groups usually ran concurrently but at different stages of development, one at 6.30-7.45 p.m. and another at 8.30-9.45 p.m., thus allowing some comparison to be made. The setting was a room in the out-patient department, at times very basic in its fittings. Each group included a non-participating regular recorder/observer, who recorded sessions verbatim in abbreviated longhand. From this recording and discussion, recorder and therapist evolved the Focal Conflict and

Resolution for each session, based on the model of Whitaker and Lieberman (1962). From these summaries, it was possible to monitor group development on a cognitive level. The recorders' contributions were invaluable apart from their explicit function. They provided support and discussion of counter-transference, and provided a balance between anxiety and smugness. The experience of recording in a therapy group has offered a valuable opportunity for training for group therapists, and been sought after eagerly by social workers and junior doctors, to whom I am much indebted.

Group process and content

The group analytic model of Foulkes (1957) was used with all these groups. The therapist's role throughout was that of a facilitator of understanding of self and key others, in the here-and-now and in relation to the there-and-then. Swapping of symptoms was discouraged and the group encouraged to look for meanings. The regular attendance of medical student and social worker observers provoked the expression and further examination of concealed paranoid feelings and provided a link between the outside world and the 'inside' world of the group. In addition to its function of testing motivation for membership of a group, the group contract had an additional importance. Group patients experience relationships largely as transference ones and have highly ambivalent feelings towards parent and authority figures. The breaking of contract rules was usual and invariably flagrant. Developing groups acted out their rebelliousness and ambivalence to authority/parent figures in the here-and-now of the group, and this flagrancy enabled the group to use the experience to resolve the conflicting needs for the all-powerful parental control and support, but also for healthy independence and potency. Rebellions within a group were noted to herald the desired basic change, and these involved stress for the therapist and recorder. The Focal Conflict scheme at these times proved invaluable, as also when groups appeared static.

These groups all showed important characteristic phases of changing relationship with therapist, therapy and other members. At first the group was seen as the magical solution, and the therapist as 'the one who knows'. Within the group, however, were the familiar infantile needs of each member – that he should have what he wanted now from the magical therapist and therapy. The response was anger and rebellion when this was not forthcoming.

This was succeeded by a period of considerable and collectively shared depression, with accompanying restatements of hopelessness, suicidal threats, increased complaints of symptoms and talk of impending disasters at work and at home. It was at this phase that members were likely to withdraw. During the next phase, sibling rivalry became overt, and in spite of the apparent regression of the group, it seemed a great deal had been happening beneath the surface. As withdrawal of projections from each other and the therapist promoted an ongoing process of individuation, members began to recognise a self as separate from others and at the same time to be able to relate as individuals, one to another with shared understanding. In the last phase, the introduction of the element of time passing by the conductor and of the ending of the group enabled patients to look back and to look forward in time, to see a 'me', a 'you' and an 'us', to see the therapist in the here-and-now, and to remember as adolescents do 'how it used to be when we were very young'. They begin to see the therapist in reality, as opposed to fantasy – as human! The ending of a group, always an emotional experience, begins as a mourning of time past, but ends with hope for time to come, a true reflection of the passing from childhood and adolescence to maturity.

These phases I have found to be regular phenomena in groups which are 'working well'. I see this as reassuring, in terms of understanding what are undoubtedly painful developmental processes during the group life, which correspond with the phases on the Tuckman model of group sequence (Tuckman, 1966).

Termination procedure

At termination, each patient was seen individually by both therapist and recorder and, where possible, another colleague. A questionnaire was completed by therapist and recorder and by the patient independently. Information was sought on the same eight parameters used at the start of therapy.

In addition, each patient was asked to record the help received through the group on a three-point scale concerning understanding of self and understanding of others. General comments on the experience were requested also.

Ex-members were then offered three possibilities:
(a) An appointment in six weeks.
(b) An appointment in three months.

(c) An opportunity to make their own appointment at a future date if required.

Few patients requested the first of these, and, as in the case of those who requested the second, few appointments were kept. They appeared, however, to represent a lifeline and an indication of residual separation difficulties.

In addition, ex-members were asked to agree to complete and return follow-up questionnaires. These were completed six months, eighteen months and two and a half years after termination.

Method of assessment of change following group therapy

In the reported five initial interviews, specific areas of disturbance of patients were identified from an early stage, as relating to eight parameters of the life situation. The parameters were:

1 Marital, or in single patients, parent-patient relationships.
2 Work.
3 Sex relationships.
4 Physical health.
5 Leisure.
6 Self-image.
7 Self-understanding.
8 Symptoms.

The first three of these parameters were based on Freud's description of successful outcome to therapy – 'to be able to love and to work'. Physical health relates closely to these. Leisure involves the dimension of self-actualisation, as opposed to survival (Goldstein, 1940; Argyris, 1968).

Prior to therapy, distortion and conflict were seen to be most marked in the areas of relationships, self-image, and self-understanding and, as indicated earlier, effective therapy in this study implied the ability of the patient at the end of therapy to see himself and others appropriately, in the here-and-now free from the transference experience. Symptom evaluation was included specifically to enable patients to evaluate their dependence on psychiatric treatment.

Ratings were as follows:

A   All eight parameters of the life situation, as indicated above, acceptable to the patient.
B7 Seven parameters of the life situation acceptable to the patient.
B6 Six parameters of the life situation acceptable to the patient.

B5 Five parameters of the life situation acceptable to the patient.
B4 Four parameters of the life situation acceptable to the patient.
B3 Three parameters of the life situation acceptable to the patient.
B2 Two parameters of the life situation acceptable to the patient.
C   All parameters unacceptable to the patient.

The rating before the start of the group was made by the therapist in the five individual sessions and derived from the clinical notes with the help of the patient. The post-group rating was made at the termination interview by discussion with the patient and through his questionnaire response.

Change here was seen to be largely global in character. One parameter would appear to affect another and throughout the centrifugal affect of each on all other parameters was marked. All parameters, therefore, received equal ratings.

Before the start of the group, ninety-three patients were rated in terms of the acceptability to them of these eight aspects of their experience of themselves. Fifty (53.7 per cent) were rated C (all parameters were unacceptable); only sixteen (17 per cent) were rated above B2. No patient was rated higher than B4 (four parameters acceptable). (See Table 4.4).

Ratings at the group end

Seventy patients (75 per cent) were assessed at the termination of the group, and these included sixty-four who completed the full group life and six others who terminated before the end of the group by agreement with the group and therapist and who had attended more than thirty sessions.

Table 4.5 shows the rating of these seventy patients after group therapy. Sixty-seven (90 per cent) were rated above B2 by contrast with 17 per cent who were rated before group therapy.

From Table 4.6 it will be seen that sixty-one patients (87 per cent) showed positive change, and one patient showed a negative change. Eight showed no change. Change was recorded as equivalent to alteration of three or more points in rating, e.g. B2 to B5 or B4 to B1.

Negative change (K.S.)

The potential of a therapy group to produce negative change is important.

Table 4.4 Pre-group rating of total series

Rating	A	B7	B6	B5	B4	B3	B2	B1	C	Total
Number of patients	–	–	–	–	6	10	15	12	50	93

Table 4.5 Post-group rating of 70 patients (75%) who completed GT

Rating	A	B7	B6	B5	B4	B3	B2	B1	C	Total
Number of patients	4	21	18	13	5	6	1	–	2	70

Table 4.6 Change* in pre- and post-group rating

	Positive change	No change	Negative change	Total
Number of patients	61	8	1	70

* Change = an alteration of 3 or more points in either direction, e.g. C-B3 or B4-B1.

A 34-year-old housewife, an ex-pharmacist, presented initially complaining of obsessional rumination concerning her intellectual attainments and suitability for teacher training. She developed acute paranoid delusional symptoms and made a serious suicide attempt during the holiday period after the thirty-fourth session. A diagnosis of acute schizophrenia was made by one of my colleagues while she was an in-patient. This patient had demonstrated her lifelong difficulties in personal relationships while in the group and was constantly destructive to other members and the therapist and there was a considerable drop-out rate within this group, which seemed related to her group behaviour.

After in-patient admission, K.S. was treated with phenothiazines and seemed to respond. She failed to complete her second follow-up questionnaire, but in returning the third one she reported herself much better. She requested an appointment and she and her husband both agreed that for the first time she was free of her obsessional self-concern to be the 'top dog', both within her marriage and within her family of origin. Both husband and wife expressed their shared conviction that her group experience related to this change. A further psychiatric episode and serious suicidal attempt occurred five years later. Ten years after the group's end, she has maintained positive change on Anafranil medication. I do not know how to evaluate the effect of the group on K.S. The onset of her symptoms occurred when she felt used and rejected by the leader of a group run by the WEA after a secret sexual affair with him. Certainly, she unconsciously vented her anger on her new group leader. A second significant factor occurred to me later. She had had only one preliminary individual session owing to the initial referral being immediately before the group's start. The basic relationship-making procedure here was lacking.

This group offered a considerable learning experience for the therapist in the full recognition of how one severely disturbed patient (with whom the therapist is unable to cope) may produce excessive insecurity within a group. In fact the three members who completed therapy in this group all showed marked and surprising positive change. For me this group emphasises the considerable importance of careful selection.

Unchanged patients

There were eight of these patients. Three failed to reply to any follow-up questionnaire. They were all exceptionally regular attenders and this was perhaps indicative of their inability to rebel against the authority structure and break out of their old dependent identity. One was reported on by his GP as being well and free of psychiatric symptoms. Another was discovered later to be a member of Alcoholics Anonymous, whose objective, the acceptance of the patient role for life, conflicts sharply with that of an analytic group. A third appeared to be deriving considerable secondary gain from his marriage partner through his physical symptoms. Two of the others who replied to follow-up, described positive change at first and second follow-up and appeared to have made marked changes in their life at the end of the group. A further patient, a very regular attender who replied to follow-up, showed no change in spite of attending for Behaviour Therapy and hypnosis elsewhere later. He was a considerable alcoholic also. Of the other two K.V., although showing no change at termination, appeared to have been able to review his symptoms and assessed them as being basically trivial, and their onset related to deterioriated family relationships. He was referred for behaviour therapy and reported himself well and symptom-free at third follow-up. B.D. showed signs of euphoria and elation while in group therapy, but at the end of the group was unchanged. At first follow-up he reported considerable depression and negative change. A previously made diagnosis suggested a manic-depressive condition and he was given lithium therapy, but complained that this dampened all his feelings and declined it. At third follow-up he reported himself well and related his depression to his mistress having married. He was amazed to encounter himself as capable of being emotionally involved with a woman, having previously seen himself as a 'gay Lothario' and playboy.

First follow-up

Of the seventy patients assessed at the end of the group, fifty-three (75 per cent) replied to the questionnaire. Three had improved on their end of group rating, and forty-eight had maintained their positive change. In addition to K.S., who was known still to be a negative changer, two others had negatively changed. M.G. had become severely depressed, and her marriage relationship had endured a tornado, the balance of power having been upset. She responded well to ECT some-what to our surprise, as she had previously not responded. At second follow-up she was delighted with her sense of confidence. However, subsequently her husband requested psychiatric help and received it. Following his recovery, she again became very disturbed and this pattern continued until further daily group therapy for twelve weeks at the Wilton Unit for Group Psychotherapy was offered. This patient would have benefited from Family Therapy initially, and the inclusion in therapy of her family through the Wilton Unit seems to have been crucial to subsequent change within the extended family as well as in the marriage.

A second negative changer at first follow-up (E.M.) was awaiting a mitral valvotomy operation. She recovered well, but her marriage ended in divorce – an outcome she had previously been unable to envisage. She then showed marked positive change at subsequent follow-up.

Second follow-up, eighteen months after the group's end

Questionnaires were sent to sixty-one patients. Forty-five (73 per cent) replied. Three patients showed increased positive change on their first follow-up rating, and these included the two negative changers, M.G. and E.M. B.D., the only negative changer at this follow-up, recovered shortly afterwards, relating his depression to his girl-friend's marriage.

Third follow-up, two and a half years after the group's end

At the time of this study, 54 patients were eligible to be followed up and 44 were accounted for. Twenty-five had completed question-naires, two had died, five were known to have left the area and nine were reported on by their GPs. Further information was available concerning three more. Of the twenty-four patients who completed forms and two of the patients about whom information was forth-coming, all showed maintained positive change. GP reports revealed no symptoms requiring psychiatric treatment in their nine patients who failed to reply. Only one patient was referred back to the depart-ment with identical symptoms to her original ones, and here the whole family nexus through three generations, as well as the GP, were highly involved in her illness. She is one of three patients who, at the time of the study, had completed group therapy and was still intermittently attending the department. Since the study was completed, a further fifteen patients have become eligible for third follow-up, and all have maintained positive change and remained free from the patient status.

Early terminators

Twenty-three patients who attended less than thirty sessions were not included in this study and were described as 'early terminators'. They do, however, provide a small control group.

Eight of these were members of the same group which included the patient K.S., who became psychotic at the thirty-fourth session, and whose aggression was highly destructive to the other members.

Follow-up was done on the twenty-three patients who failed to complete thirty sessions. Information was received from sixteen. Seven (44 per cent) have since sought psychiatric treatment and medication from GPs or psychiatrists, compared with 7 per cent of those who completed treatment. Early terminators showed from their follow-up questionnaires that they had little cognitive awareness of the group experience or change in self-understanding.

Patients' comments in the questionnaires

These are revealing in that they indicate change of stance rather than the 'swealing away' of symptoms and life's difficulties ('swealing away' in Salford is done by magic wands). Here are some examples of comments at the group's end:

'I still get days when I am depressed, but not severe like before. I get confused with myself at my lack of communication, but I accept a lot of things that happen to me, whereas before I would get depressed' – from a 26-year-old secretary and unmarried mother with a three-year history of severe agoraphobia and incapacitating depressions, who had lived a life of fantasy.

'I honestly don't know how much the group has helped. I feel rather bitter and upset at the minute and don't know if this is good or bad. I do seem to have learned that logic as I saw it doesn't solve problems and also that the human mind can be very stubborn against conscious wishes. I hope one day I can 'phone and say I am really better' – from a 29-year-old clerk with two and a half years of severe obsessional rumination concerning death.

At follow-up, the following are typical comments:

'I feel I have progressed more since I left the group. I still daydream, but not so much. I'm still shy and sensitive, but not so much. Thanks, Doctor' — from a 35-year-old engineer with long-standing anxiety symptoms and paranoid ideas.

'A cathartic experience. I find my B.Ed. philosophy course has a similar atmosphere. One has to be precise, particularly about 'ought' and 'should'. I have learned that the use of conversational terms rather than so-called scientific labels about symptoms makes me feel more human. I am more motivated and self-reliant' — from a 32-year-old teacher with a psychiatric treatment history and repeated hospital admission for paranoid delusions since the age of 8.

I find these modest submissions strangely moving in their acceptance of reality, and I am reminded of William Blake's 'Auguries of Innocence':

> Man was made for Joy and Woe
> And when this we rightly know
> Thro' the World we safely go.
> Joy and Woe are woven fine,
> A Clothing for the Soul divine
> Under every grief and pine
> Runs a joy with silken twine.

Was this what one patient meant when he said in his questionnaire at the end of the group: 'I feel I've learned something I somehow missed at school'?

Discussion

The patients involved in this study had lived for years with considerably disabled lives within the 'closed society' of their families, their GPs, their social workers and their psychiatrists. Paradoxically they have, through the experience of a closed analytic group, been exposed to an 'open society', the effect of which would seem to have been liberating. This exposure, it would appear, has facilitated a gradual thawing of the 'frozen, closed position' described by Yalom (1970). A patient in the later stages of the group expressed this as follows: 'The child inside me is waiting to be born. I think it is my mother. I'm terrified and yet I know it has to happen.' This was a young woman who had parented her parents since she was a young and only child. At the end of the group

Table 4.7 Key relationship changes during or after group therapy

Separated or divorced during or after group therapy	9
Requested conjoint marital therapy after group ended	6
Spouse requested therapy after group ended	4
Single patients left parental home	2
Reported anti-depressant therapy in close key relations	2
Total	23

Table 4.8 Life situational changes during and following group therapy

Married or formed stable relationships	11
Housewives started work or training	7
Changed jobs or promoted	8
Moved house locally	3
Left district	4
Achieved desired pregnancy	2
Took children out of care	1
Total	36

she recognised change, but only gradually became aware that she felt herself at last a married woman responsible for a new developing relationship.

From Tables 4.7 and 4.8 it can be seen that there are painful reactions within the family and marked changes in life situations following group therapy. The *General Systems Theory* of Von Bertalanffy (1971) postulates precisely this effect. The individual changing within the closed family system will inevitably discomfort the other members.

The successful treatment of a patient in a therapy group may have painful repercussions on the other family members (Malan, Balfour, Hood and Shooter, 1976). 'Close' was frequently the term used by patients in this study to describe their family. The task of the group process was to free members from this closeness and for the individual to become differentiated as a person rather than the sick member. Minuchin (1967) and other family therapists have described the 'enmeshed' family system which precludes the development of individuals within the family.

Freud's revelation that symptoms have meanings and that these meanings for a neurotic patient are his individual creation just as his dreams are, has opened up a vast new field of enquiry through psychoanalysis and psychotherapy. It has left us, however, with the question of how to evaluate the experience of Therapy, and the outcome of that search for meaning. These group patients have been encouraged to seek their own evidence of change and to evaluate their own experience, as the therapist has also done through this study. This is certainly not the science of Isaac Newton nor the medical model. Nevertheless, the scientific method has been adopted, a problem has been stated, a hypothesis made and tested.

The hypothesis that was the starting-point of this study would appear to have been validated and this is in sharp contrast to the outcome of the study made by David Malan and colleagues at the Tavistock Clinic (1976). Important and basic differences in the two studies are relevant here. Malan's patients were randomly selected and only a few had preliminary individual psychotherapy. Those became 'star patients' and derived exceptional improvement and insight development. They were described as having 'exceptional aptitude'.

These findings confirm the importance of selection, the concept of suitability for group psychotherapy and the value of preliminary individual psychotherapy. There were other differences in the two studies, in that the Tavistock groups were leader-centred and based on the model of Eznel and Bion as opposed to Foulkes. There were also a number of therapists involved, in contrast to this study where one therapist has been involved from selection, through group therapy, to assessment and follow-up and in this sense, there is considerable therapist 'contamination' of the results. It must also be said that the therapist here, as always, was inevitably a part of the group process, and, like most of the patients, evaluates herself as having changed.

In spite of this disadvantage, the continued patient/therapist relationships seem likely to have been a factor in the promotion of a basic security and facilitated change through the group experience. As Malan noted, his patients valued personal attention and relationship. In 1963, while watching *The Tempest*, and having just terminated a therapy group, I was caught by Prospero's words:

> Our revels now are ended. These our actors,
> As I foretold you, were all spirits and
> Are melted into air, into thin air;
> And, like the baseless fabric of this vision
> The cloud-capped towers, the gorgeous palaces,
> The solemn temples, the great globe itself
> Yea, all which it inherit, shall dissolve
> And, like this insubstantial pageant faded,
> Leave not a rack behind. We are such stuff
> As dreams are made on, and our little life
> Is rounded with a sleep.

At the end of an analytic therapy group, these express much of a conductor's feelings. A tempest has indeed blown up and much has happened. The fantasies have come and gone. We have been intimate strangers and the group has vanished. But I would challenge Prospero – experience at depth does not dissolve without trace.

The urgency to ask and answer questions concerning what happens on this island of group therapy and what remains when it has vanished into thin air, promoted this study.

References

Argyris, C. (1968), 'Conditions for competence and acquisition therapy', *Journal of Applied Behavioural Science*, 4.

Bertalanffy, Ludwig von (1971), *General Systems Theory*, London, Allen Lane.

Foulkes, S. H. (1975), *Group-analytic Psychotherapy: Method and Principles*, London and New York, Gordon & Breach.

Foulkes, S. H., and E. J. Anthony (1957), *Group Psychotherapy*, Harmondsworth, Penguin.

Goldstein, K. (1940), *Human Nature in the Light of Psychotherapy*, Cambridge, Mass.

Goldstein, A. P. (1962), *Therapist-Patient Expectancies in Psychotherapy*, New York, Pergamon Press.

Jung, C. G. (1923), *Psychological types*, International Library of Psychology, London, Routledge & Kegan Paul.

Malan, D., *et al.* (1976), 'Group psychotherapy. A long-term follow-up study', *Archives of General Psychiatry*, 33, No. 11, pp. 1303-15.

Minuchin, S. (1974), *Families and Family Therapy*, London, Tavistock.

Tuckman, B. (1966), 'Developmental sequence in small groups', *Psychological Bulletin*, 63, pp. 384-99.

Whitaker, D. S., and M. A. Lieberman (1962), 'Methodological issues in the assessment of total group phenomena in group therapy', *International Journal of Group Psychotherapy*, 12, no. 3.

Whitaker, D. S., and M. A. Lieberman (1964), *Psychotherapy through the Group Process*, Atherton Press.

Wolff, H. H. and Solomon, E. C. (1973), 'Complementary growth experience', *International Journal of Group Psychotherapy*, 23. 2.

Yalom, I. O. (1970), *The Theory and Practice of Group Psychotherapy*, New York, Basic Books.

Chapter 5
Some contributions of general systems theory to psychoanalytic group psychotherapy

Helen E. Durkin

Foreshadowing of change

Group therapy in the 1950s was marked in America by the impact of the 'group dynamics' movement on traditional analytic group therapy. For a long time these two disciplines had run along parallel lines without significant interaction. Kurt Lewin's application of gestalt psychology to small work groups, which was not at all concerned with therapy, nevertheless brought the two fields much closer. After Thelen's (1954) research to discover the dynamics of therapy groups, however, a small number of group dynamicists began to apply their findings therapeutically. M. Lakin and W. H. Dobbs (1962) and later D. Stock and M. Lieberman (1963) were examples. They put primary emphasis on the 'group as a whole'. Soon the voices of many traditional analytic group therapists were raised in protest. For example, S. R. Slavson, the father of American group therapy, denied that group dynamics could be employed as group therapy (1953). The field of group therapy was divided on the issue. But Saul Scheidlinger (1960) and I came to the conclusion that the two sources of information were complementary (Durkin, 1957). We kept the question open.

It was in 1957 also that Dr S. H. Foulkes, who had already incorporated gestalt psychology into his psychoanalytic theory of group therapy, came to New York City to present his 'Group Analytic Method' to the American Group Psychotherapy Association. He emphasized the influence of the group constellation on its individual members. E. Schwartz and A. Wolf (1960) were the chief contenders for continuing the American form of 'Analytic Group Psychotherapy' without change. They did not want it to be 'contaminated' by group dynamics. They insisted that the individual members, rather than the group as a whole, must be the target patients. I agreed with the latter point.

Nevertheless, I felt that Foulkes made a distinct contribution to the effectiveness of group therapy, when he insisted that intragroup interactions must always be viewed in the light of the total current group situation.

Following this meeting a number of us, including Milton Berger and Jean Munzer, joined Dr Foulkes in a seminar which he gave at Duke University. There we came to understand the technical application of his group analytic theory. It became evident that he had successfully blended the dynamics of group process with analytic interpretation. Unlike the Tavistock approach, Foulkes addressed his interventions interchangeably to the group as a whole or to any individual member, especially if he seemed to be the 'spokesman' for the group at the time. In this respect Foulkes was clearly ahead of his time. He was the first to transcend the futile dichotomy between the individual and group factors.

In the next few years Michael and I continued our correspondence. At the time I was preparing a chapter about American group dynamics for my book *The Group in Depth* (1964) and was struggling with the problem of how their findings could be incorporated into analytic group therapy. My discussions with Michael helped me enormously to put my chapter into shape. I had assumed that he too had been influenced by 'group dynamics' so that I was chagrined to learn, years later, that that had not been the case. He had based his work on the gestalt psychology of Koffka and Kohler. How could I have made such an error? The mystery was cleared up when I realized that it was because, of all the group dynamicists, the gestalt approach of Kurt Lewin had seemed to me to be most relevant to group psychotherapy.

Although I did not realize it at the time, our continuing talks and correspondence turned out to be the first step in a long path that led me eventually to general systems theory. I knew that Dr Foulkes had incorporated some new ideas from communications theory (Foulkes, 1964), so I was not surprised when he became interested in what I had been writing about GST. He suggested that we undertake a systematic dialogue via GAIPAC. Unfortunately, the exigencies of geography and our disparate professional commitments prevented us from carrying out this collaboration toward a unified theory of group therapy. Now, of course, I deeply regret the lost opportunity.

Although he did not claim the title, Foulkes's thinking is along the same lines as GST. His brilliant concept of the group matrix is a case in point.

In the present chapter I shall recount my progress along the path to

GST, and try to show what I learned and in what way it contributed to the theory and practice of analytic group therapy.

I shall begin with the conditions in America and the exigencies of my practice which led me to my present theoretical position.

The reasons for searching out a more comprehensive theoretical framework

The rapid social, economic and scientific changes which had taken place in twentieth-century America and the consequent nation-wide turmoil, had their repercussions in every field of human endeavour. In group therapy they led simultaneously to its vast expansion and to its conceptual fragmentation. The Federal Law of 1963 extended mental health services to big hospitals and to the community at large. These new populations were not readily accessible to the analytic group therapy approach which had dominated the field since its inception. Thereafter it was challenged on several fronts. New techniques, such as gestalt exercises, encounter tactics, and scream therapy proliferated in an attempt to meet the needs. A period of theoretical confusion and sharp dissension followed, which seemed to me to interfere with giving optimal service to patients and to test the credulity of the scientific community.

Most of the 'innovative' techniques aimed to increase the emotional intensity of treatment. It seemed a useful contribution until it began to be carried to the extreme of replacing analytic technique and ruling out thinking as antitherapeutic. At that point, a bitter controversy arose which once more split the field apart.

I was very much concerned about the conceptual fragmentation that was taking place in our field, and with the antianalytic attitudes that went with it. But I was equally concerned about the unwillingness of some analytic group therapists to examine the validity of the new approaches.

Edgar Levinson (1972) succinctly put into words my own still inchoate thinking about the situation. He wrote 'Paradigms are time and space bound'. It struck me that if we are to meet the changing needs of our patients in a rapidly changing world, we must review our theoretical models from time to time. And the time was at hand. I was not alone. By the 1970s a growing core of group therapists was beginning to search for a way to incorporate some of the new ideas and techniques into the traditional model (Mintz, 1975).

In my opinion, however, only a more comprehensive theoretical framework at a higher level of complexity could solve the problem. It would function as a larger conceptual umbrella under which the best of the new techniques could be logically incorporated, and the major current approaches might be encompassed on the basis of their common ground, without eliminating their valid differences.

Problems within psychoanalytic theory which limit therapeutic effectiveness

In the meantime, my personal experience had also suggested the advantage of using a more generalized theoretical framework. Ever since the late 1930s I had employed a psychoanalytic model in the practice of individual and, with some modification, of group therapy. I consistently found the technique of analyzing transference and resistance, as these occurred in the group interaction, to be dynamically effective in changing both the personality structure and the behaviour of the members. But as time went on, I became increasingly aware that certain limitations of psychoanalytic theory seemed to detract from the outcome. My chief concern was the fact that behaviour change tended to lag well behind self-understanding.

Inadequacies

It is generally conceded that psychoanalysis does not provide an adequate theory of energy. Freud had relied on the First Law of Thermodynamics to develop his libido theory. Although it was expressed in terms of nineteenth-century instinct theory, it *did* account for the biological drives that motivated behaviour. It also spoke of the objects of that drive but it did not account adequately for the part played by the environment. The emphasis was strongly on the intrapsychic factors which motivate behaviour. In practice, linear interpretations predominated. The fact that both parties in a relationship have a mutual influence on one another (even in the infant/parent interaction) was underestimated.

Closely related is the fact that psychoanalysis has clung too long to the principle of homeostasis in accounting for man's behaviour. Need gratification is seen as his only motivation and tension reduction has, therefore, remained a goal which determines our therapeutic measures.

The human being's powerful interest in mastering his environment has not been taken into account. Neither has the significant role which tension plays in these creative capacities. For this reason growth and creativity had too often played a minor role in traditional group therapy. Too many group therapists, that is to say, really earned the nickname 'shrink' instead of becoming the mind expanders that the founding father of psychoanalysis had intended. GST fills in these theoretical gaps as I shall show in a later section.

Conceptual ambiguity and imprecision leads to faulty techniques

In the course of my own early years of practice I detected certain theoretical pitfalls which I gradually learned to avoid. Later in the course of supervising trainees and less experienced individual and group psychoanalysts I discovered that many of the most common technical errors seemed to grow out of certain conceptual imprecisions.

The intricacies of psychoanalytic theory are, in themselves, difficult to translate into 'down-to-earth' clinical interventions. It is not easy to bring its abstractions of the actual phenomena into genuine connection with the patient's subjective experience. Yet it is essential to do so, if 'insight' is to bring about changes in behaviour. But when the concepts are ambiguous or imprecise, or are described in reifying terms, they allow for a variety of interpretations including those that are incorrect and/or idiosyncratic. Such errors detract from the therapist's therapeutic effectiveness. The consequences include: anthropomorphism and vitalism; making more content than process (i.e., transference) interpretations; overemphasizing the intellectual aspects of insight at the expense of the more dynamic emotional factors; getting caught up in history for history's sake without regard for the goal of change; adopting the role of the all-giving parent instead of adhering to a steadfast concerned neutrality; carrying understanding to the point of 'being permissive' with resistance even when there is a plethora of 'preconscious derivatives' or viewing resistance as a personal affront and analysing it in a pejorative manner; becoming so engrossed in correcting transference behaviour that interventions to facilitate new growth are rarely made. This last is particularly damaging to narcissistic and borderline patients who have not the capacity without help to develop new spontaneous and more realistic patterns of interacting. I shall try to show that GST helps to reduce such errors.

The selection of a more comprehensive framework

In teaching, I tried to clarify these concepts and correct their technical fallacies. In my own practice, I began to make technical changes which would avoid the theoretical pitfalls. In some cases I adapted analytic techniques to the group situation. For instance, my basic rule became 'try to tell us whatever you are experiencing while we talk'. I incorporated whatever changes developed within psychoanalytic theory itself, such as ego psychological (Hartmann, 1974) or object relations techniques (Bergler, 1949; Guntrip, 1969). And I did not hesitate to draw on some of the more recent non-analytic approaches, such as group dynamics and humanistic experientialism. Later I included some of the so-called innovative techniques of the 1960s which seemed to me to serve the function of countering the tendency of the group members to talk about feelings, instead of experiencing them, and thus to bring about change as well as understanding. Eventually, however, I became convinced that in order to avoid arriving at a hit or miss eclecticism we would require a more comprehensive theoretical framework at a higher level of organization which would solve a number of the existing problems.

Systems science

There were such frameworks available, for during the decade in which group therapy was struggling with change and dissension, several forms of systems thinking were becoming prominent in scientific circles. They had certain basic ideas in common. Von Bertalanffy defined a system as 'an order of parts and processes standing in dynamic interaction' (1968). Other definitions varied, but not significantly. Not all the phenomena of existence are systems. Sums and aggregates exist as well, and both occur in therapy groups. The crucial difference between them lies in the nature of their interaction. A system is the product of its parts which have a mutual influence for change upon one another. The parts of sums or aggregates interact additively. Their interaction does not produce significant changes.

Each category of system is composed of smaller wholes, called subsystems, and may itself become part of a larger suprasystem with new characteristics of its own, called 'emergents'. The interacting wholes form hierarchies. For instance, living systems from the 'cell to society' form a continuum. Thus, systems thinking constitutes a holistic synergistic point of view.

Such systems thinking gradually filtered into the literature of group therapy as it did into other fields. But at first the terms, such as boundary, input, and feedback were used loosely. Their relation to the therapeutic process was not precisely delineated. Later, however, it proved useful to group therapists who work in large mental hospitals or community clinics. They became increasingly aware of what it means to be a part of two or more systems, such as administration and group therapy, or research and group therapy. And they learned to shift their priorities in order to work together, to serve their function as part of a complex interrelated whole, instead of engaging at sword's point with one another. Several members of the Task Force including Thomas Dolgoff (1975) and Otto Kernberg (1973) made significant contributions along this line.

Two particular branches of systems theory, however, *cybernetics* and *general systems theory*, have had a more organized effect on group therapy. It is important to distinguish carefully between them when investigating their relevance to group therapy. The influence began after N. Weiner (1948) had called together a number of scientists to find out, among other things, whether or not the cybernetic application of information and feedback theory to systems might be applied by a wide variety of social sciences. Bateson and Ruesch (1951) were the first to apply cybernetics to therapeutic communication. On the basis of their findings a number of psychiatrists including Paul Watzlawick (1967), Donald Jackson (1967), Jay Haley (1963) and others developed a new 'communications' approach to family therapy. They regarded the family as the target system which must be treated as a whole rather than the designated patient. Changing the family was reported to bring about rapid changes in the individual family members. Group therapy could no longer ignore the new systems modality. During the 1960s training in family therapy was accepted as partial fulfilment of the requirement for group therapists. Most of the articles on systems theory in the group therapy literature concerned themselves with this communications approach.

Upon close examination, however, the family model did not seem to me to provide the solution to the problems of group therapy, for the following reasons:

1. The family therapist is confronted by a system that is already tightly organized, while the group therapist must deal with systems which are in the *process of formation*. Group members repeatedly attempt to re-establish their family-induced systems with the group members (Ezriel, 1959). The therapist's long-range task is to transform

such patterns of interaction step by step and also to foster the formation of brand new systems of interacting.

2. In applying cybernetics to family therapy the Palo Alto group became so engrossed with the family as 'The System' that they paid relatively little attention to the *influence* of the individual members in forming or in changing it, and still less to the role of their personality subsystems. Yet traditional group therapy has amply demonstrated that changing the personality subsystem of a single member is regularly translated into his interaction with others. It brings about changes in them and in the group as a whole.

3. Cybernetics is based on a machine model, while GST employs an organismic model, which, of course, is able to account more adequately for the most typically human behaviour, such as growth and creativity. It applies equally well to the group suprasystem, to its individual members *and* to the personality subsystem which we believe critical to the outcome of group therapy.

The formation of an AGPA Task Force to study GST

For these reasons I undertook a more intensive study of GST, beginning with the work of Ludwig von Bertalanffy (1956, 1968, 1969), an eminent biologist and the father of GST, and that of J. G. Miller (1965, 1969), a psychiatrist, who had done ten years of systematic research in order to build a systems view of human and social interaction. Von Bertalanffy provided a convincing exposition of the new orientation. He viewed the interaction among living systems primarily as metabolic processes. Their permeable boundaries permitted exchanges of energy. Miller added the idea, taken from cybernetics, that information was also exchanged. His research provided a detailed and well organized account of how systems operate which stressed their isomorphic characteristics throughout.

As I read, I became increasingly convinced that GST could provide some solutions to the problems of group therapy. It was for this reason that I suggested to the Long-Term Policy and Planning Commission of the American Group Psychotherapy Association that further exploration of this subject might ultimately have a significant effect on the future direction of group therapy. The chairman, then Dr Harris Peck, promptly set up a Task Force. Our directive was to make an in-depth investigation of the implications of GST for group therapy. We hoped it might clarify the theory and increase the effectiveness of its practice.

The Task Force consisted of interested experienced group therapists and general systems scientists.

We started out as a group of individuals with a wide variety of backgrounds and very different interests, attitudes and approaches to our common goal. For the next couple of years we pooled our knowledge, greatly widened the scope of our reading, and narrowed the differences in our views sufficiently to perform our task. We began to identify those general systems principles which appeared to have a significant bearing on group therapy. During our meetings and 'think sessions' we monitored our own intragroup relationships in the Bionic fashion, in order to iron out the usual interpersonal problems that arise during group formation and interfere with the task. Gradually we became an open, working system ourselves. Our findings, as I see them, will be summarized in the next section.

Why GST can illuminate the theory and practice of analytic group therapy

Whereas psychoanalytic theory focuses primarily on the structure and content of personality systems, GST is based on a comparative study of the structure of the whole range of systems without regard to content. For this reason it is able to provide us with that larger conceptual umbrella, capable of filling in theoretical gaps, transcending our paradoxes, and bringing some unifying trends to bear on the currently conflicting theories of group therapy.

Secondly, general systems scientists went on to establish the laws of organization according to which systems operate. In pursuing this course, they were able to generate a great deal of fresh information about the common characteristics of systems in general. It supplements what we already know about the special characteristics of personality systems.

What GST can contribute to analytic group psychotherapy

One result of the comparative study of systems in general was the profound and revolutionary discovery that systems, across the board, are 'isomorphic'. They share certain structural features together with their basic functional aspects. For instance, the boundarying function serves to maintain the identity of systems. The synergistic interaction of the

parts welds them into a new whole. Bringing attention to the phenomenon of isomorphism had widespread scientific consequences. It can be
crucial to the work of the group therapist for the phenomenon applies
equally to the three systems with which the group therapist is concerned. For the first time he will be able to view the group, its
members, and their personality structures as three levels of systems
which can be treated in a uniform way.

For example, heretofore group therapists thought that psychodynamics and group dynamics derived from totally different structures and followed divergent modes of operating. It created a problem
for the therapist, who felt he had to treat them differently. Moving
back and forth was distracting and discontinuous. Consequently, a
counterproductive controversy of no small dimensions developed as
to whether the individual or the group factors were the 'real' agents
of therapy. There still remains an uneasy truce between these two
conflicting schools of thought. But the trenchant discovery of their
essential isomorphism will enable us to eliminate this false dichotomy.
Moreover, the therapist will have at his command a single uniform
method of dealing with the three-tiered organization of the therapy
group. He can bring about transformations in their respective patterns
of interaction by regulating the permeability of their boundaries, and
cut through the diversity of the content to their common structural
features.

Even more vital to working group therapists is von Bertalanffy's
development of a new paradigm of living structure. Von Bertalanffy
was the first to distinguish between the static structure of closed
homeostatic systems and the dynamic structure of living systems. He
delineated those unique characteristics which 'emerged' at the level
of living systems and account for their dynamic quality. They are
open because their boundaries are permeable, which enables them
to engage in a continuous exchange of matter/energy and information with both their external and their internal environment. They
are *autonomous* because they have the inherent capacity to control
the permeability of their boundaries. They can close any boundary in
order to shut out incompatible input when their stability is threatened, or open them in order to import new energy and information.
This capacity enables them to be *active* so that they can influence the
environment as well as being influenced by it; to be creative because
they can process the energy and information they import to restructure themselves, and grow to more complex levels of organization.

Moreover, as living systems carry out their *boundary function consistently over time*, they develop a steady state by maintaining an optimal but ever changing proportion of open and closed boundaries. He called this phenomenon *Fliessgleichgewicht*, i.e., a flowing or dynamic equilibrium, which insures the system's stability throughout its succession of transformations. It calls attention to the importance of the fact that some tension continues to exist in these systems. It produces a quasi-disequilibrium which accounts for its capacity to transform itself, to be creative, and autonomous. It includes, but goes beyond, homeostasis. Living systems are heterostatic.

GST also supplements psychoanalytic energy theory. It utilizes the Second Law of Thermodynamics which states that without the application of energy in the form of work, systems are subject to entropy. Their organization gradually deteriorates and they begin to move toward randomness. Living systems have the capacity to counteract the forces of entropy by importing energy and information from the environment. They are negentropic. They process the input, transform themselves and spiral to a higher level of organization. This theory adds substantially to libido theory and contributes to our understanding of change and growth in human individual and social systems. It provides a sound metabolic (von Bertalanffy, 1968) and communications (Miller, 1969) base for their laws of operation. Thus GST explains autonomy and transcends the old mechanistic/vitalistic dichotomy.

These three strong characteristics depict a robust view of living systems, which, in my opinion, will profoundly affect the clinical effectiveness of group therapy. They can no longer be ignored.

It must not be forgotten, however, that GST is a general, not itself a group, therapy model. Both von Bertalanffy and Miller have pointed out that anyone who works with a given system (or series of systems), will fail to give an adequate account of it, unless he takes into consideration the 'emergents' or new characteristics which came into being at its particular level of complexity. Fortunately, psychoanalysis, other current personality theories, and group dynamics have provided much of this information. The group therapist who wishes to expand his analytic model or to build a new one must find a way to incorporate this special information.

In summary, GST does not itself provide a new theory of group therapy nor a set of ready-made techniques, but it makes available a new way of looking at the clinical events and a solid foundation of new information, from which we can construct, if we wish, a more inclusive model of group therapy. The creative therapist will be inspired to devise new techniques based on its principles.

The continuing work of the GST Task Force: how to apply GST clinically

A whole new body of information was opened up to us. Our discussions continued to be exciting and productive. Once we had reached a consensus that GST could indeed clarify our theory and add to our knowledge, we had to tackle the much more difficult problem of how to translate it into clinical practice. In the process, most of our members modified their theories and added to their techniques in varying ways and to different degrees. A number of us reconstructed our models or built new more strictly GST models. They differed somewhat according to the training, experience, and style of the authors, but, in general, they adhered to the structural principles of GST as I have described them. Personally I decided to employ an overall GST framework and to incorporate the psychoanalytic model as a core conceptual subsystem. The reorganization is, of course, still in progress.

The clinical application of GST to group psychotherapy

The next question is exactly how the analytic group therapist can apply the new orientation and the information it has generated in his daily sessions. Instead of trying to generalize from the work of others, I shall suggest one answer to the question by describing, as I have experienced it, the role and function of the analytic group therapist who works within a general systems context.

Since applying any new paradigm to a given set of empirical data involves making some basic premises about their relation to each other, I shall try to make my assumptions explicit as I go along. I think you will agree with my first assumption, that anyone who wishes to apply GST must first of all take into account the fact that it describes the way normal living systems operate, whereas the therapy group is composed of members who, in the course of their ontogenetic experience, have, to varying degrees, become dysfunctional. Some of them may in their earliest exchange of energy and information with their parental systems have been unable to close enough boundaries to maintain their stability as separate systems. They were too frequently flooded with excess input. Others may have overprotected their identity during these early contacts (object relations) by closing too many boundaries to keep out input from parents that was inharmonious with their inner state. Their capacity for change was diminished. If their boundary functioning was not remedied as they matured, both kinds of persons might as adults become candidates for group therapy. As group members, the former would be suggestible but erratic in their interaction with others. They would lack a firm sense of identity. The latter would be constricted in their interaction. Their exchanges with others would permit very little new input. Instead, they repeat many mechanized patterns and tend to communicate mostly with those members whose patterns complement their own, so that very little energy and information would be exchanged. Analytic group therapists will recognize that such dysfunctional boundarying lays the foundation for the development of transferential and defensive patterns of interacting which will be re-enacted and subject to change in the therapy group. When I put them into a therapy group, however, I make the assumption that in spite of their dysfunctional aspects, they retain the latent capacity of all living systems to become more active and autonomous than they have ever been.

The new goal

Viewed from this perspective the therapist's goal is to remobilize the member's full original system potentials as described in the paradigm of living systems. It is, therefore, more broadly conceived than that of the analytic group therapist. Bringing the unconscious processes to consciousness is no longer the goal but a means of increasing the exchange of energy and information within the personality subsystem. Analyzing the transferential and defensive exchanges between two or more group members becomes but one way of opening boundaries and stimulating change and growth.

How does the group therapist implement the broader goal?

The group therapist may take his cue from the way normal living systems change themselves. They stabilize or transform themselves by monitoring the permeability of their boundaries and over time develop their own flux equilibrium or steady state. For this reason I make the assumption that the therapist may temporarily assume the role of the organizing *subsystem* (J. G. Miller calls this the 'decider system', but in my opinion the term smacks of vitalism, so I have taken the liberty of changing it) and temporarily take responsibility for carrying out the boundarying function for all three of the interacting systems. When any given system is unstable and reveals a weak sense of identity, he facilitates the closure of whatever boundary is endangering its stability by permitting excess input. The input will forthwith be diminished and the system will have time to reorder its internal dynamic interaction. Its exchanges with others will become more selective. On the other hand, the therapist will facilitate the opening of whatever boundaries seem to constrict a given system's potential for growth. It will thereafter be able to import new energy and information, to process it, and restructure itself. Whether the therapist chooses to intervene in the group suprasystem, the members, or in their personality subsystems, the influence of the resulting transformations will be circular and will affect them all.

His primary focus is to facilitate change in the member systems because it is they who have come for help. He may choose to catalyze their capacity to move towards flux equilibrium by bringing about change in their personality subsystems or he may achieve a similar effect by dealing with boundaries in the group suprasystem. Whatever his decision may be, from moment to moment, he will continue to observe the state of the group suprasystem as a whole because it is a powerful force field whose continuing influence on its members he wants to maximize. When its exchanges are flowing freely, and its stability remains strong, it can be said to be in a steady state and its influence on the members will be potent. When an individual member can demonstrate that *he* has finally achieved a steady state, he will be ready to talk about leaving the group.

At this point, we must take account of a new and significant GST contribution to psychoanalytic theory, which enables us to increase our members' growth, creativity and autonomy. These characteristics of normal living systems are the product of consistent boundarying which brings about a flux equilibrium or steady state and assures it of maintaining an everchanging but optimal proportion of open and closed boundaries and a consequent stability in spite of its progressive transformations. For this reason the therapist makes his decision to intervene, not in terms of a single dysfunctional boundary taken in isolation, but in relation to the state of the whole system's momentary equilibrium. His aim is to maintain a quasi-disequilibrium because a certain degree of tension is essential to growth.

This then is the function of the GST group therapist. But analytically oriented group therapists will want to know just what the boundarying process and the exchanges of energy and information it regulates have to do with their own usual procedure.

The boundarying process

The analytic group therapist is familiar with the clinically useful concept of ego boundaries. GST extends that notion to the interpersonal and group boundaries, but shifts the emphasis to the *process* of boundarying. This generalized concept provides a more comprehensive governing principle for the selection of techniques than does analytic theory. The therapist may employ any of the current techniques, if he feels they will open or close boundaries, or he may devise new ones based on GST principles. He is not limited to the special techniques of any single theoretical approach. Although he may continue to analyze transference and resistance as the soundest way to open intrapersonal boundaries, he may employ role playing, an appropriate gestalt exercise, or an encounter technique when he is confronted with exceptionally impermeable boundaries in any of the systems. Or he may use an ego-psychological technique to increase stability. His technical options are thus increased without destroying the internal consistency of psychoanalysis or the more comprehensive GST framework.

J. G. Miller, who distinguishes between structural and functional systems, views the boundarying process as the function of the decider, or as I prefer, the organizing subsystem. The latter has generally been considered to be the equivalent of the analytic concept of the ego. K. Menninger was among the first to take note of that fact in a paper proposing a personality theory in general systems terms (1963). The advantage of the GST language is that it is less abstract and, therefore, less prone to anthropomorphic or vitalistic interpretation.

What crosses the boundaries in therapy groups?

Because changing boundary permeability is only *the means* of regulating which exchanges of energy and information are permitted to cross them and which are locked out, we must ask what crosses the boundaries in the process of group therapy. So far, we have been indicating that it is patterned matter/energy and information. But this very valuable bit of knowledge is couched in such general terms that it appears to have little to do with the task of the analytic group therapist. But GST deals with systems in *general* and, therefore, necessarily employs very general terms. Each *particular* category of system, however, *encodes* its energy and information in terms of its own characteristic processes. A plausible answer to our question is suggested by the

work of W. Gray and J. Durkin, who came to grips with this issue as
they constructed their GST models of group therapy around the part
played by emotion and cognition in the therapeutic process. Durkin
arrived at the conclusion that, on the whole, genuine spontaneous
emotions (in contrast to cover-up emotions which attend the defences
and serve to maintain the status quo), tend to open boundaries while
cognitive processes serve to maintain existing boundaries or to draw
new ones, after an emotional shift has been experienced. Both processes are essential for achieving therapeutic transformation in the
members (J. Durkin, 1975). I have tested out this hypothesis and found
it reasonably valid – examples which provide clinical evidence will be
found in a book by our Task Force – James E. Durkin (ed.), *Living
Groups: Group Psychotherapy and General Systems Theory*, Brunner/
Mazel, New York, 1981 – although I am sure further work in this
area will be necessary. I thereupon made the *assumption* that in human
individual and social systems, energy and information are conveyed by
emotional and cognitive processes. Once this is understood, I believe
that analytic group therapists will be better prepared to apply GST
concepts.

I believe that from the beginning of life these processes interact in a
system-forming way to exert mutual influence on each other. They
organize each other. Cognitive input has the effect of differentiating a
human system's originally global emotions into a series of graduated
feelings. The global emotions affect the infant's early perception of
reality. Later the graduated emotions increase the precision of the
growing child's ability to think (W. Gray, 1973). In the course of
development a variety of emotional/cognitive systems are thus formed
which may be thought of as patterns of transacting. In the group situation these complex patterns convey the energy and information that is
exchanged in all living systems. Those patterns that are dysfunctional
may be identified, by the therapist, experienced by the members, and
then gradually transformed.

Some of these patterns are restructured as the child's organizing subsystem and its functions mature. But others, because of frequent
repetition, became automatic. In the group these dysfunctional patterns
will be transformed as reboundarying is facilitated.

Thus, GST illuminates the analytic concept of transference and of
character resistance by describing the mechanisms by which they
come into being. They can then be conceptualized in language which
brings them into closer proximity with the empirical facts.

The merging stream of psychoanalytic and general systems theory in group psychotherapy

According to my experience there is significant reciprocal interplay between psychoanalytic and general systems theory in the process of group psychotherapy. For instance:

1. Libido theory accounts for the members' intrapersonal sources of energy and is significantly supplemented by GST's ecological theory of energy according to which living systems may repeatedly replenish their energy, as needed, by means of their emotional/cognitive exchanges with one another, and the environment.

2. Psychoanalysis provides a theory of the dynamic unconscious which accounts for the numerous degrees and varieties of 'pathological' behaviour which we encounter in the group interactions. But because it relies chiefly on tension reduction to restore homeostasis, it does not provide standards for normal functioning nor give an adequate explanation of the members' creative capacities. Von Bertalanffy's discovery that normal living systems operate on a flowing or dynamic equilibrium provides the new information that a certain amount of tension or quasi-disequilibrium is a prerequisite for their mastery of the environment, their capacity for self structuring and their autonomy.

Thus, GST, which is based on the normal functions of living systems in general, is able to fill in the information gap, left by the psychoanalytic model which was based primarily on the exploration of pathological behaviour. It extends the area of the group therapist's function and suggests the possibility of devising new techniques which harness tension and disequilibrium to increase his therapeutic effectiveness. (A number of our Task Force members have devised such techniques. They will be described in detail in James E. Durkin (ed.), *Living Groups: Group Psychotherapy and General Systems Theory* Brunner/ Mazel, New York, 1981.)

In practice, the results of psychoanalysis were not as far-reaching as had been anticipated. It had been assumed that explicit changes in behaviour and general growth would flow naturally from genuine insights, experienced in vivo, so that no special techniques were devised for this purpose. Nor had the long-range goals been persuasively articulated. The primary emphasis was on analyzing transference and resistance. This strategy seemed adequate for the hysterical patients who were treated in those early years, but there were many exceptions even among these patients whenever undetected character problems interfered with their ability to change. The various reasons for these unexpectedly attenuated results have been described earlier.

The heightened interaction in analytic group therapy improved the situation, but the problem was by no means solved. Its 'graduates' still showed a tendency to excel in self-understanding, but their ability to change their behaviour lagged far behind. For today's group therapist the problem is more serious, because his members include a large proportion of narcissistic, borderline, and orally or anally regressed patients whose capacity to change their patterns of interacting without further help is sporadic and undependable.

Attempts to correct this deficiency have been made both within psychoanalysis and by nonanalytic approaches. Ego psychology, object relations theory, Schaefer's development of an action language, among others, have served the purpose up to a point. So had the 'innovative techniques' of the 1960s, which tried to increase the emotional experience of the treatment. However, these were uncoordinated attempts and produced new controversies rather than a unifying theoretical framework.

Because GST puts a premium on *structural transformation* and *organic growth* as natural characteristics of living systems at the intrapsychic, interpersonal, and group levels, it provides a potentially unifying framework within which the original intentions of psychoanalysis to stimulate change and growth can be given a new clarity and a new impetus in clinical practice. The synthesis of psychoanalysis and general systems theory adds a dimension to the work of the therapist who becomes a coordinator in the world of action as well as a guide in the world of meaning. The new emphasis puts his work directly on the task of bringing about change and growth, and serves to increase his therapeutic effectiveness in a more modern context.

Summary

The first section describes the conditions which led me to take my present theoretical position. They include my discussions with Dr Foulkes, the changing socioeconomic conditions which splintered the group therapy movement in the USA after the 1950s, and the fact that GST seemed able to correct certain limitations of analytic group therapy theory which prevented its optimum therapeutic effectiveness.

The second section examines this structural metatheory and the new information it has generated in order to assess its relevance for and its contributions to the theory and practice of group psychotherapy. The third section addresses the problem of applying GST to group therapy. It indicates the basic premises involved, and describes the function of the group therapist.

Conclusions

1. GST has the capacity to bring unifying trends among the current 'group therapies' while allowing for their valid differences. If adopted it could greatly improve communication with other social sciences and make collaborative research possible. It might even serve the function of an integrative group therapy theory.
2. Von Bertalanffy's new paradigm of living systems applies equally to the therapy group, the individual members and to their personality subsystems. It delineates the common structural characteristics of living systems which *supplement* the information which psychoanalysis and group dynamics have already provided. Together they will provide the basis of a more comprehensive model of group therapy and an opportunity for increasing our therapeutic effectiveness.
3. The new information illuminates such analytic concepts as the ego, transference and resistance, makes it possible to increase their precision and to bring them into closer approximation to the empirical data.
4. The more generalized model would have the capacity to transcend several of the controversial dichotomies which have had a decisive effect on theory. Examples are the role in treatment of: individual vs. group factors; emotional vs. cognitive factors; intrapsychic vs. interpersonal factors; and biological vs. cultural factors. GST views these as essential complementary pairs.

Appendix

Dear Helen,
    I wanted to thank you for sending me your first progress report on General Systems Theory. I find this very interesting and am looking forward to what follows. I would very much like to take this up by way of discussion in GAIPAC if you would agree. I think for me

alone to answer at the present stage would be premature. I wish, however, to let you have a few points for personal use.

First, your concept of boundary: this plays a big part throughout my writings and I have used the very same words in describing it as having quasi- or semi-permeable membrane. I see the relationship of the whole and the parts in very much the same way and I think I have expressed this clearly enough throughout. I am not so sure about what you call the 'decider subsystem at the apex' with which I cannot at the present either agree. However, this would lead too far to go into this now.

Another important point is the idea of a dynamic equilibrium. In my very first book *Introduction to Group Analytic Psychotherapy* which appeared in 1949, I say on the very first page the following:

> The healthy organism functions as a whole and can be described as a system in a dynamic equilibrium. Dynamic means that it is never in a state of rest, has constantly to adjust to the ever changing circumstances, milieux, conditions in which it lives. Such adaptation, however, does not take place mechanically, following chemical or physical principles merely. There is always a creative element present, even in the simplest adaptation. . . . On the highest level creative activity seems to be an inevitable ingredient, the hallmark of healthy life. Dynamic equilibrium, therefore, means the active and creative maintenance of a good balance. From the point of view of the person such a state is described as being 'well, healthy, feeling happy, contented'. Disturbed function is due to disturbances in the equilibrium of the total situation. . .

As you can see, I add the creative element as an essential one.

Now to turn to what you talk about as 'emergents which appear at each level', this corresponds exactly to my concept of different levels of communication, different keys, different depths, in which the communication should be understood.

This is enough for today, in order to indicate to you what sort of thing I would like to discuss. There is far more than that and I think we should combine our efforts in this field to achieve a unified theory.

Once more, with kind regards,

Yours sincerely,
Michael

Bibliography

Bateson, G., and Ruesch, J. (1951), *Communication: The Social Matrix of Society*, New York, Norton.
Bergler, E. (1949), *The Basic Neurosis*, New York, Grune & Stratton.
Bertalanffy, L. von (1956), 'General Systems Theory,' *General Systems Yearbook*, 1, p. 110.
Bertalanffy, L. von (1967), *Robots, Men and Minds*, New York, Braziller.
Bertalanffy, L. von (1968), *General Systems Theory*, New York, Braziller.
Bertalanffy, L. von (1969), 'General Systems Theory and Psychiatry: An Overview', in ed. W. Gray, *et al.*, *General Systems Theory and Psychiatry*, Boston, Little Brown.
Dolgoff, T. (1975), 'Small Groups and Organizations', *General Systems Yearbook*, vol. XX.
Durkin, H. (1957), 'Toward a common basis for group dynamics', *Int. J. Group Psychotherapy*, vol. VII, no. 7, pp. 115-130.
Durkin, H. (1964), *The Group in Depth*, New York, Int. Univ. Press.
Durkin, H. (1971), 'Transference in group therapy revisited', *Int. J. Group Psychotherapy*, vol. XXI, no. 3.
Durkin, H. (1972), 'Group therapy and general systems theory' in *Process in Group and Family Therapy*, C. Sager and H. Singer (eds), New York, Brunner/Mazel.
Durkin, J. (1975), 'Group systems therapy: the structure of thinking and feeling', invited Paper presented at AGPA Conference in San Antonio.
Ezriel, H. (1959), The Role of Transference in Psa. and Other Approaches, Zurich, *Acta Therapeutica*.
Foulkes, S. H. (1949), *Introduction to Group-Analytic Psychotherapy*, New York, Grune & Stratton.
Foulkes, S. H. (1964), *Group Analytic Psychotherapy*, New York, Int. Univ. Press.
Gray, W. (1973), 'Emotional/cognitive structures', General Systems Yearbook, vol. XVIII, p. 167.
Gray, W. (1977), 'System formation/system precursors', presented at Sixth International Congress of Group Psychotherapy, Philadelphia.
Guntrip, H. (1969), *Schizoid Phenomena, Object Relations and the Self*, New York, Int. Univ. Press.
Haley, J. (1963), *Strategies of Psychotherapy*, New York, Grune & Stratton.
Hartmann, H. (1964), *Essays on Ego Psychology*, New York, Int. Univ. Press.
Kernberg, O. (1973), 'A systems approach for priority setting of interpretations in groups', *Int. J. Grp. Psychoth.*, vol. 23, no. 2.
Lakin, M., and Dobbs, W. H. (1962), 'A study in group process', *Int. J. Grp. Psychoth.*, vol. 12, pp. 64-74.
Levinson, E. (1972), *The Fallacy of Understanding*, New York, Basic Books.

Lewin, K. (1951), *Field Theory and Social Science*, New York, Harper & Row.

Marayuma, M. (1963), 'The second cybernetics', *American Scientist*, vol. 51, no. 2, p. 164.

Menninger, K. (1963), *The Vital Balance*, New York, Viking Press.

Miller, J. G. (1955), 'Toward a General Theory of Systems', *AJP*, vol. X, p. 513.

Miller, J. G. (1965), 'Living Systems: Basic Concepts', *Behavioral Science*, vol. 10, no. 3, July, and no. 4, October.

Miller, J. G. (1969), 'Living Systems: Basic Concepts' in ed. W. Gray *et al.*, *General Systems Theory and Psychiatry*, Boston, Little Brown.

Mintz, E. (1975), 'Group therapy techniques and encounter techniques, comparison and rationale', *AJP*, vol. 25, no. 1.

Reusch, J. (1964), *Therapeautic Communication*, New York, Norton.

Reusch, J., and Bateson, G. (1951), *Communication: The Common Matrix of Psychiatry*, New York, Norton.

Scheidlinger, S. (1960), 'Group process in group psychotherapy, I and II', *AJP*, 14, pp. 104-20; 346-65.

Schwartz, E., and Wolf, A. (1960), 'The mystique of group dynamics', in *Topical Problems, Psychotherapy*: II, New York, Karger.

Slavson, S. R. (1953), 'Common sources of error and confusion', *Int. J. Grp. Psychoth.*, vol. 3, pp. 3-28.

Thelen, H. (1954), *Dynamics of Groups at Work*, Chicago Univ. Press.

Watzlawick, P., Beavin, J., and Jackson, D. (1967), *Pragmatics of Human Communication*, New York, Norton.

Weiner, N. (1948), *Cybernetics*, New York, John Wiley.

Whitaker, D., and Lieberman, M. (1964), *Psychotherapy Through Group Process*, New York, Atherton.

Chapter 6
Adolescent group therapy and its contribution to the understanding of adult groups

John Evans

I first met Michael Foulkes in the Maudsley in 1957. However, while I trained to be a child psychiatrist and a psychoanalyst, contact remained minimal. My interest in group therapy was to develop later — quietly and slowly, but therefore persistently. As a result I came into more contact over the years with this pioneer and became increasingly aware of how much he had contributed to the development of the group therapy movement in the United Kingdom and the very considerable affection in which he was held. Amongst his qualities he allowed others to hold opinions of their own, he listened to them as well as expressing his own. That is, he created a growth-producing climate for young group therapists. It is with that in mind that one feels privileged to contribute to this memorial volume.

Sylvia Plath, in one of her last poems, said that 'Perfection is terrible — it cannot have children.' For a group therapist such an achievement, with its consequent sterility, can never be — as group therapy is too complex. This contribution is written with the hope that it will enable the interested reader to develop the subject further.

In 1961 I began group therapy with delinquent adolescents. Possessed with a fantasy life which alternated between providing insight into life and producing nightmares, I was as anxious as any neophyte. Although I was aware that there were nine forms of anxiety common to beginners that had been described by Berger in 1958, and which included the anxiety of the therapist to impress the group with his ability to provide leadership and his difficulty in providing it, anxiety that the group may not turn up or, alternatively, that the group may get up and walk out or, even worse, that the group will get up and walk towards the therapist, I was comforted by the realisation that I had only four of these anxieties.

Fully aware that all new adventures create anxiety, I remained in need of a conceptual framework — a survival kit which would help me to select and organise my understanding of the group activity that I was about to experience.

Being employed at that time in the Tavistock Clinic, inevitably I was greatly influenced by the work of Bion, Ezriel and Sutherland. As a consequence, I was sensitive to the need for facilitating development of a group which worked at its problems, but aware how such attempts to work are constantly interrupted by the appearance of basic assumption groups. That is, that as a group attempts to work at a task, certain basic anxieties or needs of the group will begin to appear that impair the group's work-effectiveness. The group then takes up either a dependent attitude towards the leader whom they hope will provide them with solutions, or, alternatively, there will be flight away from the situation or, thirdly, the group will become spectators as a pair in the group participate in some form of interaction. The remainder of the group watch as if their unconscious anxieties or needs could be relieved in some magical form by this pair.

My subsequent experience with groups of delinquent adolescents was that basic assumption groups in the form of fight or flight were a frequent occurrence, but one was equally impressed with the constant appearance of a dependency group. Experience with groups of adolescents of varying ages over the years showed that the younger the adolescent group, the less relevant appeared to be the concept of a group working at a task and the more apparent was the presence of a group playing.

As a child psychiatrist, I was fully aware of the therapeutic effects of play therapy with children, and I also knew of Slavson's activity groups with children. Nevertheless I retained the feeling that adolescents should, like adults, be working on their problems in the group and not playing.

Over the years that followed, I found myself constantly returning to the theme of establishing and maintaining the adolescent group's capacity to work at their difficulties, as I considered that the ability to talk about one's difficulties was an important aspect of group therapy. This could have led to my selecting only adolescents capable of using a technique devised essentially for the treatment of adult neurotic disorders. The alternative was to attempt to modify the existing techniques so that they became relevant for adolescents who needed help. Discarding the concept that adolescents are not suitable for treatment, I attempted to make the treatment suitable for the adolescent. In the years that were to follow, when I was treating younger and older delinquent groups, and then mixed neurotic and personality-disordered adolescents, I chose to establish groups in which youngsters worked at their problems through the use of directions and using confrontation techniques and limit-setting. This allowed me to survive and continue group work, although one was very much aware that by abandoning the non-directive approach, one could be focusing on the conscious content of the group, and thereby ignoring what could be more important dimensions.

However, adolescents have a mind of their own and in spite of my wish for them to work, play constantly intruded into the group. Sometimes the play that took place in the group was perceived as a means of avoiding anxiety; that is a flight away from reality. On other occasions, on good days, one felt that play was an indirect way of dealing with anxieties. For example, one delinquent boy asked, 'What if all male genitalia had right-hand threads and all female genitalia had left-hand threads?.' One's comment that he was really asking whether he was a sexual misfit allowed a more direct discussion of the problem. Likewise, another youngster's story of how an Arab sheikh had gone to a marriage bureau and looked at the photographs and decided to buy the lot could be used to explore their feelings of how they would like to be able to deal with girls in a similar way for they wouldn't then have to be concerned about whether girls were interested in them.

In my experience of play in adolescent groups, interpretations of their activity as a defence against anxiety does not always result in the group working more effectively at its basic problems. Indeed, such insight often appears to be persecutory; for example, I have interpreted to a group why they chose to sing songs rather than discuss problems. Giving an appropriate insight into the defensive manoeuvres of each participant, it brought the singing to an end and enabled the group to be in touch with its anxieties. Comforted by the maxim of strength through misery − their misery − I was not deterred by their feelings of persecution, but I have also noticed that on such occasions the group misery does not always last long enough for real growth to take place. Indeed, new defensive manoeuvres appear almost invariably in the direction of activity away from the anxiety. In comparison with adult therapy groups, adolescents appear to have difficulties in persisting at problem-solving activities which require some intellectual insight, while remaining emotionally involved in them.

It is true that adolescents − especially older ones − as they become

16, 17 and 18, can talk about their problems in greater depth, but it is rare for them to do so for periods of more than ten minutes at a time. Their limited capacity for articulate introspection and its communication to others, their limited awareness of the universality of so many emotional problems, their general lack of experience of life can result in group impotence and consequent group desire to move away from their difficulties and the establishment of basic assumption groups. Considerable activity on the part of the therapist with the provision of appropriate words and concepts and an insistence that the group continues to work at its anxieties, rather than take flight, may enable further insightful discussion to take place. However, the price that may have to be paid is that the therapist is exceedingly active and controlling with the group which then becomes dependent upon him so that the actual work of the adolescents in fact diminishes.

Thus, if I may summarise my early views on adolescent group therapy, I considered one of the important tasks of the group therapist was to facilitate the development of a work group and to minimise inappropriate defensive manoeuvres. Instead, the priority was to tolerate anxiety while seeking optimum solutions. In practice, the development of work groups was far less successful than one would have wished. The group members did not help each other as auxiliary therapists under the benevolent eye of a group conductor and yet the group members appeared to enjoy the groups, and to obtain considerable support from each other. Very clearly there was a culture gap between the expectations of the therapist and those of the adolescents.

If one examines the literature related to adolescent groups, the problem of work versus play is a recurring theme and adolescent groups take on the quality of the playground, rather than a workforce. It is common for adolescents to bring books, comics, radios, knitting, playing-cards, coffee and toast into a group, especially in a residential setting. The message is that the youngster finds the group boring and a waste of time and the problems are the therapist's, not his. In passing, my practice has been to forbid radios and playing cards, while knitting is usually allowed. An example of its therapeutic benefit arose with Pauline whose anxiety about her departure from an in-patient unit and becoming independent resonated with her struggle for independence from her mother. She asked female members of the group to knit some squares to make a woolly blanket to take away with her to keep her warm while living in the cold world outside; that is, she asked the group to provide her with a transitional object. The group recognised her need and met her request but in fact they also discussed her problems. As for the reading of comics and books, it is a perennial problem. The value of tolerating it is that it provides a frightened, inarticulate adolescent with an escape route which is usually abandoned spontaneously. It may also result in reading extracts aloud to the group and the spontaneous development of a group theme. The drawback is that it may escalate into a group activity and total abandonment of any work. When this threatens, I tell the group to put its reading material down and, if necessary, I tell them I will look after it on their behalf during the session.

My digression was to illustrate the type of play as opposed to work that may appear in an adolescent group. I have also found that to concentrate on the establishment of a work group introduces an intellectual focus which can be controlling and even moralistic rather than therapeutic and can overlook the experiential benefits of such a group experience. Thus, I was faced with the dilemma of believing that to allow a certain amount of play in the group was beneficial, and lacking a theoretical framework which supported this viewpoint.

It was Winnicott's theoretical statement on playing in his last publication, *Playing and Reality*, that enabled some of the confusion to disappear. He stated that:

> Psychotherapy takes place in the overlap of two areas of playing —
> that of the patient and that of the therapist. Psychotherapy has to
> do with two people playing together. The corollary of this is when
> playing is not possible, then the work done by the therapist is
> directed towards bringing the patient from a state of not being
> able to play into a state of being able to play.

Although Winnicott had in mind the rather rigid, inhibited personality, it did allow me to bridge the gap between the concept of adult work groups and adolescents at play.

From this followed the realisation that the adolescents' playing with the therapist was a highly important aspect of their therapy. The fact that I felt rather like a battered teddy bear at the end of many a session was proof of being involved in this play.

In passing I should say that adolescent play not only keeps the therapist fit intellectually, but can also do so physically. On more than one occasion I have chased an adolescent out of the room and down the corridor, wondering whether to hit him when I caught him or content myself with an interpretation straight between the eyes, using the milk of one's interpretation like a water cannon. I have also had to consider the fact that if I did catch the adolescent, he might feel that he had to defend himself physically and that he and I could then get ourselves into a corner, play would cease and we would find it difficult to extricate ourselves in such a manner that therapy could continue.

On return to the group therapy, with or without the youngster, one has to decide quickly on (1) how to maintain self-esteem, (2) how to turn the whole incident to therapeutic advantage, (3) how to deal with the group's anxiety and (of greatest importance) (3) how to help the particular youngster so that his own self-esteem is maintained and, with luck, the whole experience turned into emotional growth.

At one stage I would have considered the above event to be verging on a therapeutic disaster. I am now far more aware how the actual incident is better seen as a form of play which can be turned to therapeutic advantage for that individual, and for the group.

It is not uncommon with adolescent in-patients for a member to refuse to come to the group. Again, this can be perceived as a form of play. Although I have, on occasions, been prepared to take the group to the youngster as opposed to having him dragged into the group, to hold a group with the adolescent sitting in the toilet, and the therapist and other group members remaining on the outside, has distinct limitations, for he doesn't know whether the adolescent is listening inside or merely reading.

The examples given underline the fact that the behaviour of adolescents in group therapy, and towards the group therapist, differs from that existing in adult groups. That difference can be understood through introducing the concept of play, whose dimensions need to be explored.

I wish to discuss a number of these dimensions; namely, play and its relationship to acting out; its relationship to primary and secondary process functioning; to basic assumption and work groups; and to maturational tasks, especially that of separation individuation, before discussing how this can illuminate the functioning of adult groups.

The term 'acting out' was first used by Freud to indicate actions which the patient produced as substitutes for memories. However, the use of the term has limitations. With pre-school children, the chief mode of communication of their feelings and impulses is through action and not through verbalisation so that acting out is age-adequate for young children. Indeed, play therapy evolved from that recognition. In contrast, latency children have the capacity for verbalisation as well as of enactment, the balance depending upon the age and the child's personality — some being verbalisers and others being enactors. In the clinic setting, Anna Freud has commented that with such enactors the therapist must be content with striving to contain the patient's expression and reducing reality actions to play activity, thereby finding his way via fantasy elaboration to verbalisation and secondary process thinking. In other words, traditional psychotherapy focuses on getting a child to talk about it or play it out symbolically, rather than do it.

With adolescents, the problem is more complex and most therapists use the term 'acting out' both in the treatment situation and outside it. For example, Peter Bloss (1963) calls acting out 'a phase-specific mechanism of adolescents'. Indeed, a major problem in the treatment of adolescents is how to handle their capacity to act out; for example, how to deal with age-appropriate tendencies of detaching themselves from adult figures, and achieving their own independence, but which are expressed in inappropriate actions. Thus, separation can be achieved by running away from home, but there are better solutions.

As for acting out in a therapy session (some call this 'acting in'), it certainly exists in plenty, but conceptually I prefer to regard it as a form of play. It is handled best when the underlying anxieties are appreciated and interpreted, although other techniques, such as confrontation and limit-setting, are valuable, as I will describe.

I would now like to compare work groups and basic assumption and play groups.

Work groups focus on secondary process functioning, in contrast with basic assumption groups which focus on primary process functioning and are essentially unconscious in origin. In the pioneering days of psychoanalysis, the task of the early therapist was considered to be making the unconscious conscious, so that reality testing could be applied to formerly repressed primitive wishes and drives so that sublimation could now take place. Primary process functioning was seen as relieving tension immediately as it was independent of and ignored external reality. In contrast, secondary process functioning involved delay as it was concerned with reality testing and time was needed to carry out checks. The advantage was that it could result in tensions being permanently relieved as realistic means of dealing with particular stresses were found.

However, attitudes have changed towards primary and secondary process functioning and I think that our attitudes towards work and basic assumption groups are also in need of change. It is in this area that I find Rycroft's views particularly illuminating. He sees primary process functioning as essentially autistic and connected with feelings. Secondary processes lead more .to communication with external objects. He sees primary process functioning as often unconscious but, at other times, alien or not self. He considers, and I agree with him, that it is better to say that in human functioning there are two types of thinking which co-exist. The relationship between the two depends upon the maturity and the security of the individual. In a normal, secure infant, primary and secondary process functioning are integrated and harmonised, and the infant feels both at home in the world and in his fantasies, which remain to some extent bound to external real objects. Thus, he can fantasise a breast (or feeding bottle) and the reality is sufficiently close to his wishes for him to be satisfied. However, if the imaginative capacity of the child becomes disengaged from external reality and operates on a psychic level in which images cease to represent external objects and instead become substitutes for them, there is consequent impoverishment of psychic development. This is what exists in many disturbed adolescents. So what now becomes the task? The consequence of accepting Rycroft's hypothesis is that the aim of psychotherapy should be considered not only of making the unconscious conscious, and of strengthening the ego, but also of reestablishing connections between dissociated psychic functions so that the patient ceases to feel there is an inherent antagonism between his imaginative and his adaptive capacity.

Play is influenced to a great extent by primary process functioning which is the language of one's inner life. Secondary process functioning has a greater relevance in communicating with the outside world and meeting the needs of external reality. The aim of the therapist is to integrate them. With adolescents, their capacity to play in groups and with the therapist is potentially capable of being used by the therapist as a move through their age-specific maturational tasks.

In other words, I have reached the position where I do not see work groups and basic assumption or play groups as automatically antagonistic towards each other. I see them as illustrating two aspects of the adolescent's functioning – a preoccupation with work and the cognitive aspect of one's psychic functioning which can, if carried to excess, stifle an individaul's primary process functioning which is the source of their feelings and of their imaginative capacity.

Let me give you an example. A therapist may wish to be uninvolved in the play, preferring to view himself as a spectator or skilled facilitator, but this is not sufficient for adolescents as they will actively involve him in the play, experimenting in the safety of the group with their feelings towards authority figures. One day an adolescent group was so chaotic, over-active and disorganised and Elsie interrupted me so continuously that eventually I had to tell her to come over and sit by me. On the spur of the moment, I told her to stand and face the corner. Elsie had manoeuvred me into the role of a confronting, controlling parent and I had accepted that role. In turn, she continued to play, conformed with my ruling and thereafter, standing and continuing to face the corner, made occasional constructive comments on the group. She had manoeuvred me out of being a benevolent, detached, thoughtful therapist and showed me to be critical, controlling and restrictive. She had used me like a teddy bear, making me act out a role while she, in turn, played at having a new relationship with an adult male figure. Failing to recognise her motives at that time, I did not interpret that she was playing and experimenting with me, as she would have liked to experiment with her opinionated, rigid, dogmatic father. If I had been aware, I would have given her such an interpretation, but optimally not to stop her playing and experimentation. Nor would I have wished to prevent emotional release at the price of intellectual insight. The task was to formulate the interpretation in such words that would help her 'play' with her feelings towards her father and facilitate flexibility, separation and growth.

What is the function of this play in adolescent groups that so often interrupts the work groups that do occur? Apart from its defensive quality, I also see play as the capacity to experiment in relationships, the freedom to adopt a variety of roles on an experimental basis; that is, an adolescent play group is experimenting with a variety of identities. In contrast, cognitive discussion of problems allows only a limited type of experimentation although its value is not to be despised.

The play group has an experiential quality which is satisfying and liberating. Those of you who have experimented in encounter groups or, even more so, in role-playing or psychodrama, will know exactly what I mean. Play is an experiment. It is the capacity to be tentative and explore in an indirect or symbolic manner certain instinctual or infantile needs. However, if that experimentation is excessively fragmented, then no exploration that leads to integration can take place and it remains a limited learning experience. It is here that the psychotherapist has a function as a caring auxiliary ego, and it is why limit-setting, interpretation and confrontation are so important as they enable outer aspects of life to be brought into juxtaposition with the adolescent's inner reality, and reduce the splitting.

Play which can mean the presence of a basic assumption group does not automatically imply chaos, only experimentation. The play, of course, takes in the therapist and allows exploration of the relationship with adult figures. I do not consider it wholly appropriate to call it a transference relationship, as the adolescent is concerned with his developmental tasks, not mere repetitions of previously unresolved conflicts.

Good group therapy occurs when the therapist is able to guide this play and experimentation so it does not come to a halt. It is his task to facilitate the play and experimentation, not to win or lose the game. In order to do so, however, he must implement certain rules. Some of these are, of course, fundamental, such as that the adolescent players must meet regularly at the same time and be involved in the play for several months. Confrontation is one of the important rules of play but it must be remembered that the confronting role is one that the group often imposes upon the therapist, turning him into a controlling, confronting authority figure but, at the same time, making sure that he is fairly ineffectual. What is bewildering, however, in such circumstances is that, having succeeded in making the therapist ineffectual, the group may then change rapidly so that it requires a benevolent, caring, paternal figure that protects the group as they regress; that is, the adolescent must feel free to kill the therapist over and over, but he must resurrect himself on each occasion. In that sense, adolescent group therapy is more like war games or an adventure playground than a work group.

Before we terminate this discussion of play, let us ask when is it non-constructive? I think it is, first, when flight is allowed on a permanent basis and, second, when the sequence of events of play is so rapid that it becomes disruptive. Third, it is when the therapist is so demoralised that he withdraws.

I will summarise by saying that with the passage of time and the accumulation of experience, my basic approach to adolescent group therapy has not changed to any extent. Working in a variety of adolescent groups and supervising others, the basic themes that have been described have been repeated over and over, but what has emerged is a more firmly based theoretical framework.

I now wish to link these statements up with adult work groups.

The beneficial effects of group therapy occur, not only from a conscious discussion of an individual's problems, and perhaps the contribution of other members of the group and the use of sharing and empathy, coupled with interpretations, from the conductor, but because there is also room for play. Although more subdued than with adolescents, it does exist. The adoption of the various roles does take place both on a conscious and an unconscious level and helps adult patients come to terms with what I would call delayed maturational tasks, which may also be termed previous fixations and unavoidable regressions.

In my opinion the use of play and role playing in adult groups deserves more attention.

References

Berger, M. (1958), 'Problems of Anxiety in Group Psychotherapy Trainees', *Am. J. Psychotherapy*, 12, pp. 505-7.
Bloss, P. (1963), 'The concept of acting out in relation to the adolescent process', *Journal of the American Academy of Child Psychiatry* vol. 2, 1.
Rycroft, C. (1968), *In Imagination and Reality*, London, Hogarth Press.
Winnicott, D. W. (1971), 'Playing: a theoretical statement', in *Playing and Reality*, London, Tavistock.

Chapter 7

Analytical psychology and group-analytic psychotherapy: convergences

Romano Fiumara

Introduction

Certainly resistance on the part of analytical psychology with regard to group psychotherapy has not been negligible. It seems, however, that if we refer to the latter with the specific meaning of analytical group psychotherapy as defined by its founder, S. H. Foulkes, it can be seen that the theoretical body of Jungian psychology actually demonstrates points of substantial convergence.

The present work attempts to bring to the fore these points of convergence by comparing the two lines of thought in a synthetic manner.

As a preliminary step it seems relevant to cite one of the works of Erich Neumann, *The Origins and History of Consciousness*,[1] which among the works of Jung's followers was perhaps evaluated most positively by Jung himself.

In Neumann's work the basic thesis is that the individual's consciousness goes through the same stages of development that have marked the history of consciousness in humankind as a whole: phrased in a well-known term borrowed from biology, 'ontogenesis sums up philogenesis'. In his presentation of the work, Jung noted with pleasure how the author had, among other things, completed a project that he himself had intended to pursue but had not at the time been able to carry through: that is, to gather into a unified structure 'the dispersed components of research'.

Neumann, in fact, knew how to clarify and develop what already existed at the core of the master's writings, and thus was able to create the premises for further research and development, especially with regard to the subject at hand.

Neumann's work was published in 1948 and in fact ends with two appendices, the titles of which are, 'The Group and the Great Individual' and 'Mass Man and the Phenomenon of Recollectivation'. It seems timely at this point to mention their content.

In the first appendix Neumann demonstrates the positive significance of the group understood as a living unit in which all members are involved in such a way as to develop, through participation in the group itself, their individual capacities to adapt and thereby reach a condition of 'normalcy' suitable to the existing cultural canons. Within the group, however, along with the various members' drives to relate and adapt, which are valid in terms of a collective norm, Neumann also finds another line of developmental direction which he terms the 'great individual'.

This category represents the 'self' of the group as well as the unconscious 'self' of each of its members, and therefore contains the potentials not as yet revealed nor realized at a conscious level.

The 'great individual' thus defined is therefore the opposite extreme of the group, an immaterial and transpersonal entity, a category that exerts an evolutionary stimulus which only rarely can materialize in a concrete individual: the 'great individual', then, becomes the conscious carrier of the unconscious projections of the members of the group itself, and serves as a reference model for the development of independent individual identities.

> The figure of the great individual is of crucial importance for the development of every single individual. His crystallization from the collective is obviously an evolutionary advance, since the progressive differentiation of the individual and the infinite variety of ego systems it produces lead to an infinite variety of experiments within the life of mankind. Whereas formerly only the 'great man' possessed a consciousness and stood for the collective in the role of leader, the further course of evolution is characterized by a progressive democratization in which a vast number of individual consciousnesses work productively at the common human task. In this sense the leader who is saddled with collective responsibility is an atavism, and democracy the future form of humanity, regardless of the political expedients that may be chosen.

In the second appendix Neumann emphasizes instead the dangers of the mass collectivity with respect to the group and the individual. He in fact notes how in the development of western civilization the essentially positive process of the emancipation of ego and consciousness from the tyranny of the unconscious has tended to become negative: on the one hand, just as specialization has degenerated into an alienating over-specialization, so the emancipation of the ego has often degenerated into an atomistic and absurd individualism; on the other hand, ever greater sectors of the population have detached themselves from the original situation of the primary group and have flown together *en masse* into the historical process.

Both these developments tend to lower the significance of the group as a unit composed of persons consciously or unconsciously bound together, and to exalt the mass as a conglomeration of unrelated individuals. . . . As a result the ego-sphere of the human and personal is lost. Personality values no longer count, and the supreme achievement of the individual − his behavior as an individual human being − is broken down and replaced by collective modes of behavior.

The only solution that Neumann appears able to give at this point is to make a sort of declaration of principle in defence of the individual in his or her totality. 'The quality of the individual is indeed decisive, yet this is formed not so much by the quality of consciousness as by the quality of the whole personality, which for that very reason must be the psychological basis of the new ethos.' But in the dichotomy of the individual versus the collectivity, the author actually seems to have overlooked the 'third way', that is, the group.

It seems to us, however, that the seeming lack of an intermediary hypothesis, which had already been underestimated by Jung, is actually contradictory to the premises on which analytical psychology is based. Not by accident did Neumann, who, as Jung recognized, 'has placed the concepts of analytical psychology − which for many people are so bewildering − on a firm evolutionary basis', also state that: 'The group contains its own regulator not only in the form of the ruling canon, but in the mutual knowledge all members have of one another.'

It seems reasonable to hypothesize the existence of elements in Neumann's work that were preliminary to the clarifications and further developments that can be found in Foulkes. Not by chance perhaps was Foulkes's *Introduction to Group-Analytic Psychotherapy*[2] published that same year.

Analytical psychology

Jung's theoretical system seems to be centred around the supposed existence, in the sphere of the human psyche, of complexes that are reciprocally interrelated. The term 'complex' was introduced for the first time by Jung to indicate the basic structural element of the objective psyche, that is, of the collective unconscious. Composed of a group of representations characterized by a strong emotional charge, the complex enjoys an autonomy of its own, which makes it appear to be detached from the rest of psychic totality. Primarily, the complex is an ideo-affective 'psychic object' which is repressed by consciousness, or which has not reached the conscious level, and is therefore unconscious and uncontrollable; it becomes sensitized and powerful through successive individual experiences of equal affective tonality.

The behaviour of the individual is the direct result of the behavioural drives that are derived from his inner complexes, which interrelate not only reciprocally but with the socio-cultural norms as well.

In contrast to the opinions of other analysts, the complex then is not pathological in itself: in fact, since it does compose the basic structure of the psyche, it is its most wholesome maturational component. It only becomes pathological to the extent that its original informatory nucleus, or 'archetype', gets diverted or distorted by the conflicts that stem from the individual's personal life. Such conflicting contents, which in practice are in the hold of the personal subjective unconscious, constitute the 'shell' of the complex, while its 'core' is made up of the archetype, to use the terminology introduced by Whitmont.[3]

Therefore, whether a complex as a centre of energy promotes or disturbs psychic life depends on the nature of the personal associative materials that constitute its shell. To this process is to be added, according to Jung, the capacity of the ego structure to assimilate and integrate the complex itself, in other words, the strength of the ego.

Ultimately, Jung's theory distinguishes, on the one hand, the personal subjective unconscious, which consists of the shells of the various complexes and is correlated to the experiences of the individual's developmental age, traumas, difficulties and early conflicts. As such, the personal unconscious can always be traced back to its own past, where explanations can be found in terms of cause and effect. On the other hand, the existence of a collective unconscious is hypothesized: it is composed of the cores of the various complexes each of which, by its nature, is considered as having 'precipitated' from the universal human experiences that have constantly been repeated over many generations and is the 'carrier' of drives that tend to reproduce and elaborate the same experiences in every generation.

The collective unconscious, then, consists of *a priori* categories, 'archetypes', which are expressed in terms of dream images or fantasies, or through emotional and behavioural attitudes which, nevertheless, are shaped by the personal experiences of the individual, as previously mentioned.

The concept of the archetype and the term 'collective unconscious' as originally used by Jung have often been misunderstood and erroneously interpreted. For example, an acknowledgment of the supremacy of the collectivity or of a mass or racial psyche has been read into them: consequently, in his later writings Jung substituted the term 'objective psyche' for 'collective unconscious'. Making use of concepts taken from physics, Whitmont notes that what Jung intended by the objective psyche can be assimilated 'to an encompassing energy stratum from which arise varying field activities', and that 'Jung has called these psychic field expressions complexes and archetype'.

Whitmont's conceptualization which, as seen above, distinguishes within the complex the shell as pertaining to the personal unconscious, and the core (the archetype) as pertaining to the objective psyche, seems particularly clear and exhaustive in regard to the aims of the present work.

It can now be understood how the two components of the complex are strictly interrelated and to such a degree that, in the course of an analysis, it is only when the personal ontogenetic contents of the complex have been revealed that the actual archetypal nucleus can be reached. The personal shell is in fact the form in which the eternal archetypal motif is incarnated and through which our personal lives and natures are influenced. And it is, to repeat, precisely the shell, the structural component of the personal unconscious, that determines whether the complex in its totality intervenes as a wholesome or as a pathological element of the personality.

The manner in which the archetypes, expressions of the potentials of the individual, have been activated during childhood determines whether the contents of the complex will be able to achieve harmony with the other contents of the personality and the conscious ego, or whether they will remain isolated, and, therefore, as autonomous entities, interfere with the overall psycho-physical equilibrium of the individual.

Ultimately the complexes, and in particular their archetypal nuclei, are bearers of significance and of the personality's potential drives:

such 'drives' can be implemented to the extent that the archetypal nuclei become adequately integrated by the conscious ego and utilized for a better definition of the identity of the individual.

The utopian goal of Jungian analysis is well known and termed 'individuation'. By this is meant the progressive harmonization and reciprocal integration of the archetypes which, through a successive enlargement of the contents of the conscious ego, procure that the personal identity becomes substituted by the regulatory centre of archetypal nature that Jung has called 'self'.

This is an appropriate point to make several clarifications with regard to the 'self'. In the schools of psychoanalytical orientation, it is well known that the ego does not represent the human being in his or her totality. In Jungian terms it is possible to propose the hypothesis that, at the level of personal identity, an 'identity complex' exists which, it can be assumed, functions as all the other complexes do. It attempts, therefore, to manifest its own propulsory drives in an autonomous manner, with little regard for overall psychic equilibrium. In this sense, what is usually indicated as 'ego' represents only the shell of the previously mentioned identity complex. It is instead the archetypal nucleus of the identity complex, as the all-inclusive unit of the real potentials of the individual, that actually constitutes the 'self'.

Citing the words of Jung

> The ego, ostensibly the thing we know most about, is in fact a highly complex affair, full of unfathomable obscurities. Indeed, one could even define it as a relatively constant personification of the unconscious itself, or as the Schopenhauerian mirror in which the unconscious becomes aware of its own face.[4]

> I discriminate between the ego and the Self, the ego is only the subject of my consciousness, while the Self is the subject of my totality: hence it also includes the unconscious psyche. In this sense the Self would be an (ideal) factor which embraces and includes the ego. The ego is the only content of the Self that we do know. The individuated ego senses itself as the object of an unknown and superordinate subject.[5]

Here we see the attention directed by Jung to a superordinate organizational centre of the personality, that is, to an archetypal drive towards psychic totality and integrity of which the ego is only a limited and partial actualization.

This poses a particularly delicate epistemological problem, the essential difficulty lying in the fact that, as indicated by Kant, 'the Self is attempting here to observe itself'. Since the psyche exists as both object and subject of research at this level, the problem constitutes a critical point for all of psychology.

The acknowledgment, however, of a 'self' as the archetypal nucleus of the identity complex, of a superordinate organizational centre of the global personality, is of considerable heuristic value. This is so above all in the context of an 'analysis' which by its very nature is directed towards 'individuation' and for which the 'self' represents, in a manner of speaking, the final stop, the point where, in Goldstein's terminology, the concrete 'self-realization' of the individual occurs.

In order to reach self-realization the Jungian theory consequently provides for the successive analysis of the various shells of the complexes, which, through their reciprocal interaction, constitute the personal unconscious: through this process it becomes possible to achieve the progressive integration of the archetypal nuclei of the objective psyche. It is in this progression that we find the fundamental archetypes, to which Jung gave particular consideration, and it is here that they can be pointed out in a synthetic manner. We are referring to the archetype of the 'person', the 'shadow', the 'animus' and the 'anima'.

The 'person' is a mask that the individual wears in order to respond to the exigencies of social conventions and of tradition. The 'person' is the public personality that exists in opposition to the private personality behind the social facade.

The 'shadow' represents the 'inferior' or least developed aspect of our personality. The archetype of the 'shadow' consists for example of the animal instincts inherited in the process of human evolution from lower forms of life, and therefore represents what the individual habitually hides from the public eye. In this sense the 'shadow' is in dynamic opposition to the 'person'.

'Anima' and 'animus' are instead the archetypes of what is for each sex totally other. Such archetypes, even though conditioned by chromosomes and sexual glands, are the products of the relational experiences of man with woman and vice-versa. It is a well-known fact that at the physiological level men secrete both male and female sexual hormones and that women do too. Also at the psychological level, masculine and feminine characteristics can be found in both sexes. At the risk of oversimplification, the feminine archetype in the man is called the 'anima', and represents 'eros': the masculine archetype in the woman is called the 'animus' and represents 'logos'. In this case, as well, the two archetypes are in dynamic opposition, and therefore it is also possible to find here what is considered to be a basic principle of Jungian psychology, that is, the principle of correlation. For Jung, no aspect of human reality is conceivable unless the aspect that correlatively opposes it is taken into immediate consideration: all elements of existence are unthinkable – as Trevi[6] notes – unless both opposite and correlated elements are immediately taken into consideration in the thinking process. Such dynamic correlation of opposites is to be found, therefore, between the conscious and the unconscious, between superior and inferior psychological functions, rational and irrational functions, extroverted and introverted attitudes, just as we have shown is the case between the archetypes of person and shadow, anima and animus.

From this it is easily arguable that the activity of the archetype, or of the complexes in general, must be of the relational type. In order to be actualized in terms of normalcy, it must be relational in the sense that every archetype is to be considered in dynamic relation to the others, in a continual balance of opposites that may culminate in the final complete equilibrium to be found in the integration of the 'self' at a conscious level, however utopian that might be.

When such a 'dynamic relation' is obstructed, when a complex and its archetypal nucleus function in an autonomous manner, isolated from the rest of the personality, the pathological condition arises. In terms borrowed from communication theory, normalcy is linked to the free and balanced flow of communication; illness instead is linked to its closure. The realization of 'self', in other words, provides for a constant flow of communication, free and yet organized at the same time.

In this context the archetypes are to be regarded, therefore, as models not only of communication but of behaviour as well, recognizable through observation. Their organizational structure, for which is hypothesized the archetype of the 'self', promotes a reciprocal dynamic equilibrium, together with growing differentation, that is, progressive 'individuation'.

Group analysis

In one of his works Foulkes,[7] in synthesizing the basic assumptions of his theory, states:

Things are not either biological or cultural, no: what is and what seems to be inherited is transmitted socially and culturally. . . . This transmission from generation to generation is an unconscious process. The individual tends to remain unconscious of it in his own person, and well defended against its recognition. I have called this the 'social unconscious'. In the therapeutic group this is the unconscious of the 'here and now'. . . . The ego cannot see itself, just as one cannot look into one's own eyes, except in a mirror.

With the risk of oversimplification, we can consider these statements as the basic foundation of Foulkes's theory and of his practical application of it.

The primary goal of group-analytic psychotherapy is in fact to investigate and reveal the intrapersonal, interpersonal and transpersonal conflicts that unfold in a group situation where care is taken to facilitate free communication among members and render it significative in a network of exchanges that progressively come to make up the common 'matrix' of the group.

The concept of 'matrix', as a psychic network of communication, enables us to outline, theoretically, a 'surprising discovery': what we are used to considering as intrapsychic, a phenomenon that concerns only the individual, is in fact a property shared by the group. The individuals are key points in the network of communication, producing it while at the same time being permeated by it. In this sense the intrapsychic is not distinguished from the interpersonal nor from the transpersonal since what belongs to the individual is shared by the group, and 'society' shows itself to be inside the individual just as it is outside of him or her. The group 'contains' the individual while the individual 'contains' the group.

The 'matrix' is therefore inseparable from the process of communication, and it is at this level that Foulkes's theories manifest their fundamental elaboration. It becomes possible to examine the 'communication' going on in the group through free-floating discussions which are comparable to the free associations of individual analysis. In the group, however, 'communication' is in the form of significative associations within the context of the group itself, and permits us to find 'location points' for the various interventions in reference to the complete communications matrix. Within the group it is precisely communication that, as the central factor of therapy, is used as the fundamental intermediary for the maturational change of the participants.

In this regard it seems useful to note how the contemporary theory of communication demonstrates that the message is not communicative unless there is participation. Only with participation does the message acquire significance and assume a relational, meta-communicative aspect. In fact, the essence of therapy in groups rests precisely in significative participation: it is participation that makes active and efficacious the informative messages members exchange.

As de Maré notes,[8] it's not very important, in fact, who communicates, nor what is said nor how it's said nor what the intention of the communication is, as long as some means exists suited by its nature to facilitate participation. The intermediate space, the 'open system' formed by the small group, is as important as the people in the group themselves. This brings to mind, continues de Maré, the observation made by Einstein that it is not energy and particles which are essential for the description of physical phenomena, but rather the field formed by the interposed space. In physics this field is the electromagnetic force and in human associations it is information and audio-visual contact. In the context of the group, in short, attention is shifted from the flux of energy to the flux of information. Speaking in broad terms, a 'bit' of information is therapeutically effective since it brings negative entropy to the 'system' in which the therapeutic process is in course, whether this be 'system man' either as individual or as group.

'Negentropy', as defined by Shroedinger, does in fact oppose a system's habitual tendency towards disorganization and stasis, both of these tendencies being conditioned by the second principle of thermodynamics. Since it constitutes information, negative entropy is used towards the end of better differentiation as well as towards a more complex organization of the system in question. Applied to the 'system man', in short, negative entropy is a third alternative with respect to the cult of the personality or to the undifferentiated mass. It is perhaps worth while at this point to remember that it was the physicist Brillouen[9] who demonstrated mathematically the equivalence between information and negative entropy.

All the events, occurrences and verbal exchanges in the group are considered as communication, which means that they are accepted as signs, symbols and other messages that become significant when decoded and inserted in the appropriate context. The spontaneous responses of the group members are fundamental for the process of decodification, and with his or her interventions, every single member makes a contribution to the work of interpretation.

The sort of communication that emerges during group analysis permits interpretation at various levels; as is well known, Foulkes[10] distinguishes five of them, as follows:

1 The superficial level, or the level of transference in a broad sense, indicated by the internal and external experiences of the group and in which the group represents the community, society, public opinion.

2 The specific level of Transference: at this level Transference with a capital 'T', is intended in its strictly psychoanalytical meaning, in the Freudian sense. The group represents the participant's family and most intimate environment.

3 The level of projection: at this level we can observe mirror-like phenomena indicated by the emergence of the participant's primitive fantasies, and his or her relationship to objects; in such mirror-like phenomena the 'intrapsychic' is shared with the matrix which results in a process of reciprocal projective identifications. Internal and partial objects, in the Kleinian sense, are represented in the group.

4 The corporal level: it is expressed by physical manifestations, plastic attitudes, illness. At this level the group represents the schema of the body.

5 The primordial level: as Foulkes agreed, it corresponds to Jung's collective unconscious and is expressed by universal symbols. In this case the group represents archaic images such as, for example, the 'great mother'.

The process of communication, therefore, must always be considered in the appropriate group context. Every reaction, every occurrence is to be considered principally as something that concerns the whole group, although not necessarily in a uniform manner. The specific event under observation can in fact be distinguished as a close-up image with the rest constituting the background of the entire configuration. The relationship 'foreground/background' is, however, continually changing; and the same is true for the limits between what is 'inside' and 'outside' the single member as well as the group in its entirety. The experience of these changes holds a great deal of significance in the *hic et nunc* of the moment in which they take place.

The use of free communication in the relational context of the group matrix opens the road to the possibility of 'transformation', that is, the transformation of symptoms, dreams and other manifestations into significant messages; and these consequently allow a psychic displacement 'from the symptoms to the problems', which is the primary aim of analytical psychotherapy.

Within this sphere, within the group, the therapist is of primary importance. Following Foulkes's teaching, the therapist constantly encourages the independence of the group and its members and opposes the role of omnipotent father that the group assigns him. His fundamental task is to promote free communication, without imposing any choices and without any preconstructed direction. 'The therapist must control and assure equilibrium', Foulkes[11] states, 'between the analytical processes that disturb the patient's psyche and the integrative processes that strengthen it.' His essential task is to clarify and interpret whatever opposes the integrative processes, analysing resistance and defences as they appear during the therapeutic process. This allows for the spontaneous activation of the therapeutic factors common to all forms of analytical therapy, and above all of those specific factors that can be found in the analytical group situation.

Here we will mention these factors in a synthetic manner by reporting the fundamental ones spelled out by Foulkes[12] from the beginning of his work with groups.

1 The group favours social integration over a state of isolation.
2 Mirror-like reactions take place within the group by means of which the individual 'knows' him or herself through the others.
3 The most profound levels of the unconscious are activated, and they exert a specific 'condensing' action on the themes at hand, and in this manner all the participants may come to recognize the pertinence of the themes for each one of them.
4 The group fosters situations of 'exchange' with particularly important emotional aspects that are efficacious in influencing the individual.

Other specific factors of the analytical group situation could be described, but the important thing to mention here is that all factors are addressed to the members in their individuality because the declared concern of group analytical psychotherapy has always been the individual participant.

Convergences

The elements taken up here from the theoretical constructs pertaining to Jungian analytical psychology and to group analysis according to Foulkes, however incomplete and in need of further elaboration they may be, seem nevertheless to provide already at this point useful indications for a reciprocal comparison. Such a comparison seems, in addition, to show substantial convergence as much at the theoretical level as at the level of clinical application.

As previously mentioned, Jungian psychology, which, as its author explicitly declared, is intended to be a general psychology rather than a psychopathology, is centred on the existence, in the human personality, of complexes in reciprocal interrelation.

The uniqueness of the concept that Jung used in his work lies in the fact that such 'complexes' are not to be considered as pathogenic in themselves: they become so only when they are completely autonomous, split off from and no longer in dynamic equilibrium with the internal and external environment of the individual. In this sense, 'complexes' in the Jungian meaning of the term are to be considered as 'behavioural models' which become part of the individual's history (the 'core' and the 'shell' of the complex) through experience.

The other 'methodological novelty' – to use Trevi's[13] words – introduced by Jung in his psychology is the use of the principle of correlation. In Jung's view, in fact, no aspect of human reality is thinkable unless the aspect that is correlatively in opposition to it is taken into immediate consideration; no element of existence is thinkable unless our thinking immediately includes those elements opposite and correlated to it. As a consequence this is principally applicable to the archetypal components of the personality, components which, as the a priori nuclei of the complexes are in reciprocal correlation. The above-mentioned principle of correlation is equally valid in reference to the pair of opposites individual/collectivity.

Even though Jung's attention is primarily focused on the individual personality, the concept of the individual – as Progoff[14] has noted – is not a predominant fact but rather a derivation from the more fundamental category of the society to which the individual is continuously correlated.

In this regard Jung's own words are to be taken into account: 'The individual is a social microcosmus reflecting on the smallest scale the qualities of society at large.' Even more significant are the statements made in an article written in 1916, rediscovered and published posthumously only in 1970. In the article, titled 'Adaptation',[15] Jung affirms that 'in certain and not too uncommon cases . . . demand for individuation is against all adaptation to others'. But in such cases, Jung continues, the individual 'must bring forth values which are an equivalent substitute for his absence in the collective personal sphere. Without this production of values, final individuation is immoral and – more than that – suicidal.'

Consequently, in the cases where individuation requires a total breaking with social conformity, it is not to be taken as empty individualism, but rather as the creation of positive values for the individual as well as for the collectivity since the individual and the collectivity are reciprocally correlated.

The principle of correlation, therefore, serves not only to explain the intervening dynamic relationship between the single components – complexes and archetypes – which constitute the individual, but also to imply a reciprocal exchange between the individual and the collectivity.

At the time Jung was elaborating his metapsychology, epistemological formulations that have only recently made progress in the contemporary 'philosophy of science' were not yet available. We know, for example, how essential to the goal of individuation the Jungian concept of 'self' is, which, as the archetypal nucleus of the 'identity' complex, is in practice the most fundamental and all-inclusive 'model' of the individual. In reference to the general theory of systems, 'born' only in very recent times, the 'self' can be seen as an organizational pattern that creates and maintains order in a system – the case in point being the 'system man' (von Bertalanffy)[16] – through the sequence of differentiation and 'development' of its components, or its 'subsystems'; in this way it can also be seen that the complexes and archetypes, whose behavioural patterns are of Jungian formulation, are the subsystems of the general system of the 'self'.

Consequently, if we take the 'system man' as the prototype of an open system, even the system's 'relationship to society' can be seen as fundamental in the maturational process toward self-realization. It is not by chance, in fact, that in an article in 1974, Seiffert[17] stated preliminarily that 'the pair individual/collectivity is "archetypal", even though at this point we are unable to attribute either one of them to any determined archetype'.

In reference to the concept of the archetype as a behavioural model, the pair individual/collectivity appears related to the contemporary tendency towards dialogue and parity in relationships, towards the change from the flux of energy to the flux of information, towards 'democratic' relations.

Considering in a synthetic manner the theoretical-practical foundations of group analysis according to Foulkes, we find that they are concentrated – as has been noted in another work[18] – on two focal constructs, one of which is the importance given to the 'here and now' of the group as a fundamentally therapeutic agent, the other 'free communication' within the context of the group. Both are reciprocally connected and equally active in constructing a common 'matrix' of communicational relationships, a network of exchange the key points of which are represented by the single participants of the group, who produce it together while being permeated by it.

It seems worthwhile to report here, in addition, Foulkes's[19] statement concerning the participants of an analytical group: 'Collectively they represent the "norm" from which each of them individually deviates.'

The group, therefore, proves to be homologous at its organizational regulatory 'centre'. The single components of the group can make reference to this 'centre' in the effort to maturatively modify their behavioural patterns, their personality complexes. This conceptualization of the group seems to open the road towards a substantial analogy with the Jungian concept of the 'self': the 'self', in fact, also seems to be a superordinate and all-inclusive 'centre', a general organizer of the single parts that constitute the individual, his or her 'complexes' and 'archetypes', in other words, the individual's behavioural 'patterns'.

It could be objected that Jung's 'self' refers to a single individual, while Foulkes's group, even a 'small group', refers to several individuals. It appears, however, that the objection can be overcome if we keep in mind how Foulkes himself denied the distinction between 'intrapsychic', 'interpersonal' and 'transpersonal', and saw one sector as being closely correlated to the others, continually shifting from foreground to background, from internal to external, from container to contained, among the individual, the group and 'society'. It seems, therefore, that we can actually give emphasis to the analogy between the 'self' according to Jung and the 'group' according to Foulkes.

But perhaps another doubt arises; if the group is a 'normative' regulatory centre for the single members, are the members supposed to submit themselves to the group to the detriment of their individuality? This doubt has probably been at the root of the suspicion expressed up until a short time ago by Jungian psychology with respect to group psychotherapy. On the other hand, Foulkes himself has at times been misunderstood in regard to his previously mentioned statement concerning the way in which the group members 'collectively' compose the norm from which each one of them departs. The meaning of his words, which he himself clarified, is to be found in the fact that 'no matter how much the individuals may struggle for or against certain tendencies, or how clearly different their responses and reactions may be from those of their fellows and the culture to which they belong, they nevertheless accept those same parameters, those same basic rules of social life as the fundamental standard of judgment.'[20]

This can be seen to be true above all in group analysis, where the object of concern is always the individual participant and where the individual experiments with a specific condition that Heigl has defined as 'plurality'.[21] Conditioned by 'plurality', the single individual in the group must refer to him or herself in terms of the others, in relation to whom he or she defines him or herself as unique and unequivocable: in addition, the single individual must also renounce omnipotence and absolute autonomy. This means, in the final analysis, that the individual must verify whether he or she is 'correlated' to the others, to the overall environment, but always with respect to his or her individuality. The principle of 'correlation' cited for Jung, then, demonstrates its operative validity in the group according to Foulkes as well, who, as we've seen, attributes the greatest importance in terms of therapeutic goals to free but participative communication which is therefore 'correlated' among group members.

In the final analysis, the analogies found up to this point, in particular, between the 'self' and the principle of 'correlation' in the Jungian sense on the one hand, and 'participative' communication in the group according to Foulkes on the other, seem to demonstrate substantial convergence between the two theoretical constructs. At the level of clinical application, such convergence is found to be even more manifest when we take into consideration the fact that, for example, Jungian analysis is defined as dialectic, with a deep, reciprocal involvement between patient and analyst, and that in group analysis the participative exchange among single members is 'dialectic'. Jungian analysis aims to unveil the 'here and now' conflicts of the patient. Group analysis aims to unveil the 'social unconscious', the unconscious of the 'here and now' of the group situation.

Jungian analysis, particularly as far as the interpretation of dreams is concerned, is based on an intensive examination of the psychological 'context', or the network of relationships in which a dream or any other element to be interpreted is naturally included. In group analysis communication, the messages of the single members, find a natural collocation in the 'context' of the group itself, and therefore Jung's technical 'prescription' is automatically met. It can also be hypothesized that the therapeutic situation of the group offers structural coordinates that provide the means for working on through the various analytical stages pointed out by Jung.[22] The first stage is characterized by 'confession' or catharsis, and this is extremely significant in the realm of the group; the second stage, which concentrates on 'interpretation', finds a significant multi-dimensional richness in the participation of all members; the third stage, the so-called educational one, is connected to the most rigorous and profound meaning of the term 'education' (*ex-ducere*), since it 'draws out' the subject's adaptive capacities with respect to interpersonal reality; at the fourth stage, that of 'transformation', the single individual finds within the group the opportunity to make progress on the road toward individuation, but always with respect to the reality of the others. The group thus fulfils the Jungian requisites, since it functions as a structure of encounter between the individual and the collectivity and constitutes the testing-ground for individuation, since it is only within a community that the individual can offer to others the 'values' which compensate for detachment from collective conformism and make it possible to reach individuation.

Finally, the convergence between Jung's and Foulkes's theories is even more manifest at the level of clinical application[23] where their operative affinities are actually demonstrated. At this point, however, it is still possible to ask why Jungian psychology has at times demonstrated suspicion with regard to group psychotherapy.

We have noted above how the doubt that the 'group' might be able to prevail over the 'independence' of the individual has played a major role. But it is also possible to hypothesize that 'group' has not been understood as the specifically therapeutic group it was in fact intended to be, and that a categorical extension has led to confusion between group and 'mass', certain attributes of which are highly 'de-structuring' and regressive for the individual. But above all, the lack of adequate epistemological models, absent at the time Jung was elaborating his formulations, has created the obstacle to discovering the positive potential of the group intended as a structure and as therapeutic process.

As previously mentioned, the contemporary general theory of systems has now made it possible to see the substantial convergence between the two psychological constructs when both the 'individual' and the 'therapeutic group' are considered as 'open systems': the 'therapeutic group' in Foulkes's theorem shows itself to be analogous to precisely such a system.

The premises for further developments were already contained in Jung's theoretical constructs and in their clinical applications. Credit is due, however, entirely to Foulkes for having known how to gather what was already in the air and, although departing from the positions of a more orthodox psychoanalysis, how to arrive at a formulation of group analysis which does include an effective third way that lies between senseless individualism and confused and massifying pseudo-sociality.

For having taken upon himself the projections of a society and an historical epoch that seemed decisively to want to recuperate an authentic dialogue among human beings, with good reason do I maintain that Foulkes should be attributed that categorical quality defined by Neumann as the 'great individual'.

Notes

1 Neumann, E. (1948), *Ursprungsgeschichte des Bewusstseins*, Zurich, Rascher Verlag. English version (1954), New York, Princeton University Press.
2 Foulkes, S. H. (1948), *Introduction to Group-Analytic Psychotherapy*, London, Heinemann.
3 Whitmont, E. C. (1969), *The Symbolic Quest*, London, Barrie.
4 Jung, C. G. (1955), *Mysterium Coniunctionis*, Collected Works, XIV, London, Routledge & Kegan Paul, 1963, p. 209.
5 Jung, C. G. (1925), *Psychological Types*, Collected Works, VI, 1971, p. 540.
6 Trevi, M. (1973), 'Struttura e processo nella concezione Junghiana dell'inconscio', *Riv. di Psicol. Anal.*, 4, no. 2, p. 520.
7 Foulkes, S. H. (1968), 'Dynamic processes in the group-analytic situation', *Group Process*, 1, no. 1, p. 63.
8 de Maré, P. B. (1972), *Perspectives in Group Psychotherapy*, London, Allen & Unwin.
9 Brillouen, L. (1953), 'The Negentropy Principle of Information', *J. Applied Phys.*, 24, 9.
10 Foulkes, ibid., p. 70.
11 Foulkes, S. H. (1964), *Therapeutic Group Analysis*, London, Allen & Unwin, p. 65.
12 Foulkes, S. H. (1944), 'Group-analysis: studies in the treatment of groups on psycho-analytical lines', *B. J. Med. Psychol.*, 20, p. 175.
13 Trevi, ibid., p. 522.
14 Progoff, I. (1973), *Jung's Psychology and its Social Meaning*, New York, Anchor.
15 Jung, C. G., (1970), 'Adaptation', *Spring*.
16 Bertalanffy, L. von (1967), *Robots, Men and Minds*, New York, Braziller.
17 Seiffert, T. (1974), 'Die Gruppentherapie im Rahmen der analytischen Psychologie', *Z. Anal. Psych.*, no. 5.
18 Fiumara, R. (1976), 'Therapeutic group analysis and analytical psychology', *J. Anal. Psych.*, 20, no. 1.
19 Foulkes, S. H. (1964), *Therapeutic Group Analysis*, op. cit.
20 Foulkes, ibid., p. 326.
21 Heigl, F. (1972), *Indikation und Prognose in Psychoanalyse und Psychotherapie*, Göttingen, Vandenhoeck & Ruprecht.
22 Jung, C. G. (1929), *The Problems of Modern Psychotherapy*,

Collected Works, XVI, 1969, p. 290.
23 Foulkes, S. H. (1975), *Group-analytic Psychotherapy: Method and Principles*, London, Gordon & Breach.

Chapter 8

Group analytic therapy of university chaplains — the therapy of a group

David R. Hawkins

In traditional group therapy a number of people, preferably strangers, come together on a regular basis with a trained leader solely for therapeutic purposes. Similar groups may be composed of people not seeking therapy *qua* therapy but seeking experience in order to become therapists themselves[1, 2] as one undergoes a training analysis in order to qualify as a psychoanalyst. The model also appears in somewhat more attenuated form among other groups with special learning objectives, such as those wanting short-term, concentrated experience to enhance insight (sensitivity or 'T' groups) or in need of learning more about group dynamics, leadership techniques, or the skills involved in working with the mentally ill.[3] When a consultant meets regularly with certain professional teams, such as those staffing a renal dialysis unit or a psychiatric in-patient ward, with the goal of improving intra- and inter-personal processes, therapeutic functions are involved. In such an instance, one is more apt to use the term 'staff relations group' rather than 'group therapy'.

In this paper I propose to discuss a unique group experience which served several of the purposes described above. The group consisted of 13 students' chaplains in a university of about 8,000 students located in a small town. The chaplains met regularly once a week to discuss matters of mutual interest. A so-called Christian Association (CA) consisting of three full-time members, two men and a woman, was provided with space and part financing by the university. This organization served as a non-denominational religious focus for the university and sponsored a variety of social functions and provided some counselling. It served as a focal point for integrating similar activities of the chaplains from various churches in town. The churches with large congregations usually had a special student chaplain in addition to its minister or priest. In small churches the minister also served as student chaplain. All of the student chaplains, including the only local rabbi but with the exception of the single Roman Catholic priest, met once a week to coordinate their activities and discuss mutual problems. The members of the group were all highly intelligent and more sophisticated and liberal than the average small-town religious leader.

This group asked the psychiatrist of the Student Health Service if he would meet with them once a week to discuss problems of counselling. He agreed. Soon after they began meeting, they asked the leader to conduct their meetings in actual therapeutic style rather than in a didactic fashion. The psychiatrist then available was experienced in dynamic psychiatry but had not conducted group therapy previously. His style of therapy involved a rather intellectualized approach. Under his leadership the group continued to the summer holidays, after which it became necessary to find another leader because the psychiatrist took a year's leave at that time. I was approached by John, one of the CA and the youngest permanent member of the group, to see if I would work with them in place of the original leader. I agreed to meet with them to explore the possibility. The therapy group consisted of the following members:

Saul		Rabbi
Billy	over 45	Community Church (pastor and chaplain)
George		Society of Friends (CA)
Mary		Episcopal (CA)

John		Protestant (CA)
Henry		Chaplain to large Protestant Church
Ed	26-33	Chaplain to large Protestant Church
Joe		Chaplain to large Protestant Church
Adam		Pastor and chaplain to small Protestant Church

Jack		
Ruth	21-25	Interns
Sally		

Only one member of the basic group did not attend the therapy group. He was the chaplain for what was probably the most prestigious church in town and in many ways the one most closely connected with the university. Significantly, as will become apparent, John did not attend the initial sessions. The chief theme in the first session was what the role of the leader should be. In spite of verbal approbation of a democratic and self-effacing leader, it seemed clear that they were really looking for a powerful chief with strength and authority. A major preoccupation, which continued, reflecting an occupational dilemma for the clergy, was the conflict between whether it was desirable to have or be a strong authoritarian or self-effacing egalitarian leader.

There was much initial comparison of my behaviour with that of the previous therapist, who had been perceived as being quite authoritarian. Some members described with considerable glee how they enjoyed sparring with him verbally and indicated that sometimes they were able to get his goat. There was speculation about whether or not he had talked too much and whether or not he had been a good or bad leader. Towards the end of the first session there were some complaints of my not talking enough.

I was quite aware of strong counter-transference problems during this session. I had worked closely with the previous therapist and there were strong issues of competition between us. The chaplains were a well-read, sophisticated group representative of a major segment of the relatively small community in which we lived. A number of the group were personal though not close acquaintances. The therapist had not had much experience in group therapy and was concerned with his performance.

The first session dealt also with goals, about which, as might have been expected, opinions differed. The group's original purpose had been to get instruction in how to counsel. The initial switch to group therapy had not been very clearly defined beyond learning to do by being involved oneself. They discussed with me the feeling that they could learn more and particularly improve their working relationship utilizing group therapy. They felt there were feelings generated towards each other which could be discharged with minimal disruption in a therapeutic session. A number expressed the wish to learn more about themselves and human psychology generally. Some clearly wanted a therapeutic experience for themselves. The consensus was that the primary goal was to improve the group's functioning in its various activities. They discussed the importance of setting limits on what sort of personal material might be discussed since they were involved with each other both professionally and socially, often including families. It was agreed that interpersonal issues in the group could be explored as deeply as possible, professional problems discussed, but other personal matters were not to be dealt with. A few individuals wanted to have no restrictions placed on what matters could be expressed.

The initial session had been defined as exploratory. I consulted with Dr S. H. Foulkes, who was then serving as Visiting Professor at the University. It was agreed that this group promised to be interesting and that a strong motivation favoured real achievement. The decision was made to work with them using group analytic principles[4] but respecting the prohibition of bringing up and analysing personal issues outside the immediate group interaction. Dr Foulkes agreed to continue to supervise me in working with this group.

During the next few sessions, members of the group continued to test the limits, both with regard to each other and the therapist. Subgroupings and polarizations within the group began to become apparent. One of the members of the youngest group suggested he couldn't fully involve himself because he was so different in age from some of the others and also because he expected that members of the group would be making reports about him to the agency which sponsored his internship. The older members insisted that this was not a problem worthy of discussion. One of the middle-aged group made the comment that he felt the group was ageless. Nevertheless, the insecurity of the younger members persisted and raised problems intermittently for the group. Similar problems with newcomers presented themselves the following year. The group itself eventually learned some things about assimilation of newcomers and juniors into an ongoing group.

It was typical of Saul to set himself apart from the rest of the group. One example of this was his discussion of his early bohemian life in which he indicated that the others obviously couldn't understand his experience. Frequently he emphasized his being a Jew in an otherwise Christian group. This technique of using a role behind which to attempt to hide individual motives was seen frequently in this group. Others in the group were quick to point out Saul's defensiveness and emphasized his hiding behind attitudes.

The imagery employed in the group's discussion was strikingly that of aggression and competition. Members often spoke of the group process as a ping-pong match and at other times talked about 'sparring with long poles'. It was clear that members of the clergy, at least of this group's status, have a very difficult problem appearing to conform to society's expectation that they be tolerant, peaceable and forgiving. In fact, they were generally active, ambitious, aggressive individuals.

Eventually Adam tentatively said there was something about which he was very disturbed but which he felt he couldn't discuss because the group ignored him. After encouragement, he went on to say there was a strong possibility that he would be fired as pastor of his church. There was a well organized group within the church who desired this and what little support he had was not organized. He went on to say that one of the interns who was supposed to rotate among all of the churches had slighted his programme because he had been warned against it. Adam's remarks were met by a prolonged and uncomfortable silence broken at last by Saul, who demanded to know why nothing was being offered to encourage a member in trouble. The intern said he felt accused but then pointed out there was some reality to Adam's feelings, in that the group had subtly let him know that they didn't think much of Adam's programme. When group members suggested that individual expressions of regret and/or encouragement might be offered to Adam privately, I raised the question as to whether the issue was not one calling for group consideration. Billy then wished aloud that I would emulate my predecessor and point out to Saul that he was trying to be the therapist. I asked Billy why he didn't do this himself. Others expressed desires as to how I should act. Testing to see if they could get me into an authoritarian role continued.

In the fourth session many of the important stresses for the group became more obvious and in retrospect one could see quite clearly the divisive forces which were an unfortunate combination of roles, situations, and specific interpersonal problems. John had finally returned to the group and a discussion arose in which the chaplains attached to churches in town asserted that the Christian Association situation as an 'establishment group' had unfair advantages. George alluded to an episode in the session from which John had walked out; in this Billy had expressed considerable anger over what he discerned to be competition for the attention of university students. After making his remarks, which stirred up a hornet's nest, George tried ineffectually to seem a peacemaker by explaining that John's abrupt departure on that occasion had been necessitated by an appointment elsewhere. It became gradually evident that George characteristically avoided any direct aggressive confrontation but sought his ends more subtly in that his remarks had been made as a rather sly, undercutting of his junior associate. The social institutional friction between the Christian Association members and the town clergy was aggravated by the interpersonal problems between the senior and junior male Christian Association chaplains.

When Adam did lose his pastorate, this event influenced much of the group's interaction for several sessions. During the first session after his dismissal, Adam accused the group of guile and was thereupon attacked by his fellow members. It was not until the following session that the therapist was told of Adam's dismissal. Adam's ouster was finally mentioned by Henry, who constituted himself the most vocal of the group. He himself had attempted to act out on two occasions. First, he called the therapist asking him to read the part of the psychiatrist in a performance of Eliot's *The Cocktail Party*, which was being put on by another group. Then he invited the rabbi to read aloud a bitter satire on Christmas written by a Jew to a group of faculty members and students. In both instances he was quite unconscious of the hostility involved, which was interpreted by the rabbi and other group members. The therapist interpreted Henry's need for criticism by a Jehovah-like father figure whom he could then consider unjust and depreciate. In retrospect, it is evident that I was too aggressive in my interpretations. Although they were accurate, the group was not yet ready for anything so searching and blunt. Counter-transference was involved here. I had seen Henry professionally as a consultant during a time several years earlier when he was severely ill. He was one of a group of unselected medical patients whom I saw as part of a study. Subsequently I had seen him on a number of occasions through mutual friends. His emphasis on Adam's troubles led Adam to counter-attack and accuse Henry of many of the faults of which he himself was being accused. Henry gradually became aware of his need to use biting criticisms of colleagues, which he actually turned on himself as much as others.

When in another session one of the woman interns pointed to the subgroups that could not be identified chiefly on the basis of age, she failed to mention where Adam belonged. He noticed and was upset at her omission and began to talk about how the others wanted to steal the few sheep (students) he had in his care. He then announced that he planned to become a graduate student and qualify for work with the mentally ill, abandoning his career in the church. This announcement led to a discussion of differences in role between the minister and the psychiatrist that revealed much of the doubt present-day clergymen have about their appropriate role in society.

Adam suggested that he leave the therapeutic group and at first its members demurred energetically but when the discussion clarified that its purpose was to improve function as a professional group, it began to seem inappropriate for Adam to remain and it was suggested that he join another group. Although I felt that this was for the best at the time, I wonder in retrospect whether some important material might not have been worked through by his staying. At the last session he attended the group discussed clothes and went on from there about conflicts between the ministerial stereotype and the need to be one's self. At this point, attendance began to drop off remaining low for about five sessions. The group was greatly depressed during the first session without Adam.

In the meantime, Jack had spoken about going to a national meeting in which university chaplainships were under discussion. He asked permission to report on the therapy group and thus aroused considerable indignation. Two senior men accused him of being self-seeking in making such a report and indicated that he was ill-qualified in any case because of his lack of experience and the short history of the group's therapeutic enterprise.

During the unhappy meeting after Adam's defection Mary, who spoke little but maintained a friendly and compliant manner, came under discussion. This led her to say that behind her silence a great deal had been going on. It seemed clear that the focus on Mary had been a projection of the rest of the group's feelings about not being able to talk themselves.

A meeting several sessions later, which was the poorest attended of all, marked the low point of the morale of the group. It turned out that the professional meetings were also being poorly attended and there was a general expression of disgust by members of the group for what they were doing. Henry focused the feelings of the group when he talked of his feelings of inadequacy and lack of accomplishments. Ed commented how different a picture he had of Henry and how much he admired him and envied his programme. The others picked up this positive note and morale and attendance subsequently rose in both kinds of meetings.

John appeared at a meeting from which George was absent, and spoke of dissatisfaction and frustration with the group. The other members clarified John's problem vis-à-vis George, and showed how he had displaced this to the group at large. When George returned to the session that followed, the group turned on him, citing institutional problems as the cause of their annoyance with him at first, but then pointing out to him that he kept himself aloof from the others and avoided involvement with them. He exemplified this way of operation during this session, remaining silent in spite of being largely the focus of discussion. The material developed during the next several sessions dealt with the inhibition of aggression and how hard it was to reconcile their avowed goals of love and cooperation with the basic drives of personal aggression and rivalry that continued to make themselves felt.

Strong differences were reported to have been expressed between

John and Henry at one of the Tuesday sessions, which had been tense on that account. In the following analytic session George zeroed in on Henry, but subtly undermined John at the same time by emphasizing his recent graduation from seminary. The issues became obscure, and when the therapist pointed this out, George's resentment at his younger colleague came into the open, permitting the group to discuss the problem of improper communication. The George-John problem was not referred to directly again that year, but the focus for some time was on the wielding of power and the struggle for control. A student leader at the Tuesday meeting had said that students saw the chaplains as striving for control. This the chaplains were unwilling to admit. The analytic group began speculation about my management of its members.

During the last sessions members wanted to discuss what had been accomplished, and tried to get the therapist to make a summarizing statement about each. An intern who had extravagantly praised the programme to his sponsor was now disillusioned with it, seeing divided loyalties and internal friction. He spoke of his agonizing search for a church home, and his inability to find it within this group. Other members pointed to his fear of being really engaged, and his yearning for a mother. This individual had left the clergy at the time of follow-up.

When the group was discontinued for the long summer holiday of the university, interest in continuing during the year to come was expressed, along with a general sense of accomplishment. After the holiday Mary and several of the middle-aged members made an effort to recommence. Everyone but George and the interns (for whom there were replacements) came to the first meeting of the new year. It was clear from what he had said that George did not plan to return. John said that he couldn't because of professional and personal reasons which obviously had to do with his relationship to George. The relationship between George and John underwent discussion at the first sessions of the analytic group, which now had eight members; it was felt that this had affected the functioning of the whole group.

During its second year the group tended to deal much more directly than before with one another and with important interpersonal issues. The group's assimilation of new and junior members was dealt with at some length, along with the situation of the newcomer himself. Such exploration was particularly helpful to one of the new interns who experienced many of the vicissitudes experienced previously by Jack. His reactions seemed more intense than Jack's, and his working through was more complete, so that by the end of the year he had matured considerably and had become an integral part of the group.

Unable to attend the last session of the year, Saul sent a letter that seemed to express the feelings of many of the others:

> I am grateful to all of you for whatever I have gained from our sessions — and I believe I gained a great deal. I think I have been able to work through serious aggression and effectively dull the edge of anger. There are areas of myself that could never come into direct play but whose periphery touched and intruded into the sessions. Nonetheless, my experience there echoed back into the deeper chambers of that self. For the part each of you played in this vital drama of establishing identity and relationship, I can only offer honest thanks. All that I have said includes Dave too.

About a month after the group terminated, Mary gave a dinner-party for the members of the analytic group and their spouses. It was a warm and happy occasion at which there was considerable expression of enthusiasm for what the group had been able to accomplish. I continued to see members for a number of years thereafter, and heard that the larger group continued to function well. From time to time members returning from national meetings of students and chaplains have reported how much better members of this group get along than their counterparts in other universities.

Follow-up

A follow-up questionnaire was sent to the group's members seven years after it terminated. Twelve out of the 14 persons questioned responded, there having been 12 in the analytic group in the first year, and two newcomers in the second.

Questionnaire

The questionnaire consisted of 29 items, a combination of specific yes-no, graded, and open-ended questions. The following were answered specifically:

1, 2   Rate the group experience on a 6-point scale from 'extremely beneficial' to 'extremely harmful' for the group as a whole and for you personally:

		For the group as a whole	For the individual (1 'no answer')
(a)	Extremely beneficial	6	4
(b)	Moderately beneficial	4	7
(c)	Fairly beneficial	2	1
(d)	Fairly harmful	0	0
(e)	Moderately harmful	0	0
(f)	Extremely harmful	0	0

9   Would you recommend this program for similar groups?

10 yes   *1* no   *1* no answer

14   Was it an emotional experience for you?

8 yes   *2* uncertain   *1* no   *1* no answer

15   Did it change any of your relationships with other members of the group?

6 yes   *4* no   *1* uncertain   *1* no answer

Eleven felt that the therapy changed their attitude both towards other members of the group and towards themselves.

26   Did you feel that the therapist's attitude towards you was in any way different from that shown other members?

Only one, the individual who had to leave the group, felt the therapist's attitude towards him was different from that shown other members.

27   Do you feel you changed as a result of your group therapy experience?

9 yes   *1* no   *2* no answer

Other questions dealt with such issues as previous or subsequent personal experience with psychotherapy; expectations about the group; the degree to which it helped in personal or professional life; the implications of association with other group members; attitudes toward the therapist and ways in which these underwent change; changes in attitude toward one's self and others in the group. Most members felt that they had had an experience useful in their individual lives and in their functioning within a group. It had stirred strong feelings in most, and many felt that changes were apparent not only to themselves but to their friends and family. A number had liked the more personally focused and didactic manner of the first leader, but felt that more had been accomplished by the even-handed, neutral attitude of the second. Several members, notably those in the middle-aged group, who were still associated with the University at the time of follow-up, stated that the chaplains had been at their best during the years in which the analytic work was going on, and recommended a repetition of the experience. Those who had gone elsewhere since the sessions took place wanted a like experience. On the basis of the questionnaires, the group experience seemed less useful to the younger members. Jack had almost forgotten his experience when he was asked to fill out the questionnaire, and wondered at the vague memory he still had of the enthusiasm he had felt at the time; his replacement in the second year was lukewarm, probably because he had an almost identical experience later and several subsequent involvements in considerably more intense group experiences. The defecting member seemed to be still embittered toward the group and its therapist, but felt nevertheless that it had facilitated considerable growth within himself.

Saul, who wrote the grateful letter and whom I had perceived as among the most involved, was the least enthusiastic in retrospective evaluation, probably because at the time he had felt a strong need for major psychotherapy and found what was offered in the chaplains' group insufficient. He subsequently underwent personal psychotherapy. A senior member, probably the best-known of the group, had previously taught or advised most of its middle-aged members, and was viewed by many people with something approaching reverence; he had found his experience with the group humbling but rewarding, one that led to a better self-understanding and was useful in a subsequent career outside the ministry. Other members reported the significance of having seen this former father figure as a human being with feet that were at times made of clay.

The senior member who had aroused the most hostility and who had not returned during the second year had perceived the experience blandly and seemed to remain unaware of the strong feelings that had been directed towards him. He regarded the analytic group as worth while in clarifying some of the institutional problems with which its members were at the time grappling. He felt that he had never been fully involved, and had some rationalization for this detachment; he felt that two unnamed members had dominated the discussions, and that they were too excitable. He preferred the group when it was dominated by calmer members devoted to serious discussion.

Surprisingly, John, the member most often absent, wrote with considerable feeling about how important the group experience had been for him and for the group as a whole. He felt in retrospect that he had been mistaken in not continuing in the group for its second year, but at the time he had felt that he was heading for a confrontation that would have caused too much pain and presented too much difficulty in his daily work. At the time of the questionnaire he was less of a stranger to himself than he had been, and in counselling students he was more personal – but less involved emotionally.

It was Henry who had had the most overt antagonistic encounters with other group members. He indicated that the experience taught him much about his ways of unconsciously annoying others, and that it led to greatly improved functioning with friends and colleagues in after years. Other members attested to improved relations with him, but Adam continued to see him as an enemy. Henry was aware that this was so, commenting that he felt improvement in all of his relationships with the group's members but Adam, with whom his relationship had been destroyed by their engagement in group therapy.

Discussion

The question originally posed in my mind when I was approached to work therapeutically with this group of chaplains, had to do with the feasibility of dealing therapeutically with a group that met constantly for professional reasons and the members of which had in many instances close interpersonal relationships. Since that time, there has been a lot more experience with group work and we now know that it is feasible to work therapeutically with people who either constitute a group or know each other well. One approach would have been to deal with the group at a supportive level utilizing reassurance and explanation in a generally intellectual approach. This would have been one step removed from group education. I was aware at that time of another group in which an attempt at insight group therapy had led to much resentment and fragmentation of the group. It was possible with some specific modification to deal with the chaplains' group using group analytic techniques.[2] The group made the decision not to deal with intimate personal details and especially with current family relationships. However, interpersonal relationships between the members of the group were considered 'fair game'. Within this frame-work, the therapist was able to maintain a constant analytic attitude. There was no didactic material, advice was not given, and the therapist did not direct the choice of topics. The behaviour of the subgroups and individual members was consistently analysed as it seemed appropriate to do so. Such issues as the father transference were interpreted although no member was asked to supply information about his experience with his own father. It seemed to me that working in this fashion presented somewhat more counter-transference or at least personal anxieties for the therapist than would ordinarily be true when leading a therapeutic group. The therapist operated analytically but restricted the breadth of the analysis. This was therapy in depth but in a special sector.

In discussing any therapeutic venture two important questions should be asked: was any harm done; was there any benefit? First I will consider harm. The analytic group work did bring out in the open differences between George and John leading to their defection from the analytic group in the second year. It is clear that this problem was in operation before the analytic group work began so that whether the clarification and bringing out in the open of these issues were helpful or harmful remains an unresolved question in absolute terms. As will be discussed later in this section, I believe this was advantageous to the overall function of the group. In retrospect one wonders if there could have been some way of more adequately dealing with the conflicts so that George and John could have been kept in the group. I think it's quite unlikely that it would have been possible to keep George with his own well-defended character structure. The questionnaire clearly indicates that John came close to remaining in the analytic group a second year and in retrospect wishes he had.

Adam's pain over having to leave his church was probably exacerbated by his not being allowed to continue in the group but the extent of this damage is unknown. His own assessment of the group experience provided at a later date was that it had been highly important to him in changing his ways of dealing with others. On the questionnaire no one perceived damage.

What about the benefits for the group? It was clearly the impression by a majority of members that the experience had been useful for the group as a whole and no one saw it as harmful. Those who went elsewhere wished that they could have a similar sort of experience. Those who remained in the same town reported that their overall functioning as a group seemed to have gone best during the years that the analytic group was functioning. Anecdotally, the group members report that discussions with colleagues in other institutions have led them to believe that their collective functioning was more successful than in most places.

It is clear that at the time that I began work with the group there were serious, divisive forces at work which seemed on the surface to involve differences between the Christian Association and the parochial chaplains. As it gradually became apparent that behind this was the more crucial problem of interpersonal difficulties between George and John, the group seemed better able to deal with the total problem. Once the rest of the group was aware of what was going on and could make allowances for it, they were protected in a fashion similar to that afforded the psychiatrist when he has some understanding of the neurotic behaviour of his patients and is not unduly troubled personally by behaviour which otherwise would be upsetting. As was noted from the questionnaires, there was wide variation in the degree to which the experience was judged to have benefited individuals. Clearly no one felt that it had been a meaningless experience. No one felt damaged by it and several individuals perceived it as a major growth experience for themselves individually.

Lastly, I felt that a number of things were learned from the experience of working with this unusual group. The special problems of the clergy in our present-day society came into sharp relief. Broadly these revolved around the conflict between authoritarianism and egalitarianism and aggressive-competitive behaviour versus passive-non-competitive operation.

Traditionally the rabbi, priest (father) and minister have been the designated leaders or paternal figures who established standards of conduct for their congregations and communities. Now, in keeping with our times, there is strong pressure for the clergy to be egalitarian so that the minister can be one of the crowd. This conflict between the wish to have or to be a strong authoritarian leader as compared with an egalitarian social facilitator was particularly evident in the group's manner of dealing with the therapist. The pressure to deny and to feel guilty about their strong aggressive-competitive drives also was an especial problem because of the perceived requirement that a clergyman be non-aggressive and interested primarily in the welfare of others and not personally ambitious.

An especially fascinating aspect of this experience was the opportunity to observe the interplay between issues that had to do primarily with the impact of one unique personality on another and those which had to do with societal roles. In the usual group therapy situation societal roles play relatively little part in the functioning of the group. The definitions 'lawyer', 'clergyman', 'housewife', for example, have meaning in terms of identity but minimally influence behaviour in the group. In operational functional groups, one is aware of the fact that the personality dynamics of individuals in the group play an important part in the group process as well as the individual role. However, it is not usually possible to understand individual dynamic personality operation except as obliquely inferred. By virtue of the combined operational and therapeutic function of this group, role and personality interaction was more clearly discernible. An example of the use of role for individual needs was Saul's polarizing the group along Jewish-Christian lines. This afforded him an apparent justification for overtly expressing hostile aggression. In actual fact, there was no evidence for antisemitism in this group. There was little basis for competition since there would have been no expectation of the Christians recruiting Jewish students to their programmes or vice versa. A plausible role difference served as an easy vehicle for personal needs.

The most complex, the most interesting, and for this group the most significant intertwining of intrapersonal dynamics, interpersonal relationships, and social role was the George-John relationship which markedly accentuated the CA-non-CA division and rivalry. It was inevitable because of the social structure that there would be envy of and rivalry with the CA by the parochial chaplains. What became apparent only gradually were George's dynamics. The implication of that for his relationship with his junior colleague, John, and the way in which it affected CA-non-CA relationships and reverberated throughout the entire group slowly evolved.

George, the oldest member of the group, a member of a denomination which especially espoused non-violence and togetherness, kept the others at a distance and allowed no direct confrontation. His behaviour stirred up considerable guilt in many of the others for whom he served as a father-transference figure. John, who was the youngest of the permanent group, was extremely ambitious, talented, and attractive. He promised much as a leader but frequently did not live up to expectations. Their professional relationships were vaguely defined. While by implication and seniority George was the leader of the CA, they were technically peers. In many ways by his aggressive activity John took over leadership on certain issues.

Difficulties had broken out shortly before I started work with the group. This led to a temporary rejection of the group by John presumably as a displacement from his frustration with George. Under the guise of being a peacemarker, George frequently got John in trouble with the others. The gradual unfolding and eventual exposure of this relationship made it too painful for them to continue in the group the second year. Had they been comfortable, united, and open in their relationship to each other and the rest of the group, the built-in complications of the establishment backing of the CA would have been less threatening to the rest of the group. The analytic work was not capable of resolving the interpersonal problems of George and John so that the group's integrity remained completely intact. However, it did clarify the situation sufficiently so that the rest of the group could take the problem into consideration and the total chaplains' group was able to go on functioning reasonably effectively in spite of the George-John problem. Individual personality conflicts and their covert effects on others probably affect group processes much more than is generally realized.

References

1 Yalom, I. D. (1970), *The Theory and Practice of Psychotherapy*, New York, Basic Books.
2 Foulkes, S. H. (1975), *Group-analytic Psychotherapy: Method and Principles*, London, Gordon and Breach.
3 Volkan, V. P., and Hawkins, D. R. (1972), 'The Learning Group', *Am. J. Psychiatr.*, 128, p. 9.
4 Foulkes, S. H., and Anthony, E. J. (1957), *Group Psychotherapy: The Psychoanalytic Approach*, London, Penguin.

Chapter 9

The effect of numbers on the basic transference pattern in group-analysis

H.J. Home

New discoveries in psychoanalysis seem closely related to the acceptance of new situations as offering the possibility of conducting effective psychotherapy. The dyadic situation with adults discovered and refined by Freud opened up the way for the first breakthrough in the understanding of psychogenic symptoms and their treatment. The development of child analysis with its new situation of active play enormously increased our understanding of unconscious fantasy and the defense mechanisms. The development by Foulkes of group analysis in the small group has allowed us to understand better the way interpersonal relationships are used for the expression of tension, and this in turn has led to the possibility of therapy in natural groups such as the family. The acceptance of new situations for therapy rids us of suggestions and ideas about the unique efficacy of the earlier ones. It enables us to see that while the basic identity and principles of psychotherapy are constant, the treatment situation can usefully vary and the so-called technique of psychotherapy will vary with the context in which it is practised. It also shows us that different situations both favour the psychotherapy of different conditions and can offer possibilities for therapeutic intervention that are not available in others. Yet again the relative importance of various factors differs from situation to situation and their difference can become observable. In what follows I shall look at some varying aspects of transference to the therapist.

The classical situation of psychoanalysis requires the analyst to see one patient alone for five or six sessions of fifty minutes every week. The classical situation of Foulkes's group analysis requires us to see the patient once weekly with seven others for a session of one and a half hours. Frequency of attendance in the one situation is substituted by a multiplication of persons in the other. It is interesting to note that emotionally or in terms of feeling/meaning one and several (including two) do not seem to exist in a continuum but often in strong contrast. As an English song puts it: 'One is one and all alone and ever more shall be so'. One of course means one of a kind – one patient and one analyst. Two, three or even four do not quite make a group. To my feeling a group exists with five of a kind, e.g. five patients. Six, seven and eight consolidate the group and beyond that number the character of the phenomenon again begins to change, though slowly. At about fifteen a new character emerges, a medium-sized group and, at about twenty-five, a large group. This is a subjective statement based on my own feeling on the matter, but I think nevertheless that anybody can distinguish these qualitative changes though probably at slightly different points.

Since the establishment of Foulkes's analytic small group as a basic psychotherapeutic treatment situation, group therapists have treated groups meeting up to five and six times a week. For some reason nothing very significant seems to have arisen from this practice, perhaps because they have usually been in-patient groups. This is not the case with psychoanalytic practice, at least in England. The frequency of treatment is regularly held to be important and a treatment is not considered to be fully psychoanalytic at a frequency of less than four sessions a week. In my own experience it seems to be true that the therapist's style requires to change if frequency of treatment is less than four weekly sessions, though this will partly depend on the character of the patient.

This contrast between the group situation and the individual situation interests me here; the former varying with numbers, the latter with frequency of meeting. Theoretically the psychological root meanings of all interpersonal situations must be related to developing childhood experience. It therefore seems reasonable to relate root meaning of the individual situation in psychotherapy to early situations with mother from the time of feeding at the breast. The breast situation is one in which proximity to mother is the main controller of infantile anxiety and it seems natural to see this as related to the effect of frequency of sessions in individual psychotherapy. When the anxiety level is high it is very difficult to think calmly and, conversely, when proximity of object is achieved anxiety diminishes and thinking becomes more possible. Taking this point of view, increases of numbers to two, three and four are essentially modifications of the individual situation as it is felt. Two and three are potentially situations of rivalry for the one. The feeling of proximity to (possession of) the object is undermined and anxiety rises. The central conflicts of individual therapy will therefore be concerned (1) with the establishment psychologically of a constant separate object which is not disastrously split into good and bad, and (2) with that rivalry which emerges in the Oedipus complex as described by Freud. This situation of rivalry is stimulated by the unavoidable increase of perceptual and cognitive awareness which is part of growing up. As eyes and hands coordinate, the space-time world comes into being and the situation of many people can be appreciated more fully.

Now if the conscious and unconscious meaning of the situation of one is rooted in early object relations culminating in the Oedipus complex, the meaning of the group situation seems specifically rooted in adolescence and the central conflict is a conflict about authority.

At about the number five a group exists and this marks a qualitative change. It is a qualitative change like that which we experience when, at a certain frequency, separate taps become a continuous noise. In a therapeutic group the patients belong to the group as a felt entity and the conductor does not belong in the same sense. Because he occupies a role which is different from that of the patients he of course appears as different. What is surprising and belongs to the transference is that he appears as personally different and not simply in respect of his role. He is felt to know all, and to be healthy. Beyond that, at a deeper level, he is felt to be powerful and to be capable of changing (i.e. helping) the patients. Cure is very easily felt to be something that has to be elicited from the conductor and that it will be a reward for pleasing him. The precise emphasis in any group on this or that aspect of authority will depend on its composition, but as Foulkes very early saw, 'progress' in the group is expressed by a modification of the need to attribute undue personal authority to the conductor. This is achieved by the conductor's interpretation of the group attitude to himself and by all interpretations, interventions, and contributions, whether by the conductor or others, which lead to increased communication in the group. Increased communication does not simply mean more talking, it means also better listening, more relevant response, more honesty about what members think and feel about the world generally, about one another and the conductor. Increased communication is a qualitative term. The better the quality of communication the easier it is for members of the group to understand one another and for the conductor to interpret the unconscious communication. As the conductor participates more fully in the group communication and especially through his interpretations, the nature of his authority can gradually change in the direction of becoming an 'authority' in the sense of being expert and potent in the situation and away from being an authority in the sense of being the one who imposes his order and his orders. Order in the group then becomes a function of the increasingly appropriate relationship between members of a group of people seeking insight for the sake of healing.

I feel that in the 'large group', i.e. the group of more than twenty-five relative strangers, the problem of authority is so acute that communication is at first reduced to almost nothing both quantitatively and qualitatively. This drastic reduction in communication, which is part of the intense and pervading paranoid anxiety arising in the large group, makes it particularly liable to acting out as the only available means of emotional catharsis. In the small group the members from the beginning are able to feel one another as recognisable 'persons' with whom communication will be possible even if, at any moment, it is extremely difficult. One can note here that even one very paranoid character in a small group can hold up its development for a long time so that it behaves like a large group in restricting communication.

When Freud coined and used the word 'transference' for his psycho-analytic work he was thinking wholly in terms of the dyadic situation, the situation of two. Transference was therefore the transference, by the patient onto the analyst, of infantile wishes and expectations. Perhaps in relation to the small group we should restrict the idea of transference to transference made towards the person of the conductor either by individuals or by the group as a whole. The use made by group members of one another in recreating past patterns of relationship would be excluded from the meaning of the term. Strictly then, transference in the small group usually begins with transferring qualities of authority onto the conductor. Colleagues often speak of this as transference of the father image. I find the usage misleading because the father figure of classical psychoanalysis belongs to the Oedipus complex. The authority figure of group transference is a grown-up among children. He is essentially a figure excluded from the group (of children) and is created as a defence against the small child's wish for 'my Daddy'. The authority transferred to the conductor is a defence against regression. He is felt to be the object of obedience and not of love or understanding. This transference of the authority figure in the large group takes an extreme form and is more god-like than human. In the small group the closeness of the physical situation operates continually to modify the extreme authoritarian projection. Nevertheless the authority figure is someone from whom one conceals things, but who is always liable to find out. The authority figure is also seen as a-sexual and anti-sexual by contrast with children guilty of sexual play and knowledge.

It has always seemed to me that both in individual analysis and in group analysis the relationship between the patient associating freely and the analyst interpreting appropriately is an analogue of sexual intercourse. This is not a difficult idea in English where one can speak ordinarily of social intercourse and verbal intercourse between people. It seems to me thus because an interpretation is not the communication of knowledge, i.e. of a proposition, but it is a response to a situation as it arises in treatment. It is a response made possible by the patient's communication and its quality will depend on the quality of the communication. The projection by the group onto the analyst of a-sexual authority acts as a resistance in treatment because it prevents the analyst from making interpretations which are satisfying and mutative responses. The analysis of this projection, which is a group transference to the conductor, is necessary to make possible fully mutative interpretations. It is equivalent to the analysis of transference in the situation of two when transference acts as a resistance and impedes the patient's developing free association. As a group matures it can use the conductor realistically as someone whose presence focuses feelings of many kinds and makes them conscious and so available for interpretation and understanding. The group itself provides a situation in which communication can develop and insights can be shared. Communication offers an alternative to the catharsis which is otherwise offered by projection and 'acting out' inside or outside the group.

In addition to the central dynamic, group transference to the group conductor, the group like any other social situation in which several people take part together is a field for the expression of transference phenomena between all its members. Many of these transferences become obvious, many simply exist unobserved and many are observed by people other than the conductor. A great deal goes on in any group meeting of which the conductor is unaware, partly because of what goes on between people in a way that is not visible. In this the group situation is very unlike the individual situation where everything in the session goes on in the field of force surrounding the patient and analyst. When moving from psychoanalysis to group analysis this is experienced by the therapist as a loss just as, when moving in the other direction, the therapist misses all the information which comes from seeing someone respond to other people. It follows that details of any individual's transference, whether to the conductor or to someone else, can never be worked through in a group, although they may momentarily come into focus and be interpreted. The transference that can be worked through is that between the group as a whole and the conductor, though not every group member may share equally in that working through. It is the working through of this transference which seems to be the essentially therapeutic process leading to that modification of the super-ego, which in strict psychoanalysis is achieved by analysis of the transference when it acts as a resistance, and which leads to insight and understanding of individual and group behaviour.

The therapist who uses an analytic technique and attitude in the small group, that is who takes up a quiet, observing attitude in the group and who confines himself to interpretive comment, will find himself excluded from the comradeship of the group at first. If at this stage he makes interpretations to individuals in the group he is likely to make the individual to whom he interprets feel 'picked on' and also to arouse great sibling rivalry. He may even encourage anti-therapist feelings which are akin to those feelings which can develop towards a school teacher in a class. All 'decent' children are against the teacher. Anyone who is for him is seen as 'teacher's pet'. In a group of adults the development of such feeling is a regression of group consciousness. Progress in the group shows as the acceptance of the therapist in his role, and the development of this acceptance appears as a willingness to tolerate individual interpretations both from the therapist and from members of the group. Gradually the therapist is seen as a helpful person and his personal skill and insight is valued instead of feared. But quite particularly he is experienced as a friendly person capable of giving and receiving enjoyment as a loved father instead of being experienced as a remote and feared teacher; as someone who will understand (that is identify with the patient) rather than as someone who will discover sins; as a human being and not as a god.

In individual psychoanalysis things seem to develop differently. Regression is towards dependence on an idealised therapist and 'progress' in treatment is marked by an increasing capacity to accept the therapist in his *professional* role and in the reality of his *professional* relationship with the patient. The patient grows up and becomes his parents' equal. He turns away from the treatment as a young man turns away from home in order to satisfy his erotic needs and to establish a life intrinsically related to his own personal desire.

In the group situation it seems as if the conductor as an authoritarian super-ego melts in the group communication, or is it that the rising level of communication dissolves his authoritarian quality? Ideally the patient in the group comes to accept the conductor's total identity and his own and leaves the group to establish it in the world outside where to verbal communication can be added sexual communication in activity. When he goes he will remember especially the group like a family and only secondly the conductor as a father.

Chapter 10
Meaning and information in the group process

Ernest H. Hutten

The small group is biologically, psycho-socially, and historically the most natural form of association for human beings. The very large group, say a people, could only be formed after millions of years when their number and technical civilisation had reached a certain size and level. The very small group – the so-called nuclear family – is the result of recent, technological and urban development and, in fact, represents a kind of alienation from the natural, biological order; and the same holds for the very large group, a people or nation. The natural organisation for human beings is, then, the small group, the 'extended family' or the small herd or tribe. The very fact that originally we were, and sometimes still are, born into a small group, live and love within it demonstrates that this group provides the proper setting for our well-being and, therefore, for therapy.

How can we characterise, or make explicit at least, what features of human association constitute a group? Modern science has stimulated much thought about it. In the natural sciences, too, we have reached a point where it is no longer reasonable to treat of the single individual, and the whole group of them – the system – has become the 'carrier' of the action. The stage of classical physics where an isolated piece of matter – the 'mass point' – is the representative of a natural phenomenon has been passed. With it, the conventional type of energy transmission – or causality – as the basic relation linking mass points in space-time, or events, has been greatly changed. The need to treat a group of individuals which are connected by numerous, strong and complex interactions – and not an isolated individual acted upon by a single force – provides the motive both for a psychological group theory as well as for physical systems theory, from thermodynamics, via quantum mechanics, to the most recent symmetry group theory.

1 I want to point out first, that communication rather than mere

physical causality forms the link between human beings. Communication is meaningful information; and information is more than causality which is, in the strict scientific sense, energy transmission between two space-points, through action-by-contact. Information, too, is energy flow but the energy is 'modulated', a special pattern is impressed upon it. This represents the message, as in radio transmission, in which the speaker's voice changes the shape of the electromagnetic wave.

Moreover, when speaker and receiver do not have a language in common, we need as well another 'dimension' in order to speak *about* the signal transmitted and so to establish its meaning. This can be achieved – and genetic information transmission by means of DNA is the natural model – by constructing a system of choice that allows us to compare the unknown signal with a known symbol, to 'look it up' in a dictionary; and so the meaning is found. Energy transmission, codification into a set of conventional signs like the alphabet (the four-letter genetic code), and 'translation' or interpretation into a meaningful sentence are the three steps of communication that we find in the DNA model.

2   Conventional information theory arose from physics, for the improvement of telephone and telegraph technology, and so is concerned only with the amount of electromagnetic energy, not with its meaning which remains implicit on the assumption that sender and receiver employ the same language. Information, verbal and non-verbal, has long been recognised as the natural, most important link between human beings. The concept of information has been widely applied in psychology, though with little success, and most scientists have given up its use. The reason for the disappointment is clear. Conventional information theory has remained within the domain of classical physics whose causal mechanism does not suffice to describe human behaviour. Communication, meaningful information, goes beyond mere energy transmission and represents the natural generalisation of causality. A vertical informational level scheme, a hierarchy, is required so that we can find the meaning of information on one level by reference to a higher, meta-level. An unknown message is deciphered by comparing it with another, similar one already known. Linear causal order must be replaced by non-linear, informational organisation.

3   This introduces an important idea. A group is an organisation, not a mere physical system. Again, conventional systems theory has been employed to explain human behaviour, with no more success than conventional information theory. Physical systems theory is, indeed, a great advance relative to Newtonian 'individualism'.

Thermodynamics, quantum mechanics, and symmetry theory are the three steps in its development up to now. It is true, when we 'abstract' from our laboratory results the role the experimenter plays, necessarily, in obtaining them, information and its storage remain outside the theory; and we deal only with a physical, causally ordered, system. Relationships between men, however, are not like the single, causal encounter between Newtonian particles. Mutual action between human beings cannot be cut up into a series of one-sided, physical actions as is possible, approximately, in most fields of physics; its strength makes the interaction truly non-linear, and its meaning is lost without the stored information this relationship includes. Organisation, an organism, implies complex, hierarchical structure, flexible function, and memory. It is information rather than causality that rules the organised system; moreover, it is meaningful information – the meaning a message has for the individual determined by his inborn needs and acquired knowledge – that is required by an organisation.

4   An organisation is always an open system made up of individuals that have joined together for a purpose, for achieving a common task, for at least trying to move together in the same direction and to survive. Unlike the physical system, say the atom, an organised system, or organism, can move under its own power. While an atom is a system of discrete energy levels, the organism is a system of information levels. The very many levels, or layers, of which a human being is made – from the 'lowest' chemical level of atom and molecular compound, via macro-molecular (genetic), cellular, physiological, organ levels, etc., to the mental-emotional level – are not merely energetic but, increasingly, informational. With the 'higher' levels come more 'degrees of freedom', the control of the muscular and organ levels making self-movement possible.

A physical system, even when 'open' to the outside world, is always in its equilibrium state; and it cannot by itself initiate any reaction. An atom, for example, possesses a store of energy; but it must be excited from the outside before the electron can make a transition to another energy level and emit or absorb light. The open, physical system is in a steady state since the rate of increase in energy must equal the rate of outflow from the system: energy must be conserved. Moreover, in any process the system may carry out, some of its energy – though not lost – becomes unusable for further work. The increasing disorder or 'entropy' within the system is the price to be paid for the work done.

There is, however, no conservation principle of entropy and, hence, also not for information which represents, *cum grano salis*, the order-liness of the system energy; mathematically, entropy and information have the same form, though with opposite sign.[1] Both entropy and information, therefore, can be created or destroyed within a system. It implies that the open, biological system may contain non-equilibrium states for which the so-called 'free-energy' has a higher value than for the equilibrium. The difference in free energy between non-equilibrium and equilibrium then defines the capacity of the system for initiating an action by itself. Without discussing details, it is clear that the diverse behaviour of energy and entropy, of causality and information, or of order and organisation explains why biological systems can do what physical systems cannot.

5   The very moment we have an organised system, organism, or human group, there is activity; choice between various actions becomes possible and this indicates the meaning the course chosen has for the organisation. Meaning rules human actions while cause determines physical processes. Rules of Meaning rather than Laws of Nature explain human behaviour. The capacity for meaning is a natural charac-teristic inherent in a highly organised, informational system.

The information (and misinformation) stored within the organism, arising from past experiences and inborn needs, sets the standard by which to evaluate new experiences and to establish their meaning. It is a kind of, never quite perfect, fitting-in process into a classification scheme of stored information. Meaning, when unknown, can only be 'specified' by reference to a meta-level on which we can describe and explain the lower object-level of an experience. The accumulated infor-mation stored in the organisation is used in this manner. We do so in everyday life, after all: when we encounter a new, or surprising, or otherwise unknown experience, we find its meaning by comparison with known experience remembered. 'Where there is smoke, there is fire', etc.

However, there are at least two sources of error. Either our present, unknown experience is incorrectly perceived; or our known experience was falsely interpreted when originally put into our store of informa-tion. Thus, the correct meaning may require either present experience to be repeated in order to ascertain its characteristics; or, we may have to change, or re-interpret, our stored information based on past exper-ience since it turns out to be mis-interpreted. The criteria of formal semantics are satisfied when we can specify the possibilities for correct meaning, for false meaning, and for no meaning at all. Taking a Carnap language-system as representing the classification for information stored and received, the criteria can be made more explicit. The main argument is this. Learning involves the acquisition of new information; it also requires us to change old misinformation, to correct infantile misunderstanding, and to abandon immature prejudice.

6   Let me try to say something about the process of communication in a group. There are always two levels: unconscious and conscious, non-verbal gestures and verbal expression, physical signs (or their tokens) and abstract symbolism. Our unconscious, irrational fantasies determine most of our conscious, rational actions. The task is always to make the unconscious conscious: 'Where Id was, Ego shall be'. It is on the conscious, verbal, symbolic level that meaning is attributed to the unconscious, non-verbal, physical signal. The transmitted energy — by gestures, sounds, etc. — carries the psychological meaning as expressed by the symbolism, or by the semantics of linguistic communication.

Conscious communication specifies meaning when we can speak *about* the unconscious mechanisms that activate human behaviour. The meta-level allows us, through interpretation of the object-level, to establish meaningful communication. If we could not become aware of the unconscious processes, we could not find the meaning either of action or of linguistic expression. Words, too, have meaning only if they can be related to the unconscious, bio-psycho-social, ambivalent forces that provide the basic tension of life. (Once a language is established, meaning becomes conventional in most instances since its grammar and the semantics are known to speaker and listener. We need no longer make the special effort to find the meaning of word or deed by interpreting personal, or unknown, unconscious motives by reference to conscious, known, stored information.)

Since free association is the 'royal road to the unconscious', we become aware of our unconscious processes in terms of a direct interpretation of the internal stimuli, a simple symbolism — the symbolism of the unconscious — that represents a kind of *Ursprache*, codified already in terms of primitive, rather 'concrete' signs. This 'deep level' of language needs transcription, in terms of the cultural and social codex of 'mature' symbolism, to transform it into the expressions of ordinary language. Chomsky's Transformational Grammar is a formal reconstruction of this process.

The informational level structure characterises any organisation. Sherrington already spoke of the integrated levels of the human organism, from the chemical to biological and cellular level to, finally, the mental-emotional levels. The more integrated a level, the more information it can store. The cell is the pre-eminent example: a membrane enclosing several substructures has greater informational potential than its separate constituents alone. In the human being, perception can control behaviour since the mental-emotional level of the brain which is made up of innumerable, complex, interacting, and highly integrated substructures has a greater capacity for storage and reception of information than any of the other levels. Feedback from above to the low levels can then control and direct the organism's behaviour while the energy flow from the lower levels upwards, produced by the chemical-physiological metabolism, keeps the organism alive. This rough sketch of the Model of Man will also serve as a model for any organisation.

7   When individual organisms come together to form a group we have a vastly enriched informational structure. The group becomes a super-organism. The group process of communication produces still higher levels of organisation than the individual can achieve and, therefore, offers also the possibility to obtain a higher degree of integration (and differentiation). From a certain viewpoint it would not be wrong to say that the problem of health and happiness – the problem of life – is integration. We are never completely or successfully integrated, however healthy we may feel. All illness, mental-emotional and physical, is fragmentation of the psycho-physical personality; malfunction, pain, and death is the result. The evolutionary need for increasing integration, for improving our capabilities and capacities, brings about growth and development: and this is the principal task for a living being, whether human, animal, or plant.

A group, when highly organised, is an organism, a living entity like a poly-cellular animal. It is an integrated system that, as does any organism, responds to the reality of its ambient world. Both 'reality' and 'pleasure-pain' principles exist then. The response to reality – both external and internal – represents the ego process that can make sense out of non-sense, or convert the irrational and unconscious fantasies into rational and conscious thought. The cortical brain, with its power of inhibition, selection, and control, gives the individual his basic ego-function. The well-integrated group can develop a similar function and so facilitate conscious, reality-directed, thought arising from unconscious, pleasure-pain activated, fantasy.

Groups of people, under uncontrolled conditions, always act in such a way that their behaviour is determined by the 'lowest common denominator'. Crowd behaviour is notorious for that. The most infantile, immature levels of every individual unite in organisation and reinforce primitivism. This demonstrates, however, how groups of people form an organised system, a level-structure not dissimilar to that of the individual. Their unconscious strivings – being immature, they are invariably destructive, in the main – turn into murderous action. This is how armies are formed and wars manipulated by 'statesmen'. The presence of more mature individuals – the conductor of a small group – may raise the common denominator to a higher value by his, presumably better integrated, personality; or he may, like Hitler, lower the group levels still more by his destructive, psychotic fragmentation. This explains why, in the family or ordinary group, the sickest individual often is also the most powerful one. Group organisation is easier through the sharing of lower, rather than higher, levels of integration; the 'activation energy' of formation is lower, regression is easier than progress. The simpler structure already exists and so the pathway to it is facilitated, while progress requires us to find a new way to arrive at more complexity. Higher, more integrated, levels force us to overcome barriers of anxiety since more integration also brings more differentiation, if it is correctly done; and differentiation always includes some destruction of 'false' integration, i.e. of integration on a more primitive level or of premature integration forced by anxiety. The 'false ego' of Winnicott exemplifies this idea. We can never learn anything new unless, at the same time, we unlearn something; new meaning always involves abandoning old, more primitive, meaning. This produces anxiety.

8 Within the enlarged organisation of a group, however, new meanings of old experiences or new, meaningful experiences can be produced as well. Here we come to the therapeutic action of the small group. Creation – the production of genuine novelty out of pre-existing material – is a natural process in the universe, from stars and galaxies to men, animals, and plants – without which no evolutionary progress would occur. Although the specific mechanism must vary depending on whether creativity in the physical or in the mental-emotional-social sphere is concerned – just as the evolutionary mechanisms differ in these spheres – original novelty is the result. Every insight and therapeutic improvement is creative since new meanings are found from old, mis-interpreted experiences and 'false' meanings are abandoned. A new, more realistic, level structure of meaningful information is so created and a better integration (and differentiation) of the individual sharing the group experience is achieved.

Integration, on any level, is never perfect or total; and death – final disintegration – is always present. The greatest integration we can achieve is the moment of creation – of the maximum of creativity of which, individually or in a group, we are capable. Biology is always the basis on which, with higher integration, more complex level structure and, finally, the mental-emotional-social characteristics appear. Birth is the very epitome of creativity. Eros and Thanatos, though, are twin brothers, inseparable. Creation cannot be achieved without death: integration is not possible without some fragmentation of the previous, incomplete, or incorrect, integration of a level, or set of informational levels. Only in this manner, too, can differentiation − the more varied and flexible use of information on a given level − go together with increasing integration. I know that many people do not wish to accept the 'death instinct': but all the cells of our bodies are mortal, they die and are shed all the time, and how can this natural process not be represented in our unconscious fantasies? To accept the biological reality of death and its emotional consequences is an indispensable requirement, in my view, when processes, both in the individual and within the group, are discussed.

9   From the evolutionary viewpoint, too, biology comes before psycho-social, extra-somatic, development. Only when the animal body is sufficiently organised can the first, unconscious mental-emotional strivings arise: our most primitive, unconscious processes that represent the Ancestral Ape. This idea may be trivial; but it is too often forgotten; and with it, the reality of the unconscious, even of the whole inner world of man, is lost.

All these points, I feel, are important when we want to explain in more detail how group processes, and their specific mechanisms, affect the participants and, sometimes, have therapeutic effect. Just as a molecule is formed from atoms such that the energy levels of the several atoms come together to make new, common, and more numerous levels, so the informational levels form a common system, at least when the group works properly. Like all human beings, the participants in a group have defective integration and information levels that differ from one person to the other. A common organisation will include 'good' and 'bad' levels lying close together − as molecular levels are closely spaced relative to the atomic level scheme. Communication is thus facilitated when the group directs its attention to these, similar, levels.

Or, mis-information and mis-interpretation of early experience that produced the 'bad' level can be more easily corrected by transfer of correct information from a neighbouring level. Group members who have the same fantasies dominating them, suffering from the same mis-information, misled by false meanings, could easily mutually reinforce each other and, thus, grows a 'false ego' of the group. The behaviour of one participant, in a special respect, can be changed only when he recognises the mis-information – the unconscious mis-interpretation of an infantile, pre-verbal experience. Neurosis, completely, and psychosis, to a large part, arise from mis-interpretation of early experiences. The group facilitates its recognition.

10   The two basic unconscious mechanisms, the schizoid-paranoid and the depressive, are visible in the group process; and the hierarchy of integrated, meaningful, information levels allows us to see how these mechanisms affect group communication.

Obviously, to give a very brief characterisation only, fragmented information gives rise to schizoid behaviour; the separate parts are in conflict with one another and so become persecutory to the person. Mis-interpretation forces diverse information into a false integration on one level, or several neighbouring levels, that cannot hold together. This is a very early, and primitive, mechanism, still very close to the somatic levels of biological organisation. Yet differentiation – the more advanced kind of splitting – is always necessary as well, provided it is a process contained within limits. After all, the basic integration must be maintained: it is the wholeness that is provided by the mother's body and, later, by her personality (as long as she is herself sufficiently healthy). Thus, information cannot be cut into bits totally, meanings cannot fly about divorced from inner and external reality, from genuine experience.

If this happens, we have psychotic behaviour that is difficult, if not impossible, to change. This kind of behaviour, on a small scale, can be observed with an individual or within a group, when meaning and actual utterance of a word are cut off from one another and gestures, facial expression, and sudden outbursts of laughing show up the split. A group, particularly in its beginning stage, often behaves in this manner, when the individual contributions to the group discussion fail to connect and everyone has to resort to physical behaviour to express his embarrassment at the lack of group cohesion.

While the schizoid person is not sufficiently connected with his inner and external world, the depressive is too much burdened by it. His experiences weigh him down and he carries an enormous burden of guilt; he can barely move. Eros and Thanatos, good and evil, are so close together for him, compressed, that he can hardly see the difference between them. Such behaviour is equally visible in the group at a later stage, when – for no obvious reason, after a number of lively sessions – the group becomes mute, the whole hour passes without anything being said, everyone is miserable and wants to escape. Yet something happens all the same since, in the next session, a new topic arises and a lively discussion ensues. The integration of each informational level and, perhaps, of the whole hierarchy is too strong and, therefore, false since it does not allow for freedom and flexibility in the use of information. It is rigidity, not proper integration. The informational level structure is compressed as are the energy levels of an atom when it is subjected to high pressure. The levels are squeezed and overlap, by 'pressure broadening'; and diverse levels of information are forced together making it impossible to make sense of either. Confusion and subsequent mute silence characterise the individual and the group in this condition.

Integration without differentiation solidifies but does not lead to group formation. This false integration is linear and causal – forming larger aggregates, with loss of function of the components and rigidity of structure as a whole. We see this phenomenon before our eyes every day: it is the most common occurrence in Mass Society trying to save itself, by Bureaucracy and Establishment, by institutionalisation.

But proper group formation increases differentiation and allows its participants greater freedom within the group than they have as separate individuals: all integration is based upon this fact. For relationship between members is by communication, meaningful information, and not through causality. It is not linear: mere plurality of connections – branching causality – does not suffice. Meaning requires multi-dimensional relationship – a hierarchy of levels since the meaning of a message on the object-level can be specified ('spelled out') only on the meta-level. Meaning implies hierarchy, a multi-dimensional organisation of information levels. In this way integration is achieved with differentiation; it is vertical, not a horizontal, organisation. The higher levels, the meta-meta-levels, etc., provide meaning by virtue of memory, of the stored information within us, of the many layers of experience that we build up in the course of growth and maturation.

It is not an accumulation of smaller parts on the same level. The cell, for example, is highly integrated as well as differentiated, capable of a wide variety of functions; it contains substructures that enhance its informational power and flexibility and so the cellular level plays as important a role in the organism as the atom does in a piece of inert matter.

11   In the hierarchy of well-integrated, independent information levels the higher exercise some control over the lower levels by feedback. However, it is information, not energy, that relates the levels

and the feedback is an information processing, not an energy controlling device here. Each level, though, also functions autonomously, to some extent, on its own energy supply and stored information. (It is a hierarchy of feedbacks in which the higher level determines the 'setting', or 'reference condition', of the lower level. Each level has access also to the energy it needs to function and possesses the degree of organisation appropriate to it. The physiological level is controllable by the processing of information received by perception; the subsequent physiological reaction, say of the stomach, may increase acidity or arouse hunger, etc. At the same time the physiological level, through the stomach, is maintained by the causal energy supply, i.e. food. And, in turn, the physiological level exercises control over the chemical reactions on the lower level, changing the nature or type of reaction (ion concentration, pH). What I am talking about here is, really, the Model of Man which, naturally, must be the paradigm for all organisation.)

The army, as authoritarian organisation, can be causally efficient – through the accumulation of material and men rather than through proper integration; its creative potential is zero; and its destructive aim facilitates its own disintegration. The bureaucratic organisation disintegrates into fragments when what little information it can transmit to its various levels, due to its low degree of integration, blocks up the channels of transmission. Obviously, between poorly integrated information levels there is, equally, poor communication. The information processing feedback between them works badly, and the bureaucratic group is solid rather than integrated, held together by energy or material flow only.

In a properly functioning group the unconscious processes of inner reality correspond well with the processes of external reality. The awareness of internal patterns and their recognition in the external world – the meaning of an experience – depends on the organisation already achieved in the inner world. We can only see what we are able to see – vision is blind without pre-vision and intuition. Thus a certain correspondence between old information stored and new information received can affect and change each other, with the resulting improvement in our knowledge of both inner and external worlds. Meanings, of course, come on many levels – from the simplest, here-and-now, 'concrete' action required for immediate satisfaction of a need, to the complex, 'abstract', thought process needed for the anticipation of the future. Imagination, the images of possible patterns of action and events, is primitive, visual communication that provides the first rungs of the ladder leading to the higher levels of meanings, of the semantic hierarchy.

12   To repeat: no integration without differentiation. Schizoid processes lead to differentiation; but if this results in a complete separation of the parts, all links being broken, then it produces death – a rattling of dry bones. Depressive processes prevent differentiation; if they result in too great a compression and bring about collapse, then they produce death, by rigidity. Bureaucracy, using mainly causal energy to transmit orders and to produce order, remains on separate, single, horizontal levels even though a pyramid of command is involved. The lines of communication are linear rather than non-linear, thus effect equals cause in strength and no 'non-linear' surprises occur. The multi-dimensionality is apparent, not real. Though the energy flows upwards, it is causal linkage that is vertical, and information flow is weak and impeded since it requires non-linear pattern and modulation. Information remains stored on a given level, horizontal. The 'abstract', higher dimensions, the special phase-space of communication and meta-communication, etc., is beyond the ordinary space-time of energy flow. Integration and differentiation require as well multi-dimensionality of the organised level structure.

At this stage of evolution of man, at least in the western world, the straightforward exploration of the concrete, terrestrial environment is exhausted. It is by constructing ever more 'abstract' levels of external and internal reality, by the hierarchical organisation of information received from experience, that we can increase indefinitely our knowledge and insight. Even the coming exploration of the solar system and of our galaxy and of the universe at large depends on our capacity for 'abstract' imagery and thought. We have first to abandon the 'concrete' conceptualisations derived from simple, everyday, experience before we can visualise the very different experiences such an exploration will bring. Even today, for example, most of us think of extra-terrestrial life and of the means by which to ascertain its presence in simple terms that are so inadequate as to throw doubt on its very existence.

Abstraction, the ever-increasing separation from the concrete experience of the child, or from the solid touch of the classical physicist, has guided scientific research and, via the non-Euclidean space of Einstein, the 'phase-space' of thermodynamic and of quantum systems, we have arrived at the exploration of the still more abstract iso-spin space of symmetry physics. We learned to organise our information by constructing a hierarchical system, levels upon levels of integrated knowledge, by increasing abstraction in conceptualisation and in theoretical explanation that are, all the same, built upon ordinary laboratory experience. This progressive process of abstraction is made possible by the use of symbolism.

13 An organisation is a system in which symbolisation is facilitated. A physical system only requires signs – signals – that is, a physical link between parts of the system so that it can hold together. An organised system, an organism or a human group, requires symbols whose transmission provides the information link between the parts, or partners, of the organisation. The sign-referent relation is by convention and by definition – a codification into a convenient 'alphabet' whose suitability usually however, arises from experience. The symbol-sign relation is an interpretation, since the symbol carries meaning that, though to some extent culturally and socially conditioned, all the same may differ for different people; yet it is the basic unit of a meaningful, internal and external, reality. 'Lightning is electric discharge' is simply a transcription, or codification, though based on knowledge. ' "Lightning" means that God is angry' is an interpretation, given by a rule of meaning and not by a law of Nature, and obviously depends on historical, biographical, etc. conditions. That 'personal symbolism' is relatively uniform, all the same, expresses the fact that all human beings have much in common and that, in spite of widely different levels of maturity and civilisation, our biological needs are the same.

This brings my discussion back to the group process of communication. The group is the natural 'matrix' in which grows the symbolism and the meaningful information that our experiences offer us; for it is within the group that we begin our lives. The group is, therefore, the most fundamental association of men in which to carry on meaningful activities and in which to live a satisfactory life. This has been discovered by many people over many years – and the commune, Kibbutz, etc. gives expression to this insight.

The group is, then, the natural mean between the exaggerated individualism of western society – a feature strongly enhanced by eighteenth-century revolution – and the mass society of today, in which anonymity and population pressure have played havoc with our lives, through the indiscriminate and profit-seeking application of science and technology. Causal order prevails over meaningful application: energy, in every form, e.g. as money, or property, or profit, determines the social pattern.

14 In the last resort, human development is moral. We are born with a moral sense that allows us to distinguish between what we call 'good' and 'evil', although specific acts may be evaluated by us in

diverse ways, under different conditions, in different cultures, and at different times. The moral code depends on time and space.[2] The moral sense, the ability to distinguish, is inborn and developed at the mother's breast. What we feel, correctly or mistakenly, maintains and improves our life is good, what threatens or destroys it, is bad. (Only a very small percentage of people lack this sense, a genetic defect as colour-blindness or as being deaf-mute.)

Rage and revenge are the most primitive expressions of our moral sense; shame and sacrifice are the next stage; we progress to guilt and punishment; and when sufficiently mature, responsibility and reparation express our adult morality. The biological tension between the sexes, the internalised conflict between good and evil derived from it, and all the other polarities to which this tension has given rise, is the mainspring of human evolution. A great deal can, and perhaps ought to be, said about the problem of morality since, in our present western culture we will keep to the Two-Worlds theory according to which Value and Fact, or 'is' and 'ought', etc. are totally separate and 'never the twain shall meet'. All I do want to say here is, once more, that the small group is the natural ground in which individual, moral growth can most easily occur. Of course, this is closely connected not only with the anthropological fact that, in evolution, the human group was the association for survival. It is also that only a small group allows proper organisation in which meaningful information, or communication is the main feature: its reception, its storage and its transmission between members are at a maximum.

In the mass society, especially today's Admass society, social pressure, economic tension, and the rat race − with its total alienation from inner and even external reality − force the individual back to the more primitive, moral stages of rage and revenge. Urban terrorism is one symptom of it. The 'nuclear' family is too small a group in which a sufficiently rich organisation can arise. Isolated, being thrown upon themselves, the members of a family fall prey to the family conflict, with illness and even death in its wake. Again, only the most primitive dominance is established, an order and not a proper organisation in which meaning and mutual understanding prevail. There is good reason why, today and for some time, the 'death of the family' has been announced. Alternative structures of society and of individual life styles have to be found to make modern life safe and creative. The small group, from all we know about it today, appears to be the most successful association of human beings that our evolution has brought about so far.

Summary

This is only a proposal for a theoretical model by means of which to explain the general, non-specific functioning of a human group. The specific, clinical use of the model must depend on the special, psychoanalytic interpretation of the information stored and transmitted within the organised system. These are the main points.

1 Causality as explanatory principle is replaced by communication, the flow of meaningful information.

2 Meaning requires a hierarchy of information levels.

3 The group is an organised system, with complex and strong interactions between members. These interactions cannot be cut up into single, one-sided, causal actions. The group produces a 'force field' or, rather, an information network. Information instead of causality rules human behaviour.

4 An organised system, or human group, is open and dynamic in the sense that it is always a bit 'off' its equilibrium, so that it can change under its own power. This is unlike the physical, causally ordered system which, even when open, is always in equilibrium and changes only through external force.

5 An organism or group is capable of activity, therefore, e.g. learning. The group is the natural biological organisation of life.

6 In the group process there are at least two levels — communication and meta-communication. Thus the meaning of unconscious motives can be made conscious, explicit.

7 The group is a superorganism. The informational levels of individual members merge into a common level structure. Thus, the individual's information, or mis-information, can be changed through the group process. There is a 'reality principle' that brings about the group ego-function.

8 Insight and therapeutic improvement result from the group's capacity for creating new information.

9 Both schizoid-paranoid and depressive mechanisms are seen at work in the group process. Integration requires differentiation — otherwise fragmentation or rigidity destroys the organised system. Informational organisation must prevail over causal order.

10 In the hierarchy of well-integrated information levels, the higher exercise control over the lower ones by feedback which is here an information-processing, not an energy-controlling, device. While information flow is downwards, energy flow — 'food' — is upwards, in order to maintain the organism.

11 'Abstraction' from the primitive 'concrete' experience of the child leads to the infinitely extendable, structure of levels upon levels of integrated knowledge. This knowledge is based, thus, on the solid ground of ordinary experience. Progress is upwards, through meaningful information, not sideways, through the causal accumulation of material. Symbolisation is the means by which abstraction proceeds. This process is facilitated in the group.

12 All human development is, in the last resort, moral. Our inborn moral sense finds expression through widely differing moral codes. The small group allows moral growth to occur more easily than any other form of human association since meaningful information, or communications, is maximal in it. The small group is the 'golden mean' between excessive individualism and mass collectivism, between alienation and anonymity.

Notes

1 This means, roughly, that information is the opposite of entropy, or 'neg-entropy', as it has been called. Increase in information implies an improvement in the orderliness of the system, while increased entropy represents more disorder, an increase in irregular, thermal, movement or 'noise'.

   Since there is no conservation principle for information, there is no need for the information system to be always in equilibrium; or, we need not stipulate that as much information enters as leaves the system. This is required, however, of a physical system ruled by energy alone. Therefore the information system may be slightly 'off balance', for example, in a state above the nearest equilibrium. It means that it has information (or modulated energy) at its disposal. This, in a physical system, is called 'free energy', energy that can be used to do something. The energy is inside the system and can, therefore, initiate an action when the system returns to the nearest equilibrium state. The action then ceases and the system remains in its 'natural' equilibrium.

2 The moral code depends on space and time. The moral sense, our ability to distinguish between whatever we feel to be 'good' or 'bad', is inborn. What we do accept at any given time as good or bad – or the encoding of our feelings into a system of values and commands – depends on the degree of mental-emotional integration we have achieved, on the society in which we live and the compromises we made with its values. The moral code is, therefore, the result of many factors, representing individual learning and understanding as well as social forces and cultural background. Thus, place and time enter into the formulation of the code in terms of which our usual moral sense is expressed.

Chapter 11

Group analytic psychotherapy according to Foulkes and psychoanalysis according to Lacan

M. Laxenaire

Summary

S. H. Foulkes is among those who have always tried to integrate psychoanalytic theory into group psychotherapy. But he has done so with discernment, never omitting to specify the limits of such an integration. Hence the name that he has chosen for his method: group-analytic psychotherapy, rather than group psychoanalysis. Like him, I believe that a number of psychoanalytic concepts, such as the unconscious, the transference, the Oedipus complex, identification, projection, interpretation, the primal scene, etc., are applicable in a group situation; but I also think that this group situation requires a new reading of these psychoanalytic concepts. The aim of this article is to try to show that certain of Lacan's concepts can be of help in this new reading. These concepts are little known abroad, but, in France, it is difficult to speak of psychoanalysis without speaking of Lacan. The importance accorded to language, the linguistic structure of the unconscious, the mirror stage, the trilogy of the imaginary, the real and the symbolic, the renewal of the Oedipus complex, among others, are concepts which, in my view, are of definite practical interest in a psychoanalytic approach to group therapy and psychodrama. Furthermore, these new tendencies are not so removed as might be thought from the theories of Foulkes. This, at least, is what I would like to show.

One possible ambiguity should be cleared up at the outset: Jacques Lacan has never shown any interest in group analysis. His concerns have been entirely those of orthodox psychoanalysis, as developed by Freud on the basis of the couch-chair situation. However, there is no reason a priori why these concepts should not help us to understand the process of psychotherapy at work in a group. G. and P.

Lemoine tried to confront this problem in a book published in 1972. In 1975 I myself made use of Lacanian theories in an attempt to elucidate and specify 'the processes of changes in group psychotherapy'. The aim of this article is more precise: to attempt to show that certain of Lacan's principal themes are indispensable in the practice of group analysis. Indeed, in England and France, psychodrama and group psychotherapy have become gradually imbued with psychoanalytic theories. The transference, unconscious conflicts and interpretation, to mention only a few fundamental concepts, have become accepted by all those who are concerned to distinguish between group therapy and group analysis.

S. H. Foulkes (1969), who was a pioneer in this field, locates the problem quite clearly when he writes:

Whereas other psychotherapeutic groups work only or principally with the manifest content of the group discussion, group analytic therapy uses this manifest content to arrive, through a process of analysis and interpretation, at the latent content, just as a psychoanalyst uses the manifest content of a dream to uncover the latent thoughts of the dream.

In other words, although the group situation is radically different from the analytic situation, the ultimate aim is the same: to lay bare the unconscious and to lead the subject to confront his personal truth and, in order to make his position quite clear, S. H. Foulkes adds:

In the group therapeutic situation free verbal communication is carried to the limit . . . ; there is the attitude of the conductor, which is not only directed towards maintaining the group atmosphere and the active participation of members, but which also enables him to become a transference figure in the psychoanalytic sense and to accept the various roles that the group assigns him; there is the importance given to the repressed unconscious in the psychoanalytic sense and to the interpersonal, social unconscious in the group analytic sense; there is analysis and interpretation of the material produced by the group.

Having made these points clear, I can now return to my subject and pose the problem in these terms: since more and more group therapists are integrating psychoanalytic concepts into their practice, and since Lacan has given psychoanalysis a new, very individual direction, would it not be possible to extend this renewal of psychoanalysis to group analysis? And, if so, in what way would group analysis benefit? In order to answer these questions I have chosen a number of Lacan's key concepts, such as the mirror stage, the notions of the imaginary and the symbolic, the primacy of language, the meaning of interpretation or the structuring function of the Oedipus complex, and I have transposed them to the group situation.

The mirror stage

Jacques Lacan entered psychoanalytic history in 1936 with a paper delivered at the Marienbad Congress entitled 'Le stade du miroir comme formateur de la fonction du Je' (The mirror stage as formative of the function of the I). This paper, revised and delivered in a final form to the Zurich Congress of 1949, is intended as a definitive critique of the Cartesian *cogito*. Against Descartes' 'I think therefore I am' (on which all traditional French philosophy is based), Lacan declares 'it thinks therefore I am', which, in its esoteric formulation, is an adumbration of the whole of Lacan's later structuralism.

What does it mean? Between the ages of six and eighteen months, Lacan argues, the child's brain is not yet totally formed. Moreover, the child is unable to conceive of the body as a totality. He can recognize only limbs or organs, or fragments of these: a foot, a finger, a hand, a breast, a mouth; and this is a fragmented recognition, in which no distinction is made between one's own body and the mother's body.

If the child could depict the way he sees his own body at this time, he would do so, Lacan writes, 'in the form of disjointed limbs, of those organs represented in exoscopy, growing wings and taking up arms for intestinal persecutions – the very same that the visionary Hieronymus Bosch has fixed, for all time, in painting, in their ascent from the fifteenth century to the imaginary zenith of modern man'.

By way of a brief parenthesis, I would remark that this quotation from the *Ecrits* (1966) gives some idea of Lacan's rich, complicated style which, with its unexpected grammatical constructions, leaves an impression of baffling obscurity. This style, which French people, and no doubt foreigners even more, find profoundly disturbing, has resulted in Lacan being frequently accused of pedantry, 'Gongorism' or, at least, a failure to communicate. In my view, however, this prose is worth a careful reading, for it opens up a dimension of language beyond that of mere communication: that of being a metaphorical expression of the unconscious.

But let us return to the fragmented child. One day, in front of a mirror, he suddenly escapes from the world of Hieronymus Bosch and is able at last to contemplate himself in his entirety. At the sight of his body reassembled and set within proper limits, he experiences 'intense jubilation'. He jumps for joy and smiles at his mother who, observing the scene, vouches for its authenticity. For the first time he becomes aware of his own existence. Close to his mother, but separate from her, he confusedly affirms himself as a different being. This first encounter with himself is also for the child a new birth.

It is, however, an ambiguous birth, for what the child has seen in front of him is only an image, and every image is a lure or false trail and for a long time the subject will bear the taint of having discovered his identity through the non-existence of a fleeting reflection. One thinks of Narcissus seeing and admiring himself in the water, only to drown himself in his image and die. The child, too, and the adult after him, it seems, also run the risk of drowning themselves, not in the deception of the watery mirror, but in the identifications that originate in this initial identity, if the paternal function does not perform its liberating role at the Oedipal stage.

It is also important that the child should recognize this image for what it is, that is to say, a copy or even an imitation of reality. In this he is helped by the mother's gaze, which enables him to grasp the unreal, almost hallucinatory side of what he is observing. But if this recognition of its illusory character is missing, the child will become prey to the mirages of his perception. He then becomes alienated, in the old sense of the term, that is to say, mentally disturbed, a stranger to himself, and takes the road of psychosis and paranoid aggressiveness. But what route does he take? That of the imaginary, which we shall now explore.

The imaginary double and the group as mirror

The mirror stage refers to the imaginary in so far as it introduces the notion of image: the imaginary is that which allows itself to become prey to images. No distance intervenes between the subject and his reflection. They are united in a state of non-differentiation and fusion in which no one can any longer recognize that which is his.

It is this fusion in an apparent duality that Freud defines as primary narcissism. J. B. Fages (1971) writes:

Lacan defines it as imaginary by remaining as close as possible to the etymology of the term: it is imaginary because the child identifies himself with a double of himself, which enables him to recognize himself. By doing so the child has filled a void, a gap between the two terms of the relation: the body and its image.

This allusion to the 'double' offers a way back to the group. For this is precisely one of the processes most frequently observed in the functioning of a group: identification with a double of oneself, but without being aware of it and manifesting it in behaviour that moves through a whole range of emotions, from aggressiveness to love. And this is hardly surprising, writes S. H. Foulkes (1969), who without realizing it is very close to Lacan here, since 'the group situation has been compared to a hall of mirrors in which an individual is confronted with various aspects of his social, psychological or physical image'.

Carrying the analogy still further, S. H. Foulkes anticipates later developments in therapy when he writes:

In the course of a baby's development, the mirror reactions thus described help him to differentiate between what is he and what is not he. Reflections of oneself coming from the outside lead to a greater awareness of self so that the narcissistic child finally learns to distinguish his own image from that of others. Mirror reactions are consequently essential mechanisms for the solution of this primary narcissism.

In other words, at an initial stage the group situation encourages mirror identifications involving an imaginary double and, at a second stage, makes it possible to go beyond them and to encourage in the individual the birth of a true autonomy. This birth does not always come easily and gives rise to displays of aggressiveness or, on the contrary, of love projection. Two short sequences, which occurred in different groups, will make clearer what we mean by 'identification with an imaginary double'.

To begin with, an example of aggressive duality in which a 45-year-old man, René, found himself confronted in the group 'with various aspects of his social, psychological or physical image', to use S. H. Foulkes's words. These aspects are embodied in another member of the group, Luc, who is more or less the same age, the same height and build, though slightly slimmer. René and Luc look so much alike that during the first sessions the other participants get their first names mixed up. One day they are sitting on either side of the woman monitor. 'They look like two candelabra on either side of a mantelpiece', one woman remarked. The image stuck. As far as the group was concerned, they were now twins.

From that moment on, René was constantly aggressive in his behaviour to Luc. He attributed to him all the defects he hated in a man: Luc was indecisive, soft, weak, erratic. He never stopped criticising him, ridiculing him and judging severely everything he did. The women in the group who, secretly or overtly, were on Luc's side, wanted blood. 'I wanted a duel between Luc and René,' said Marie. 'I wondered if one day we wouldn't find them both dead in a field,' added Paule. René tried to establish a virile image of himself. 'For me, a man is someone who attacks, who fights,' he said, addressing Luc. He mocked Luc's dependent attitude towards his father. 'You've behaved like a little kid with your father,' he said, 'you don't know how to stand up to him like a man'. And he concluded, with scarcely restrained violence, 'I'd like to punch you in the face.'

He did not do so, for the woman therapist intervened with her interpretation of the incident: 'You are like two twins, one of whom can live only if the other dies,' she said. 'There's an alternation between the two of you; both cannot be strong at the same time.' Thus, gradually working through the brutal expression of his aggressiveness, René discovered its cause: Luc represented and embodied that part of himself that he did not wish to acknowledge. Later he was to provide, in his behaviour, innumerable examples of the faults he criticised so vehemently in Luc.

This brief extract shows very clearly the mechanism of paranoid projection, with its aggressiveness and its identification with archaic images. The aggression towards another who is both similar and different is explained by the resurgence, in adulthood, of the behaviour of the mirror stage. Still very close to his fragmentation, the child, confronted by an image whose meaning cannot at first be grasped, no longer knows who he is and what belongs to him. He dismembers his dolls, takes his toy motor cars apart, stamps on his toys, littering the ground with their debris and recreating, in his unconscious fury, the picture by Hieronymus Bosch mentioned above. René, in words, was acting in exactly the same way towards Luc.

On a more philosophical plane, Lacan's thesis on aggressiveness is very close to that of Hegel. 'By raising the struggle of the Master and the slave,' writes J. M. Palmier (1969), a struggle of pure prestige in which each wishes to be recognized without recognizing the other, to the dignity of a symbol for the whole history of the world, 'Hegel has provided a theory for all time of the proper function of aggressiveness in human ontology that seems to foreshadow the iron law of our time'; this iron law governs groups as it does the rest of the world. In it paranoid aggressiveness is no longer seen as more or less widespread, but it acquires the possibility of being recognized and superseded. The group is first of all a mirror in which each individual finds himself again through the other with his drives, recognized or rejected; thanks to the intervention of the psychotherapist the mirror is broken and the subject finds himself again, 'through the looking glass', alone, confronting himself and his truth. From that moment, if he wishes, he can change.

The second example of mirror identification comes from another group. This time it concerns a recognition of homosexuality. Christian is about 35, but looks much younger. He seems emotional and sensitive. His language is precious and colourful. At the beginning of the group he often referred to his mother, who is possessive and authoritarian. He has never been able, it seems, to detach himself from her completely. He is obviously afraid of opening up a dialogue with the women of the group and refuses the opportunity when it presents itself. On the other hand, he seems more and more fascinated by Stéphane, a young man of ambiguous physical appearance, who so far has seemed unwilling to talk about himself. But, one evening, Stéphane finds himself sitting opposite him. At first he just looks at him for a long time and says nothing. Then the following conversation takes place:

Stéphane: I'm glad you're sitting opposite me, but what am I going to do about it?
Christian: So am I. But the problem for me is that Stéphane is good-looking, except for one. [Pause] The fact that I think Stéphane is good-looking presents problems; at the same time, for me Anita is a woman who isn't like a mother, that makes up for it.
Anita: Do you like the fact that he's good-looking?
Christian: Yes.
Sophie: Why?
Christian: It's probably because of my homosexuality. I see Stéphane as the tempting angel from the Italian film [*Theorem*], in which a young man arrives in a family and perverts everybody. There's an ambiguous, attractive side to you . . . Angel, sphynx or bi-sexual.

Stéphane: I'm quite willing to be thought bi-sexual, but
sphynx. . . . I've an older brother called Christian, as I've said
before.
Christian: No. Does he look like you?
Stéphane: Yes, but older. Have you got any brothers?
Christian: No, just a sister. She's much younger than me.
Stéphane: I've always regretted that I haven't got a sister.
Christian: I'd like to be friends with you. We could go out
together, eat together.
Stéphane: We could talk about women.
Christian: Yes . . . [rather put out] Why do you say that?
Stéphane: I always want to talk about women when I'm with a
friend I get on well with.
Christian: Friends are important to me. But I've always been too
afraid to let things get too far. I've no friends at the moment.

Christian discovers in the mirror of Stéphane the image of his
homosexual tendencies. He expresses them. Stéphane cancels them out
by mentioning women, because he is afraid of getting involved. Homosexuality and paranoia are two sides of the same symptom. The group
gives a new demonstration of this, following on Freud's interpretation
of the Schreber case. It also provides an opportunity to go beyond both
and to give the subject back his truth by getting him to go through the
mirror. After this episode, Christian will at last be able to confront the
problem of his relationship with his mother. We shall see how. Stéphane,
on the other hand, will not return to the group, having chosen flight
rather than the painful necessity of confronting his truth. In any case,
his refusal to pursue a dialogue with Christian made this outcome
rather predictable.

The theme of the double is a favourite one in literature. There are
a number of examples of what happens when someone allows himself
to be taken in by this mystification. The story of William Wilson, as
imagined by Edgar Allan Poe, ends tragically: weary of meeting his
double wherever he goes, a double who has the courage to commit the
evil acts that he could not allow himself to commit, William Wilson
provokes him to a duel and kills him. In this duel, unable to bear the
perverse part of his drives, he in fact kills himself. Thus ends tragically
the life of a paranoiac, by suicide or the murder of the hated image of
himself. As for the homosexual, he drowns in the narcissistic image
that he seeks in the representatives of his own sex. Otto Rank (1973)
has subtly analysed the fantasy of the double, with its antagonistic

paintings of love and hate, death and immortality. Fortunately the group offers an alternative to the mortiferous destiny of mirror identification, and it is here that its therapeutic function is located. W. R. Bion (1972) has stressed the way in which the group functions in terms of the three modalities of 'fight, flight and pairing'. It is not my purpose here to discuss these well-known theories, but simply to mention them in order to bring out how Lacan's conceptions may complement them.

What, in fact, is at issue in the group? Essentially, it is a question of going beyond the imaginary stage, in which the participants tear themselves apart, confront one another, flee from one another and identify with one another in twos, in order to rise to the signification that these phenomena have for everybody. D. Anzieu (1971) has laid great stress on a similar, though even more primitive, moment in the functioning of groups, which he calls the 'moment of group illusion'. He sees in this a warm moment in which the ideal ego of each individual takes the place of the common ideal ego and he concludes thus: 'Lacan, linking the ideal ego to the mirror stage, has situated it in the register of the imaginary. Observation of groups also confirms this: the group illusion is the particular form that the mirror stage assumes in a group.' I would entirely accept that conclusion.

Access to the symbolic

But the supersession of imaginary identifications must take place and it can take place, according to Lacan, only through access to the symbolic, that is to say, through language. With these two concepts, we come to the very centre of Lacan's contribution to psychoanalysis. I would now like to show how these concepts may be transposed to the group.

The term 'symbolic' is derived from the term 'symbol', but it is not to be confused with it. The symbolic order designates 'the order of the phenomena with which psychoanalysis has to deal in so far as they are structured by a language. They constitute a pre-established, structured order of interhuman relations, in which the subject must insert himself' (Lacan, 1966).

This sentence enables us to understand in what way Lacan is a structuralist. If the subject must be inserted into language, it is because language pre-exists him. The young child thus passes from nature to culture. In doing so, he alienates his personality in the symbolic code to which he belongs by birth. Moreover, this code is not made up solely of language. Claude Lévi-Strauss (1947), another structuralist, has shown in the area of ethnology that primitive peoples obey complicated codes of kinship and exchange. Without having to go so far for examples, could it not be said that certain misunderstandings between the British and the French derive quite simply from their different culinary codes? It is said that General de Gaulle concluded a long speech against Britain's entry into the Common Market by saying: 'And, anway, they don't eat like we do!'

So, Lacan argues, the subject only apparently says 'I'. He is manipulated without knowing it by his mother tongue. To begin with, this tongue is only a series of sounds associated with bodily sensations. Later certain sounds become detached and are associated with objects, but the word and the object designated by that word are connected in the most arbitrary fashion. Lacan takes up the distinction made by the linguist F. de Saussure (1965) between signifier and signified. The signified, that is to say the object, is out of reach of the consciousness. Access to the signifier only is possible, that is to say, to the arrangement of sounds that form the words. It is the chain of signifiers that constitutes the symbolic order and, consequently, the subject himself.

The unconscious is of a linguistic order

By cutting out from the signifying chain what is useful to him or more precisely what relates to his own childhood experiences, the individual sets up for himself a stock of language, his speech. This speech is the only audible sign of his unconscious. 'The truth of the unconscious,' writes J. M. Palmier (1969), 'is that man is inhabited and transformed by the signifier.'

In other words, the subject is at the outset merely a sort of improved tape recorder that records the speech of his parents. 'The unconscious is the discourse of the Other,' Lacan was to say, and added at once: 'The unconscious is structured like a language.' These two formulas provide the key to the subject's truth: through the analysis of the transference, the individual will be able to distinguish between what he owes to others (the recorded part of his mini-cassette) and his unconscious desire (the still virgin part).

In order to get there we have no need of an exploration 'in depth', which attempts to bring 'to the surface' various childhood traumas: it is enough to study the structure of the discourse in the here-and-now of the analytic relationship. To him who knows how to hear it, the unconscious is manifested in language. In order to explain what he means, Lacan uses Edgar Allan Poe's story, 'The Purloined Letter': four or five people are looking for a compromising letter, but despite the most meticulous searches it cannot be found. In fact, it is where no one would dare to imagine that it could be: clearly, for all to see, on the desk of the compromised person.

Such is the unconscious, clear for all to hear in the way in which each individual manipulates the signifiers that were once imposed upon him.

Return to group analysis

This atemporal way of approaching the unconscious suits the group situation perfectly. All group analysts stress that it is impossible for them to carry out a minute exploration of the past of each of the participants. On the other hand, all insist on the value and importance of the exchanges in the here-and-now of the session.

S. H. Foulkes (1971) thus distinguishes between vertical analysis according to the subject's past and horizontal analysis according to the system of his present relationships. 'The transference relationship between the individual and the conductor,' he writes, 'or with any other member of the group cannot be developed as fully as in psychoanalysis, nor can it be analysed vertically (to use my term) to the same degree.'

In a group, transference is multiple, affecting both the therapist and the other members of the group. In reality, the transference exists in any case, but it is the interpretation of the monitor that gives it its operational value. We can reintroduce at this point the Lacanian concepts already discussed and apply them to the group situation.

Individual analysis may be defined as the gradual uncovering of the personal signifiers of an individual until the point at which a primordial signifier, on which all the others depend, is revealed. S. Leclaire (1957) compares this verbal arrangement to the fugal development of a musical theme. The variations are often impressive, but the theme remains and provides the key to the whole.

Now, what takes place in a group? Leclaire's musical comparison is even more valid than in the case of the solitary individual. Each participant plays his part of the score on his own instrument, but on the basis of a common theme. This theme is the group signifier, proposed by a participant, then accepted and orchestrated by the others. Similarly, in ancient tragedy, the chorus and the hero reply to one another according to the fugal alternation of their lamentations. Aeschylus's *The Persians* provides an excellent example of this dramatic exchange. In the psychodramatic situation the exchanges are of the same kind. The action that takes place is intended to encourage in the subject what Moreno (1965) called 'spontaneity'. This spontaneity is true speech, relieved of the weight of 'cultural deposits'. Lacan, too, sees the aim of psychoanalysis as that of freeing speech in order to decode its unconscious signification. Although the means are different, the aims are identical and the ultimate vehicle still remains language.

'Verbal communication,' writes S.H. Foulkes (1969), 'is changed into group association. This implies that group discussion is not discussion in the ordinary sense of the word, but something that we call free discussion. It is the equivalent in the analytic group of what is known as free association in psychoanalysis.'

Whatever the mode of association chosen, what is important is that everything should take place in and through language. This point of view is accepted by all those who practise group analysis, whereas it is challenged by those who practise non-analytic group therapy. In encounter groups or bio-energy groups, for example, the stress is placed on emotional or physical liberation: liberation based on the catharsis theory.

This difference is an important one. Must we, in other words, remain in the imaginary and accept that an action contains its end in itself or must we analyse the imaginary in order to reach the symbolic? G. and P. Lemoine, defining their psychodramatic practice, while also claiming allegiance to Lacan, write: 'Unlike Moreno, we lay stress on the imaginary, thus provoking an analysis of identifications and repetitions, rather than on catharsis, which is certainly a useful effect of psychodrama, but an epiphenomenal one.' In group analysis, as in individual analysis, the aim is reached only when the imaginary has given way to the symbolic.

Group interpretation

In the last resort the difference between these two conceptions of the group comes down to the attitude adopted to interpretation. From the analytic point of view, the process of change can occur only through interpretation, and interpretation has value only in the transference. This coincides with what Lacan calls 'a moment for understanding'.

It gives meaning to an obscure situation. Without interpretation the group situation would run a strong risk of getting locked into a series of *passages à l'acte* whose meaning would be lost for ever.

Now the interpretation is addressed to a particular subject in order to emphasize his relationship with the group. S. H. Foulkes gives an example of intervention that is worth mentioning because it establishes perfectly the two indispensable factors, speech and the relationship with the group.

Foulkes recounts the incident thus: 'A homosexual, Alex, is arrested in a public lavatory for importuning a young boy. He arrives at the group session completely drunk and declares: "When I've finished talking, you'll be so disgusted with me, you won't want to see me again." It is a tense, anxious moment for the group. "We'll get you thrown out of here," says one participant. When he feels that the participants can no longer bear their anxiety, the therapist speaks to Alex: "As usual, you've managed to make your family afraid of you. In fact, it's you who are afraid. You want the group to reject you, so that you won't have to reject the group." '

In other words, the monitor's interpretation suggests to Alex the hidden meaning of his *passage à l'acte*. But the value of this intervention derives above all from its relation to the group: Alex behaves with his new family as he did with the old one; he makes himself unbearable so that others will decide matters for him. The situation is repetitive and he will become aware of the fact.

This example shows perfectly what we mean by the 'atemporal structure of the transference' — and of interpretation. It is in the here-and-now of the group that the truth breaks out and there is in fact no need to seek, in order to bring it out into the open, some memory of the individual's earlier life.

Lacan (1973) writes that 'the transference is the enaction of the unconscious' — an enaction which, in the group, is very often a *passage à l'acte*, as for Alex; indeed, the psychodrama is simply a controlled *passage à l'acte*. Like actings out, slips of the tongue, dreams, or para-praxis, the *passage à l'acte* makes it possible to reproduce in the time of the group a new version of what Freud calls 'the infantile cliché'. Lacan prefers the term *'trait unaire'*, or single stroke, an expression that is an approximate translation of the German term *'einziger Zug'*. The single stroke also designates the primordial signifier of an individual, that is to say, his fundamental structure.

In so far as the psychoanalyst's silence enables it to remain open, the transference avoids getting bogged down in love. This absence of response to the demand for love gives the subject an opportunity of discovering his true desire. As S. H. Foulkes's example shows so well, Alex's desire was in reality 'to get himself rejected by the group as he had been rejected by his own family'. Such an interpretation is 'therapeutic' in so far as it stops short of the neurotic repetition by elucidating, in a verbal explanation, the meaning of the *passage à l'acte*.

Thanks to Alex, I think I have shown that interpretation as understood by S. H. Foulkes has something to gain from the Lacanian conceptions of the transference, the structure of the individual and the omnipresence of language and signifiers.

The Oedipus complex and the law

I would like to conclude by referring to one last problem: that of the role of the Oedipus complex in the access to the symbolic. Lacan reinterprets this structuring moment of the personality in linguistic terms. Now, the group situation allows a new linguistic enactment of the Oedipal situation. That is to say, the Oedipus story is played out again through the story of the group, but with other words.

S. H. Foulkes (1975) has always insisted on the fact that psychoanalysis could not be applied to the group without undergoing certain modifications. These modifications pertain to the specific situation of the group and to the processes of communication between the participants. 'The main medium of therapeutic processes is communication, shareable after decodification (analysis) of all observable phenomena.' It is communication decodable in psychoanalytic terms that encourages change in the individual.

The processes of maturation described for the individual are repeated in the group situation, but in such conditions that they encourage a change in the personality. S. H. Foulkes (1975) writes:

While all the processes known from psychoanalysis operate – as modified by the group situation – the ego itself is regenerated, as it is confronted with the conditions prevailing in its genesis. The same is true for the superego. This fully explains the change in depth, which can be observed, and its lasting nature.

The Oedipal situation is an excellent example of psychoanalytic process reactivated by the group. We have seen that the child before the mirror became, in a group, the subject before his double. In both cases the relationship implies two similar, even 'fusional' characters. Left to itself, this situation culminates in psychosis (paranoia), perversion (homosexuality) or death. If another evolution is to be made possible, a third character is necessary. This character is the father. To quote A. Rifflet-Lemaire (1970),

He intervenes as the depriver in a double sense: he deprives the child of the object of his desire (the mother) and he deprives the mother of the phallic object (her child), so that one might translate his role as a spoilsport, in the full sense of the term, by this double injunction: you will not sleep with your mother; and to the mother: you will not re-integrate your product.

It is through the law of the father, on condition that it is recognized and accepted by the other, that the child will abandon the imaginary and enter the symbolic order. He will now at last be able to speak for himself, in the first person, and say 'I', for he will at last have access to his desire. This passage can be performed only at the price of a loss: symbolic castration. 'The father castrates the child *qua* phallus and separates him from the mother. This is the debt, what has to be paid for being oneself through having access to the order of the symbol of culture and civilization' (ibid.).

The group situation repeats the Oedipal situation in so far as the male monitor, forming a couple with a female monitor, represents the law of the father. It is to him that one pays the debt and it is he who denounces the 'group illusion'. The symbolic castration that results, split, flight or *Spaltung*, to use Lacan's terms, is the sign of a resolved Oedipus complex, the prelude to the 'regeneration of the ego', to use S. H. Foulkes's term.

Christian's subsequent history will illustrate these abstract notions. After exploring his homosexuality through the image of Stéphane, Christian sank into silence for several sessions. One day he broke out and, in the course of a dramatic psychodrama, he insulted his mother in the shape of one of the women in the group, who played her part. Exhausted, he admitted that he dared to make this scene because he felt authorized to do so by the authority of the monitor, that is to say, the father. It was his way of verbalizing his affects and of passing into the symbolic.

Throughout this article, I have tried to show that the analytic approach to the group as conceived by S. H. Foulkes is not incompatible with some of the psychoanalytic concepts as developed by Lacan. The fundamental options remain the same, but they are expressed differently. The great psychoanalytic concepts however are transposable to the group only on condition that they take the specific group situation, which gives them new meaning, into account. Lacan's contribution may help, it seems to me, to facilitate this new meaning and, judging from his writings, I do not think that Foulkes would disagree.

References

Anzieu, D. (1971), 'L'illusion groupale', *Nouv. Rev. Psychanalyse*, no. 4, pp. 73-93.
Bion, W. R. (1961), *Experiences in Groups*, London; in French, *Recherche sur les petits groupes*, Paris, P. U. F., 2nd Edn, 1972.
Fages, J. B. (1971), *Comprendre Jacques Lacan*, Toulouse, Private edn.
Foulkes, S. H. and Anthony, E. J. (1969), *Psychothérapie de groupe. Approche psychanalytique*, Paris, Epi.
Foulkes, S. H. (1970), *Psychothérapie et analyse de groupe*, Paris, Payot.
Foulkes, S. H., Kadis, A. J., Krasner, J. D., and Winick C. (1971), *Guide du psychothérapeute de groupe*, Paris, Epi.
Foulkes, S. H. (1975), 'Qualification as a psychoanalyst as an asset as well as a hindrance for the future group analyst', *Gaipal*, 8, no. 3, pp. 180-2.
Lacan, Jacques (1977), *Ecrits: A Selection*, trans. Alan Sheridan, London, Tavistock.
Lévi-Strauss, Claude (1969), *Elementary Structures of Kinship*, trans. J. H. Bell, J. R. von Sturmer, ed. R. Needham, London, Eyre & Spottiswoode.
Lévi-Strauss, Claude *Mythologiques Le cru et le cuit* vol. I, 1964; *Du miel aux cendres* vol. II, 1966; *L'origine des manières à table* vol. III, 1968; *L'homme nu* vol. IV, 1971; Plon, Paris.
Moreno, J. L. (1965), *Psychothérapie de groupe et psychodrame*, Paris, P. U. F.
Palmier, J. M. (1969), *Lacan*, Coll. Psychothèque, Edit, Univ.
Poe, Edgar Allan (1960), *William Wilson. Oeuvre en prose. Traduction de Baudelaire*, Paris, Club Français du Livre.
Poe, Edgar Allan (1969), *Selected Writings*, Harmondsworth, Penguin.
Rank, O. (1973), *Don Juan et le double. Etudes Psychanalytiques*, Paris, Petite Bibliothèque Payot.
Rifflet-Lemaire, A. (1970), *Jacques Lacan*, Bruxelles, Edit. Dessart.
Saussure, F. de (1965), *Cours de linguistique générale*, ed. Ch. Bally and A. Sechehaye, Paris, Payot.
Rank, Otto (1975), *The Don Juan Legend*, trans. D. G. Winter, Princeton University Press.
Rank, Otto (1971), *The Double*, trans. H. Tucker, Chapel Hill, University of North Carolina.

Chapter 12
Why group analysis works

Maria Rita Mendes Leal

Group analysis emerged from the theory and practice of psychoanalysts and as a 'modified technique' shares many of the concepts formulated by Freud. But, as has been shown in other papers, it is the child of a younger age. Even its definition given by its founder, S. H. Foulkes, is formulated in 'operational terms' and points in a direction unforeseen by Freud in his basic text, *Massenpsychologie und Ichanalyse*. My proposition in this paper is that group analysis works because it is grounded in scientific method in its conception and in its (correct) execution, i.e. it may be seen as a process of mobilizing natural elements, life's own maturational forces in the service of adult creative growth. When activating normal developmental dynamics through strict observation of nature's rules, group analysts enter the field of social intervention with no other preconception – political, social or other – than that of scientific determinism and philosophical pragmatism.

Group analysis was first applied to the treatment of traumatic neuroses in a war hospital and may, thus, be applauded for its seminal influence both on institutional therapy and on individual psychotherapy. S. H. Foulkes defined it from the beginning as a branch of scientific research in human social phenomena to be practised *pari passu* with treatment aims.[1] He never abandoned the basic definition of group analysis as: '*that which you may observe when*' six to eight individuals (formerly unknown to each other) meet regularly with a conductor sitting in a circle around a low table, having no other task beyond investigating their mutual communications in the here and now of their common meeting-ground. This meeting-ground – i.e., the responsibility of the conductor who convenes the group – is thus circumscribed as the group-analytic situation, and is later designated as a referent of the group-analytic 'matrix'. Whatever else Foulkes may have suggested in the effort to explain his 'invention', to my mind he seems always to have conformed to this model of: *'that' which may be observed 'when'*.[2]

Group analysis is a process of analytical investigation in the above-mentioned circumstance. By extension, the definition may be said to apply in any other rigorously defined circumstance in which independent individuals maintain ongoing relationships with each other and with a conductor in some non-task-oriented meeting-ground.[3] The object of observation is the group as a locus of interchange between individuals. Its sole aim is 'understanding', centred in the group.

Group analysts hold in common with psychoanalysts the presupposition that an 'analyst' in the act of analysing ongoing human relationship phenomena is at the same time, by the very act, treating this transaction. The inverse proposition is also upheld: 'treatment', i.e., that which promotes change and renewed mental integration of the human psyche, is illusory if the scientific attitude on the part of a participant but non-interfering (i.e. 'abstinent') observer is lacking. At the same time the term 'analytic' which is at the root of both terms, group analysis and psychoanalysis, refers to the material under scrutiny in both disciplines. The term analytic does not only designate the quality of 'abstinence', i.e. the basic scientific stance of non-interference in the object of investigation. In addition, the focus is on a specific modus in the integration of human personality, i.e. emotional resonance and its lawful characteristics, a resonance which researchers are now calling 'implicit behaviour'.

Going back: group analysis is a form of treatment and research into emotional life and interchange (implicit behaviour) and the laboratory in which this research is effected is the on-going group interrelationship in a controlled setting. Thus, in summary, the following statements can be made about group analysis:

1 From the moment that a conductor undertakes the attitude of the researcher face to face with an agglomerate of independent individuals committed to an ongoing experience, he has been noted to observe how humans are impelled to communicate when they meet. Communication may take on verbal or non-verbal form, it may be ordered in a rational sequence or follow a train of free association; it will be interspersed by silences or pauses, through which (as is testified by many) other messages will take form and be registered, but always it implicates a response. A message not received may not be designated a communication. If the conductor points out the observed forms of communication and their variances, it will be

found that he will be soliciting a key to understanding the current experience; and this suggestion will be included in the total matrix of communication in the context of which messages sent out (received or non-received) will take on specific content.

2 Group intercourse and its variance becomes the context for insight into individual personality. A generalization of the above observation may take on the form of a distinct (so-called) 'principle'. In S. H. Foulkes's wording, one may say: group phenomena are more primitive than individual phenomena. I believe that on formulating this statement he may not have been too sweeping in his stance.

In a personal encounter a few weeks before his death S. H. Foulkes reminisced on his experience of being born as the youngest in a large family. In that intensely active 'natural' group little 'Michael' (as he was known to friends and colleagues) grew and found himself the creative, authoritative but gentle individual which he was. Foulkes's contention on that day was that he could not have conceived of personality formation otherwise than against the background of that group of seven individuals. But when Foulkes centred on theory in his writings he would say that terms like 'group' and 'individual' function as complementary concepts. They make sense only as such. Like 'form' and 'ground' perception, their separation is an artefact proposing a never-ending set of pseudo-problems.

3 Analytic investigation of interpersonal phenomena requires that communication, verbal or non-verbal, may be contained in the group-matrix, i.e., that 'implicit' communication is not substituted by 'consummatory action' which lies outside the group setting as defined. Action as such may be contained in the group when reformulated in the group setting, if (and at the point where) its significance in that context can be located. In other words, outside happenings or actions may become communications inasmuch as their message may be received. By definition, Foulkes repeats again and again: messages not received do not, *a fortiori*, constitute communication in group analysis.

4 An important observation group analysts have made, following Foulkes, is that mental disturbance or suffering as communicated by the isolated individual in the consulting room may be 'located' as a symptom of a group disturbance in the group-analytic matrix. There the individual may be concretely seen evolving in a network of disturbed relationships in which his everyday life is intermeshed. Thus neurosis becomes a social, not a private phenomenon, in more than a theoretical sense.

Social scientists have enlarged on this, but the group-analytic setting best helps to pinpoint the locus where individual pathology and social distortion become tangential.

Given the above rapid excursion into the realm of concepts, I come back to my aim — which is not to trace the lines of historic influence of group analysis on social science, but to proceed further in the empirical description of the curative influence of analytic investigation in groups. Thus, my questions go back to: 'what makes well' or 'what makes better' or: 'how does group analysis work as a therapeutic tool?' My thesis may be stated in brief: Deliberate stimulation at any age of the 'search for response' reaction as seen in early childhood will act as an agent for personality growth, i.e. will induce emotional development.

The group-analytic investigation as described by S. H. Foulkes and delineated above presents a locus for optimizing the 'search for response' reaction through which the self is differentiated from the other, as I shall detail. In 'facilitating'[4] this intrapsychic activity of testing the response of the other to one's own initiative in a continuous reality-testing process (understood in Freud's terms) group analysis becomes an agent of change, and of emotional growth.

Intrapsychic change permits a new use of whatever reality is presenting itself to the individual in actual life, this being a viable concept of 'cure'.

On focusing the 'search for response' dimension, a new concept which I will elucidate further in subsequent pages, I am not setting this against psychoanalytic insights. The fact is that Freud's discoveries dealing with repressive and/or maladjustive mechanisms of psychic functioning are *confirmed in the group-analytic situation*. These mechanisms are dealt with in practice at the point where it is possible to refer the occurring processes back to the *matrix of intercourse which is the group relationship*. But, in this article, I am intent on delineating regularities of intercourse in the group, consonant with Foulkes's concept of 'ego-training in action'. This concept was abstracted from observation in the here-and-now of the group-analytic practice but was never elucidated very clearly by him or by his colleagues. It designates a form of intrapsychic adaptation or corrective experience, which I will try to set in a new language of emotional development. To this end I shall briefly describe recent research into young children's emotional-social development in which the more pertinent questions become centred on the 'search-for-response' reaction. This is a theoretical construct formed to integrate new empirical data of infant and child observations.[5]

Recent controlled observations reveal that babies are more attentive to the outside world, from early days, than was known, and present from the beginning discriminative emotional reactions to differential personal relationships, though using distinct neural registers from those that individuals may use preferentially in later waking life.[6] Further, the baby takes the initiative in the direction of establishing self-other relationships from the first months of life in the form of search for a 'responding other' with whom the child will communicate – thus, it seems, finding himself in his emerging boundaries.

The mechanism of 'attachment' which has been proposed by John Bowlby as an explanatory concept for the description of early emotional development belongs, relatively speaking, to a late age of emotional development (i.e. the last quarter of the first year of life). Earlier emotional intercourse in the form of thing-gesture-conversations needs more primitive descriptive models for clarification. We know that the toddler will not maintain a healthy interest in the outside world if real 'attachment' cannot be attained. But it is less well known that the possibility of 'attachment' is very meagre if emotional intercourse is not established much earlier between the baby and his carers in a form distinct from that seen in attachment behaviour.

We know that the child does not in the beginning apprehend himself as a mind (consciousness) or even as a distinct body (sense of self) but, on an emotional register of experiences of resonance, he does have a 'grip on the world' and is in some way 'present to himself'. As a body subject he is of necessity immersed in his emotions. He may become aware of them very early *if he has occasion to 'analyse' his experience of expressive co-action with people and things as partners to his experience.* This transitive use of the carer and of objects at each moment of intercourse provides the baby with a moment by moment matrix connecting experiences with each other and with himself. If the basic self-other exchange provided through this primitive intercourse with the carer does not take on the form of *'now you – now I'* protoconversation (or if this communication is lost) – then future emotional development cannot be expected as 'transitive objects' will not easily appear in play activity, i.e. objects will not be used for the purpose of emotional equation which is the basis of pre-symbol formation. Given the resulting emotional disturbance, first described by Spitz in its extreme form,[7] 'attachment' will not result as the externalization of an effectively established communication system – but will appear as an artefact imposed by the adult world on the child, following the paradigm that the child must 'be protected', therefore 'be dependent'.

In this way 'attachment' will take on the pathogenic anxious mode described in crisis situations. It will not function as the protective shield elicited by the self of the child to the exact measure of his requirements of an interpreter and general manager of his dependent needs. Instead 'attachment' will be a construction of a pseudo-self straining to maintain some control in a false relationship through the commitment of absolute dependency. Being held by a more 'real' carer in a consistent matrix of communication, would on the contrary leave him free to go on with the satisfying business of exploring the world of percepts in continuous flux around him.

To give substance to this account of the young child's primitive emotional and intellectual development which is rather different from the picture more usually presented, I will describe natural development with data taken from other fields. Ethologists exploring the animal world have found that every organism reacts only to the sum of potential stimuli which it selectively chooses from the environment for some aim — seemingly anticipating important species functioning. Thus, animals construct from the outer-thing world (the *Umwelt*) their own world (the *Eigenwelt*), a 'possible' environment to which they are responsive.

In analogy to this, the phenomenon of 'stimulus barrier' which appears in the human child some hours after onset of extra-uterine life — reducing the scope of his responses — has been understood tentatively in the light of the youngster's disposition to organize his own 'self world' (*Eigenwelt*) as distinct from the outside world of things mechanically taken in by the psyche.

Describing animal life in his vivid style, Konrad Lorenz pinpoints the origin of personality as another instance of selective centration: 'Personality commences,' he says, 'where, of two individuals, each one plays in the life of the other a part that cannot easily be played by any other member of the species'.[8] In other words, personality begins in the course of exchange, *as bonds are formed for the first time.*

The very young infant does not recognize his carer as a distinct entity. He nevertheless forms particular expectations in respect to that 'element' in his environment which succours him. The mother (or carer) is characterized something in the infant's experience even if on a different register from conscious percept and memory images.[9] For instance, it has been shown that distress scores (denoting emotion reaction) increase in the sequence of shift of caretakers on a hospital ward as measured for babies less than ten days old.[10] Thus, even though preference expressed in *motor* action cannot be observed on the part of very young children, distinctive emotional reaction may be recorded from the beginning. This reaction, which is not the result of perceptual discrimination, testifies to some appraisal and makes implicit some evaluation register. I have posited that this register of emotions which permits recognition and bonding is the very substrate of later emotional/intuitional expressive functioning. The emotional register tapped in distress scores by Burns, Sander and Stechler establishes the meaning of caretaker-for-infant. Emotional appraisal is, by definition, the most primitive experience of meaning. It is also the most primitive form of establishing contact with the 'other'. In other words, emotional appraisal is *expressive*; thus, it is at the same time the most primitive form of communication.

Expressive co-action in human babies, designated by psychologists as 'proto-conversations', is the outcome of appraisal exchanges, i.e., sequences of emotion responses, non-verbal in form and content (for instance smiling) or gestural playful exchanges.[11] Proto-conversations are initiated in the context of a caring partnership, long before space, time, or object discrimination have been learnt by the baby. They become structured before cortical maturation of the brain. It seems clear that lower order centres of the brain subserve 'proto-conversations'. These are distinct from cognitive exchanges in turn subserved by distinct brain structures, which mature later in time, but may build on the former.[12]

It follows that the establishment of a good relationship between baby and his adult partner and carer is extremely important for biological and mental growth of the baby in the first stages of mothering and depends essentially, at all moments, on the capacity of both partners for reciprocal feedback. This statement will now be detailed.

Innate arousal mechanisms, species bound, furnish the bases for the release of response-originating forms of reciprocal feedback (for instance mother offering breast relates to baby's rooting movement of the head). Characteristic tendencies to activity in *turning, intensity, modality*, etc. become organized and mutually regulated in the course of interchange, the role of biological rhythms for early psychological development having been well established by Peter Wolff's research.[13] Signals and signs, forming consistent connotative (non-denotative) communication of messages recorded and responded to are, in human babies, forms of pre-language. Language must build on this. Real language must be preceded by meaning formation and will take on a denotative function, i.e. will make use of signifiers.

The semantic relationship is born – i.e. the denotative function emerges — in my view, from the basis of this initiative to an encounter on the part of the human infant which I have called the 'search for response' reaction. This is, I shall now add provocatively: the baby in search of a meaningful self. Justin D. Call, presenting his data at the 23rd International Psychoanalytic Congress in Stockholm, in 1963, already called attention to the baby's spontaneous contribution to the mutuality of relationship between infant and mother.[14] This has become the locus of more recent research on early socialization processes of humans. Alongside symbiotic phenomena (later 'animism' of the young child) the essential ingredient of emotions differentiating *self* from *other* may be delineated right from the beginning of extra-uterine life. This fact has been negated, maybe because the differentiation of the baby's *own* body and *own* search is grafted on and proceeds at the expense of the adult's experience of dependency and need control.

Neurological considerations also affected the conclusions, it being pointed out that only subcortical centres are functional in the first months of life. The argument applies to the whole range of experience: thus perceptual acumen, space and object discrimination, etc., were equally not to be expected in the small baby, as science seemed to confirm.

In the meantime Fantz, Bower and many others using ingenious strategies of research have revealed what fine discrimination and judgment the baby is capable of exercising. This may result, in the neonatal period, from data like gross quantity of neural input rather than specificity of stimulus.[15] The net result is nevertheless that some appraisal of the world is on its way from the beginning. At the same time more recent studies have confirmed that the baby has much greater interest in appraising the personal, i.e. emotional, significance of the stimulus configuration — *empathic* carer *concerned* with a living infant — than in stimulus pattern configurations (Fantz's checker boards, or Bower's trains and balls).

The child's ability to perceive, explore, and investigate is not evident, in the earlier months, to the naked eye but is becoming clearer each day to researchers. In the *Annual Review of Psychology*, 1974, D. M. Baer and John C. Wright summarize that year's baby studies with the words: 'Research shows the now familiar outcomes of greater than expected orderliness and competency and earlier than expected development of skills.'

Still, research on the baby's emotional capabilities lags behind. I believe this is due, as in other instances, to the fact that research has preconceived emotional life in the context of adult emotions: structured affects contemporary with concrete imaginative contents. If we would stop to consider the *relation* the child establishes with whom or whatever is to be defined as *mental* (even remembering that this relation is served by subcortical centres of the brain) we would get much further in the study of emotional life and development.

How the child forms relations and maintains emotional intercourse with adult partners has been studied recently in many ways. For instance, research at Edinburgh University conducted by Trevelyn and his co-workers has restated that the infant is entirely self-expressive in his contacts with mother in the first four to six weeks of life. From then on he takes up mother's imitations of *his* expressions (not the contrary) and imitates them. A mutual understanding of these act-sequences is thus created. From this exchange of 'imitations' (which observers have noted presents a rhythmic sequence of repetitions and pauses) emerges for the adult a pleasurable feeling seemingly pertaining to this gestural intercourse, by some called proto-conversation. Proto-conversation is seen, for instance, ritualized in the 'peek-a-boo' game and other traditional 'games' of infancy.

Another instance of discovery of the 'surprising' initiative of infants in establishing a personal relationship through gestural dialogue is found in the research of J. B. Watson. He and his co-workers became interested in the course of studying reinforcement mechanisms in early infancy[16] in a non-solicited characteristic of their protocols and which they called the baby's 'contingency analysis' or 'for short, the Game'. The 'Game' designated an apparent seeking out and pleasure in finding, on the part of two-month-old (or older) babies, of *those responses contingent* to their own repeated *initiative*. Initiatives became interspersed by pauses and were followed, when contingency was the case, by an outburst of cooing and smiling. Conversely, pouting and even crying followed in some cases when irregular, i.e. incongruent (contingent, interspersed with non-contingent) responses were verified by the baby who seemed to reject the fact that he could not predict *a* consistency in *the* relationship.[17]

Of course this is very far from proof for the subjective 'feeling of being a self' of which J. M. Burgers writes in *Science*.[18] But we do find a distinct emotional register of personal initiative and affirmation as of boundaries of an autonomous self.

The child's 'generalized classing of all reinforcers as social reinforcers (i.e. to be smiled at or rejected) may well be a reasonable if temporary response', reviewers Wright and Baer wryly comment, using

J. B. Watson's 'behaviourist' language. In his words: if the baby is committed genetically to seeking and discriminating response-contingent stimuli, this will happen outside the laboratory only in the presence of a human partner, to establish a human relationship.

Just like monkeys in Harlow's experiments and ducks in Tinbergen's manipulations, human babies' expectations could be subjected to illusions to focus more clearly their essential need for exchange. Thus, following his basic need, a human baby will interact with a mobile and play with that construct *as if* it were a human responder.[19]

J. B. Watson, reflecting on his material, coins the important verification: it seems that people become important to the infant because they play 'the Game'. In this view, *the game of reciprocal feedback for which the human infant is genetically equipped* explains interpersonal relationships and is − by inference − the condition of personality development. Because, in the sense of implication of a responder, we are speaking of 'own-actions' on the part of the baby which are intending a relation with an intending or rejecting *other*. I am not speaking of conscious ego-function but referring to expressive co-actions described in the language of the encounter, that of initiative and intention: emotional resonance phenomena, 'implicit' (as opposed to public) behaviours, relations between *me* and the *other* who in my intention is located as *recipient* and *co-actor* of my autonomous experience. In using this wording in this paragraph I am saying that human communication (as initiated by the human infant very early) goes beyond mere interaction, i.e. exchange of signals, but may refer to the expectation of a two-sided modification of behaviours *with the implication of a mutuality*, in the sense of an expectation that the other will *complete one's own actions*. This expressive affirmation of *own self*, given in the expectation of response coming from the other, would be place for the *pause* which child workers have observed as a need of even very young infants interacting with them. This pause, felt as a question-mark by the 'participant observer' when not accepted or respected, is followed by 'fear' or withdrawal.

It seems necessary to reflect that to the emergent self of an infant (person) *relating with*, i.e. implicating another person, things also become important and become agents of intercourse in the service of play. First in mother's hands and later in the power of the more and more capable infant 'things' will enter into the 'self' constituting dialogue. Through the use of imagination the old 'now I − now you' rhythm of reciprocal feedback which implicates the 'other' (hopefully) will be observable in the use of toys. These will take on the function of sustaining the basic interpersonal relationship out of which emerged 'selfhood'. Later, the relationship with God — if searched for — will take on this same rhythm or will not be sustained.

Going back to my contentions on 'attachment' viewed by some as the earlier mode of human social intercourse, I can now make my point clearer. 'Attachment' presents a system of preferential communication. In the second half of the first year, 'mother' becomes an absolute reference point (and all-encompassing shelter) which confers consistency to the world and guarantees safety to exploratory excursions.

But attachment of the *real* self of the child to his 'mother' cannot be formed if the child's more elementary need for the experience of spontaneous initiative to implicate himself with a responder has earlier been frustrated or subjected to factors of incongruence. If some spontaneous movement to initiate and hold pre-language, gesture-act-conversation, has not been sufficiently responded to — the child will 'attach' to the 'mother' on the basis of his so-called false self. A strict bond of dependency on 'Mother's' protection then 'welds' mother to baby, and an anxious one-sided appeal substitutes for psychological intercourse. The world then becomes a dangerous seducer and novel things appear as threats to the baby's dependency needs. 'Attachment' of this kind designates a false relationship between baby and his world, and is not the necessary stepping-stone for future autonomous intercourse with a social world. One can put this in other words: children presenting high levels of anxiety in what seems 'attachment' behaviour and who will not or cannot play, are not really 'attached', that is, conscious of protection and fearful of loss, but are spectres in search of a self.

It is my contention that some anxious, dependent adults presenting different types of neurotic symptoms, but with an immense inexplicable psychic pain, are infants in search of a self who never could form a real and needed attachment. Real 'attachment' as a developmental instance only makes sense if the baby has attained the stage of emotional differentiation of self. If this is not the case, the bonding that results will function as a protective artefact, obstructing the exploratory capacity of the infant while sustaining the symbiotic unity with the mother in a disturbing fashion.

The activity called play should proceed according to the model of pre-verbal interchange dialogue between infant and mother (the duet), thus supporting the gradual differentiation of self through the use of an 'other', a transitive not in itself important thing related to mother. The toy thing may even be 'animistically' confused moment by moment with mother or parts of mother's presence — that is with those parts of the mother which are present (i.e. as 'inner objects') in the child. In this way proto-conversations with the all-encompassing mother of the symbiotic phase may in time dispense with the direct presence of the material mother. This occurs as the baby's body, his gestures and movements and later outer objects used in play, take on 'animistic' roles, in extension of the baby's *mental* movement of appraising meanings, which are in turn exchanged with the more and more externally differentiated mother.

Given this background, the mechanism of play may be seen as communication through the process of 'animistic' identification (a mental process) of the child's inner experience with parts of outer reality and the ensuing in-and-out-going dialogue between these two.

As noted, through this mechanism the child may grow out of the infant-carer symbiosis in so far as he develops new contacts with a 'third', the transitive other, the toy object. The 'third', the outside object-person, distinct from mother and distinct from self up to a point, starts out by being just part of the child's mental life (i.e. an inner object) projected on the outside in a 'search-for-response'. Mother was, to begin with, part of the feeling of totality of the child (a kernel self) but she made possible contact with 'things' outside the dual-unity. She becomes more distinct, a partner to experience, as contact with a real outside other — the 'third' — is effected. At the same time, because toys permit manipulation and exploration, perceptual differentiation and conceptual development may be set on its way. One may express these same contents in other words: 'inner objects' projected on the outside world are appraised for their meaning and compared in time and space with percepts more and more consistent. These again are responded to as to partners to the dialogue ('animism' is still effective through the years). Thus poles of in-out-going mental intercourse are constituted again and again in what Freud called 'reality testing', which is, in this view, the essence of mental development.

Here lies the importance of the social impulse and of play. In the play of very young children one can observe the rhythm of 'now-you-now-I' or 'now-there-now-gone' activities with 'contingency analysis' most clearly, taking on the format of primitive proto-conversation.

It is my contention that in group analysis the characteristic rhythms of 'contingency analysis' seen in early childhood may be re-experienced in so far as no task is set to the group outside the analysis of spontaneous communication, which may take on the form of emotion-centred proto-conversations. The group-analytic psychotherapist establishes the matrix of interchange in such a way that spontaneous initiatives of communication may find an outlet. No onus is placed on feedback needs except those pertaining to the very conditions of communicability in the setting of group meetings. In this 'matrix' channelled by the reality structure of events being communicated, a lot of exchange of personal resonance takes place. For instance, exchange which takes on the following form: *A* 'I feel sad about . . .' *B* 'You feel sad.' *A* 'Yes, I feel sad and I remember. . .' *C* 'That makes me understand. . .'

Communication of contents of experience in a free-floating manner become a form of recovery of 'search-for-response' reactions leading to the analysis of self-contingency with a sort of new encounter of the other in a common matrix. It will take on the classical form of implicit in-out-going proto-conversation (i.e., I am feeling — you are feeling; I am moved by — you are moved by; I go out — you go in; me — you), an emotional exchange rhythm from which selfhood first emerged and which, recovered in the group situation, may be seen as a form of promoting intrapsychic adaptation of ego-function.

Ego-training in action as described by S. H. Foulkes would, in this view, be understood as a bringing into consciousness the unconscious search for selfhood, an emotional activity (hopefully) set in motion in early childhood and going through many 'vicissitudes' since those early days.

Thus, in this view, going back to the title of the present paper, group analysis works in the sense of a cure for emotional difficulties because it promotes the conditions for individuals to take up again the primitive rhythms of now-you-now-I proto-conversation, thus recovering a necessary contact with the core of self-constituting experiences as they exist in nature.

Notes

1 In this he concurred with S. Freud.
2 Even though he does, sometimes, seem to propose further qualifications.
3 I.e., the 'large group' may confirm to these basic tenets.
4 Winnicott's concept of the 'facilitating environment'.
5 M. R. M. Leal (1976), 'An enquiry into socialization processes in the young child', unpublished doctoral thesis, University of London.
6 'Neural structures', in M. R. M. Leal, op. cit., p. 156. Even adult neural function oscillates between activity of a more primitive core of the brain, organized reticularly, with random connected

elements and 'tonic' characteristics of transmission of signals and that of other structures of the brain connected in parallel, showing more exact 'phasic', i.e. ordered, relationships (ref. to R. M. Bergström for the use of these terms).

7 'Hospitalism: an enquiry into the genesis of psychiatric conditions in early childhood', *The Psychoanalytic Study of the Child*, 1, 1945, pp. 113-17.

8 Konrad Lorenz (1969), *On Aggression*, London Methuen (paperback), p. 118.

9 For example: visual following is, initially, a subcortical function, like pupil dilation.

10 Padraic Burns, L. W. Sander and G. Stechler (1972), 'Distress in feeding. Short-term effects in caretaker environment of the first ten days', *J. Am. Academy of Child Psychiatry*.

11 M. R. M. Leal (1976), in her unpublished doctoral thesis (University of London) 'Social development of the young child', unfolds this view of emotional development summarized in the next pages.

12 R. M. Bergström (1969), *Brain and Early Behavior*, Resonance Mechanisms of the neocortical system may function as the first regulative centre of the brain and as releases for cortical functions. Academic Press, London & New York.

13 Peter H. Wolff (1967), 'The role of biological rhythms...', *Bull. of Menninger Clinic*, XIV.

14 Justin D. Call (1968), 'Lap and fingers play in infancy. Implications for ego-development', *Int. J. Psychoanalysis*, 49, pp. 375-8.

15 G. P. Sacket (1963), 'A Neural Mechanism Underlying Unlearned Aspects of Visually Controlled Behavior', *Psychological Review*, 70, pp. 40-50, for example points out that pattern discrimination as studied by R. Fantz could function on a subcortical level.

16 In summary: one side of the infants' pillows were wired to mobiles calculated to call a baby's attention. If the baby moved his head on the pillow, the mobile would present its tricks.

17 J. B. Watson (1967), 'Memory and "contingency analysis" in infant learning', *Merril Palmer Quart.*, 13, pp. 55-76.

18 J. M. Burgers, 'Curiosity and play: basic factors in the development of life', *Science*, 1966, 154, 1.

19 It is important to bear in mind that this project was set up in the context of real families, with mother cooperation fully solicited and obtained. Some mothers, having had other children, reported that their baby was beginning social intercourses earlier than they would have expected and with rare enjoyment.

Chapter 13
The concept of the therapeutic community: variations and vicissitudes

Tom Main

When you honoured me with your invitation to give this, the first
S. H. Foulkes Memorial Lecture, I did not hesitate to accept. I knew
Michael Foulkes for over thirty years and I decided that it would be
forgivable to allow myself certain reminiscences evoked by memory
of him; not not so much about him as about the first years when we
worked together, ate together and talked much before taking our
separate ways in friendship.

My title was offered impulsively and I shall not confine myself
strictly to it. The vicissitudes occurred before as well as after the birth
of the concept: the variations later. I should also make clear that whilst
this lecture is offered to the memory of Michael Foulkes it is not
primarily about him.

Some time in 1940 when Britain was fighting for sheer survival a
phobic infantry soldier was sent to a psychiatrist by his Medical Officer
at the request of his Company Commander. The psychiatrist reported
back as follows: 'This soldier should be excused from handling a rifle,
should be allowed to wear carpet slippers and should be given duties
within a two-mile radius of his home in Bradford.'

This putting the patient first and above all else ('*le malade, toujours
le malade*') is in the medical tradition we all hope to find in our doctors
when we are ill, and it is in this tradition that the great studies of man's
organs, his bodily systems and their pathology have been made. This
medical model has brought great benefits to mankind and it would be
folly not to value and pursue it always. But we must also respect its
limitations. My example shows how it can be inappropriate sometimes
to the point of being ridiculous, even harmful for the welfare of the
patient's fellows and for his own dignity. The idea of a soldier contributing to a desperate war effort by marching about a suburb of Bradford,

197

wearing carpet slippers and having no rifle, is not easy to contemplate without amusement. Our psychiatrist was ridiculous but only because he had been half-educated, taught to think in terms only of a single order of system — the individual — and therefore unable to respect other levels of human systems. Even a passing acquaintance with general systems theory would have helped him.

Every individual can be conceived of as a system of interacting subsystems — such as the circulatory or muscular or respiratory systems; and in bodily illness it is a matter for diagnosis which of the subsystems is disordered and needs treatment. The individual is however something more than the sum of his parts, and indeed every human system is more than the sum of its parts. This is because human systems and their subsystems are in active relations with each other, and react dynamically in complex ways to create larger systems, be it a cardiac system, a whole human system, a family system or a hospital system. In each case an understanding of the system is not to be achieved by serial study of the isolated parts.

Each human system, no matter how complex, may thus be viewed on its own, or as an interacting element in a higher-order system which itself can be studied as a whole, but which in turn will be an element in a yet higher-order system. In the hierarchy of systems each level of subsystems, systems and higher-order systems has its own legitimcy, its own unique laws and dynamics and pathology and its own claims on us for singular concepts designed specifically for that particular level. Once we have chosen one system for study — say an individual, or a workgroup — we should bc clcar that it will not be well understood nor usefully treated by techniques or insights derived from work with systems of a different order in the hierarchy. An expert on the renal system is not thereby equipped to treat a whole person's unhappiness, nor is a psychoanalyst automatically equipped to treat a family nor a family therapist a disturbed workforce; nor, to reverse the direction, is a social anthropologist automatically equipped to understand the nature of a single person. Each expert is competent only with his own level of system.

It will be clear that sometimes the disorder inside one system will secondarily disturb one or more of the systems with which it is dynamically related, perhaps of a lower order, or a similar order or a higher order. In diagnosis we therefore need to distinguish those disturbances which arise from inside a system from those which are merely reactive to the strains created by other related systems, and to be capable of locating our diagnosis accurately at the appropriate *level* of system and in the key system of that level. Put in more human terms the individual may be disordered because of matters inside himself, or his disturbance may be essentially reactive to another person's disturbance — let us say that of his wife. His own disorder, whether internal or reactive, may create strains for nobody but himself or it may affect other family members. He may again create strains for a higher-order system, let us say his employers, or be under strains from that. And so on. Our neurotic soldier was disordered within himself as a system, and this had led to his being under further strains from his relations within the higher-order system. Our psychiatrist proposed to alter only the latter, whether it liked it or not, in the interest of his patient. Hence the slippers and no rifle. He was however utterly blind to the intolerable strains in the higher-order system which this soldier's illness created and which were expressed by the Company Commander's referring him. Indeed he invited the higher-order system to accept even further strains and to alter its life-and-death aims to suit his patient. As you can imagine this invitation to the Army to alter its aims was declined and the soldier was discharged, no doubt to everybody's satisfaction.

In the scientific hierarchy of human systems, none has any particular merit over another. Each has its own right to recognition. But to make unconfused and appropriate observations about human distress we need some awareness of the different orders of system as well as observational instruments, concepts and tools of intervention singular and appropriate for each order; and now we may avoid sterile prejudgments and lofty generalisations about the singular importance of one particular preferred system for every kind of distress. And we might come to discriminate and value and cease to preach about the superior or inferior merits, for instance, of individual treatment or marital or family or group or social treatment in various circumstances. We can indeed grow the hope of respecting each level of diagnosis and treatment for what it can and cannot do, and of deciding when one level of treatment would be more appropriate than another in a given situation. But if we can make diagnoses only at *one* level then we shall only have *one* shot in the locker, and *one* automatic prescription no matter what the human trouble.

My army anecdote was from 1940, and concerned the relentless use of the medical model with which all doctors entered the Army. But we learned. By 1945 there were few Army psychiatrists who thought only in terms of personal systems, even those who worked only in hospital. Many psychiatrists were now thinking, somewhat confusedly it is true, in terms of lower- and higher-order systems —

although they did not use these words. Psychiatrists working with units in the field were all aware of certain battalions in which individual breakdown was common and of others in which it was rare. A few psychiatrists, of whom I was one, tried to find out what made this difference and began to think in terms of larger social wholes, to recognise their several identities and to study the ways management systems in various battalions improved, maintained or damaged the morale of battalions as wholes as well as the mental health of the individuals who comprised them. We had easy access to such matters as the rates of sick bay attendances, absence without leave, drunkenness, minor indiscipline, severe military delinquencies, venereal disease, breakdowns and various psychosomatic illnesses. It was not difficult to notice how these figures rose and fell more or less together, and collectively were reliable indices of unit morale. In addition it was possible to get informed opinion at various levels about which units were in bad shape. In the field one met well-run units of high group morale which carried significant numbers of men with manifest personal breakdown who refused to report sick, and who would soldier on effectively; and other units which combined to make an unhappy and inefficient whole with generalised reactive miseries, complaints, delinquencies and psychosomatic disturbances, even among men with records of stable personal health. Such facts alone revealed the limitations of the medical model of individual illness and personal treatment, and almost all field psychiatrists added to concern for the individual a concern for various social systems of the Army. This was a new world. The facts were there, the demand urgent, and we doctors were ill-trained for helping in these problems. Social science was in its infancy — was psychiatry then to become more a social psychiatry and less a medical one? We were ignorant but willing. The concept of social system had yet to be devised and we had to be content with vague ideas such as social wholes, group morale, social climate, corporate identity, although we were much helped by the generously offered concepts of social psychologists like Eric Trist and later by social anthropologists like Adam Curle.

I worked chiefly with the infantry's common fantasies and soon it was possible to ask questions, one of which is relevant for this occasion. What was it about the various battalions which made the difference in promoting or failing to promote the health of the individuals within them? It had nothing to do with social structure nor with the width or height of the administrative hierarchy. These were inescapably identical in all units. Nor had it anything to do with roles; these, and the powers and responsibilities they carried, were defined precisely and without blurring by the Army and were the same in each battalion. Nor had it to do with role relations; these too were also laid down. Thus it was not the type of social hierarchy, nor role-rigidity, nor the role relations, which explained why a particular battalion was therapeutic or anti-therapeutic. It seemed to be something both more vague and more important than these; it was the culture, the human *folk ways* by which the systems were operated, the quality of *human relations* inside the social structure. These differed widely and clearly made the difference to the humans in the several units. I shall return to this matter of culture later.

Our rather vague concepts, such as group morale and group dynamics concerned higher-order systems, and this change of system was new and far from easy for us doctors. It is difficult today to remember that at the time it involved effortful major conceptual shifts in psychiatry which had hitherto ignored groups except as the sum of personal states. Not all psychiatrists were able to make these conceptual shifts, but those who did were rewarded by a new exciting viewpoint – the possibility of a social psychiatry concerned with the study and treatment of social entities and their effects on individuals as their subsystems. This viewpoint did not require the abandoning of interest in the inner life of individuals; rather it led to an additional new major interest for those who were already committed to a psychoanalytic interest in the inner life of man. But this did not arrive suddenly. It grew slowly out of the urgent demands of the situation and the facts in the new field before us. In the Army the individual was cared for, trained, and valued highly, but only as a contributor to *group* purposes, and for the survival of his group as a whole he must be risked, perhaps even to lose his life. There were also economic pressures on psychiatrists to recognise groups. Soldiers were many and psychiatrists few. In addition the existence of groups was inescapable and insistent; sections, platoons, batteries, squadrons, companies and so on. Every man belonged to a group and derived some of his identity from it. Every time a psychiatrist saw an individual he knew – unless he was blinkered like the 1940 psychiatrist in my anecdote – that he was seeing a member of a group of singular skills and purpose. It was not surprising that under the pressure from such facts various psychiatrists began to observe and think about and to experiment with groups and to grasp at the scant available knowledge about groups. In the clinical field a little-known foreign psychoanalyst, Michael Foulkes, now highlighted as a pre-war pioneer of small-group treatment, was posted

to a hospital – Northfield – and given his majority and full facilities
to apply and develop his studies into the unconscious life of groups
and to teach. Joshua Bierer was similarly employed for a time at Northfield. And in diverse non-clinical work with groups there were more.
John Rickman, the distinguished psychoanalyst, had begun his interest
in group unconscious functioning decades before at the leaderless
meetings of the Society of Friends, and even during the 1918 revolution had studied the effects of group discipline systems in a Russian
village. Familiar with Trigant Burrow's psychoanalytic work of the
1920s on group therapy, he had become vastly experienced in the study
and resolution of unconscious tensions in the leaderless small-group
activities and group discussions devised for officer selection by his
distinguished psychoanalytic pupil Wilfred Bion. Rickman generously
taught and inspired others, especially that small band of workers who
after the war founded the Tavistock Institute of Human Relations and
became applied psychoanalysts. Henry Dicks studied the psychological
foundations of the Wehrmacht and Nazi culture; John Kelnar later did
similar although lesser work about the Japanese. A. T. M. Wilson undertook operational research into field problems and then brilliantly
devised and supervised a country-wide network of units as transitional
communities, imaginatively using small groups in the re-culturation
of thirty thousand socially dislocated soldiers – the returned prisoners
of war. It quickly became clear to all involved that to be effective in
the desperately urgent matter of war, we needed deeper understanding
of unconscious motives, fantasies and object-need in groups as well as
in individuals, and we drew heavily on psychoanalytic thought, even
developed it. We had to be practical, and as J. D. Sutherland later
remarked, there is nothing so practical as a good theory. He and a score
of others took part in this change towards a social psychiatry simply
because the work was there demanding to be done, but I will mention
only a few more. Sutherland himself worked thoughtfully and intens-
ively alongside Ferguson Roger with small groups in Officer Selection;
and H. E. Bridger, a mathematician and educationist experienced in
field command, was energetic as a military observer of groups in Officer
Selection. He was posted to Northfield in 1945 after Foulkes, and
about the same time as I was. By 1945, outside the Army, British
psychiatry went on, as it does today, in proper pursuit of the medical
model and largely untouched by interest in higher-order human systems
or the unconscious life of man. But there were a few kindred spirits.
T. P. Rees of Warlingham Park was seeking for a social approach to
avoid the anti-therapeutic and maximise the therapeutic effects of

mental hospital life. Major Elliott Jacques, a psychiatrist of the Canadian Army, was eager to join his thinking and his future with ours. Maxwell Jones, a civilian inundated with neurotic patients at Mill Hill Emergency Hospital was experimenting with psychodramatic portrayals of selected patients' individual problems followed by large-group discussion of these. And at the centre of the movement was Ronald Hargreaves, a brilliant imaginative stimulator and military administrator of this higher-order psychiatry.

In passing, most of the sixteen I have mentioned were called by Henry Dicks 'Members of the Invisible College'. Four are dead, five later became heads of Institutes concerned with groups, seven took academic chairs in psychiatry or an allied social science, and eight were or became psychoanalysts.

But now to Northfield, where the concept of the therapeutic community was born. It was a large military psychiatric hospital in Birmingham commanded, when I arrived, by a regular army medical colonel who was not a psychiatrist. The administrative staff, the clerks, orderlies, cooks, sentries, educational staff, physical trainers, paymaster, quartermaster were all soldiers of various ranks, while the Matron and her nurses were all of officer rank as Army nurses. I was sent there in early 1945 when our armies were at the gates of Germany and it was at last clear that the war was to end in victory for us. My relevant Army experience had involved studies of group morale and discipline during battle, especially of infantry in the western Desert, and I had had experience of arranging the systems of care of psychiatric breakdown in the British and Canadian armies in the battles of Western Europe. My instructions were to help the development of group studies at Northfield and I was to take charge of one of the two divisions in the hospital. The social structure of my division was clear. As a Lieutenant-Colonel I was responsible to the Commanding Officer, a full Colonel, not only for overall treatment of patients but also for promoting and directing the morale, discipline and work of all – patients and staff – in my division. I had several Majors – senior psychiatrists – in turn responsible to me in the same way for their medical and nursing officers and men and patients and in turn their Captains and Lieutenants were responsible to them. Each Major cared for one or two wards and the nurses were in military hierarchy and responsible to him. His ward patients were responsible, through their medical officers, to him. Proper saluting occurred all round, although it was not always of a kind a Guards sergeant-major would have been proud about, especially when offered or returned by unusual soldiers like Major Foulkes. Inside this clear hierarchy, as in all military units, the officers and soldiers were also people and of course variously enjoyed or disliked each other. The hierarchy was an indestructible ordered container with a prime medical purpose and what went on in it was human life, some of it psychotic, much of it severely neurotic, which could variously be stimulated, enjoyed, tolerated, disciplined or treated. When I got there I found the usual hospital convention of regarding all the staff as being totally healthy, and if wayward to be overridden, reproved or disciplined; and all patients as being totally ill, and if wayward to be tolerated as not real people and treated with charity, drugs or psychotherapy – that is to say social splitting and the projection of health and illness were part of the social order. Group-treatment abounded, based on and inspired by Foulkes's teaching.

There was much indiscipline in the patients. Their psychiatrists tolerated this and excused it on grounds of illness, but my non-psychiatrist commanding officer and his non-psychiatric military staff throughout the hospital were far from content with the psychiatrists' tolerance and sought to have soldiers who got drunk or got out at night or were violent or mutinous or had untidy wards to be put on charges and sent to the orderly room. I had a difficult time with my (superior) commanding officer over such cases almost every morning. I also had a difficult time with my (inferior) officers who were most resistant to my idea that they also should study indiscipline as a psycho-social problem. Rather they wished to tolerate it and study it only at a lower-order of system, that of individual pathology which they treated individually and in small groups. As a senior doctor I should protect the patients from the insensitive mind of the military so that my psychiatrists could get on with their important therapeutic work. After a few weeks of this heavy going I began to feel misjudged by all and grew ill-tempered.

Then I heard that a disorder in the higher-order system of the hospital had preceded my arrival. It had been treated by discipline and had been hushed up as shameful but it had not been studied as an intrasystem problem; yet once I heard about it I understood both my commanding officer's need for me to ensure more discipline and my psychiatrists' contempt for mere administrators. I report it now for it is no longer a painful matter of anger and scandal but an interesting event from which a lesson – important for the therapeutic community concept – is to be learned.

The first Northfield Experiment had already been conducted by Bion and reported in the *Lancet*. Faced with a wardful of neurotic soldiers, who in Army terms were slovenly, undisciplined, idle and dirty in ways that were outside the medical model of illness, Bion had viewed their behaviour not as the result of massed personal illnesses but as a collusion by a group with the staff requirements of the hospital where the staff are to be well and self-disciplined and patients are to be ill and disordered. He told his soldier patients at a daily ward parade that he was fed up with them, and henceforth refused to be responsible for caring about, treating or disciplining delinquent behaviour which was theirs and not his, created by them and not him. He would not punish them but would no longer visit them or their ward. He would be available for discussion in his office every morning but only for soldiers who presented themselves clean and properly dressed. In the next weeks they severely tested out his resolve. The ward became filthy, beds were not made for days, absence without leave and drunkenness increased and the whole hospital staff was alarmed and angry. It was chaotic, but Bion plainly did not get his DSO in the First World War for nothing and he stood firm. As the days passed a slowly increasing number of properly dressed soldiers began to attend his office and some NCO patients soon begged him to intervene in the chaos. He refused to take over their indignation and military ideals but discussed these with them as their property and so freed them to own the conflict between fecklessness and efficiency inside them. They slowly grew responsible for themselves and their ward comrades and now formed their own discussion groups and rotas and disciplinary systems. Cleanliness and order, no longer imposed from above, grew inside the ward group. The military super-ego, no longer projected onto higher authority, had returned to the lower-order system and Bion's ward became the most efficient in the hospital. This was a bold imaginative innovative experiment, not in permissiveness about illness but in the delegation of health and responsibility to patients. But now for the secret, the part that was not written up, but which I regard as of equal importance to that which was. The unpublished secret is that Bion was sacked from Northfield. Neither the commanding officer nor his staff was able to tolerate the early weeks of chaos and both were condemning and rancorous about Bion's refusal to own total responsibility for the disorder of others. The resultant rows in the commanding officer's office came to the notice of higher authority and after Bion had left the commanding officer of the hospital, then a psychiatrist, was also sacked, to his great indignation. Once I heard about these rows I was tempted to hold partisan views about them, but then realised that my very job was to study such higher-system tensions and that at the level of the higher hospital system this first experiment had been a technical failure although a brilliant success at the lower ward system. Bion had been therapeutic for his ward but anti-therapeutic for the military staff, successful in his ward, a lower-order system, but highly disturbing to the hospital, the higher-order system. To put it another way he had failed to work at and get and maintain social sanction for his deeds. Thus anti-social in the wider sense, he had been the author of his own social downfall.

Both abroad and in this country I have often been asked by an enthusiastic doctor, sometimes eminent, to use my authority to help him maintain his 'good' therapeutic community, in a ward or a hospital wing or a whole hospital, and to throw my weight behind him and his progressive staff in a fight with the 'bad' reactionary others in the larger whole, either inside or outside the hospital, who cannot stand the strains and want the work stopped or modified. Always the doctor has failed to get and maintain sanction for what he is doing. Usually he and his staff simply feel innocent, righteous and wronged. Sometimes the patients will join them in projecting all evil outside the community and now in idealisation of the community, all will proselytise about its benefits. There is now no hope of owning and examining the destructiveness or other negative matters inside the community — for these have been projected outside, lost to group ownership and examination and treatment. This failure to gain sanction is in the end not only destructive of wide-eyed awareness and treatment of group problems, but self-destructive for the very existence of the lower-order system; because it is anti-therapeutic for the higher-order system. It needs emphasis, and is to be neglected at peril, that every higher-order system is related hierarchically to the lower-order system and has to be studied and helped in its own right if it is to understand and support the work of the lower-order system. David Clark, author of *Administrative Therapy* and of the phrase 'Therapeutic community approach' made this very point in his first essay about educative duties of the senior psychiatric administrator who is squeezed by those both above and below him.

At Northfield I now knew that my commanding officer was aware that his psychiatrist predecessor had been sacked. I began to understand his anxieties about the therapeutic goings-on in his hospital, in which soldiers discussed things in an undisciplined way as equals with their officers in groups, questioned openly the way things were and were permitted ill-discipline by their psychiatrists. And I began to think that this was why he did not check his military staff's plain disapproval at the way psychiatrists did not stamp out their soldier patients' indiscipline. In this I was wrong and later realised it.

At this time Northfield was not a therapeutic community, only a community in which therapy was occurring, mainly in groups. I was still concerned however only to further the innovative group treatment of patients and naively hoped that if I could educate my commanding officer he might persuade his staff to be more tolerant of therapy for patients' ill-discipline. I spoke now more freely to him of the technical problems we were tackling and shared more of my uncertainties with him. At my invitation he manfully sat in on certain groups but remained sceptical and still sometimes raged at me over events in my division and at the failure of my officers adequately to discipline their men.

In both divisions of the hospital many groupy things were however happening. Psychodrama was in enthusiastic general experimental use; for it was new and had to be tested. Sociometry was used to measure and arrange groups of patients for work-tasks. Michael Foulkes, the outstanding therapist and teacher in my division, went on treating the patients of his wards in small groups. He knew much more than any of us about treatment and we leaned heavily on him and he taught us, in small staff groups. His remarkable capacity for requiring others to puzzle with him, his calm, his patience and his ability to tolerate uncertainty and confusion and to think his way through small-group events drew all the Northfield psychiatrists to learn from him. Martin James, Susannah Davidson, Mildred Creak, Stewart Prince, James Anthony, Pat de Maré, Armstrong Harris, F. R. C. Casson, Millicent Dewar and many others now distinguished and well-known workers sat at his feet as I did whenever possible. He was inexhaustible. Simple but important questions were settled. Was this not several individual treatments done in a group? Was it treatment by the group? Or was it rather treatment of the group as a whole? What did he mean by a group identity? Or a group theme? It was difficult to understand that he could think about two systems at once, the small group as a sensitive whole and its interacting human subsystems, that he could study the dynamic group matrix and also listen to the unconscious content, or follow the development of a group and also of the individuals in it. Because of Foulkes, group treatment was used for the majority of patients in every ward. In this memorial lecture I would like to emphasise that before and during and after Northfield he was blazing a trail that opened up a whole new order of human system for therapy – the small group. It was new then, indeed revolutionary. There were other trail-blazers — for instance Slavson — but it was Foulkes more than anybody in Europe (Bion never had pretensions about group therapy) who was steadily developing it as a proper clinical study. Foulkes had a later benign interest in other systems, of lower order (for instance in studies of families) and of higher order (for instance ward groups) but he did not seek to become expert in these. He *knew* about small groups and marvelled about them and could not understand why anyone should miss such a good thing. At Northfield he came only slowly to the idea and was not excited at first that a whole community might become therapeutic. Indeed he teased me and described my first efforts as 'highly organised chaos', but soon after the idea was promulgated he leapt at the thought that small-group discussion could be a basic tool for promoting it.

The work of Harold Bridger gave him further opportunity. Fresh from cool studies of the way leaderless groups tackle work problems and create their own leaders, Major Bridger with a small staff was posted to Northfield to help develop group activities. The word spontaneity as used by Moreno in his reports of children's play-groups was in vogue, part of an end-of-the-war climate which accorded Bridger freedom to facilitate the emergence of spontaneously formed action-groups of patients. I have to remind myself now that at that time of dependence on leadership it was daring to do so. Bridger however was skilful and confident about the hidden unused capacities in people. For instance he sat alone and waited for days in a large room with a new notice over the door announcing it as 'The Club', and when soldiers came in and asked him what club it was he asked them what club they hoped it was and then offered to work with them to make it so. And soon because there were many hopes there were many activities. There had been staff-organised occupational therapy but now, with Bridger, patient-organised group projects began to flourish. Hobby-groups formed, a newspaper group, a chess group, a drama group, a printing group, a typing group and so on; a painting group advised by Sergeant Bradbury, now lecturer at the Tate Gallery. Bridger also explored work ambitions and discontents and facilitated spontaneous work-groups for specific projects. Real work for the hospital and the neighbourhood began. Groups for carpentry, bricklaying, metalwork, glazing, decorating, catering, the first industrial therapy groups (at the nearby Austin Motor Works at Longbridge) now began and carried along each member; while job-trials for desired but untested jobs in civilian life were arranged through the local labour exchange.

Not all went well; because the groups contained human beings troubles abounded. These troubles were at various levels of system. Some inefficient individuals were recognisably preoccupied with intra-personal problems, such as personal mourning for multiple comrade-loss, and other such intrasystemic problems which were not *primarily* disturbances of relations with their present objects. They could be respected and supported by groups but only slightly aided by examina-tion of their present relations with groups, and individual treatment was offered to them alongside the continuing total programme. Then in some work-groups, as in therapy-groups, inefficiencies, quarrels, arguments, sulks and walk-outs occurred, and now Foulkes gladly accepted my invitation to become an *ad hoc* trouble-shooting con-sultant whenever crises or inefficiencies appeared in work-groups large or small. Sometimes he needed to do major group therapy to help groups carry disturbed individuals, but sometimes only the group-system was disturbed. I will always remember his pride at resolving before lunch a morning's lightning strike in the stage group (of painters and scene shifters), which threatened to wreck an evening's vaudeville. With Bridger he had moved on from therapy groups to the treatment of action-groups.

But now we began to use groups for a third purpose – the examina-tion of other crises and inefficiencies, whether clinical or administrative and whether these involved staff or patients or both. Once a problem was discovered an *ad hoc* group was called of all concerned and affected, to seek out what had gone wrong. Almost always we would find that interpersonal tensions inside the group were hidden behind a so-called material event (and often projected on to some superior in the military hierarchy). Thus we slowly replaced blind hierarchical discipline of un-understood annoyances by the discipline of informed common sense.

Northfield was now, by 1946, a hospital of a new kind, in which both patients and therapeutic staff sought to explore in a way never attempted before the unconscious tensions which pain the lives of individuals and of the small groups they find themselves living in. It looked – as Foulkes teased me – highly chaotic, but both hospital divisions were in fact busy, efficient and relatively free from unresolv-able internal tensions. It was also innovative and exciting. Yet in the larger hospital there were strains. Something was not right.

In the large community many of the non-therapeutic military staff, administrative, domestic, maintenance and to a lesser extent secre-tarial, were of low morale. Some openly resented patients taking the right of action or decision over matters of work or equipment and it was true that patients would organise group discussions and activities which regularly overlapped or contradicted or interfered with the military staff's wishes, duties or expectations. The staff was being ignored and after all they, not the patients, were there to run things. Treatment was treatment: fair enough; patients should be treated kindly because they were ill but they should do what they were told; when things went wrong staff should step in and correct things and show the way; it should not be left to patients to sort out troubles; things had gone too far; it was the psychiatrists. My commanding officer made it plain that his tolerance was now at an end, and I began to think about Bion's fate. I had resolved however not to share it, however noble that would be, and wondered how to preserve the tottering sanctions for our work. I tried not to feel either too guilty or too righteous and wronged − without great success − and to free myself to think about my commanding officer's plight. Why could he not control his staff and support our work? Why had this otherwise pleasant, intelligent man become regularly stupid, angry and theatening? Why did he feel himself threatened by events? With some difficulty I ceased to be so self-centred and began to see that he had troubles of his own. He was responsible to his seniors and he was also the inevitable repository for all the grumbles and discontents of his military, administrative and artisan staff which I and others, safe in our military rank and medical authority, had ignored or brushed aside as reactionary. Yet he was being fed by his military juniors with these discontents as their head of the administrative and domestic hierarchy of the hospital which was separate and distinct from the therapeutic hierarchy which I represented. I then realised that the almost daily rows he and I conducted were about unresolved tensions, not between him and me as individuals but between the lower-order systems of military and therapeutic staff fed upwards and into us. These tensions between the administrative and medical subsystems had been regarded by all in the subsystems as nuisances, issues not for open study or scientific scrutiny but for noisy argument or silent power struggles. He and I were thus being unconsciously required by our own staffs to be their champions and to conduct these struggles on their behalf; and we had been unconscious of this. So now there was a new set of problems. How to ensure that the tensions could be examined, perhaps resolved, where they began − between people in the lower hospital systems? How to put the lower-order military staff in touch with the needs of the lower-order therapeutic staff and patients? And vice versa.

What were the unconscious fantasies each system grew about the other? How much blind mutual projection of evil was going on and distorting perceptions of each other? One evening I suddenly realised the *whole* community, all staff as well as all patients, needed to be viewed as a troubled larger system which needed treatment. Could all people in it move to consideration of each other's plight and benefit from opportunities to examine the conscious and unconscious uses each was making of others? Could the total institution become therapeutic for all? Clearly we would need a *total* culture of enquiry if we were regularly to examine, understand and perhaps resolve the tensions and defensive use of roles which are inevitable in any total system. Today the concept is well-worn, and the term I coined for it – the Therapeutic Community – is now in use so widespread that the coinage is somewhat debased; but then it was new and for me at least it was a sudden insight, a major conceptual shift, a new way of viewing events in a hospital. It also demanded appropriate viewing instruments. At this level of system – a whole community – techniques of investigation and intervention had yet to be devised; indeed today argument about them still seems wholly proper. But now at Northfield interstaff relations and staff-patient relations began to be seen as legitimate matters for regular, indeed essential, study, whereas hitherto only patient-staff, patient-doctor and patient interrelations had been. This attempt to create an atmosphere of respect for *all* and the examination of *all* difficulties would be a long way from the medical model, whereby disease is skilfully treated in anonymised people under blanket medical compassion and served by a clinically aloof and separate administration.

I would like to have been able to report great things at Northfield as the result of this new concept, for the time and the climate were right. Foulkes and his numerous trainees had often had nurses sit in on therapy groups – although only as healthy beings – and Bridger had always had certain non-therapy staff sit in on task-group discussions. But I was posted to other work a few months after arriving at the notion of the Therapeutic Community and I was able to gather only its firstfruits, although I had other opportunities later in civilian life; and in 1946 I published the idea tentatively at the request of Karl Meninger who was a fascinated visitor to Northfield. In the few more months I was there military staff began to participate in examining tension systems. They slowly but increasingly joined crisis-groups and ward discussions, and now task-groups and hobby-groups with patients. It became ordinary for orderly room clerks, staff sergeants, Matron's staff, secretaries, military cooks and orderlies and night staff, yes, and sometimes my commanding officer and his adjutant, to be seen in groups alongside patients and psychiatrists. Many were raising personal issues or plans or complaints relevant for their work and discussing how they were affected by others, and were being listened to. I held two ongoing staff training groups to examine current work-tensions, one for nurses and one for orderly room and catering and artisan staff. The Rehabilitation Officer from the labour exchange (for now the war was over and demobilisation would soon begin) also sat in on a special interest group. The military staff's grumbles and ideas and problems were given equal status to everybody else's and they themselves were seen increasingly as people working in legitimate and inescapable roles and inevitably contributing to constraints and freedoms in the whole system. They now argued and discussed with patients and others and came to recognise their own total usefulness. *People* of individual style and potential and work needs were better recognised where *stereotypes* of the sensitive sick and the insensitive staff had tended to exist.

The higher-order system as a whole began to examine its tensions and became better able to understand and therefore to sanction the activities of its various subsystems. My regular Army commanding officer began to accept his proper kudos from psychiatrists who visited Northfield, but I would be exaggerating if I said he became fully at ease. Of course there were always problems to examine. When I left Northfield not all military staff were able to tolerate discussion of tensions that involved them; but, more importantly, there were similar resistances in some psychiatrists about regarding the woes of the staff as being not only inevitable but legitimate even though these had major effects on the unconscious roles accorded to their patients. It would be pleasant to think that had we worked further on this traditional split between therapeutic and non-therapeutic staff it might have been narrowed, but such a belief would also be foolish and, yes, grandiose. Every community requires and in subtle ways gets certain people to act as containers for its conservative wishes on the one hand and its progressive wishes on the other and tends to require, create and maintain various split-off sectors of itself into which it can variously project evil, disorder, financial discipline, illness, inefficiency, health and insensitivity and to encourage these in subtle fashion to create trouble. Thus internal personal conflicts are socially externalised. Indeed resolving such social splits, especially in so far as patients may be used as containers of childishness and helplessness or staff as containers of all brains and ideas is inevitably an essential never-ending task in any hospital community aiming to be therapeutic. But Northfield went quite far with this task and now I shall leave it with an anecdote about how one small split was resolved. I remember with gratitude that in a group which met to discuss a crisis over food a staff corporal-cook patiently explained to an irate private soldier that I had no choice, as a senior officer, about doing a weekly inspection of my patients' kits and personal cutlery, nor about criticising his favourite ward sister for neglect of her military duty of seeing that his own missing cutlery was replaced. After hearing the corporal, the soldier turned to me sympathetically and asked if I liked the job of inspecting kits. When I said 'No, but I have to do it', he went on, 'And you've got to do it well or you're in trouble, aren't you? And if you do it well we hate you, don't we? What a rotten job you've got.'

Certain obvious lessons from this, the second Northfield Experiment, were clear. Psychiatric patients are sick as people, but not sick all through. Their skills and healthy parts need not be ignored in daily life in hospital as in the medical model which concentrates only on their sick parts. Delinquencies, fecklessness, clinical crises, dependence and irresponsibility in patients are forms of participation in hospital systems. Informed patient participation in organising and running the ways of a hospital is possible. Staff-based discipline is mostly unthinking but will be used whenever staff anxieties are unbearable. Staff anxieties are inevitable in psychiatry and staff defences against these tend to take rigid forms. Staff anxieties are legitimate and need regular exploration and treatment. Patients and staff tend to require and become entrapped in collusive splitting and projective defences against pain; health and illness, good and evil, strength and weakness, activity and helplessness, leader and led. Heads of organisations are liable to be unconsciously required to own or act on the tensions of their staff. Groups and sub-groups and whole communities tend to project ownership of hostility outwards and so lose the hope of insight. Using group discussion a culture of enquiry can be promoted for the better recognition of the humanness of all and better understanding and resolution by all of clinical crises and social upsets. A whole hospital community can be antitherapeutic for the people in it even though the medical model is well pursued and their diseases are well treated. By altering the relations sought by staff and patients a hospital can become less antitherapeutic and more therapeutic for all the people of the hospital, and yet can still allow room for the appropriate practice of the medical model. So much for the lessons.

Since Northfield many more experiments with therapeutic

214 The concept of the therapeutic community

communities have been made. A sizeable literature has grown up, and in preparing this lecture I have much appreciated an appraisal of it by Richard Thompson which I hope will soon be published. He points out, as have others, that the term 'therapeutic community' is in such widespread and diverse use as to be almost meaningless; and has been used for many situations of which a few he quotes are: a West African Yoruba village, the school, the church, the prison, centres for drug addicts, community care programmes, general hospitals, admissions units, geriatric hospital care, the *world* and, by allusion, corrective camps. So the term is now a bandwagon, and I cannot clear up the resultant confusion.

Thirty years after Northfield the term 'therapeutic community' owes most of its meaning to Maxwell Jones whose innovative work, especially with psychopaths at the Social Rehabilitation Unit of Belmont Hospital, and voluminous writings about his own precepts and practices have much influenced others. His personal skill as head of that and other units, together with his publications, have earned him deserved status and if I have some important reservations about some matters he holds dear, I must record my admiration of his pioneer efforts. The work in the USA of Goffman and then Caudill, both social scientists, has also been powerfully influential in getting doctors to accept the propriety of viewing higher human systems as wholes with properties and laws of their own; Stanton and Schwarz have demonstrated in detail that staff relations can have massive effects on patients' syndromes and that these cannot be noticed by a non-psychological staff seeking to pursue only the medical model. In this country R. N. Rapoport, another social scientist, has also illustrated how the study of social systems can illumine many phenomena that would otherwise be regarded as due to the patients' illnesses. Yet the work of social scientists in surveying hospitals as social systems has not always been fundamental; some of it has been essentially only indignant or impatient and reformist about superficial behavioural phenomena, not truly compassionately investigative of deeper unconscious needs and conflicts. One ill-effect is that here and there one may find psychiatrists attempting to explain away interpersonal conflicts as due to defects in the social structure, rather than setting about the more painful task of examining the multipersonal origins of conflicts which often hide behind the blaming of the social structure. Criticising the structure seems often to be merely a seductive avoidance of the problem, a projective defence *against* studying more painful interpersonal conflicts in depth. The blurring of staff roles, which Maxwell Jones advocates, seems to me another device for avoidance of conflict studies to allow the illusion of staff innocence and the disownment of responsibilities when the going gets rough. Is it not an example of the defence of appeasement against persecutory anxiety, the fear of being attacked for being active and clear? Persecutory anxiety is inevitable in group life, especially in executives, as Elliott Jacques has shown; indeed this and other anxieties are inevitable in all human relations, but they cannot be resolved by appeasement, only acted out. Better if the staff fears about pursuing a role which is essential but unpopular are brought to light, discussed openly and studied in depth by all as human equals. Of course unconscious fantasy roles are always sought and offered both up and down the hierarchies of all human systems and of course they bedevil recognition of real people in real roles and thus hinder realistic relations. But they need analysis, not appeasement by role-abdication. In General Hospitals defences against staff anxieties, of appeasement and of role avoidance or diminution may not much matter (although the work of Isobel Menzies suggests that they do), but in psychiatric hospitals where emotional matters are the essence of the work, where the strains can be overbearing and where staff acting-out of anxieties is liable to be a daily event, the regular scrutiny and resolution of prevailing projective fantasy systems within groups seems essential for promoting the health of both patients and staff. Altering social structures and roles under flags of permissiveness or democracy to appease projections is liable to endanger study of the problems which arise in attempts at real adult relations between people in essential functional roles.

I agree heartily with Maxwell Jones about the need to avoid authoritarianism but again this is not, as is commonly suggested, related to social structure. Authoritarianism is a specific way of relating to people, an attitude towards them, a personal characterological or cultural but not an organisational matter. It is not produced by any particular hierarchical structure, but can operate in any. (Authority is of a different order of fact, a matter of special skill or knowledge as recognised by others. It can lead to pride or the fear of being envied, and to apology, but it is not, like authoritarianism, primarily an attitude towards others.) Responsibility downwards for tasks (that may involve care of subordinates) and upwards to *people* is however an organisational matter, and in my opinion tasks should be carefully and clearly designed in several linked roles at necessary hierarchical levels to suit the overall purpose required by an organisation so that the resultant social structure will both make sense and be clear to all. Whether the

216 The concept of the therapeutic community

responsibilities in such a clear system will or will not be discharged in an authoritarian or a humane manner will not be the result of the structure's clarity but will depend on the character of people and the *culture*, the folkways of the organisation. Clarity of structure and of roles actually enhances efficiency and minimises conflicts between roles and about responsibility and allows the examination of remote manoeuvre. I join the inability of Raskin to regard role blurring as therapeutic, for a community.

My own conclusions, from the early studies of different battalions to later experiences with different hospitals is that it is not the structure but the *culture* which is decisive for the human relations on offer. A clear known structure and appropriate roles with inescapable responsibilities is needed for efficiently operating any task; of repressing prisoners or rehabilitating them, of caring for sick children or healthy ones, of distributing food parcels or bombs, of saving lives or running an extermination camp. Efficiency requires clear unshakeable roles for all. Efficiency is relevant but insufficient for a therapeutic community. Over and above efficiency and social structure, the culture — the *ways* people in the structure relate to each other — is decisive for whether the people in the structure treat each other's roles with distance or warmth, enmity or friendliness, respect or contempt, concern or coldness. Not the structure but the *culture* will decide, for instance, how far, when the various orders of staff and patients meet together in role but in joint consultation, they will truly respect and be interested in each other's work and listen to all ideas as *personal* equals; and how far they will truly discuss doubts and resistances and enlist and evoke each other's talents and invite participation in various tasks and how far not. The culture will greatly influence how far delegation of powers and responsibilities is or is not adequate, and how far people trust each other and how far they watch each other suspiciously. In my observation, culture, the folkways of operating an organisation including the informal ways people relate to each other, is decisively influenced by the way the organisational heads relate to others. As they relate to their immediate subheads, so will these relate to their staffs and their staffs to their juniors. In a therapeutic community where a culture of patient honest enquiry into difficulty is needed, with interest in understanding in depth the personal systems, the systems, group systems and the community system, it seems essential that the culture be initiated by the heads of the community organisation. They are thus required to practise true personal respect and professional concern for each other and for their immediate subordinates. They will be ready to recognise and investigate their own and their immediate staffs' successes and failures with dispassionate interest but not blame, to share with them their own uncertainties and problems, to demand their participation in facing problems and fashioning plans and to require that their team think with them about the work to be done. The word charisma does scant justice to such an orientation of self-conscious responsibilities. I am glad to say I have met several such heads and cultures.

And now to end. The term 'Therapeutic Community' has become used so variously that it is almost meaningless today. None the less, just as it was a conceptual breakthrough when Freud through free association conceived of studying a whole human experience and not simply the parts which interest a questioner; so treatment of groups in free discussion is the extension to a higher-order system of this very breakthrough. The therapeutic community concept is, I believe, yet another extension of Freud's breakthrough, for it also rests on the study of unconscious matters. Its hallmark is not a particular form of social structure but a culture of enquiry. It both requires and sanctions instruments of enquiry into personal and interpersonal and inter-system problems and the study of impulses, defences and relations as these are expressed and arranged socially. It is good to remember that one essential instrument for it — group treatment — was fostered and nourished and defended by Michael Foulkes, in whose memory I gratefully offer these remarks.

Chapter 14
Michael Foulkes and the Northfield experiment

Pat de Maré

I first met Michael Foulkes thirty-three years ago at Northfield, during the hot summer of 1944 just before D-Day. Writing this brings back these memories with a particular poignancy. His death at the age of 77 from a heart attack was painless and occurred suddenly in the middle of answering a question at a seminar of close colleagues. He had already asked me a few weeks previously to write about Northfield and I am filled with the sad realization that the opportunity to have heard his comments is lost forever; lost, too, is the theoretical companion to his last book which was published in 1975, which he was in the process of preparing.

My first meetings with him were brief since I was *en route* to Normandy. He was, in fact, the only person who witnessed the 'North-field experiment' throughout, from his instituting it in July 1943 to his demobilization in December 1945. Even so, in the middle of the enormous tensions of war just before D-Day and before getting to know him as well as I did later, I was very aware of a feeling of intense excitement which surrounded his whole personality. He seemed to transcend the conditions of those oppressive days and sparked off in those associated with him an enduring inspiration and enthusiasm. It was not simply the charisma of an original and creative thinker which I think we all recognized, but the impact of contact with a mind that far exceeded in depth and breadth any that we had had the good fortune to come across before. This was coupled with the fact that he was in the throes of creating a dimension which was to affect the whole subsequent course of psychotherapy, for, in introducing the psycho-social level by an actual operative technique which could be simply applied, he succeeded in turning the whole direction of psychotherapy towards a new dimension. In asking us to look at the other side of the coin, which till then had been unacknowledged, namely the context within which a psychotherapeutic relationship might or might not occur – he drew our attention to this new and crucial issue, made particularly apposite by the very circumstances in which we found ourselves: war. Northfield was a building with enormously long corridors so that, busy and pressurized by his daimon as he was, he seemed always to be on the trot.

He was compactly built, his movements were quick and light and he was an excellent tennis player. He had considerable charm and was good looking in a puck-like way, with greying hair and extraordinary grey-blue eyes. He had a powerful but fine Jewish nose and sensuous lips; his teeth were set widely apart, and he would often smile with a slightly mischievous expression. He spoke English with a German accent but with an extremely good command of words, since he was keenly interested in the appropriate choice of words. He would struggle for hours at a time over a particular term – for instance the use of the word 'catalyst' or 'matrix' or 'group-analytic psychotherapy' which was the name he finally assigned to his technique. Once he had become involved with a topic, which was very often, he talked in a breathless way, breaking off with an occasional sigh, when he might look down at the floor, become quiet and absorbed (and I would wonder if he was bored by some comment that had been made). In addressing a person he would turn his head and look at them fully and directly and gave the impression of concentrating his entire attention on what they were saying. In fact his capacity for concentration was enormous, but (I think) he found it extremely tiring. For instance, once in a group a certain author had said that the book he had embarked on needed only a further fortnight's work to be completed. 'Only a fortnight's work!' gasped Michael. He had written his first book during a fortnight's holiday in 1947, more or less without a break, smoking continuously, and at the end of it he had his first, fortunately slight, heart attack.

He felt passionately about ideas – for him there was no facile split between intelligence and feeling – and he appeared to feel with his thoughts and think with his feelings, as if thinking were an instinctive, enjoyable process. If someone said something which interested him his whole body seemed to move forward as if he could actually see his ideas. When he was involved in a discussion he would talk with a rush of words, half-thoughts and free-associations, in a sort of confusion to which he would allow full range. To people's consternation he would sometimes lecture like this, baring his mind, allowing himself to be confused, worrying over an idea. In discussions he would continue tirelessly in this style sometimes for hours, which could be exhausting to others as well as to himself. Finally matters might either be left in the air, when he would be both dissatisfied and apologetic, or alternatively he would suddenly punctuate the flow of thoughts with some startlingly clear conclusion as if this had been obvious to him all along.

He would pick people's brains blatantly but would be more than happy if they returned the compliment. His manner was quiet and gentle and I never once saw him angry or harassed, but he would occasionally get ruffled by an idea. Sometimes he would ask a disconcerting or enigmatic question, the reply to which would appear to disappoint him, and this slightly ironical or mischievous smile would appear in his expression; sometimes, on the other hand, he would jump at an idea and would be flatteringly pleased. He hardly ever stopped thinking and planning, yet his thinking clearly tired him, and he would rub his eyes with thumb and forefinger and blink as if the brightness of his ideas were exhausting.

The first time I met him was in a consulting-room at Northfield. It was shortly after I had seen him in the distance at one of the long tables in the dining-room, talking to Martin James. It was a sunny spring day and he was standing over some coloured powder paints (for he said in passing that he was interested in certain colour tests). The impression he gave was of lightness, happiness and excitement and I found myself fascinated by the way he talked, by the refreshing way in which he put things, a feeling of originality and pleasure and of personal friendliness. But I was not prepared for the feeling of intense liking that I had for him. He was 45 at the time and I was 28. In the course of conversations, this faintly mysterious smile of his would often flit across his face and there would be this ironical inflection in the tone of his answer, which might be followed by a short humorous laugh. For instance, on one occasion in describing people's contributions to a discussion he commented: 'You know, some of the things they were saying made no sense – people often seem to get seriously preoccupied with absolute rubbish', and he gave this laugh, which had a peculiarly unprejudiced warmth and gave an impression of complete acceptance of them as people.

God knows what he thought of me! I do know we had a mutual regard and friendliness. I was both a communist and a roman catholic and I had started a personal psychoanalysis with Karin Stephen a year before the war. I was deeply interested in groups, in which I had participated in London and Cambridge as a medical student during the 1930s. He was obviously amused by some of my more glaring inconsistencies but he never scoffed at them. Indeed he seemed to enjoy arguing through some of my dilemmas and agreed 'in principle' (a word he often used) about some of my more radical views, particularly about banking and the economic system. Of all people, as a refugee he had reason to be sensitive to the political implications of war. I would argue that adjusting to reality implied adjusting to a status quo, in this instance a highly wasteful war. He had been in the German army in the First World War, and here he was with the British Forces in the Second World War. The issues of fascism, communism and democracy were at stake and it was only a matter of chance that we found ourselves on the side of the 'goodies'. He would tease me by saying that he had not yet analysed a communist whose political stance was not based on some form of neurotic conflict. He pointed out that we were not an experimental or research unit but a military hospital working under high pressure where the practical needs of the day had to be met. His attitude towards the Nazis was that of the psychoanalysts in Berlin who had declared that 'in good times we treat them and in bad times they rule us'.

In fact during the early 1930s before leaving Germany in 1933 Michael had been acquainted with members of a Marxist sociological group called the Institute of Social Research, which included Horkheimer, Fromm, Adorno and Marcuse and which has since become known as the Frankfurt School. They attempted to integrate Marxist with psychoanalytic theory. Their institute was in the same university building as the Institute of Psychoanalysis (in Frankfurt). Marcuse, who was a somewhat younger man, bore a striking physical resemblance to Michael.

Although the idea of groups had been very much in the air in London of the mid 1930s, Foulkes had little notion of the movements associated with them. Apart from gestalt, field and holistic theory, two papers in the mid 1920s by Trigant Burrow in which the word 'group analysis' was first used (and of whom Foulkes said, 'He was the first person to put the group into the centre of this thinking. That was and remains his great merit'), two plays, one by Pirandello and the other by Gorki, the two psychoanalysts Wender and Schilder working in the USA, he had to rely on his own resources for inspiration, and he had no direct sources of information other than the situation at Northfield itself.

The story of Foulkes's first attempts to apply group therapy in 1940 is interesting. In the late 1930s he had often considered how rewarding it would be if his patients in analysis were to hear each other's free-associations. He had always looked upon psychoanalysis in the light of life as a whole, and not upon life from the perspective of the analytic couch. Finally in 1940, in the waiting-room of his private practice in Exeter, he decided to invite his patients to carry out as far as possible 'free-associations' in a free-flowing dialogue. It was there, after his first session, held in a waiting-room at 23 Dix's Field, that he felt an historical event had taken place in psychiatry. 'But', he added afterwards to his wife 'nobody knows about it.'

After two years' work with fifteen patients in a group, he published a joint paper in 1942 with Eve Lewis, a psychologist.

> The concrete realisation of the part which social conditions play in their troublesome problems, the social front of inner conflicts so to speak, gets people thinking in a critical way and makes them experience the part they themselves are playing, both actively and passively as objects as well as instruments of these conditions – an altogether desirable contribution to their *education as responsible citizens* in participating in a free and democratic community.

> The reciprocal significance of the individual and the group was already discovered.

In the same paper they mention group association as distinct from 'free association' and go on to point out that the specifically group features are socialization, sharing, stimulation and exchange, and that the therapist slowly shifts his attention to 'the group *situation as the preferred frame of reference*' (my italics here and above).

In 1942, before Foulkes was called up and before his arrival therefore at Northfield in 1943, there had already been a preliminary attempt made by Majors Bion and Rickman to establish a group approach in one of the wards (and which I witnessed peripherally). This had lasted for about six weeks. I had been sent with some twelve other psychiatrists to a six-month course in military psychiatry which Bion and Rickman conducted. (Five were American, one was Polish and six were British.) During these six months, which were extremely stimulating and which mainly took the form of seminars, Bion and Rickman had launched the 'first Northfield experiment' as it came to be called. A ward was set aside from the rest of the hospital and a 'leaderless' ward system was set up which was designed to display neurosis in the individual, primarily not for the patient and the medical staff but as a problem for the whole group, in this instance the ward – which was then dealt with by discussions at the morning ward meetings. It was a very radical approach and was applied in a manner that proved too radical for the rest of the hospital. The problem of bed-wetting, for instance, was not left to be coped with in the secretive orthodox way by the nursing staff, which increased the soldiers' sense of disgrace and inadequacy, but as a problem for the whole ward which had to be discussed openly at the ward meetings. There was therefore a minimum of nursing staff and aides. Bion and Rickman participated as observers.

The prime reason for terminating the experiment lay in the anxiety of the 'authorities' that such a radical approach would undermine discipline and the last straw came when the dining-hall was left in a state of disorder following a film show and the floor was left strewn with newspapers and used contraceptives. Bion and Rickman were shortly afterwards posted to the War Office to set up the procedure at the War Office Selection Boards for potential officers who, amongst other things, were assessed on their conduct as observed in small leaderless groups, tackling various problems of strategy!

Late in 1944 Rickman was to revisit Northfield at the time of the second experiment of Foulkes. His visit proved highly stimulating and it was not until then that Foulkes became fully aware of the details of the first experiment.

It was typical of Foulkes's whole philosophy that he approached the problem in an entirely different and more circumspect manner in what he called Phase A of the second Northfield experiment. This involved the very modest beginning in 1943 of enlisting the enthusiasm and support of the then Commanding Officer, Lt-Colonel Rosie, a self-effacing, highly intelligent Scot, to introduce small-group weekly meetings with certain of the patients from his own ward which consisted of seventy to eighty patients.

During this phase he was observing a principle he had already thought out – namely to regard the total situation, in this instance the whole hospital, as his frame of reference, and this included *all* the hospital staff, not only the converted but

> those who were remote and stood in some kind of opposition and who made, by the way, an indispensable contribution, too, quite apart from the fact that people were of course not divided into two factions of 'pros' and 'cons' like black and white sheep. They had an overall basis of common ground and enthusiastic devotion in their duties inside the hospital as a whole – as it should be in a good group (1948).

Subsequently in my career I had occasion to regret that I did not follow this principle more fully. Where I had done so at St George's Hospital, the group work reached fruition, but where I failed to do so at Halliwick, the project eventually failed.

His philosophy was to locate the foreground figures against the background as being distinct but *essentially* related and to apply the therapeutic lever wheresoever it seemed appropriate. I am convinced that it was this dialectic duality between relationship and context that constituted the basis for his success. I do not think that this can be overemphasized and is only too often understated. What then happened were five major advances.

First, by seeing all his patients on his ward in groups of eight or ten, he was able to observe each soldier more frequently, which saved repetition and therefore time — in other words all sorts of advantages in matters of expediency.

Second, the regressive tendency activated by individual interviews, which was particularly undermining to morale, was avoided or reduced to a minimum.

Third, therefore, it became apparent that the subtle but vital phenomenon of morale, involving the whole ward, was promoted which, under those circumstances, was synonymous with improvement. It had a totalizing, as distinct from a fragmenting and isolating, effect and there was less evidence of unwilling soldiers challenging discipline on grounds of health.

Fourth, not only did this procedure have time-saving advantages but the individual soldiers did qualitatively better than those treated along orthodox individual lines. In particular, not only was the method more successful therapeutically speaking but it proved strikingly superior in finer diagnostic and prognostic factors.

Fifth, the rest of the hospital became interested and many colleagues, mostly the younger ones, from other wards became more involved and therefore more open and responsive to training. It was during the relatively muted stage of Phase A that I first met Foulkes and it was not till after the BLA campaign was over that I witnessed Phase B, when the whole ward as a community was conducted on small-group lines and which distinguished Phase B from A. Again it had started off along very modest lines when Foulkes had been given orders to take over a particularly demoralized ward where the psychiatrist had been taken ill and of which the divisional officer had said: 'It is in a dreadful condition and must be taken by storm and I have nobody else to do it.'

What Foulkes decided was to approach the ward as a group and the first thing he did was to wander round it to assess the atmosphere by talking to various patients. He realized that handling a group of this sort entailed a painstaking attention to detail. He established a nucleus of cooperative patients which he formed into a group. He initiated meetings with the nursing staff and encouraged them to participate and to take social histories. Soon the patients began to experience the value of this interest and he was able to apply a measure of discipline by posting one of the more difficult customers back to his unit. Of this ward experience he wrote:

> I believe I am right in saying that already, after six weeks or so, this ward was the best ward in the hospital, it did not matter in what terms this was measured, whether in general morale, behaviour and bearing in the hospital, regular participation in activities, occupational or social or in disciplinary matters such as absenteeism or in terms of psychiatric improvement. It is however very interesting that all these items go up and down together.

Phase B had become organized by the end of 1944 when the Second Front had become an established fact, and all the wards were now being conducted along group lines.

A military staff had been selected who had acquired positive understanding of the psychiatric point of view from experiences with the War Office Selection Boards (WOSB), and in particular of a group-psychological orientation. This enabled all those involved – military staff, psychiatrists and patients – to face the tasks of the hospital as a common concern and the invidious division within the hospital between 'Medical Wing' in hospital blues and 'Training Wing' in khaki had been judiciously dropped.

By the time I returned to Northfield over a year later, in July 1945, the BLA campaign had ended, VE-Day was over, and Phase B2 was in full swing – 'the epilogue of the Northfield Experiment' (so I was not able to see any of Phase B1). I shall never forget the change that had taken place in the meantime. If anything was inscribed on Michael's heart it must surely have been Northfield Phase B2 when the full impact of his genius made itself felt and had blossomed into fruition. The atmosphere of the hospital was entirely transformed. The enthusiasm which I had seen contained in his personality on the former occasion had now flowered and had spread throughout the whole hospital.

I do not suppose Foulkes ever again reached the same level of

intense creative excitement. Nor do I suppose for a moment that it had
that much to do with the convening of small analytic groups in a hospital
setting. On the contrary, it was more out of the application of what he
called 'group-analytic principles' to an entire context which in this
instance resulted in the 'large-scale transformation of a whole hospital'.
This represented the first occasion in which this approach had been
attempted and successfully implemented. Eventually the whole hospital
was understood to be a therapeutic group or community, 'the first
prototype of its kind', which became better known in a term coined by
Tom Main as a therapeutic community.

His capacity to make contact with others was based on this appreciation of the totality of the hospital. He wrote:

> It had been a very significant experience for all those who partici-
> pated in it. Those who did I am sure will agree that the changes
> which went on in both patients and staff alike were nothing short
> of revolutionary. From morning to night and from night to morning
> everything which was seen as relevant was used in the service of a
> true and quite radical form of therapy.

But Phase B2, like all Foulkes's undertakings, had had very modest
beginnings:

> The war was now over and a certain air of apathy had descended
> upon both staff and patients. The hospital life had become stale and
> incoherent: the activity side somewhat departmental and institution-
> alised. What was to be done? I had the good luck on my own request
> to be transferred to the activity department. It became quite clear
> that levers had to be used to bring about an effect on the hospital
> spirit as a whole. *The situation suggested the remedy*. Groups had
> to be formed whose task was directly related to the hospital itself,
> and who from their function were forced into contact and
> cooperation with others. In principle as well as in detail this new
> approach opened fascinating vistas; one had to find one's way into
> the heart of groups or remnants of them and bring them to life
> again. Their influence was felt within a week or two throughout the
> whole hospital, from the Commanding Officer to the last patient,
> orderly or office girl. New life blossomed from the ruins. These
> experiences were among the most interesting I have ever had.

This quotation is from a paper he read to the British Psychoanalytic

Society in 1945. What he wrote about the same experience thirty years later in 1975 is confirmatory of that statement:

> This was an experience which occupied me for day and night for about three years. I hope it will serve as an illustration of principles which have proved of value in psychiatric and other hospitals, as well as in prisons, industry and other institutions of all sorts, especially also educational ones. Of still greater importance are the methods and principles as they grew from the far more subtle observations in small groups, based ultimately on group psychotherapy inspired by the psychoanalytic approach. It is not too much to say that these new methods and principles will increasingly transform the whole of social life, at least in the West. Given good leadership such an objective is realistic as we showed experimentally at Northfield Military Neurosis Centre during World War II. The day will come when whole communities and nations will deal with their affairs in this way.

At Northfield Foulkes's philosophy was to allot to the social side of man the same importance as his instinctual nature:

> The conviction that man's neuroses and their treatment change their form decisively in accordance with the community in which they arise is fundamental for a group approach. This was experimentally confirmed at Northfield. In psychotherapeutic observations, both in the individual and group situations, I could observe how the patients' mind, concerns, attitudes and even symptoms, changed according to the dynamics of the hospital as a whole.

> The large-scale transformation of the hospital developed out of the idea of letting it grow into a self-responsible, self-governing community. No effort was spared to sense the patients' needs to unearth their spontaneously felt desires and urges, to create opportunities for all conceivable activities whether for work, artistic interest, sports or entertainments in and outside the confines of the hospital. . . . The importance of all this from a therapeutic point of view was that the patient was at every step brought face to face with a social situation; thus the relationship of the therapeutic group in the narrow sense towards the hospital changed, the smaller unit becoming more definitely orientated towards the larger community of the hospital. The exact way in which the small group

changed and re-circulated itself towards the new conditions in the hospital was one of the most interesting points to observe. This showed how the individual person's mind is conditioned by the community in which it exists. Groups were confronted with each other. Many patients improved so much under this management that not only individual treatment but even psychotherapeutic group sessions tended to dry up and become subsidiary to the work project, ward activities or social activities of the hospital. The effect of all these on the psychiatrists' groups was very interesting too. . . .

In 1964 Foulkes was to write, somewhat sadly it would seem: 'It happens that much of my earlier experiences and experiments were conducted under military conditions, in conjunction with the introduction of group psychotherapy into the psychiatric services of the British Army. What had been a cooperative effort during the War lost its unity afterwards.'

Certainly subsequently in my own career I was only to experience anything like the same excitement of Phase B2 at Halliwick in its hey-day sometimes, and at the social club at St George's and a large group at the Institute of Group Analysis which met weekly for a year.

What, then, are these group-analytic principles which in being applied to a hospital context had such enormous repercussions? At the time it was not possible to grasp the full implications of these events though I have little doubt that, from many things Foulkes said, he himself had a very clear visionary realization.

Since those days in which the environment had forced itself upon us in the form of warfare I think we have lost ground. We have become more academic, less empirical, superficially more established, but less rooted, less attuned to certain social realities, less political and less cultural in the best sense of being citizens, less prepared to recognize that, though the war is over, the dispute for this more dynamic and comprehensive approach is still going on but in a very muted form; the apathy which descended on Northfield at the end of the war in Europe has continued. Basically the contribution of Foulkes and Northfield was the handling of a new dimension, the social, the cultural and the political in relationship to neurosis. Neurosis in isolation is a relatively uninteresting condition and it is only when its true nature in relationship to context is 'located' that its meaningfulness begins to be revealed, when meaning itself becomes located as the experience of individual and context, establishing a relationship with each other.

This was the significance of Northfield. This was what the excitement was about but this was only a beginning!

I realize today that what I had witnessed there was a man vitalized by the discovery of this crucial issue, of the link between the deepest 'vertical' levels of the intrapersonal psychoanalytic with its 'horizontal' transpersonal social context.

His description of group-analytic psychotherapy in his last book in 1975 was that

> group-analytic psychotherapy is a method of group psychotherapy initiated by myself from 1940 onwards in private psychiatric practice and out-patients clinics. It grew out of, and is inspired by, my experience as a psychoanalyst, but also it is *not* a psychoanalysis of individuals in a group. Nor is it the psychological treatment of a group by a psychoanalyst. It is a form of psychotherapy *by* the group *of the* group, including its conductor. Hence the name 'Group-Analytic Psychotherapy'.

From this description follow the four group-analytic principles which he was to describe as applicable 'to all forms of human groups even if they are not primarily therapeutic'. These principles are:

1 The total situation is the frame of reference for all operations and for the interpretation and understanding of all observable events. Situation in this connection comprises all the objective reality circumstances and the rules, explicit or implicit, observed in the encounter. (I myself would see this as the contextual structure of the group.)

2 All persons involved in the enterprise, institution or project, must be brought together and meet regularly for full and frank discussion and interchange of information and viewpoints. Maximal mutual awareness and communication is the aim, shared as far as possible by all concerned and therefore enabling the whole group to take an active part in their enterprises. Given good leadership such an objective is realistic as was shown experimentally at Northfield. (I myself would see this as the relationship and the relating dimension, the negotiating processes, the dialogue, which takes place within the context.)

The other two principles concern the leaders using their abilities, in the best interest of the group, 'the group's servant and follower', and the exploration of the situation not as it *appears* to be but for what it really is. Both of these would seem to follow upon the first two principles and are therefore secondary and concern the psychoanalytic aspect of the group. The implication of these principles is simply that they comprise two distinct categories of an inseparable duality, two sides of the same coin negotiating with each other. Never for an instant is it feasible for one to become superimposed upon the other. In gestalt terms the background is represented by the context of the group, and the figure by the relating processes within the group; both are in antithetical interaction with each other.

In brief, what I am saying is that Foulkes at Northfield was legitimately excited not by the application of *psychoanalytic* principles to a whole hospital but by the application of small-group principles which involved the large-scale transformation of that hospital. Theoretically it is crucial to make this distinction since it has considerable implications for the future development of group analysis. This is likely to involve not so much community but a specified large group *per se* applying group-analytic principles to a large-group setting. In no other setting is the inseparable duality of relationship and context made so glaringly obvious. These two categories are distinct and constitute a consistent binary system which can, for instance, be in complete opposition in a dialectic process across a transitional boundary zone.

The psychoanalyst is a transitional object; the group, on the other hand, provides a transitional context. In analysis the relationship is displayed in the form of the transference. In groups, particularly large groups, a duality has arisen in which the context is also made clear and this should be clearly differentiated. I have called it *transposition* since it deserves a name. Freud made the astounding comment that 'hypnosis is a group of two'. Only by telescoping the relationship (of two) with the context (of a group) could he have arrived at this conclusion and only because most groups are at a rudimentary stage of relative mindlessness can the patient succumb to the mindless and ego-less state of hypnosis.

What Foulkes did was to become a liaison officer between various groups, e.g. reflective and activity, moving from 'armchair' to 'open-air' psychotherapy and fashioning a small 'co-ordination group' to do likewise.

What he did *not* achieve was the next step of putting the small groups into a direct primary face-to-face situation with each other. Rather like a shaman he himself personally took on the function of the large reflective group; the mode of communication was indirect, through the other small-group activities, via himself as distinct from a direct dialogue. As he described it (1975): 'To interpret, therefore, is to transfer or to translate from one context to another.' What still remains to be clarified is the nature of these contexts. In 1942 he was describing group therapy as an altogether desirable contribution to people's education as responsible citizens. In his chapter in *The Large Group*, in 1975, he was still writing that the group is perhaps the first adequate practicable approach to the key problem of our time, the strained relationship between the individual and the community. It is now up to us to take that step, viz., the more direct application of principles that Foulkes culled from small-group psychotherapy to larger settings, where the emphasis is less upon psychotherapy and more upon delicate civilizing processes.

Chapter 15
Historical perspectives of group analysis

Helle Munro

After an introduction, this paper summarises notes from:
I Comparative psychobiology
II Comparative social psychology
III Archaeology
IV Social anthropology
V History of attitudes to the irrational
It concludes with a summary of Freud's myth on the origins of civilisation and an alternative, based on group-analytic ideas, is suggested.

Introduction

Some years ago I spent a few afternoons with Dr Foulkes in free-floating discussions on our shared interest: how to link the new dimension of group analysis closer to scientific developments in other fields, with particular reference to the evolution of different forms of group formation, and of different concepts for thinking and communication about groups.

Foulkes, like Schilder, Eriksen and Heidegger, regards experience as referring simultaneously to several worlds (Foulkes, 1964). For the purpose of this paper it seems relevant to use four spheres of discourse: the outer physical world, the outer social world, the inner somatic world and the inner mental world. Experiences find simultaneous expression at different levels of articulation from general physiological arousal to precise manipulation, from vague representation of hallucinatory imagery to communication about recurring configurations that can be confronted with subsequent experiences. In physics as in group analysis confrontation with reality defines scientific as opposed to other approaches (Hutten, 1976). Most events combine recognisable general elements with new unique elements, the proportion determining the limitations of prediction and communication. Both the amount known, and the complexity of configuration that can be overlooked, varies within and between groups (P. Foulkes, 1976). A group may keep its specialist information shrouded in mystery. Or as Foucault suggests the strategy may be to produce new information at a rapid rate, to maintain competitive advantages (Gordon, 1977). It is easiest to maintain advantage as an entrepreneur in a relatively unexplored sphere, or on the boundary between two spheres: academic competition has resulted in many new hybrid disciplines (Lewis, 1976).

> Specialisation has proliferated like a cancer . . . the landscape is blurred by the ceaseless activity of millions of professional ants . . . the gap between professional knowledge and [information] for the masses gets steadily wider . . . this therefore, is a moment to take stock (Plumb, 1977).

My main qualification for such a task of stocktaking is, I must confess, my ignorance. At the outset I had a fairly clear vision, based largely on the brave attempts of the BBC at summarising: humanity at the threshold of a comprehensive understanding from the big bang of creation to the molecular control of human endeavours through genes, enzymes and conditional reflexes. As there was little room or sympathy for dynamic psychology in this system it seemed a good idea to attempt an integration.

I read one book and felt I gained deeper understanding based on more data. I read another – and found myself disorientated again, since the facts, the interpretation and the language all differed. When I had digested that and tried out my ideas on friends they inevitably said: 'Have you read . . .?' throwing me back into my ignorance. I can therefore only offer an idiosyncratic selection of anecdotes that seem relevant to my topic. Evolution has to be inferred: we study the living to understand the dead and interpret the remains we have dug up (Lewis, 1976).

I Comparative psychobiology

The human view of animals has varied with the ecological cooperation, competition or exploitation, from the hunter's keen observation to the farmer's dominance of domesticated beasts and extermination of vermin. Collection of specimens for entertainment was fashionable in Egypt at Ankhenaten's time (Hawkes, 1977). More recently we have relied on animal surrogates in rigid medico-biological experimentation which usually is not allowed on humans.

We are reluctant to abandon the Aristotelian postulate that animals can be treated as things as they have no rational minds, though they share with humans the passions that motivate movement (Rohde, 1966). The psychobiological approach has led to impressive advances both in agriculture and medicine. But despite changes in terminology (instinct, drive, release mechanism, regulator) it is still rarely known how 'vapour from the somatic humors penetrate the pores of the brainmatter' and interact with impressions from the physical and social outer world to regulate behavioural processes. The one exception is the carefully studied relationship between sweetness and foraging in the blowfly. Biological needs which are similar in a wide range of life forms may employ very different psychological drive systems. All must be compatible with the habitat to allow survival, but many are totally unsuitable outside a narrow range of variation. In this respect investment in more modifiable learned regulation is superior to inherited 'hardware' programmes (Brown and Herrnstein, 1975). The cost is bigger vulnerability through a prolonged immature stage, and the high fuel consumption of bigger brains (Griffin, 1976).

The physiology of learning is poorly understood but learning and hedonism are related in the very general law of relative effect: a behavioural response varies directly with its own reward and inversely with the totality of rewards acting at the same time (Brown and Herrnstein, 1975). Excitation and inhibition can both be learnt just as both can be innate: it is not more ethical to be inhibited, nor more natural to be uninhibited as has been argued since the time of the Cynics (Rohde, 1966). Some connections seem to be learnt quicker than others, but many animals can learn to respond to arbitrary signals, including such abstractions as colour or form, number or sequence of elements. Learning under high arousal tends to be rapid and rigid. Eventually discriminant inhibition disintegrates with paradoxical or primitive innate behaviour emerging (Brown and Herrnstein, 1975). It is quite easy to give animals irrational, neurotic habits, not quite so easy to cure them again (Tinbergen, 1951).

The problems get much more complex when we consider conspecifics as the stimulants as we must for, for example, reproductive or aggressive behaviours. For the stimulus changes as much as the specimen, with complex interlocking complementary behaviours.

Thus normal copulation in cats depends on the queen repeatedly throwing off the tom, rolling on the floor and hissing, before she allows him to mount again. Without this behaviour the tom carries on and on with intromissions and ejaculations. The oestrus cycle of the female cat, previously regarded as an invariant in behaviour studies, depends on the proximity of other females with a tendency to synchronicity (Larsson, 1973). The duration of the cycle is altered if a male is present. And the effect is altered again if a better smelling male is introduced. Males from a different strain are preferred, to the point of miscarriage if the possibility of a more exogamous pregnancy smells possible. This tendency is stronger in females reared with access to their father (Parkes, 1976). Bowlby's paper on maternal deprivation at the World Health Organisation conference in 1951 inspired much research on rearing (Rutter, 1972). In rhesus monkeys isolation results in severe pathology. With access to peers some heterosexual activity may slowly develop, with immature patterns remaining. Non-genital homosexual friendships include more dominance-submission behaviour than where there has been free access to mother (personal communication, Larsson). The mother reassures her angry or frightened son by sucking his penis or encouraging him to mount (Anthoney, 1968). This may facilitate metabolising of androgen to oestrogen which seems necessary for reproductive activity in males as in females: possibly it acts via a preoptic centre in rats (personal communication from Larsson).

II Comparative social psychology

Laboratory studies are increasingly being supplemented by field studies to compensate for the one-sided, if not pathogenic, conditions of the laboratory. Here the leitmotif is the relationship between the articulation of social space and the ecological balance in physical space. A social group is characterised by the proximity and frequency of interaction between members (Crook, 1968). During ontogeny traditional culture imposes behaviour modifications within the limits given by the phylogenetically evolved gene-pool. The overall group techniques of adaptation must be sufficiently functional for survival (Kummer, 1973). Maintaining group cohesion consumes a lot of time so presumably these recently evolved mechanisms have compensatory survival value (Griffin, 1976).

Field studies are full of methodological problems (Crook, 1968). Subtle communications of intent while on foraging trips are far harder to study than dominance, sex, grooming etc., occurring during rests (Kummer, 1971). Our stupidity in picking up animal communication is shown by the imperfections even of a surrogate bee (Griffin, 1976). We are far from learning chimpaneese, but a chimp can quite quickly learn pidgin Ameslan, with sufficient grammar to satisfy Chomsky's syntax demands (Linden, 1976). Presumably the hope is that creolisation will make it a native language in the chimp colony so we can study natural chimp communication (Trudgill, 1974). The chimps had no difficulty picking up derogatory expressions like 'you nut' or 'black bug'. Uneducated chimps express the same sentiment by throwing excreta at unwelcome intruders. The language of aggression seems to some extent interspecific: birds of many species heed each others' warning shrieks, rabbits ignore a casually strolling fox – sometimes to their cost, as foxes may cheat (not even that is a human prerogative). However, aggression is usually defined as angry, but usually ritualised and not too dangerous, communications between conspecifics (Brown and Herrnstein, 1975). Such aggressive encounters establish dominance rank with precedence for a class of objects, like food, mates, rest-places. But dominance is usually subordinate to possession which is defined as actual, proximal interaction with a specific object (Kummer, 1971). Mates are mutual possessions. Thus a juvenile has a chance of getting a mate if he settles for an immature female who doesn't appeal to the dominant male. One dominant male inhibits dominance behaviour in other males, making larger bands possible. On the other hand a dominant female tends to inhibit mutual attraction between males, so more dominance-submission rituals occur (Kummer, 1971). A breeding population distributes itself over the available habitat according to some territorial arrangement, ranging from the ferocious loner like the spider for whom breeding is a hazardous business, to the megapolis of identical sisters in an anthill. Boundaries are established through aggressive displays with space-related intolerance depending on scarcity of vital resources (Lack, 1966). Less dominant members of the species are therefore either prevented from breeding, or pushed outside the usual habitat where they may succeed in developing new coping mechanisms. With the artificial limitation of space in a laboratory excessive numbers of mice result in such aberrations as impotence, homosexuality, cannibalism, withdrawal or crude heterosexual assault without the usual courtship niceties (Parkes, 1976). Primates show a variety of group formations: monogame pairs, one-male groups and multi-male groups. Sometimes they congregate in larger bands around a scarce resource like a waterhole in drought (Kummer, 1973). For long foraging trips in

open country a large band is most functional, indeed the battle formation of rhesus monkeys make them a formidable fighting force. Such
cooperative defence is based on learning in consexual peer groups,
following rejection of incestuous overtures. The incest taboo seems as
widespread in other social animals as in humanity. Fairly stable rank
order reduces the amount of aggression, but dominance is neither transitive nor total. Rowell suggests that each encounter enforces or inhibits
a dominance pattern. Dominance, initiative and decision-making may
be separate functions (Kummer, 1971).

Opinions differ about the degree to which group structure is determined genetically, by traditional cultural patterns, or by frequent
revised 'contracts'. Crook suggests that protocultural traditions mould
both the social structure and the methods of subsistence. Kummer finds
at least in baboons a hereditary bias; both more agonistic plains
baboons and more hedonic forest baboons have survived in the boundary space without modifying their social order. Tradition has more
survival value than invention where experimentation is dangerous and
learning slow. In the Japanese Macaques juveniles were the innovators
while dominant males were most reactionary, i.e., the last to adopt
habits of food-washing and bathing.

The current evidence is that animals have internal maps or schemata
of spatial-temporal configurations, with recall, anticipation and intention communicated in complex, flexible and versatile systems. It therefore seems an unnecessary complication to postulate discontinuity and
ascribe awareness to humans only (Griffin, 1976). Sherrington complained that Descartes wrote about a dog as though he had never been
friendly with one (Sachs, 1976). Perhaps modern biology is becoming
aware that the reification of organisms under a microscope can be as
misleading as the anthropomorphism of folk-beliefs in other cultures.

In the process of speciation ritual mating communications are of
crucial importance: when two dialects have diverged beyond a certain
point cross-breeding no longer takes place, e.g., in chaffinches who
learn their dialect by hearing other chaffinches – but not by hearing
any other species (Brown and Herrnstein, 1975). The evolution of our
own species is the subject matter of

III Archaeology

Archaeology has recently unearthed much new evidence about the
evolution of Homo Sapiens Sapiens. The picture is rapidly changing

and the old sharp concepts are getting blurred boundaries. 65 million years ago some cataclysmic event ended the Mesozoic era and the 200 million years' dominance of the very successful dinosaurs as well as many other plants and animals. During the Cenozoic era the continents gradually drifted, tore and folded into their present location and shape. The climate was restless, gradually worsening, culminating in a succession of a dozen or more ice ages over the last million years. During this period mammals rapidly spread and diversified (Spinar, 1972). Carbon dating is difficult because of variations in cosmic radiation. This may be related to sun spots and solar winds and could affect climate and mutation rates (Lamb, 1972). In a mosaic of diversifying gene pools cross-breeding may speed up differentiation (Leakey, 1977). Selective mating could have favoured certain traits, e.g. mental agility in hominids (Bronowski, 1973).

The Primate order is first in evidence about 40 million years ago. The Anthropoid sub-order emerged a good dozen million years ago. In the same period the hominid family is represented by Ramapithecus whose bones are found in Asia, Europe and Africa. Around 6 million years ago diversification of many species appears to have been rapid. But there is a fossil gap in the hominid record until the appearance in Africa of four distinct varieties in layers dated 2-4 million years old. While Boisie and Africanus are Australopitheci, Habilis may be classified as a member of the genus Homo. A.Africanus used crude pebble tools, while H.Habilis used sophisticated hand-axes and other tools, varying locally. Together with surviving Ramapitheci these tribes lived side by side until the more primitive members became extinct about a million years ago. Meanwhile Habilis changed into — or gave way to — Homo Erectus whose oldest skeleton (so far) is about 1½ million years old. With a brain capacity some 775-1300 cc, Erectus had technology sufficient for migration over the next 50 millennia to the far corners of Asia and Europe. They appear to have been hunter-gatherers, returning regularly to favourite campsites, where they lit campfires and built shelters. They carefully removed the brains from some of their dead — possibly for ritual consumption. Ochre may have been used for decoration. Homo Sapiens, the Neanderthaloids, may have evolved gradually in several places about half a million years ago, giving way to Homo Sapiens Sapiens over a period from 50 to 30 thousand years ago (Leakey, 1977).

With Neanderthaloids we have moved to the middle Paleolithic period, from the Acheulian to the Levallo-Mousterian lithic technology. This consisted of an elaborate stone tool kit with local variations. The dead were now tied up in foetal position and fenced off from the living space, the body strewn with ochre and medicinal herbs. Care for the disabled is shown by the skeleton of a cripple who reached the respectable age of forty. The modern human seems to have spread through the Neanderthaloid population with resulting hybrid cultures like Mousterian-Aurignacian or Mousterian-Gravettian. Both show chiptools like knives and burins, requiring bifacial elaboration with a toolmaking tool, such as a punch. This stage also sees the combination of materials as in woodlances with flint heads.

The East European Gravettian culture was based on mammoth-hunting, perhaps causing the extinction of the mammoth: one building in South Russia was found to contain parts from ninety-five animals. From this culture come the first preserved art-works: animal and 'Venus' figurines in burnt clay or carved ivory, as well as decorative patterns on ornaments which now accompany the ochre-strewn body in a covered grave. Descendants of this group seems to have populated Asia, Australia and America while the low ocean levels of the last Ice Age still made crossing fairly easy, using some sort of raft or boat (Clark and Piggot, 1970).

In south-west Europe the Magdalenian culture became predominant during the last glacial period. Here the reindeer was the prime, but not the only, target. Technology was mostly characterised by harpoon developments, while religion cum art cum natural science is reflected in the famous cave paintings. As the ice receded these hunters probably pursued the game north, and some 10,000 years later we see similar sequences of pictures on the Norwegian rock faces (Broby Johansen, 1967): naturalistic animal outlines trap the game in imagination and perhaps in magic. Shamans – both male and female – cast their nets, and prey is shown wounded, snared or hung for drying. Outlines are gradually supplemented with surface detail and later occasionally body interiors, e.g., a dolphin is drawn with a foetus inside. A dance costume (hides) with an exaggerated phallus suggests fertility rites – this may be after Aryans introduced horse-worship, which included ritual royal sodomy. As in the caves, artists have used the same surface over thousands of years, and the imagery may be part of some historic consciousness.

The rock pictures in Australia are linked with the myths from the dream time (Lewis, 1976) explained bit by bit to children as they approach initiation.

In south-west Europe culture stagnated or deteriorated. In the northern temperate zone the Maglemosians developed the mesolithicmicrolithic culture by rivers and lakes – plentiful in the post-glacial floods. They perfected bows and arrows with microlithic tips, axes for tree-felling, and boats. Thanks to a thorough multi-disciplinarian approach with pollen counts and carbon-dating accompanying all digs, Scandinavia gives perhaps the most detailed information of the cultural-ecological development over the last dozen millennia (Glob, 1969). As park tundra turned to dense forest, the hunters concentrated on shell-fish by the northern shores, as witness their enormous oyster-shell middens. Both they and the inland bog people were gradually pushed out by the neolithic farmers, slowly migrating from the Middle East, cereal growers were quickly followed by cattle ranchers, with their ox-drawn carts.

The neolithic revolution, agriculture, started in the Middle East where wild cereals and easily domesticated goats and sheep are found. At first it was swidden cultivation: an area was cleared and cultivated for a few years till exhausted. The group then moved on, returning perhaps after a generation when the soil had recovered. The many excavated tells show layers of intermittent habitation over very extended periods.

At the end of the neolithic period Aryan tribes, spreading from the overpopulated South Russian steppes, reached Denmark. Having domesticated the horse and perfected the battleaxe (after which they were named), they established themselves as a small upper class. Their enormous cattle herds threatened the small farmers, and clearing most of the remaining forests they quickly exhausted the soil. At first they fought their cousins the beaker people in Germany. But with the coming of bronze technology they established trading alliances and monopolised the Nordic export of fur, amber and high quality flint which was superior to bronze for many everyday tools. Judging by the ever growing burial treasures, the bronze market collapsed with the introduction of iron. A wetter climate had washed minerals out of the exhausted topsoil and deposited iron in locally mined sand layers under the spreading moors. The final immigration came with the Teutonic tribes that conquered all of northern Europe and brought the Roman empire to its knees. But Mediterranean trade and culture seems to have flourished, absorbing newcomers, until the Muslim conquests cut or threatened sea routes, causing frequent costly battles till the end of the Crusades. This South European recession gave the Vikings their chance for plundering cum trade cum colonisation from South Russia to North America (Brøndsted, 1965). Naturally enough they are described by their victims in most unflattering terms, but the evidence is that they were not only superb sailors, but also good administrators and town planners. For the upper class tools and adornments were well designed, there was a democratic constitution, women had considerable responsibility, freedom and power, and their epic prose and poetry is second to none (Wahlström & Widstrand, 1967).

We have no means of knowing the communications and thoughts of past pre-literate humans, but we can to some extent reconstruct the scenario from artefacts and re-enact a plausible drama. Thus Thor Heyerdahl has made the cultural diffusion theory more feasible by his voyages on balsa rafts and in papyrus boats (Currey, 1977). There seems little doubt that humans were intrepid travellers at an early date, carried goods, skills and knowledge with them, and colonised or established trading relations where possible. But equally, new invention or fundamental revision of ideas took place. The Sumerians invented the earliest monumental constructions we know, the ziggurat. The Egyptians, however, elaborated this into the far more developed pyramid, which has an interior as well as an exterior. With the annual Nile inundations washing away any boundary markings, standard measures based on Pharaoh's royal body dimensions were a must for peaceful coexistence (Lorenzen, 1976). And exact measurement, as well as the invention of stone masonry, was necessary for Imhoteb's impressive structure that has rendered him immortal to this day (Hawkes, 1977).

In European monumental architecture, the first aesthetic articulation was of walls defining an enclosed outdoor space: the royal courtyard of the Minoan trading empire acted as scenario guiding the rigid observances and regular processions from the Royal to the Great Mother's apartments. Articulation of an indoor space is impressively achieved in the Mycenaean graves, originally tiled with gleaming bronze, that reflected the treasures of the entombed, living king in the rays of the rising midsummer sun. When the recycled everlasting deity is displaced to heaven, divine wishes cannot be construed and the interior of a God's earthly visiting chamber is of no consequence: in the Greek temple it is the exterior of the building that is articulated with superb mastery of the three-dimensional effect, e.g., complex compensation for optical illusion: the purpose is to inspire awe in the visitor who may dwell without, but may not enter. It is only with the Roman Pantheon that a building achieves both outer and inner articulation, where we can take possession by a total drama, dwell successively at outer and inner vantage points (Cornell, 1969).

The ancient monuments in Denmark show alternations in burial fashion that almost certainly were imported: some brought by immigrants, others perhaps taught by 'free masons' coming with traders. The un-covered early neolithic cairn surrounded by a henge rises monumentally on a hill top, while the megalithic barrow is covered by earth and only the articulation of the inner space impresses. The flat-topped bronze-age barrows with ramps leading up suggest processions for the Great Mother whose insignia is everywhere (Glob, 1969). Still in the North, primitive dwellings similar to reconstructions of stone-age structures have remained until recently in some areas: the Eskimo igloo and the Lapp skin tent are so perfectly adapted to the ecological niche these people occupy that improvements are hardly possible. In an isolated community in Sweden where Finnish labour was imported in the seventeenth century you still find the odd log cabin with an earth hearth in the middle, a smoke hole above, with ledges and pegs in the wall as the only furniture. In such a hut mother and children would spend most of the long dark winter months, with father venturing out for food and fuel. There was only room for mother to move, and as a witch she magically transformed the raw materials father brought from the wilderness into light and heat, food and clothes. Culture was largely verbal, a rich tradition of tales and myths in poetic language offered the only entertainment during periods of forced idleness (Sundquist, 1962).

By drawing inferences about stone-age life from still existing struc-tures and living memory of their usage we have now come to

IV Social anthropology

Some cultures have continued at a hunting-fishing-gathering, or a nomadic herding and trading, or a migrant swidden cultivation level of subsistence long enough to be described. All seem to be western-ised and disintegrating now. There are, of course, difficulties in linking this material to prehistory. Firstly, many descriptions may be mis-leading because we are too bound by our own concepts, and because our tribal informants may only know part of their own culture and may be unwilling to share their most important knowledge with us – indeed they may realise (like Don Juan) that a PhD student would be unable to understand the tribal mysteries even if the tribe were willing to initiate him (Lewis, 1976). Secondly, all societies today have as long a history as we have, and even if a simple technology serves their survival strategy, they may well have a highly developed, and recently elaborated, culture. This certainly seems true for the totemism of North

America and Australia (Clark and Piggot, 1970).

Like any other species, humanity survives through some good enough arrangement for a breeding population with access to vital resources in its territory, a point stressed by Malinowski. There is no simple relationship between method of food production, surplus wealth, and social organisation. By and large, if the chosen subsistence economy requires continuous strenuous effort (as for the sea indians by the Magellan Strait), little elaboration occurs (in this case the life-style may have deteriorated as they were pushed further south by new arrivals). The more mobile and scattered a population, the more loose and egalitarian the social structure usually is.

The incest taboo is claimed to be universal (Brown and Herrnstein, 1975). Monogamous pairs seem the most widespread basic breeding unit. But a variety of other forms occur, depending on the conditions of ownership (Engels, 1902). The sexual division in the reproductive function is apparently nearly always accompanied by a division of gender roles in productive labour (usually not, as some males would postulate, to protect women, particularly when pregnant or nursing, from physical strain). Hence with changing circumstances men or women may produce and possess the more lucrative surplus commodities. Amongst hunters, as for anthropoids, a territory belongs to a larger band. Game belongs to the owner of the first arrow to hit it, and can be pursued into somebody else's territory. Recurrent wild crops may belong to individuals who first claim possession. At the next stage, nature modified by human labour belongs to the family who did the work originally – e.g., a dug well, domesticated cattle, a sown crop on cleared land. Humans have long memories so claims based on ancestry become very complex, unless priority is given to one line or other, e.g., father's father's . . . father, or mother's mother's . . . mother. Even if the ownership is traced matrilineally, and sisters stay together, a male, e.g., mother's brother, is usually in control and owns the offspring, while the genitor, though known and recognised, may have few rights. With memory of ancestry instead of simple dominance, possession becomes property that can accumulate over generations. The oldest clan member, being nearest to the ancestors, may more or less autocratically communicate how the ancestors want their property administered, or else. . . . The social position of other clan members is defined hierarchically, in terms of distance from some ideal such as the elder-ancestor. Hence a death may dislocate everybody, requiring prolonged rituals till all have passed to their new positions. All important changes of social position may require rites of passage: giving up the old identity, floundering in no man's land, being reborn in a new identity (Lewis, 1976).

With varying individual skill in producing consumer goods, there is usually some system of sharing within the clan. Among the Kwoma of New Guinea the successful pig-hunter never eats his own kill, as he thinks his arrow has polluted it with his own waste which is poisonous to him. It is shared out amongst his relatives according to fixed rules and thus eaten before it rots. The hunter gets prestige for his skill. We may find the reasoning odd, but the custom is functional within that society (Brown and Herrnstein, 1975). With accumulated inherited property a man may let poor relations herd his cattle or cultivate his soil giving him right to tribute while they have right of usage. Similar arrangements of patron and client may be established between conqueror and vanquished. Collecting tribute when there is plenty usually carries an obligation to keep the clients from starving in hard times. Prestige may also be attached to generosity beyond obligations, at festivals where all comers are fed. Overlaying these systems for sharing resources, surplus production often gives rise to a system of exchange of useless luxury goods, that carry much higher prestige value, i.e., define ones identity in the hierarchy. Such exchanges facilitate trade in consumer goods and mutual cultural inspiration. Alliances are also useful in territorial and other fights, which often do not involve much bloodshed. Alliances may be further cemented by proscribed exogamous marriages that also involve gifts in the shape of bride wealth or dowry. But often endogamy is preferred, to prevent 'pollution' and division of wealth. A community is formed by a peace-group within which homicide is disapproved of and requires compensation in the shape of blood-money – this may be the source of money-economies. The amount of compensation depends on the social distance horizontally in terms of kinship, or vertically in terms of prestige. Blood-money is paid by the clan rather than the individual; a habitual killer in the family would be expensive and might meet with a sudden death – if possible blamed on the opposition. The currency for gifts, bride wealth and blood-money may be quite separate from the currency for commodities – 'nothing money' that even nothing men have. Inflation may occur in one but not the other currency (Lewis, 1976).

Settlements, whether temporary or permanent, usually have a clear physical boundary, a ring of stones or a fence, or the huts face inwards encircling a safe place. What is inside the boundary is understandable culture, what is outside is nature, wilderness with unknown dangers that would pollute if they got in. In daily life friendly neighbourhood bonds may override kinship bonds. But in times of hardship the domi-nant clan is likely to claim territorial priority and chase minorities into the wilderness (Lewis, 1976). Prolonged overpopulation may even put a strain on kinship bonds, so a splinter faction is formed and migrates to set up a new settlement (Brown and Herrnstein, 1975). People from the wilderness may be regarded as unpredictable, like wild animals, fair game for plundering, eating, or domesticating as slaves. A trip into the wilderness carries the danger of pollution and is surrounded by cleansing ritual, even if it is a daily trip for hunting (men), foodgather-ing (women) or trading (either sex). On the other hand considerable wealth and prestige may be gained within the community, a 'nothing' man may become a big man, from daring entrepreneur initiative. Amongst gypsies women are considered more prone to pollution, e.g., from promiscuity, because their genitals are parts of the inner body which cannot be purified as easily as the outer body can be cleansed (Okely, 1977). Some social anthropologists, notably in America, lay much stress on the linguistic-conceptual aspect of culture. Ideas that seem weird to us may have a rational function within the total conceptual system of the culture, and accurate observation may be expressed poetically-metaphorically. The place of witchcraft and possession, of magic and mystery, is where nature refuses to fit justi-fied expectations, e.g., by producing unclassifiable monstrosities. The Lele tribe regard the Pangolin as a totem, associated with virility and dangerous to women, for 'it has the tail and scales of fish, climbs trees with four prehensile limbs like a monkey, and produces single off-spring like a human' (Lewis, 1976).

Ideas of witchcraft often function to improve on unfair distribution of luck. A lazy man blaming witchcraft for crop failure would be laughed out of court, but a conscientious man may be given compen-sation from a luckier neighbour. If nobody in the group can be blamed, the witchcraft is obviously caused by a hostile tribe or an offended ancestor. In the latter case the elder or shaman who wrongly conveyed the ancestor's wishes may be deposed, though he, of course, in turn will maintain that somebody knowingly or unknowingly must have broken the regular cycle of rites that give reality to the eternal 'living dead'.

In many societies only dominant property-owning members have a voice and articulate important deep structures. Aliens, slaves, 'nothing' men and women — like animals — find themselves trapped in the dominant conceptual structure making their position a matter of definition. Undercurrents in the subcultures may then find symbolic or behavioural expression, maybe in noisy rebellion with exaggerated allegiance to the wilderness (dirty, long-haired, ragged, obscene etc.). In West African tribes women in a trance are seen as alienated by the men, and a witchdoctor is called in to cure them.

The women reinterpreted the witchdoctor's exorcism as part of their initiation ritual into a sisterhood, complete with secret language and prepared to defend the dignity of womanhood with considerable force (Ardener, 1977). Such a sisterhood offered the only vigorous rebellion, when British colonialism threatened their basic value system (Ifeka-Møller, 1977). Clashes of ideology are common in the field of mental health. In Papua New Guinea some 800 distinct language-culture groups each have their own health care system. Often a concerned relative brings the sufferer to an expert who is supposed to recognize the condition and know a tested cure. If the expert is trained in alien (Western) concepts mutual misrepresentation of meaning of syndrome and cure will occur. This may threaten the whole social fabric; for example, if a prophet of the Cargo cult is treated for megalomania the Pacific islanders may lose the hope that keeps them going in a very deprived economy (Burton-Bradley, 1981), Psychiatric intervention in cases of possession is always a delicate matter. Possession occurs only amongst believers, and while devils should be driven out, gods may be welcome, even voluntarily invoked. Possession by a god may give powers of prophecy and healing, and therefore high status and a steady income (Chandra-shekar, 1981). When doubtful the church may try to pass responsibility for deciding the merits of a miracle to the medical profession, as happened with a Jesus possession in Singapore. As no major psychiatric disorder was found the evaluation problem was handed back to the church (Ngui, 1981). Psychotherapy must be modified for other cultures. Hong Kong Chinese are reluctant to be seen without a relative present, and expressing emotion would mean loss of face – shame being more important than guilt. Understanding the culture-specific somatization is essential for meaningful communication (Wai-Ho-Lo, 1981). Written evidence inevitably comes through the educated elite and reflects their ideology. Nevertheless it is the major source for the following section.

V History of attitudes to the irrational

In concentrating now on the development of ideas I am not denying that ideas reflect and depend on the socio-economic structure of the society in which they arise (Marx, 1963). But space permits only the briefest mention of the rapidly increasing complexities of material life. Probably overpopulation drove Iranian farmers into the twin river valley where they joined up with tribes from upriver, already mastering simple irrigation. This growing culture rapidly developed when the Sumerians, of unknown origin, took over control. The annual inundation kept the land fertile, so permanent settlements were possible: villages grew to towns which grew to cities. With cheap labour to harness the irascible rivers through an irrigation system, surplus grain could form the basis for trade with the many commodities they lacked, from timber and metals to cotton and spices. Trading with Egypt, Syria, Arabia, Persia and the Indus valley (which again perhaps traded with China) was sufficiently developed for foreign quarters to have been established in Ur. The temples and chieftains extracted taxes for their work of placating the temperamental Gods that, for example, had caused the big flood burying the original city. And the tax collector needed accounts – hence the development of arithmetic and writing – which again led to private colleges for the training of an intelligentsia. It is from school libraries, as well as temple accounts and royal proclamations, that our knowledge of Sumerian and subsequent Accadian culture comes. Already at this stage we find two types of medical practitioners: the *asipu* carefully checked the patient's symptoms, on a par with horoscopes as omens of divine displeasure or demoniacal possession, due to a breach of religious observance committed knowingly or unknowingly. Treatment consisted in pacifying the Gods and driving away the demons. The *asu* was concerned with pharmacological remedies for the patient's suffering. The *asu*'s bag contained such powerful ingredients as opium, hemp, belladonna, water hemlock, hellebore, as well as milder camomile, mustard seeds and ingredients for enemas. Surgery was practised, for there is mention of specified fees for different operations on noblemen, freemen and slaves – with corresponding scales of punishments for negligence. Apparently surgery was a craft without academic training – no texts have been found. Midwifery and nursing were, as was brewing, innkeeping and prostitution, female occupations. But there is at least one record of a lady *asu*. In Egypt, medicine, like architecture, was ascribed to the immortal Imhoteb. Here surgery had a higher status, and anatomical texts are found; mummifying involved considerable dissection of corpses. The differences between Egyptian and Mesopotamian cultures is partly explained by different roots: the Hamites of Africa were organised under semi-divine chieftains in direct communication with the ancestors and their totem animals. Also the predictability of the Nile inundation fitted an ordered pantheon, with stress on recycling as a form of immortality. But even if the divine ruler's spirit is re-incarnated in his successor, you never know if he will want his old body, so it is safest to preserve it with all it might want, securely petrified and entombed (Hawkes, 1977).

In classical Greece we also find two distinct medical schools: the Asclepius cult involved dream interpretations, possibly drug induced, as most prophecies were. In Delphi vapours from *Hyoscyamus* (henbane) are reputed to have been used for oracular trances. The snake-god's cures were probably largely cathartic, as was the preventive mental hygiene of participating in religious rites. From this sports competition and drama gradually separated out with a stress on excellence as the chief virtue. On the other hand Hippocrates' prescriptions were based on observational and internationally collected information, an empirical trend started with the Ionian nature philosophers who tried to break away from narrow religious dogmas.

This split in medicine reflects the general split between mythos and logos which we associate with the establishment of a rational ego separated from irrational animal passions. Plato was trained in down-to-earth Socratic dialectics, but became increasingly interested in the Pythagorean combination of mathematics and Orphism, which related rebirth to morality − excellence in the pursuit of harmony, beauty, justice and truth. With poetic vision as much as clear logic, he wanted to prop up the collapsing city-state ethics, but came close to destroying the traditional brotherhood gods in his thinking about the absolute, i.e. monotheism. (Such abstract monotheistic ideas may well have been inspired from abroad − they are first known from Amenhotep IV's Aten cult, and bear similarity to Oriental Taoism as well as Zen Buddhism. Trade during antiquity in goods and ideas both north and south round the Himalayas is nowadays seen as a plausible hypothesis.)

Following Plato, the Gods became increasingly redundant amongst intellectuals. Plato's most famous pupil, Aristotle, was an alien in the city-state and adhered more and more to the empiricism of the Ionian nature philosophers (Rohde, 1966). In his metaphysics he argues that language and logic must reflect the external order. A string of predicates without a substantial thing to which they belong would be as meaningless as the silence of an animal. With an as yet weak boundary between the rational ego and the inner, unknown, passionate wilderness it was safest to fix attention firmly outwards where structures and boundaries could be clearly perceived and defined (Bertelsen, 1974). Aristotle's medical texts, as so much of his thinking, known only through lecture notes, are rather dry descriptions, classifications and prescriptions.

Amongst many variations some diagnostic labels recur frequently from the Greeks onwards: epilepsia, toxic states (e.g. alcohol+ mandragora officianalis), phrenitis (feverish state), hypochondriasis, melancholia, mania, and lycanthropia (werewolf behaviour – at times epidemic). Therapies included drugs such as helleborus (to cause sneezing and other inner cleansing) and opium (to stop nocturnal wolfhowling). Dietary regulations included plenty of alcohol for the wealthy Roman clientele for whom soothing conversation and entertainment was also prescribed. But other writers were more in favour of fright, pain (e.g. cauterizing the shaven crown) and bloodletting (particularly beneficial for haemorrhoids). The debate on location and mechanisms of mental disorders reflects disagreement between spiritual and somatic models right up till modern times. Plato took the head's near spherical shape as proof that it must be the site of divine ideas battling against chaotic matter. Aristotle located reason in the heart. The Hellenistic Alexandria-schools dominated through most of the Roman period. Methodics, represented by Asclepiades and Soranes speculated on solid atoms passing through tight or loose pores in the brain causing hyperstenic or asthenic states. Pneumatics like Archigenes and Rufus searched for humoral-pneumatic links, as Erasistratos found airbubbles in the arteries in post-mortems. Claudius Galenos became the most quoted authority for over a thousand years. He followed Aristotle and Hippocrates, systematizing the humoral-temperament theory. During the Middle Ages the Arabs preserved much classical knowledge and Ibn Sina (Avicenna c. 1000 AD) was a major source for later European studies – with religious distortion in translations through both Muslim and Christians. Avicenna reintroduced the pneuma idea, taken seriously enough for Rondelet to use trepanation to let out the black fumes of melancholia (ca. 1550 AD). Medicine was studied by the Benedictine monks at Monte Casino. But by and large the church saw mental illness as divine punishment or – more pronounced after the reformation – demoniacal possession to be treated by prayers, exorcism, or torture and death. Over a three-hundred-year period some 3 million witches were burned, mostly women. This probably exterminated most deviant as well as countless normal females. The spread of syphilis may have contributed to fear of the seductress.

During the renaissance neoplatonic, kabballistic and hermetic thinking spread, with a search for human perfection. The Essene therapists had a high reputation for their powers of healing through touch or thought alone. The powerful touch was interpreted as animal-magnestism by Mesmer and his followers. In 1520 Paracelsus burnt Galen and Avicenna, introducing instead his own alchemical theories, with stress on macrobiotics (acid-alkaline balance), the harmful effects of sublimation and distillation of sulphur in the body, and the Archaeus (microcosmic soul) fighting Tartarus (waste-products). Later fermentation became the in-word. Descartes located the spirit in the pineal gland, but post mortems, e.g. by Steensen, failed to locate the pores it should flow through. Hoffmann tried to be strictly materialistic, introducing a nerve aether to carry ideas round the body but his pupil and adversary Stahl regarded this as secreted by the soul. The soul was definitively located in the brain during the French revolution when it was found that the guillotined head would look at you when spoken to and grimace terribly when a finger was poked up the medulla (Beyerholm).

During the Middle Ages recorded European thought is firmly anchored to the Christian mythology, incorporating various aspects of Greek, Persian, Jewish and later, through the crusades and more peaceful trade links, Arab philosophy. Monastic orders usually sought an experience of the infinite and divine through observance of a strict diurnal pattern of actions towards God. Such predictability is the foundation for experienced constancy and hence for substantial existence of the eternal in the stream of changing phenomena (Williams, 1977): This approach was during the upheavals of the fourteenth century combined with mystic contemplation, tearing attention from worldly emotional attachments to enter 'the cloud of unknowing'. From this position, by divine grace, it may be possible to enter the inner mansion and communion with the Godhead. Corresponding scholarship was obsessed with the ratio of the finite and infinite, i.e., the problem of convergence of an infinite series and a measure for irrational fractions. This problem came up in speculation on the unity of a manifold, such as the Eucharist; on diffractions and refractions in lenses and prisms, and reflections between countless mirrors true or impure; on perspectives, viewpoint and symmetrics; on squaring the circle, which was necessary to rationalise the perfect motion, from which other motions could be derived (Harrison, 1978). The cult aspect of medicine, and some of the most potent pharmaka, survived in sub-cultures. Witches were supposedly well versed in the use — and abuse — of digitalis. Ointment from *Hyoscyamus* (used by the Delphic oracle for inhalation) can be absorbed through the skin and was perhaps rubbed on a broomhandle for rectal insertion to give kinaesthetic hallucinations of flying. Nowadays minute amounts are used homoeopathically in seasickness pills. 'Angel-dust' (Phencyclidin) in the 1970s USA epidemic of flying trips seems to have related properties (Pittel and Oppendahl, 1979). With the increase in witch covens Luther's interest in the anality of the devil may have had some foundation in reality (Brown, 1959).

With increasing trade, the feudal system (based on kinship and neighbourhood ties) was eclipsed by the alliance of merchants and monarch, witness the growth of royal boroughs. The corresponding changes in ideological superstructure are reflected in the theological debate leading to the Reformation, as previously suppressed sects surfaced and proliferated.

During the Middle Ages fools had been tolerated in the community, whether amongst wandering pilgrims, beggars, gypsies, actors and tinkers, or as entertainment at noble castles and market fairs. Their ravings made sense in terms of the iconography of the village church. Now towns began to refuse entry to madmen, they were either detained for display within the city gates, or sent by ship from town to town, as eternal travellers. At the same time literature and art were intensely preoccupied with the subject of madness. Erasmus opened a discussion on the wisdom of fools; Brant's *Narrenschiff* of 1494 was illustrated by Bosch by the turn of the century (Foucault, 1967). With folk symbols taken out of their contextual restraint they developed monstrously, like drug-trip visions without a ritual framework. People saw in madness a mirror of their inner doubts and confusion. 'Here shall he see gross fools as he', reflects Shakespeare's recurrent preoccupation with madness, real or pretended (*As You Like It*).

Towards the end of the sixteenth century allusions to 'fallen noses' were added, reflecting the spread of syphilis. As in classical Greece the classical post-Renaissance period took time to separate logic and empiricism from mysticism and poetical vision. Newton achieved a workable model of fluxion (Leibniz's formulations of a differential calculus had a better logical structure) – the same point which Archimedes had reached when his circles were destroyed as the economy and culture of the Hellenic sphere collapsed. But confronted with the strange transformations of substance in the chymical crucible (and perhaps inspired by toxic fumes, with mercury and sulphur as favoured ingredients in the *prima materia* to be sublimated), Newton still relied on the allegorical language of alchemy – a language which tells more about the sexual and spiritual fantasies of the experimenter than about the substances examined (Jung, 1966). As the new order became established, the need for safe trade routes resulted in increasing pressure to rid the country of vagrants. The seventeenth century saw a proliferation of establishments for the confinement of the poor, the petty criminal, and the mentally alienated who didn't even possess himself in the world. In accordance with the morality of the times these prisons became workhouses, supposed to be self-supporting and keep their inmates industrious. When it was found undesirable to upset the sensitive market with the cheap output of forced labour, useless occupations were invented. Rehabilitation only became an aim of occupational therapy when manufacture created a demand for manpower. Those unwilling or unable to conform contributed to the economy by being displayed for a penny on Sundays – safely chained or locked in bare cells, as, like animals, they were supposed to lack sensibility to discomfort. Their grotesque and degraded behaviour was a good moral lesson in the ultimate consequences of idle imagination.

During the eighteenth century, with farmers impoverished or dispossessed, court fashion was to glorify the purity of country living, as reflected in idyllic paintings of courtiers disguised as shepherds and milkmaids. The workhouses got blamed for polluting the air with decay – as had the leprosy colonies in medieval times. Some health inspection and stress on hygiene was introduced under medical supervision (Foucault, 1967).

With an ordered society, rational science, and madness locked away, it became increasingly safe – and necessary – to question the inner basis for knowledge and morality. In Kant's formulation: a statement is based on the simultaneous presence of a manifold in one temporal unit. The components are successively examined, so one element must remain present, and must be judged to have remained the same, while attention turns to another. This sequence of imaginative synthesis requires a continuous, unaltering centre containing but not contained in experience: a transcendental apperception with modes of synthetic imagination given as an a priori category (Bertelsen, 1974).

By now the chemical transformation of substance was fairly well mastered. Medical innovations started with Paracelsus' alchemic mercury cure for syphilis (Bronowski, 1973). Successes with digitalis from folk-medicine and quinine from the Incas (James, 1961), was followed by medical enthusiasm for the newly rediscovered opiates as cure-alls. A new vision emerged in art and literature, a vision of the forces of wild nature (hitherto feared and despised) that could be sublimated when safely viewed from a prospect tower or framed by a folly. Simultaneously, commercial interests turned those romantic visions into scientific-technological transformation and exploitation of energy (Bronowski, 1973). In philosophy, too, the problem of sublimated, spiritual energy, became paramount.

Kierkegaard is mostly concerned with the categories of energy transformation, expressing his phenomenological analysis in the language of traditional Christian mysticism. As the rational ego pursues its intellectual passion towards a climax, the passion (like all passions) is transformed to its opposite and the ego collides with the irrational hermetically sealed intensities in the dimension of the unknown (Eternal). Through the original sin of refusing surrender to God's will the ego lost its innocence and immediate unity. In the struggle for possession of the world the ego repeatedly denies demands from the unknown, only to find at the peak of its power that it is enslaved by its possessions with no free passion to invest. Fear, despair and guilt may then tempt the ego to renounce the world and approach the encapsulated intensities. Remembering and repenting the accumulated sins may lead back to a state of innocence where the grace of God may re-establish unity. Inspired by the newly translated Indian scriptures, Schopenhauer was more interested in the universal energy of the inner unknown: Eros in many disguises blindly and greedily seeking *lebensraum*, destroying what gets in his way. Rationality to enhance his rule can turn against him and win access to Nirvana beyond recycling (Bertelsen, 1974).

The humanitarian reforms at the end of the eighteenth century separated the mad, who by now had been reasonably well described and classified, from the poor and the criminals – to protect the latter. The new retreats or asylums largely did away with chains, as madness was no longer respected as a fearsome power. It was found that most inmates could be controlled like children simply by the personal authority of the director – sometimes, but by no means always, a medical man. The madman regained a place in reasonably comfortable surroundings, at the cost of becoming an obedient minor. The chains were exchanged for the internal constraints of guilt and fear. Attempts at curing had previously been based on interaction, such as confronting the deluded with the folly of a similar delusion in others. Now it became a matter of careful observation with prompt punishment of any transgression from the narrow path of normal behaviour. Some punishments, such as icy showers, might be based on older medical theories, e.g., of mania as a hot, dry condition caused by sulphurous vapours penetrating the pores of the brain, the locus of interaction of reason and passion, of mind and body. But the moral implication was clear even here, for the nerve fibres got their excessive sensibility from idle indulgence in fantasy.

The nineteenth century industrialisation and urbanisation brought overcrowding of the asylums and decline of moral treatment (Greenblatt and Levinson, 1965). Between 1875 and 1910 London secretly bought part of Lord Rosebery's estate and built three mental hospitals, a defective colony and an epileptic colony – still the major industry of Epsom, apart from racehorses. It was obvious that nobody else would want to mix with mental hospital staff so at least there should be enough close together for internal community life! During this period psychiatry became increasingly respectable, succeeding in classifications and with every hope of finding physiological explanations and cures on a par with other branches of medicine. After the link between syphilis and general paresis of the insane was discovered, as many as 50 per cent of inmates were given this ignoble diagnosis, until the advent of the Wasserman test for syphilis. Mental aberration and deviance was firmly ascribed to neurological dysfunction, a nuisance to orderly society, and only on very rare occasions the starting-point of intellectual or cultural innovations (Maudsley, 1939). This trend has continued into the twentieth century: patients are still often expected to follow a prescribed daily round, work diligently and behave as minors vis-à-vis staff (Goffman, 1967). The introduction of effective drugs has now made it possible to normalise behaviour with a biochemical strait-jacket. Theoretically this should empty the mental hospitals except for a residue of geriatrics with irreversible brain decay. Interestingly, this reactionary trend (basically money-saving) has the same social effect as the left-wing liberation and self-help trends, away from mystification by and dependence on the medical profession (Illich, 1973): increasingly the psychotic, the addict, the unemployable and the rebellious mix with Romany and Diddicoy wandering the country. With the recession of the 1970s the number of hostels has dropped, sites and squats are cleared and long-haired louts are ordered outside the town limits by the police.

Conclusion: psychodynamic theory and history

It is against the historic background of police suppression, followed by moral repression of the irrational, that we should evaluate the revolutionary impact of Freud re-establishing a dialogue with folly (Foucault, 1967). From this dialogue it rapidly became obvious that it is as practical to say that the outer physical world disappears when I am not looking at it, as to say that the inner mental world disappears when I am not conscious of it. But if mental processes can continue without awareness, then there is a whole new subject to be approached scientifically: the unconscious. Freud devoted the majority of his life to establishing this new science, with practical application in clinical work, a method of investigation through loose chains of ideas, elaborating the hidden meaning of dreams, errors of actions, and neurotic symptom formation, and a gradually clarified (though never very clear) theory, linking the emerging findings. A theory of unconscious mental processes is a theory of internal continuity, which for Freud meant the lasting effect of the early childhood experiences which establish the supremacy of rational, orderly human behaviour. This infantile drama is continuously re-enacted in a silenced internal discourse employing the primary process language of metonymy (displacement) and metaphor (condensation) duplicating the secondary, rational and intentional, processes (Lacan, 1979) with the ordering language of a phallic-dominated society (Althusser, 1969). When these processes from the inner wilderness beyond the repressing defences are allowed a voice in the analyst's consulting-room, (transference) re-enactment in a dialogue takes place, with articulation and subsequent integration.

The metaphor, dream or myth, does not distinguish inner and outer, material and mental: dreams can simultaneously be interpreted as relating to somatic processes and social relations. Having to borrow concepts from biology and sociology, Freud at one time attempted to derive unconscious mental processes from biology and their inhibition from society, but in later works he abandoned the former as premature and reversed the latter: society is based on the repression of pleasure-seeking. Freud's last statement of these views is as follows (Freud, 1940).

According to Darwin early humanoids lived in hordes dominated by a brutal male, possessing all females and liable to kill, castrate or chase off the younger males. From Atkinson comes the idea that the sons joined forces to kill and eat the father, while Robertson Smith contributes the idea that a totem animal is substituted for the father as sacred protector to be killed and eaten only at an annual totem feast. Together with this development comes the prohibition of incest and the rise of the matriarchal organisation as a means of preventing the rise of one brother as the new father. But potentials for the suppressed original order survive and eventually re-emerge in the shape of the patriarchal chieftain, at first with limited power, later as a pharaoh or emperor. Under Amenhotep IV the system of one universal ruler on earth was reflected in the decree of one universal God above, symbolised by the sun as lifegiver and enlightener: a religion of truth and justice instead of magic. This religion perished as quickly as it had arisen in the Egyptian power game, but was forced by Amenhotep's son or courtier Moses on the Jewish labourers in the Nile delta. In return for conversion symbolised by circumcision, he promised to lead them from slavery to a fertile land of their own. The Jews eventually got fed up with Moses' rigid demands, killed him and joined other semitic tribes in the worship of Jahve, a primitive local Baalat. However, the Mosaic tradition was kept alive by a few priests, and eventually gained supremacy with the joined force of guilt over the primal and the Moses murders.

Freud has no doubt about the validity of similar concepts in ontogeny: the son desiring his mother, develops a murderous hate for his father, but in fear of retaliation he renounces and forgets this wish and seeks instead to gain the approval of the father or the super-ego, the inner representation of ideal and authority. The repressed may return in adolescence, distorted by the repressing reaction formation and hence acted out in apparently meaningless symptoms or over valued beliefs. Often it is again repressed, to re-emerge under emotional stress or lowered strength in later life. When it comes to a phylogenetic mass psychology Freud is explicit about the lack of detailed evidence. He acknowledges selecting from among conflicting views that which suits his thesis. He regrets the incompleteness of his ideas of the great man as history maker without adequate attention to the social network. And he is well aware of the dubious nature of racial memories and a group unconscious. He attempts several formulations, but cannot avoid a theory of the return of the repressed in history with a biological as well as traditional basis.

At a time of threat not only to the Jewish people, but also to intellectual and spiritual values, it was important for Freud to stress how he saw the dynamics of truth and justice. This starts with the stress on deduced paternity as against observed maternity, and is much reinforced by the prohibition of magic rituals and sensory representations of the God idea.

The strict adherence to this sets the Jew apart from Christians who incorporated many elements of the Great Mother's religion, such as salvation through the sacrifice of the son – which Freud sees as an unconscious expiation of patricide.

To Freud psychoanalysis was firstly a tool for scientific investigation. Secondly, by offering articulation to hitherto repressed and distorted forces it might bring about social liberation. Thirdly, it sometimes brought about an improvement of individual disease.

I have elsewhere outlined subsequent developments in dynamic psychology (Munro, 1973-4). Suffice it here to say that Jung was most radical in pursuing a pure science of psychic phenomena and resisting temptation to either a biological or sociological reductionism. He used Freud's analytic method of attending to fleeting hunches, normally treated as background noise causing random errors in intended functions. With attention the complexes (locked intensities) gained increasingly articulate representation in consciousness, using the culturally available symbols – in Jung's case Platonic-Christian. Mental energy (libido, passion) is channelled and converted through archetypal categories in the unknown (unknowable) region. The archetypes have psychic reality in their representations, predictably recurring, with experienced eternal numinosity, as from beyond finite individual experience. At first archetypal representations are personifications, but behind the human masks occur representations of a self-structure in abstract configurations like the Pythagorean tetrakyst or the Tantric squared circle (Jung, 1959). Cyclic, repetitive recurrence is the immobile mover, the intersection of permanence and flux, of divine and human. Jung's historic comment is concerned with shifts in the concept of spiritual force. At a magic fetish level mana is located in a specific object. The spirit of ancestors, linking a kinship group together, is shared by all but most fully incarnated in the elder. With larger groups inhibited endogamous libido is increasingly converted to power invested in the divine monarch. As rational thinking splits from myth, spirits become homeless, displaced first to mountain tops, then to heaven. Simultaneously the inner irrational becomes less accessible (Jung, 1956).

Jung's purely phenomenological approach has often earned him the label of mystic. But exactly because he did not use neurological hypothesis (which by now would have been old-fashioned), his formulations have been more consistent with data from other fields, where he and Freud differ in terms of a testable hypothesis, e.g. typology (Foulds). Basic psycho-analytic meta-concepts developed to account for irrational acts and were related to infantile memories and biological necessities. They are not easily modified to account for the complex experiences of an adult ego. Seen in Darwinist perspective as an organization for increased survival fitness, the ego becomes a collection of apparatuses linking the innate drives and their phantasy-representations to potential sources of gratification in the external world. These concepts, developed by the American ego-analysts describe the ego as object (Guntrip, 1977) but can fit in with current technological research. From logical analysis of a function (such as stereoscopic vision) an algorithm can be tested against a micro-chip model and the actually occurring braincells with their neuronal and enzyme connections. However such research still only illuminates fragments of the awe-inspiring capacities of the brain. On the motivational side biochemical studies suggest a complex system of endogenous opiates and their antidotes (linked to the old acupuncture principles) underlying the pain-avoidance/pleasure-seeking principle (Maddocks, 1979). The altered manner of experience of an ego with damaged apparatuses is convincingly described e.g. in connection with a gun-shot wound (Luria) or inflammation (Sachs, 1976).

In Britain the Kleineans tended to label hypothetical dynamisms synonymously with their phantasy-contents. This led to a theory of inate imagoes, modified by experience to form internal objects, internal representations of outer objects, and ego-precipitates modified by fusion with internalized objects. Guntrip, following Fairbairn, discusses how the infantile ego splits in its relations to outer and internalized bad (tantalizing or frustrating) objects. His descriptions of the experiencing, rather than experienced, ego come close to the formulations of the early dissenters (Adler, Jung, Rank) and the existentialists. But the early Freudian condemnation of unorthodoxy still seems to prevent psycho-analysts from drawing on such heretic sources. Winnicott, while acknowledging object-relations theory, develops his ideas of the experiencing subject from observations of the social mother-baby unit. With a good-enough facilitating environment the baby can gradually emerge, feeling that he can BE as a person and has a space in which he can DO. A space which both separates and unites him and mother, a space which is neither inner nor outer, neither created nor found, a space for playing alone or with others (Winnicott, 1974). By this circuitous route we seem to have arrived back in the naive-realistic world of everyday life, where we have developed our shared language and culture, the world we had to split and examine imaginatively and scientifically to account for inexplicable phenomena and thwarted expectations.

Both Freud and Jung stressed the importance of mass psychology and the primacy of the collective, but neither made direct observation of groups. They seem to have feared that the ego would be submerged beyond reprieve in a collective, reducing behaviour to a low common denominator. While this obviously can happen, orderly groups have been the rule long before man appeared on earth. Despite acknowledgment of Darwin, Freud as much as Jung regarded animal behaviour as crude and instinctual. We must now acknowledge that animals, too, have inhibitions, social structures and language. If anything, human civilisation is accompanied by increasing disinhibition of sexual and aggressive drives, and fusion of the two does not appear to occur amongst animals.

Both Freud and Jung also underestimated the degree of cultural exchanges from the earliest times, and the longevity of tradition even in informal subcultures like children's playgroups (Opie and Opie, 1977). It was with the high numbers of traumatic breakdowns during the war that earlier experiments in group therapy really got under way. The results of various community and group approaches were encouraging, but formulations tended to get bogged down either as psychoanalysis in group or as social rehabilitation. Only Foulkes saw this clearly as an entirely new field of study, calling for new concepts to describe the new observations, building on and related to but different from psychoanalytic techniques and formulations.

The subject-matter, the universe of discourse, for this new science Foulkes calls the group-matrix, the sum total of known and unknown events during a group's history (Foulkes and Anthony, 1957). Unfortunately this term is dropped in later publications due to persistent naive misunderstanding. If the group conductor can ensure a regularly recurring situation where exploitation and dominance cannot be instituted, the group can be encouraged to engage in free-floating conversation, each member expressing whatever ideas occur to him. The conductor, listening with evenly hovering attention, will then discover transpersonal structures and processes, as shared themes are expressed now by one and then by another individual.

Individual contributions link together in chain associations, with resonances, mirroring and contrapuntal dialectic. The theme is unfolded with both manifest and latent contents, resistance to further exploration, etc.

The group brings strangers together, all seeking to belong and be understood. Each expresses himself in terms absorbed in his infantile and current real-life network (Foulkes, 1975), from symptoms and gestures to poetic imagery or stringent logic. Gradually the group develops a shared, remembered culture and language, with increasing articulation of shared, previously to each unknown, deep structures.

Masks and fences are communal structures that can come down when exploitation and accumulation of wealth cannot split through greed on one side, envy on the other. Verbal symbols reach past the isolating feelings of guilt and shame to the most intimately personal, yet most universally shared, experiences. Ego differentiation and cultural development occur simultaneously. As defences within members are resolved and integrated, previously latent contents become manifest, verifying or refuting the conductor's hypothesis. As resistances between members are resolved and as members learn to pool their individual unique knowledge, consciousness extends into a new dimension, where the collective knowledge, the common multiple, far exceeds any individual capacity.

Group-analytic formulations about the interface between the inner and outer mental worlds could not begin till fairly clear, independent disciplines of psychology and sociology had developed. Group analysts are still groping for theoretical formulations, with temptations to short cuts such as wholesale adoption of models from other fields: for example, many writers conceptualise events in large unstructured groups in Kleinean terms: the individual regresses to the helpless state of an infant at the breast. What we need are concepts allowing us to translate between the models of the inner and outer mental worlds, something like an interface chip for decoding or a semi-permeable boundary where synchronicity can be induced.

From a group-analytic theory we would need a revised myth on prehistory, accounting for the evolution of secondary processes but not through the sequels of the incest taboo. The latter, but not the former, we seem to share with animals. Imagine that inclement conditions (such as an ice age) forced two (or more) variants of hominids together – at a point of the speciation process where they had developed separate, mutually incomprehensible, languages. One tribe, the Barilli, might have lived in wooded country, with predominantly hedonic communications, and survival techniques mainly stressing recurrent rhythms of crops, etc. Visible dangers were easily avoided, but invisible dangers could lurk anywhere. The Ammonars, on the other hand, came from open savanna country where survival depended on accurate hand-eye coordination, speed and endurance in the hunt and an agonistic social organisation. If two such tribes could only survive by cooperating and interbreeding, they would have to invent a new, second order, pidgin language, translatable into either Ammonar or Barilli – a pidgin court-ship ritual maybe, allowing transformations between Ammonar and Barilli identity. With misunderstandings likely to be fatal, since outsiders were hunted and eaten, it would be necessary to reinforce the learnt language through some sort of imaginative, yet rigid and serious game: a tribal rite. In the rite group members jointly recall the past, which no one could do alone, and they jointly give here-and-now reality to the absent, re-enacted past and the hidden, latent future. From the rite it is, therefore, possible to develop symbolic language and accumulation of skills, knowledge and property over many generations, i.e., to initiate the history of civilisation and culture. And through the continued development of articulation and cooperation we may ensure that this history does not end in genocide.

References

Althusser, L. (1969), 'Freud and Lacan', *New Left Review*, Spring 1969, pp. 189-219.
Anthoney, T. R. (1968), 'The Ontogeny of Greeting, Grooming and Sexual Motor Patterns in Captive Baboons', *Behavior*, 31, pp. 358-72.
Ardener, S. (1977), 'Sexual Insult and Female Militancy' in Ardener, S. (ed.), *Perceiving Women*, London, Dent.
Bertelsen, J. (1974), *Ouroboros*, Viborg, Denmark, Borgens Forlag.
Beyerholm, O. (1937), *Psykiatriens Historie*, Copenhagen, Levin & Munksgaard.
Broby Johansen, R. (1967), *Oldnordiske Stenbilleder*, Copenhagen, Gyldendals Forlag.
Bronowski, J. (1973), *The Ascent of Man*, London, BBC.
Brøndsted, J. (1965), *The Vikings*, Harmondsworth, Penguin.
Brown, N. O. (1959), *Life Against Death*, New York, Vintage.
Brown, R., and Herrnstein, R. J. (1975), *Psychology*, London, Methuen.
Burton-Bradley, B. G. (1981), 'The traditional nosology', paper presented at symposium on Transcultural Psychiatry, Macau.
Chandrashekar, C. R., *et al.* (1981), 'Prevalence and nature of possession in Rural India', paper presented at symposium on Transcultural Psychiatry, Macau.
Clark, G., and Piggot, S. (1970), *Prehistoric Societies*, Harmondsworth, Penguin.
Cloud of Unknowing, The (anon.) (1961), Harmondsworth, Penguin.
Cornell, E. (1969), *Humanistic Inquiries into Architecture*, Gothenburg, Sweden, Gunperts Forlag.
Crook, J. H. (ed.) (1968), *Social Behaviour in Birds and Mammals*, London, Academic Press.
Currey, A. (1977), 'Interviewing Thor Heyerdahl', *Scanorama*, November, pp. 65-6.
Engels, F. (1902), *The Origin of the Family, Private Property and the State*, Chicago, C. H. Kerr.

262   *Historical perspectives of group analysis*

Foucault, M. (1967), *Madness and Civilisation*, London, Tavistock.
Foulds, G. A. (1965), *Personality and Personal Illness*, London, Tavistock.
Foulkes, P. (1976), 'Cannon or Creed', *Group Analysis* IX/1, pp. 15-16.
Foulkes, S. H. (1964), *Therapeutic Group Analysis*, London, Allen & Unwin.
Foukes, S. H. (1975), *Group-analytic Psychotherapy: Method and Principles*, London, Gordon & Breach.
Foulkes, S. H., and Anthony, E. J. (1957), *Group Psychotherapy*, Harmondsworth, Penguin.
Freud, S. (1940), *Moses and Monotheism*, London, Hogarth Press.
Freud, S. (1950), *The Interpretation of Dreams*, London, Allen & Unwin.
Glob, P. V. (1969), *Danske Oldtidsminder*, Copenhagen, Gyldendals Forlag.
Goffman, E. (1967), *Asylums*, Harmondsworth, Penguin.
Gordon, C. (1977), 'Birth of the Subject', *Radical Philosophy*, Summer, no. 17, pp. 15-26.
Greenblatt, M., and Levinson, D. (1965), 'Mental Hospitals' in Wolman, B. B. (ed.), *Handbook of Clinical Psychology*, London, McGraw Hill.
Griffin, D. R. (1976), *The Question of Animal Awareness*, New York, Rockefeller University Press.
Guntrip, H. (1977), *Schizoid Phenomena, Object Relations and the Self*, London, Hogarth Press.
Harrison, A. (1978), 'On Scholastic Physics', PhD thesis in preparation.
Hawkes, J. (1977), *The First Great Civilizations*, Harmondsworth, Penguin.
Hutten, E. H. (1976), 'The Scientific Status of Psycho-analysis and of Group-analysis', *Group Analysis* IX/2, July 1976, pp. 109-14.
Ifeka-Møller, C. (1977), 'Female Militancy and Colonial Revolt' in Ardener, S. (ed.) (1977) *Perceiving Women*, London, Dent.
Illich, I. D. (1973), *Deschooling Society*, Harmondsworth, Penguin.
James, D. (1961), *Folk and Modern Medicine*, Derby, Conn., Monarch.
Jung, C. G. (1956), *Symbols of Transformation* in *The Collected Works of C. G. Jung*, vol. V, London, Routledge & Kegan Paul.
Jung, C. G. (1959), *Aion*, in Collected Works, as above, vol. IX.
Jung, C. G. (1966), *The Psychology of the Transference*, in Collected Works, as above, vol. XVI.
Kummer, H. (1971), *Primate Societies. Group Techniques of Ecological Adaptation*, Chicago, Aldine & Atherton.
Kummer, H. (1973), 'Dominance versus Possession' in Montagne, W. (ed.) *Symposia of the Fourth International Congress of Primatology*, Basel, S. Karger.
Lacan, J. (1979), *The Four Fundamental Principles of Psychoanalysis*, Harmondsworth, Penguin.
Lack, D. (1966), *Population Studies of Birds*, Oxford University Press.
Lamb, H. H. (1972), *Climate: Past, Present and Future*, London, Methuen.
Larsson, K. (1973), 'Sexual Behaviour, the Result of an Interaction' in

Historical perspectives of group analysis 263

Zubin, J., and Money, J. (eds), *Contemporary Sexual Behaviour: Critical Issues in the 70ies*, London, Johns Hopkins University Press.
Leakey, R. E., and Lewin, R. (1977), *Origins*, London, Macdonald & Jones.
Lewis, I. M. (1976), *Social Anthropology in Perspective*, Harmondsworth, Penguin.
Linden, E. (1976), *Apes, Men and Language*, Harmondsworth, Penguin.
Lorenzen, E. (1976), *Technological Studies in Ancient Metrology*, Copenhagen, Nyt Nordisk Forlag.
Luria, A. R. (1975), *The Man with a Shattered World*, Harmondsworth, Penguin.
Maddocks, J. (1979), 'Mind, Matter and Mechanism', BBC Radio 3, 16-20 July.
Marx, K. (1963), *Selected Writings in Sociology and Social Philosophy*, Harmondsworth, Penguin.
Maudsley, H. (1939), *Natural Causes and Supernatural Seemings* (Thinker's Library no. 73), London, Watts.
Munro, H. (1973-4), 'Developments in Dynamic Psychology', Part II-IV, *Group Analysis* VI/2-VII/1.
Ngui, P. W. (1981), 'Hysterical possession syndrome', paper presented at symposium on Transcultural Psychiatry, Macau.
Okely, J. (1977), 'Gypsy Women: Models in Conflict' in Ardener, S. (ed.), *Perceiving Women*, London, Dent.
Opie, I., and Opie, P. (1977), *The Lore and Language of Schoolchildren*, Frogmore, Paladin.
Parkes, A. S. (1976), *Patterns of Sexuality and Reproduction*, Oxford, Oxford University Press.
Pittel, S. M., and Oppendahl, M. C. (1979), 'The Enigma of PCP', in R. L. Dupont *et al.* (eds), *Handbook on Drug Abuse*, US Department of Health and Welfare.
Plumb, J. H. (1977), 'Introduction to the History of Human Societies', in Hawkes, J., *The First Great Civilisations*, Harmondsworth, Penguin.
Rohde, P. P. (1966), *Den Store Moders Genkomst*, Copenhagen, Thannin & Appel.
Rutter, M. (1972), *Maternal Deprivation Reassessed*, Harmondsworth, Penguin.
Sachs, O. W. (1976), *Awakenings*, Harmondsworth, Penguin.
Spinar, Z. V. (1972), *Life Before Man*, London, Thames & Hudson.
Sundquist, M. (1962), *Bostaden i Tärendö*, Göteborg, Licentiat thesis, Chalmers Tekniska Högskola.
Tinbergen, N. (1951), *The Study of Instinct*, Oxford, Clarendon.
Trudgill, P. (1974), *Sociolinguistics*, Harmondsworth, Penguin.
Wahlström and Widstrand (eds) (1967), *The Viking*, Göteborg, Tre Tryckare A.B.
Wai-Ho-Lo (1981), 'Culture and depression with special reference to treatment', paper presented at symposium on Transcultural Psychiatry, Macau.

Williams, D. (1977), 'The Brides of Christ' in Ardener, S. (ed.) *Perceiving Women*, London, Dent.
Winnicott, D. W. (1974), *Playing and Reality*, Harmondsworth, Penguin.

Chapter 16
The contribution of S.H. Foulkes to group therapy
Malcolm Pines

The first group-analytic group that S. H. Foulkes conducted was in his consulting-room in the small West Country town of Exeter. The date was 1940 and for the first time a psychoanalyst trained in the classical tradition had brought his individual patients together in a group so as to listen to the way in which they communicated with each other, and saw his role as the facilitator of communication and understanding between the members of the group. What, then, had brought this man to this innovative, even revolutionary, practice in a small provincial town? To give some sort of an answer to this question we must retrace the steps of his personal and professional life.

At that time Foulkes was a refugee German-Jewish psychoanalyst who was soon to take his place in the British Army as a military psychiatrist. It might well be that the relative professional isolation of his situation at that time enabled him to free himself from the psychoanalytic context with its emphasis upon the two-person relationship and the classic psychoanalytic technique of interpretation. But the ideas had been burgeoning for many years in Foulkes's mind. It is clear that he had been influenced in the progress of his thought by the sociologist Norbert Elias whose two volumes, *Über den Prozess der Zivilisation*, he reviewed just before the war in the *International Journal of Psychoanalysis*.[1] In this work he found steps towards the synthesis of the study of society through sociology[2] and the study of the individual through psychoanalysis that could lead to a new form of psychotherapy. Prior to this he had already been exposed to modern sociological thought through the writings of and discussions with members of what were later to be known as the Frankfurt School. His first years as a psychoanalyst were spent in Frankfurt where the Institute of Sociology and the Institute of Psychoanalysis had close physical and cultural connections. The works of Fromm, Marcuse, Horkheimer and Adorno all derived from that source. Indeed, much of Foulkes's thought reflects directly that view of man which derives from Marx and his predecessors. To quote Marx: 'only in community with others has each individual the means of cultivating his gifts in all directions. In the real community the individuals obtain a freedom in and through their association'.

Interest in the psychoanalytic study of man in society was developed in the two decades preceding the Second World War by such anthropologists as Malinowski and Roheim, and by psychoanalysts who were greatly impressed by the effect of culture upon the personality and emotional conflicts of their patients. This historical point of view was most clearly to be found in the works of Eric Erikson, to whom Foulkes referred in his earliest book, and in the writings of those who later came to be known as the neo-Freudian school, such as Fromm, Horney and Sullivan, though Foulkes makes little reference to them in his work. In the book by Foulkes and Anthony there is recognition of the importance of Kurt Lewin's work to group-analytic psychotherapy. They acknowledge that it was Lewin who first put forward the idea of the group as a dynamic whole operating in a social field. Though Foulkes and Anthony acknowledged that the field situation is an expermental and not a therapeutic situation, they were prepared to borrow concepts from Lewin's studies.

They refer to studies on the analysis of group tension and to Lewin's concept of boundaries that separate the members and which regulate the distribution of tension within the group. They refer to the authoritarian and democratic group atmospheres, to the analysis of roles and to Lewin's concepts on time perspective. In their summing up they state that:[3]

> field theory has made a major contribution to the study of group dynamics and social fields which is of interest for a theoretical framework of group analysis. Its concepts of the dynamic whole, of figure and background, of belongingness, of tension and conflict, of the various types of leadership and 'atmospheres', of the time perspective and the here and now of cohesive and disruptive forces, of valences and of integrated and leaderless groups, have been incorporated as part of the group analytic system. The gestalt conception of the group is logically developed from basic gestalt theory and is unrelated to holistic ideas that naively transfer to the group properties that belong to the individual.

They quote with approval Lewin's statement that 'in the social as in the physical field the structural properties of a dynamic whole are different from the structural properties of the sub-parts. Both sets of properties have to be investigated.'[4]

From our present vantage point it is clear that there is a common viewpoint shared by all these writers which rose from a shift in psychodynamic thought, away from the study of the isolated individual and away from the earlier psychoanalytic viewpoint which saw the individual primarily developing through the impact of the primitive instinctual drive upon the developing mind, with personality resulting from the outcome of the inevitable conflicts between drive and defence. In Freud's later formulations the influence of culture and society was made explicit through the development of the super-ego, which represents the internalization of the parents and the creation of a structure within the mind of the individual which represents the viewpoint of that society of which he is a member. However, in classic psychoanalytic theory the influence of society came relatively late in the development of the child. At this time the psychoanalytic study of the family was in a very elementary phase. Foulkes brings the influence of family and of society into the foreground from the background position in which it was then regarded within psychoanalysis. In Foulkes's theory the individual is not prior to society; society and individual are artificial abstractions and are only apparently and semantically separate. 'Psychodynamics are rarely if ever confined within the boundaries of the individual but regularly include a number of inter-connected persons. They are transpersonal manifestations.'[5] Any one individual is born into a network of communication processes which inevitably and profoundly affect his nature from the moment of birth and even in all probability prior to this. Naturally, the new-born also contributes to the network of communications by its own unique actions and responses.

This viewpoint gives primacy to communication. It leads to a great emphasis on the importance of language and non-verbal communication and Foulkes was influenced by such work as that of Ruesch and Bateson.[6] We can go further back in the development of Foulkes's basic approach to psychology and see the profound influence of the work of the neurologist Kurt Goldstein. For two years Foulkes had worked as assistant to Goldstein, whose classic work on the effects of brain damage had led him to develop his own version of a gestalt-based psychology. In his own way Foulkes also was developing a dynamic field theory of personality which, although not based upon experimental psychology as was that of Lewin, and coming as Foulkes's work did from clinical practice with neurotic patients, was to lead to certain similarities. In this, Goldstein's influence was powerful:[7]

> From training and insight acquired in neurobiology assumed by my teacher Kurt Goldstein I held a conviction that the situation in which one works, the situation as a whole, really decided all part processes and their meaning, all part processes which one can observe. Naturally in a group the total situation is a group situation.

Goldstein's view of the integrated action of the central nervous system was that any individual neurone functions not in isolation but always as part of a communicating network. Each neurone represents therefore a nodal point within the network of the central nervous system. Foulkes took this viewpoint and applied it to the concept of the individual. The essence of man is social not individual. 'Each individual – itself an artificial though plausible abstraction – is basically and centrally determined, inevitably, by the world in which he lives, by the community, by the group of which he forms a part'.[8] Inside and outside, individual and society, body and mind, fantasy and reality, cannot be opposed, all separation is artificial isolation. The individual is a part of a social network, 'a little nodal point as it were', and can only artificially be considered in isolation like a fish out of water.

In Goldstein's major work *The Organism* he strongly emphasizes his viewpoint that the organism reacts altogether as a whole entity:[9]

> A specific performance is a specific pattern of the whole organism. Each stimulation always causes a change in the entire condition and only apparently a locally confined change. The reaction to stimulation is always determined by the functional significance of the stimulus in that part of the organism within reach of the stimulus. In the intact organism this reaction is determined by the whole; in the injured organism by the part which is relatively isolated.

Foulkes essentially saw the sick individual as the relatively isolated part of the organism. The organism is the social group, basically the family, from which the person derives his personality and his identity. This way of thinking is rooted in a Hegelian, holistic gestalt epistemology. It begins with the search for the significant whole and only later attempts an analysis of the component parts. The significant whole with which Foulkes begins is the social group and this view pervades both his theories as to the therapeutic effect of group psychotherapy and his views of the personality of the individual. Starting from this point of view, the sick person is like an isolated, injured part of the organism.[10]

> The neurotic position in its very nature is highly individualistic. It is group disruptive in essence for it is genetically the result of an incompatibility between the individual and his original group. It is at the same time an expression of destructive and aggressive tendencies.

Thus, what was in the healthy individual a social situation, where he or she represents a nodal point in a healthy and openly communicating social structure, becomes for the neurotic individual a focal rather than a nodal point for destructive and aggressive tendencies.

On the basis of this Foulkes describes the neurotic symptom as a disturbed expression of the patient's conflicts. Arising as they do from the position of isolation of the individual from the healthy context of his network, they can be described as follows: 'Symptoms in themselves autistic and unsuitable for sharing exert for this very reason an increasing pressure upon the individual for expressing them. As long as he cannot express them in a better communicable way he finds no real relief.' This leads, inevitably and logically, to the fashioning of a situation in which people can communicate better — more freely — to the small group as a therapeutic framework.

Group association

What Foulkes initially called free-floating discussion, which follows the invitation by the therapist to the group to 'talk about anything which comes to your mind without selection', he later called free association. Free association refers to an individual's stream of consciousness as it appears, either in the psychoanalytic situation with the analyst as audience, or in the mind of any individual who learns to practise the technique. In the move from individual free association, 'originally a one person concept, almost on a brain physiological level', Foulkes felt that he had made a historic and decisive step:[11]

> In the group the minds of strangers with a totally different individual conditioning are reacting and responding to each other. If

we find — as we do — that their responses, verbal or non-verbal, conscious or unconscious, to each other's productions can be used as a quasi-association to a common context, we make a totally new assumption. We now treat association as based on the common ground of unconscious *instinctive understanding* of each other. We no longer take as our basis of operation the conditioning of old experiences based on traces in the brain, on memory traces. Instead we accept that ideas and comments expressed by different members have the value of *unconscious interpretation*. The therapist's job is now to maintain an analytic attitude which enables him to understand the relationship of the members of the group to each other, to the group and to himself. This is a complex and mutual inter-reaction between members. It is impossible for the therapist to follow each individual separately at the same time and therefore he focuses on the total inter-actional field, on the matrix in which unconscious reactions meet.

Foulkes was fascinated by the interplay of personalities, of their words and actions within a shared context. He had the ability to stand back from the actions of the individual and to try to conceptualize patterns that were emerging within the boundaries of the given situation whether it be a social group or one taking place in a planned therapy situation. The significant difference between these two situations, social and therapeutic, is that the therapist submits all communications to the process of interpretation. Meaning is sought for in the understanding of the patterns of interaction, of process derived from studying content. Foulkes would, in all likelihood, have been in agreement with Whorf, who wrote:[12]

we all hold an illusion about talking, an illusion that talking is quite untrammelled and spontaneous and merely 'expresses' whatever we wish to have it express. This illusory appearance results from the fact that the obligatory phenomena with apparently free flow of talk are so completely autocratic that the speaker and listener are bound unconsciously as though in the grip of a *law of nature*.

The power of the community

In his first book Foulkes described what he called a basic law of group dynamics:[13]

The deepest reason why patients can reinforce each other's normal reactions and wear down and correct each other's neurotic reactions is that *collectively they constitute the very norm from which individually they deviate*. Each individual is to a large extent part of the group to which he belongs and this collective aspect permeates all through to his very core. Insomuch as he deviates from the norm of his group he is a variant of it and it is this very deviation that makes him into a unique individual. Thus within a group individuality manifests itself as variations upon a common ground. The sound part of individuality is both supported in the group and as a therapeutic culture develops the further growth of healthy individuality, is approved and supported by the group as a whole. Neurotic processes, that is symptoms and neurotic aspects of individuality, diminish as their individual meanings become communicated and understood, both by the patient and by the other members of the group. As the process of communication moves individuals and the group as a whole from the exchange of autistic un-understandable experiences, communicated by symptoms and by neurotic behaviour patterns, to shared, articulate, understandable communication, so there is a freeing of individual energies and potentialities which can be used now in the creative development of the group process itself and of the individual's own personal growth and change.

The group can only grow by what it can share and only share what it can communicate and only 'communicate' by what is has in common, e.g. in language, that is on the basis of the community at large. In that sense group treatment means applying 'common sense' — the sense of the community — to a problem by letting all those openly participate in its attempted solution who are in fact involved in it.

This can be done either by taking into therapy all those persons who are involved in the establishment of the original problem, that is the family group or the family plus its close associates, the 'root' group, or in a therapy group in which all members of the group eventually become involved in a re-creation of the original problem through the repetition compulsion. Thus again we must understand that Foulkes saw neurotic and psychotic problems as arising always within a network of interpersonal relationships and never within the individual in isolation. The group situation is therefore the natural forum for therapy, and the person's emotional problems will always reveal themselves in the pattern of disturbances of interpersonal relationship, within the network and the matrix of a group situation.

In a very interesting way Foulkes saw the group-therapy situation as one in which aggression and destructiveness, always part of the dynamics of the neurotic position, were being transformed into a more healthy form of aggressiveness and assertiveness. He described the neurotic position as being group destructive because *genetically* it is the result of incompatability[14] between the individual and his original group, primarily his family, and it was as a result of this that the neurotic position expresses aggressive and destructive tendencies. Within the group situation this destructive tendency, showing itself through disturbances in interpersonal relationships and communication, is forced into the open and does not receive the sanction of the group. The healthy aspect of the person's individuality, which must include his aggressive and assertive energies, is however both supported and accepted. Each person in the group eventually will find himself attacking the neurotic defences of his fellow-patients because these defences are group disruptive. In this way destructive energies are used to undermine the neurotic position of the other, i.e. are converted into constructive energies in relationship to the group processes; the constructive efforts within the group combine and support each other: 'Disruptive forces are consumed in mutual analysis, constructive ones utilized for the synthesis of the individual and the integration of the group as a whole.'[15] One of the most important functions of the leader is to use this tendency for progressive integration of the group to allow aggressive energies to be set free in order to serve constructive ends. There is a strong 'socio-biological' aspect of Foulkes's formulations. In an evolutionary sense he saw constructive tendencies having such great force because they will slowly but inevitably lead the group towards the norm of its own collectivity of which it is in itself a smaller part: 'The group has an inherent pull towards the socially and biologically established norm.'[16] Though he wrote that adjustment in a therapeutic group means social adjustment, he was very far from meaning that this meant adaptation to the superficial aspects of communal life.[17] The type of social adjustment that he had in mind was one that would enhance each member's creative individuality and potentiality and which would reduce neurotic inhibition of spontaneity, sensitivity and capacity for full emotional participation and relationships.

The group-analytic situation

The group-analytic group is a small face-to-face group of seven to eight members. Its arrangements are informal, no procedure is prescribed by the therapist for the participants to follow, they are not offered a programme or a plan on matters which are to be discussed. The conductor encourages spontaneity, in order to voice thoughts freely, and the development of a culture in which all contributions are admitted at any time and in which the members are free from the usual social censorship of their thoughts and of their feelings. If the group has an occupation it is to bring out verbally anything at all that the members wish to speak about. An essential part of the group-analytic situation is the conductor's attitude, as distinct from his technique. His technique should arise from his attitude, which is that of acceptance and encouragement of the members' communications. The group-analytic situation can be analysed into three component parts:

1 *Structure.* These are the patterns of relationships that are relatively stable and continuous and which arise out of the continuing interaction of the members of the group. These patterns of relationships take shape as habitual roles taken up by the individuals, as configurations between several members of the group. Alliances, subgroups, divisions, are examples of these.

2 *Process.* This is the dynamic component of the situation and is manifested as the interaction of all the elements of the situation in their reciprocal relationships and communications, verbal and non-verbal.

3 *Content.* Content is transmitted through the channels described above. It is through the analysis of the content, transmitted through structure and process, that psychopathology is revealed. The content that will emerge is determined by the structure and process already described. It is for this reason that the group analyst pays fundamentally more attention to structure and process than content.

The structure of the group, that is the patterns of relationships that are relatively stable and continuous, can be altered either by bringing about planned and deliberate changes in these patterns, as for instance by Moreno's use of the sociogram to clarify to the participants the nature of their relationships, or by the group-analytic method of the gradual evolution of awareness by the members of the group themselves of the ongoing patterns of relationships.

Inevitably any one individual in the group will participate and operate against the background of the total network of communications that has evolved in the group. This total network of communications is what Foulkes called the group matrix. The matrix is a slowly developing specifically group phenomenon, in which the meaning of individual neurotic responses can be mapped out against the group context. This brings in the dimensional aspect of foreground and background, again a phenomenon to which Foulkes paid great attention[18] and which arose from his background in gestalt psychology. The individual's contributions and participations stand out against the background of the group as a whole and represent his unique, as it were 'finger- or voice-print', his own unique style of participation. In group-analytic terms individual or group resistance is manifest as attempts to break the mandatory framework of the group-analytic situation. This is seen by such behaviour as latecoming, absenteeism, irregularity, meeting of members outside the group and so on. Transference in the group situation by virtue of its repetitiveness and exclusiveness tends to block group processes and becomes a problem for the group as a whole.

Once the group-analytic situation had been evolved, Foulkes was then able to consider what were the specific therapeutic factors that arose in this situation.

Definition: 'Group analytic psychotherapy is a form of psychoanalytic therapy which takes as its frame of reference the group as a whole. Like all psychoanalytic therapy it puts the individual into the centre of its attention.'[19]

As with all psychotherapy it has many factors that are similar to those of psychoanalysis. These are: greater consciousness of what were previously unconscious forces, catharsis, working through, insight and analysis of defence mechanisms. Besides these there are therapeutic factors which are group-specific arising out of the group situation in itself with all its social factors and forces.

Foulkes differentiated therapeutic factors in group-analytic situations from group-specific factors. Group-specific factors are:

1 *Socialization.* Through the process of sharing, through the experience of group acceptance and belongingness, the patient is brought out of his isolation into a social situation in which he can feel adequate. 'He is a fellow being on equal terms with the others.'[20]

2 *Mirror phenomena.* The patient can see aspects of himself

reflected in the image, behaviour and problems of the other members of the group. Through this he is enabled to confront various aspects of his social, psychological and body image through identification with and projection on to the other members of the group.

3 *Condenser phenomena.* Foulkes observed that even deep unconscious material is expressed more readily and more fully in the group through the loosening and stimulating effects that the persons have upon each other. Collectively, through the pooling of associations in the group, the meanings of symbols that appear in dreams or which manifest themselves through such symptom formations as phobias can be more readily understood. It is as if what the group holds in common through their dreams and symptoms can suddenly be understood, the symbol having acted as a 'condenser'.

4 *Exchange.* Not only do the members of the group often have a lively exchange with each other of information which leads to understanding both of oneself and of the meanings of emotional interactions and problems, but this also can lead to chain phenomena and resonance. Each member of the group will reverberate to a group event according to his currently displayed level of development. Thus, for example, if a theme evolves in a group that has to do with violence, one will see how some members withdraw into silence, others display a marked interest in the behaviour of the other persons, i.e. sharing the use of projection, others can be self-revelatory about their own fantasies. Themes that arise in the group that have to do with such issues as parting, loss, grief, mourning, are rich sources of information as to the current fixation and developmental level of the members of the group.

In trying to summarize therapeutic factors to be found in a group-analytic situation, Foulkes added to these four group-specific factors a number of others

1 *Group as support.* In any therapeutic situation there will always be a balance between the integrative and analytic forces at work. Analysis and interpretation inevitably arouse anxiety and can lead to further defensive activity on the part of the individual. The fact that the individual in a group situation is not alone in his attempt to resist, as well as to uncover, his inner world gives him support in this endeavour and lessens some of the inevitable narcissistic mortifications that arise through the acceptance of interpretation. The

group members will support each other through painful periods and members actively help each other towards the integration of the conflicting factors in their ongoing dynamic conflicts and situations. Often one sees patients accepting interpretations and comments from other members of the group which they would be very unlikely to accept from a therapist. This is because the person giving the interpretation or the confrontation will often offer himself as a person to be identified with, saying: 'I know from my own experience, I say this as one who has the same experiences as yourself and this is how and why I understand you so well.'
2 *Communication.* 'Working towards an ever more articulate form of communication is identical to the therapeutic process itself.'[21]

Foulkes described the therapeutic process 'from symptom to conflict' in terms of a growing capacity for communication. The therapist's role was seen by Foulkes as that of a person who facilitates the processes of communication in the group, that is the process of 'analysing' took precedence over that of 'interpretation'.[22]

The conductor strives to broaden and deepen the expressive range of all members, while at the same time increasing their understanding of the deeper unconscious levels. The zone of communication must include the experience of every member in such a way that it can be shared and understood by the others, on whatever level it is first conveyed. The process of communication has much in common with making the unconscious conscious and with the concepts of unconscious, pre-conscious, and conscious in topographical and dynamic sense.

Thus Foulkes described the work towards greater communication as going parallel with the process of analysis. In his thinking, neurotic and psychotic disturbances were always linked with a blockage in the system of communication and socialization of the patient, and the aim of the analysis was to translate the autistic symptom into a problem which could be verbalized. Each patient benefits through working towards a freer expression of conflicts within the group situation, both his own and that of his fellows. Neurotic and psychotic disturbances are bound up with deficient communicability and are blocked both intrapsychically and interpersonally. 'The language of the symptom, although already a form of communication, is autistic. It mumbles to itself secretly, hoping to be overheard; its equivalent meaning conveyed

in words is social.'[23] By increasing the range of communication that
can be communicated and understood in the group, Foulkes was concerned with two different aspects. The capacity of the members of the
group to speak at a higher level of communication, that is with more
sophistication, subtlety and comprehension, is a process fundamentally
akin to education. At the same time, however, the equally important
process of deepening understanding takes place:[24]

> The group has to go downwards and to deepen its understanding
> of the lower levels of the mind by broadening and deepening its
> vocabulary until every group member also understands these levels.
> Ideally the whole group should learn eventually to move over the
> full range of the scale.

He differentiated the rising level of communication in the group from
intellectualization in the following manner: 'Intellectualized discussion
is suspended, as it were, in mid-air, whereas true communication in
the group is firmly rooted in the experience of the group, and grows
from it.'[24]

The functions of the therapist

Foulkes differentiated between 'dynamic administration' and 'therapeutic activity'.

1 *Dynamic administration.* By this he meant those activities of the
conductor by which he creates the group-analytic situation itself.
This includes not only selection of patients and composition of the
group as a whole but also consideration of the social situation of
therapy itself. The therapist is the responsible administrator and has
to be aware of the interface between the group-therapy situation
and the social situation in which it occurs. Thus the therapist as
administrator has to take care of his relationships with the hospital,
clinic or other situation in which therapy takes place. He has to
guard and define the external boundaries of the group situation
itself. There are always powerful dynamic forces at the boundary
of the therapeutic situation, with pressures that will both support
and disrupt. The therapist's function as administrator is to enhance
the constructive and to diminish the disruptive forces. Thus he will
be concerned with the relationship of the psychotherapeutic unit or

department with the other departments and personnel of the hospital or clinic, so as to ensure that therapeutic factors within the group-analytic situation itself are allowed to flourish. He is concerned with such very basic factors as accommodation, that is having a room with the correct furniture, quietness and freedom from disturbance. The essential furniture is identical chairs arranged in a circle and in the centre of the space of the group Foulkes preferred to have a small round table which acted both as a focal object of the group, diminished the empty space and could even at times act as a transitional object.

2 *Therapeutic activity.* As conductor of the group he distinguished between leadership, analysis and interpretation.

As a *leader* the therapist is not primarily concerned with the formation of a good, efficient group. He is not out to create a team, to encourage good morale, friendship and bonhomie. As a leader he puts the group as a whole into the centre of his attention, tries to let the group speak to bring out agreement and disagreement, repressed tendencies and resistances against them. He activates and mobilizes that which is latent in the group and helps in the analysis and interpretation of content and of interpersonal relationships. He encourages the active participation of the members of the group and uses the contribution of the members in preference to his own. Inevitably he has a powerful effect on the evolving culture of the group. He emphasizes the 'here-and-now' aspect of the situation and stands for an attitude of tolerance and appreciation of individual differences. The conductor helps the members of the group to become active participants in the process of group maturation through which individual change then takes place.

Inevitably the group will in the first place look to the therapist as to an omniscient and omnipotent figure from whom they expect magical help. In that sense the group may look to the therapist as a father or a primordial mother. Foulkes did not go far into discussion of the symbolism of differences between the therapist as the father and the group as the mother.[25] What he did pay much attention to is the process of maturation that occurs as the group is gradually weaned from its dependence upon the therapist as leader. As Foulkes put it, one cannot be weaned from something that has not previously been there or powerfully established. To begin with the therapist should accept the exalted position that the group puts him into, not because in this way it gratifies his own wishes for power but because from this position he can lead the group into a process of analysis, insight and, eventually, more appropriate adult behaviour. To begin with he accepts whatever position the group chooses to confer on him, realizing that this gives group security. It is a position that he accepts in order eventually to liquidate it, to change from being a leader *of* the group to being a leader *in* the group. Eventually, as the group replaces the leader's authority by that of the group itself, there is a process that leads to a change of the super-ego relationship both of individuals and of the way in which they collectively act in relationship to these powerful forces in the group situation itself. The power of the leader is based upon projections of such super-ego components of each person's personality. Gradually, as they wean themselves from dependence upon him and as he uses his power not destructively or coercively but in order to liberate the group's capacity for emotional communication, understanding and growth, so leadership, his or theirs, becomes an ego rather than a super-ego activity.

Foulkes saw *interpretation* as a perceptive and creative act which arose from the receptive, passive attitude of the therapist. The conductor allows the interpretation to come to him from the contributions of his patients. Basically he differentiates the therapist's interpretative activities into the following three types:

1 Interpretation which enables unconscious processes to become more conscious.
2 Interpretation of resistance and defence.
3 Interpretation of transference reactions.

The group itself develops an interpretative culture which can often be useful but sometimes is defensive and a manifestation of resistance and this has to be interpreted.

Foulkes felt very free to make interpretations to individuals as well as to the group as a whole. He considered that interpretations were always significant to the group as a whole as well as for the individual. Thus, they could be addressed to any particular individual, could refer to any configuration or relationships within the group, between the group and the conductor, could be concerned with the here-and-now or range over the whole history of the group. They should preferably be based upon the available experience of the moment and on the level at which the emotion is most active.

He advises the conductor to direct his interpretations towards:

1 On-going group interactive processes.
2 Repetitive conflict situations.
3 An understanding of the past experiences which spring to the mind of the patient in association to the group situation.

4 Current experiences in the life of the patient both within and without the group.

5 In particular what he called 'boundary incidents', events taking place at the interface between the ongoing group and the outgoing life of the individuals comprising it.

Foulkes saw no essential distinction between processes inside the group and those going on outside, for inside and outside to his mind were false dichotomies. Boundary incidents therefore could involve the relationship of a patient to any member of his own social group, to his body, as manifestations of illness, psychosomatic or otherwise.

Transference

It should be clear from what has been said so far in this article that in Foulkes's theory and practice, the therapist does not confine his activities to interpretation nor are his interpretations always directed to transference, to himself as the central figure of the group. To do this would be to maintain the therapist in the role of the central figure, as a projection of super-ego fantasies on the part of the individuals. The therapist's activities are directed towards liberating the members of the group from primitive and powerful forces, which he does partly by interpretative activities, but to a very considerable extent he aids in this process by facilitating the maturation and development of the group as a whole. He therefore opposed the argument that only transference interpretations are mutative, and because he did not draw a rigid distinction between events occurring within the group situation itself and those occurring outside, he felt free to pay attention to these 'external' events. For him the equation for therapy was $T = (t + X)$. T stands for the total therapeutic situation, small t for the transference and X the current interpersonal and life situation of the patient outside the group. In Foulkes's view a situation had developed within psychoanalysis where, as he put it, the transference can swallow up the neurosis. By this he meant that the transference process, which should be the main vehicle of liberation for the individual from his neurotic conflicts, can become so powerful and so resistant to change that it largely replaces the illness and does not give way to a healthy resolution. This could arise from a faulty technique, that of exclusive attention to the transference. This can have the effect of infantilizing the patient and maintaining him in a dependent, neurotically gratifying position and one which also gratifies the therapist's unconscious counter-transference.

The culture of the group

Thirty years after Foulkes's first explorations in group-analytic psychotherapy we may find it hard to recapture the significance of that
experiment. Now that group psychotherapy is so firmly established
as a major form of psychotherapy, it is difficult to imagine its non-
existence – that on one particular day in Exeter in the year 1940
S. H. Foulkes invited the patients whom he was treating individually
to come together and to 'free associate' together, as a form of free-
flowing dialogue. After his session, evidently elated and relieved, he
said to his wife that an historical event had taken place in psychiatry
that day 'but', he added, 'nobody knows about it'.

Psychotherapeutic techniques are special forms of human interaction and association, that is to say of relationship. They are situated
in a cultural context from which they can only be artificially isolated,
when they are to be seen as foreground without background. If the
move from individual to group psychotherapy is seen solely as a change
in technique, this ignores the significance of the background, of the
cultural context. The significant move is from individualism to pluralism,
and to a significantly different use of space and time in the psychotherapeutic context. The time and space dimension of a psychotherapeutic situation is now shared by a number of individuals, not solely
by one expert and by one patient. These individuals have the shared
responsibility of creating the psychotherapeutic situation. This is a new
form of human association with new potentialities; a group that can
form its own culture, one that is concerned directly with issues of the
emotions and of attitudes towards them. The group 'decides' what is
to be admitted and to be left out of its discourse and on this basis
develops an unique culture. Foulkes's approach was to go along with
whatever his groups wanted to bring in or to leave out and then to
work with the consequences of their actions.

The significance and influence of the work of Foulkes

Within *group psychotherapy* Foulkes's influence has been very considerable, though it often goes unacknowledged. Many persons are
unaware of the fact that even our terminology, when we classify
groups as open, slow-open and closed, was devised by him. The stan-
dardization of a small group as a regular once-a-week form of psychotherapy with a group composed of seven or eight individuals carefully

chosen so as to represent a balanced and heterogenous group is based upon his experience. The technique of group association, the therapist's role of listening to the group as a whole and understanding patterns that develop within the given context of the group, was his most significant contribution. As one of his close associates, Dr de Maré, has described it, he introduced for the first time into psychotherapy a 'movable context'. The group-analytic situation is not a static situation. As the group develops its network of communication, so it forms its matrix which, given the appropriate conditions and technique, extends the range of communication and of understanding of all the members of the group. Here the work of Foulkes differs significantly from that of his contemporaries Bion and Ezriel who do not allow for progressive maturation of the group and of the significant change in context.

Family therapy

Foulkes laid a theoretical foundation for family therapy. Though he did not himself practise family therapy at all extensively, he made reference to it in his writings and encouraged his colleagues in this direction. The work of A. C. R. Skynner[26] is a significant contribution in this direction.

Network, theory and therapy

Here again Foulkes was a pioneer, bringing as he did the concept of the network of communications into the foreground and by describing the individual as a nodal point in this network. In group therapy a significant part of the person's social world is brought into the therapeutic situation with the aim of uncovering conflicts and misunderstandings within that group, which then becomes in itself the process of therapy.

The therapeutic community

The 'second Northfield experiment' laid the foundations for a most significant development in hospital psychiatry. This work, carried out in a British Army military hospital between 1940 and 1945, led to the development of the concept of the therapeutic community.[27] After the war Foulkes was no longer directly involved with in-patient psychotherapy but his example and his influence can be seen in the work of David Clark.[28]

The large group

Though Foulkes's main writings were concerned with the small group and he was not over-enthusiastic about the application of group-analytic theory to large groups (upwards of twenty-five persons), he significantly influenced those persons who had begun to develop the large group as a significant therapeutic situation. The leading proponent and theoretician of large-group psychotherapy is P. B. de Maré.[29, 30, 31] Persons who have themselves experienced the confusions and difficulties of a large-group situation and seen how these can be resolved and that a new form of social organization can arise in these particular circumstances, are firmly impressed with the therapeutic potentialities of the situation where, in the words of de Maré, the individual can discover what it means to be a citizen. In this way some of Foulkes's hopes that through group psychotherapy mankind can achieve a better understanding and a more harmonious and less destructive pattern of relationships may some day come closer to reality.

Notes

1 Foulkes, S. H. (1938), *International Journal of Psychoanalysis*, vol. 19, p. 263.

Elias named his approach 'socio-genetic'. It is an argument about internalisation through the process of civilisation. What had previously been an external conflict, a 'real' one in the life of the individual, becomes, because of the historical and cultural process, an internal one. Aggression which at one time was freely expressed by the individual in his relationship with others gave him freedom of expression at the expense of being at the mercy of his fellow-beings. As the application of crude physical force and violence is monopolised by the state, aggressive impulses have to be directed inwards and fear becomes internalised as well. As there is less to project on to externally in the form of real dangers, inner objects become the containers of aggressive and persecutory fantasies.

Foulkes comments that psychoanalysis has tried to trace the

284   *The contribution of S. H. Foulkes to group therapy*

sources of the super-ego in the human species, mainly in two
directions, firstly the phylogenetic and secondly the psycho-
genetic. In addition, we should now add the socio-genetic. The
consequence of this is that the psychoanalyst needs to consider
the whole network of the social inter-relationships in which the
individual is involved and to accept the fact that there is no sharp
line of demarcation between what we are accustomed to describe
as inside and outside, individual and environment.

2 Foulkes, S. H. (1942), *International Journal of Psychoanalysis*,
vol. 23, p. 94.
3 Foulkes, S. H., and Anthony, E. J. (1957) *Group Psychotherapy:
The Psychoanalytic Approach*, Harmondsworth, Penguin, p. 39.
4 Ibid., p. 40.
5 Foulkes, S. H. (1964), *Therapeutic Group Analysis*, London,
Allen & Unwin, p. 180 (German edn, p. 89).
6 Ruesch, J., and Bateson, G. (1951), *Communication: The Social
Matrix of Psychiatry*, New York, Morton.
7 Foulkes, S. H. (1973), Address to 1st European Workshop on
Group Analysis. *Group Analysis*, VI, p. 73.
8 Foulkes, S. H. (1948), *Introduction to Group-Analytic Psychotherapy*, London, Heinemann, p. 10.
9 Goldstein, K. (1939), *The Organism. A Holistic Approach to
Biology*. New York, American Book Company.
10 Foulkes, *Therapeutic Group Analysis*, op. cit., p. 89.
11 Ibid., p. 4.
12 Whorf, Benjamin (1973), 'Linguistics as an exact science' in *The
Silent Language*, ed. Edward T. Hall, New York, Doubleday
Anchor Books, p. 123.
13 Foulkes, S. H. (1948), *Introduction to Group-Analytic Psychotherapy*, London, Heinemann, pp. 29-30.
14 'Incompatibility' can refer both to an environment failure, that of
the 'facilitating environment' (Winnicott) leading to cumulative
trauma (Khan) or to the infant's or child's inability to make the
best use of what was offered or available.
15 Foulkes, *Introduction to Group-Analytic Psychotherapy*, op. cit.,
p. 31.
16 Foulkes, *Therapeutic Group Analysis*, op. cit., p. 90.
17 Ibid., p. 90.
18 It is interesting to compare this formulation of transference in
group-analytic terms with the recent formulation by George
Klein in his revision of psychoanalytic theory. Klein defines
transference as 'the peculiar mixture of over-estimation and affective evaluation bestowed upon people in significant positions
without consideration of the *context* of the relationship'. By
emphasizing the concept of *context* Klein is drawing attention
to the importance of the figure-ground relationship, as did Foulkes.
19 Foulkes, *Therapeutic Group Analysis*, op. cit., p. 39.
20 Ibid., p. 33.
21 Foulkes, *Introduction to Group-Analytic Psychotherapy*, op. cit.,

p. 169.
22 Foulkes, *Therapeutic Group Analysis*, op. cit., p. 112.
23 Foulkes and Anthony, op. cit., p. 259.
24 Ibid., p. 263.
25 Slater, P. (1966), *Microcosm*, London, Wiley.
26 Skynner, A. C. R. (1977), *One Flesh, Separate persons*, New York, Brunner-Maazel.
27 Main, T. F. (1946), 'The hospital as a therapeutic institution', *Bulletin of the Menninger Clinic*, vol. 10, no. 3, pp. 66-70.
28 Clark, D. H. (1964), *Administrative Therapy*, London, Tavistock. Social Science paperback, Tavistock 1971 and various contributors to *The large Group – Dynamics and Theory*, ed. L. Kreeger, London, Constable, 1975.
29 De Maré, P. B. (1972) *Perspectives in Group Psychotherapy*, London, Allen & Unwin.
30 De Maré, P. B. (1975) in *The Large Group. Dynamics and Theory*, ed. Lionel Kreeger, London, Constable.
31 De Maré, P. B. (1977), 'Group analytic principles in natural and stranger groups', *Group Analysis*, vol. 10, no. 1.

Chapter 17
Affective warp and metascience
Juan Rof-Carballo

The radical factor of constitutive affective warp

Science being a product of human activity, the purpose of which is a better knowledge of reality, one may legitimately examine it, according to the form it takes, with regard to its relationship with the social structure in which it develops, the psychology of those who cultivate it and the conceptions of the world which underlie it and covertly determine the policies which stimulate and develop it. All of these facets which allow us to reflect, in a critical manner, on science as a human product that is characteristic of our times, and which, in reality, complete and even overtake the so-called Philosophy of Science, are based, to my way of thinking, upon a radical biological factor which I have named constitutive affective warp. S. H. Foulkes has been kind enough in his *Therapeutic Group Analysis*, to link his key 'network' concept to my 'affective warp' pp. 147-8.

The basic fact that human beings are born prematurely does not have a solely biological significance. The cultural repercussions of this, although they have become increasingly widespread in recent years, have not yet reached their final peak.

This 'biological prematurity' corresponds, from the neurophysiological point of view, to the immaturity of large and important areas of the brain, mainly in the so-called inner brain or limbic cortex. From the genetic point of view more importance is being given each day to the epigenetic processes which take place in the development of the newborn child, either through the activity of latent genes or the action of development genes or because of reverberant readjustments between the milieu and genetic factors which, as long as the living being does not fully constitute itself, continue to regulate and determine its development.

The extraordinary influence which 'early experiences' have on the animal world and also on primates, programming certain important enzyme systems, such as those which govern the activity of the endocrine glands and the nervous system, is reflected in the observations made by psychologists on children who have been abandoned or who lack affection, and is linked to the importance of 'attachment behaviour' which has been analysed by many researchers and which, in the field of psychoanalysis, is equivalent to the superior functions known as the pre-object and object relationship.

Studies of severe psychotic and neurotic cases have unanimously placed great emphasis on the importance of disturbances produced during what some call the 'symbiotic phase', that is to say, during the early and extremely close mother-child relationship. To explain the dynamics of the constitution of the human psyche during the first months of life, some famous psychoanalysts, such as Spitz, use terms taken from embryology or genetics, such as 'organizers' and 'proto-organizers' and so on. Elsewhere I have pointed out the importance of this 'convergence' of results which is graphically expressed in the similarity of concepts used by researchers coming from a wide range of backgrounds:

1 Symbiotic relationship; first dialogue – Spitz, M. Mahler (psychoanalysts).
2 Pre-object relationship; particularly favourable environment – Winnicot, etc. (psychoanalysts).
3 Early experiences (biologists and psychologists).
4 Primary or programming conditioning (reflexologists and behaviourists).
5 Neuro-endocrine programming (endocrinologists and neurologists).
6 Epigenetic period; activation of development genes (geneticists, evolutionists, embryologists).
8 Socio-genetic inheritance (cultural anthropologists).
8 Imprinting, 'Prägung' (ethologists).
9 Basic defect; basic fault (psychotherapists).
10 Basic matrix (group psychotherapists).

Each one of these concepts defines a reality which cannot be exactly superimposed on that defined by the others. Therefore they are not synonyms. However, all of them, to some extent, embrace a common ground to which all these studies lead and which I have called the 'affective warp', that is, the basic fabric which is later completed by a 'social weft' (P. de la Quintana), the one shaping the other and vice versa.

To give an idea, however superficial, of the complexity of this radical affective warp factor, I have isolated, within it, a series of parameters or functions (see my book *Violencia y ternura*) namely:

1 The *protection* or *defence* function. Bowlby's attachment behaviour or support behaviour.

2 The *liberating* function. The child's exploratory or investigatory urge. The withdrawal or separation impulse (Bowlby).

3 The *structuring* function. The first arrangement of the child's world, by the mother.

4 The *linking* function. The patterns for care (suckling the child, holding the child in a certain way, speech accents, the language and so on) are passed on from one generation to another (Boszormenyi-Nagy's 'hidden loyalties').

5 The *life-giving* function of the world of objects. When this is lacking, the child cannot distinguish between the 'animate' world of living objects and the 'inanimate' one of lifeless objects. The mother acts as a 'mediator between the child and reality'.

6 *Basic confidence* or *basic trust*. The precise adjustment of a child's needs, including the low development of cerebral neurones, constitutive enzymes and something which complements and satisfies these, creates a basic sense of confidence, disturbances of which are revealed in human pathology.

7 The *horizon* function. The 'emotional period' with its tendency to wandering, to leaving home, when the warp is deficient, demonstrates a radical vector of the human psyche which oscillates between the need for proximity and the need for remoteness.

8 The *integrating* function. The 'Ego' is, in fact, the expression of the fact that, as a child grows, increasingly complicated and better integrated systems of unitary control of the psychosomatic reality are developed.

9 *Biopsychic unity*. This is expressed in a more or less successful harmonization of the neuro-endocrine controls.

10 The need for backing — in other words, a person's whole life subsists on a support base. One of man's tendencies is that, as soon as he becomes independent, he re-creates support structures of a more permanent nature, such as institutions and companies, giving rise to a 'family', a stable organization and so on.

This first relationship is transactional, that is to say, it is not one of cause and effect, of the mother or environment on the child, but one of a mutual and intricate interaction. This presupposes an instinctive diatrophic impulse in the people responsible for the child's welfare, this being different from the procreative sexual impulse but related to what I would call diatrophic sexuality. Biologically speaking, this is evidenced by the fact that, on the one hand, the body contains progesterone, needed for the implantation of the fertilized ovum in the womb and the first stages in its development, and lactation hormones, while, on the other hand, mothers (and also males) have an impulse to protect, help, educate and, above all, *pass on* their behavioural patterns, their habits and customs and their value systems to their new offspring.

Man is born of this first complementarity, in a dynamic ensemble of extraordinary richness which I have researched in my books. However, let us not forget that protection is as essential as separation to the affective warp. The classic example of Freud's grandson who, at an early age, left the side of his mother who, apparently, was not paying him any attention, going further and further away, exploring the world around him, until a moment was reached in which the anxiety of the child and the mother became unbearable and both rushed towards a mutual encounter, is a living expression of this twofold aspect of the affective warp, in which the desire for independence and autonomy is as vital as the urge to pass on cultural guidelines.

This is what Lichtenstein failed to take into account when he coined the term 'identity' (basically superimposable on mine of the 'affective warp'), to indicate an 'objective structure of early childhood'. It is important to make this quite clear from the very beginning, because this concept of identity (very different from the sense in which Erikson used the word) is the basis of Hans Kilian's *Dialectic Anthropology*. For this author, the child is socially 'stamped' by this first tutelary relationship and immersed in the dominant cultural system in such a way that he will more easily sacrifice his life than his unconscious identity. He also sides with the point of view of Lichtenstein who states that while admitting the pleasure principle, there are even more powerful reasons for admitting the principle of identity. The latter would be a more powerful factor of human motivation than the pleasure principle. 'Identity', for both of them, represents that human structure in which the psychic life of a person is linked to his social life and his social life to his psychic life. The two are thus institutionalized and, throughout the course of a lifetime, reinforced, just as the different layers of the bark of a tree consolidate and strengthen the trunk, year after year, by being laid down, one after another, around a basic nucleus. Both writers forget that this basic nucleus is, by virtue of the very essence of the concept of an affective warp, revolutionary

Figure 17.1

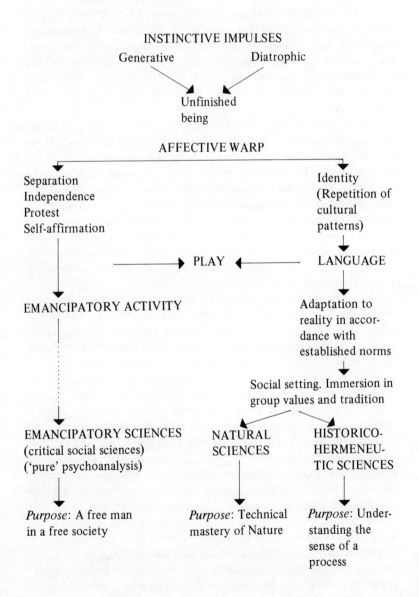

and innovatory, since in it is reproduced the 'desire to explore and be independent' of the young child who, biologically speaking, is based upon the autonomous development of his own particular genes which weave their own neurone programming within the subtle modifications which the environment is continuously overprinting. Together with 'basic confidence', this leaves the new being with a radical sense of autonomy which may even include a desire for protest and independence.

Therefore, even at the very beginnings of human life, we have both basic instinctive impulses: the generative and the diatrophic, converging on the 'unfinished being' or child and producing the phenomenon of the affective warp, with its two radical aspects: the one in which there is a tendency to repeat cultural patterns and the other of protest and affirmation of the 'self'. In Figure 17.1 I have tried to outline my ideas a little. It will immediately be seen how the area which, in metascience, is made up of the so-called 'emancipatory sciences' starts out, in a straight line, from this 'emancipatory desire' which is already biologically implanted in the human being.

Scientific endeavour, according to Radnitzky and Törnebohm

Radnitzky and Törnebohm conceived of science as 'an endeavour which produces and improves knowledge'. They illustrated their ideas with the following diagram (Figure 17.2), which I have slightly modified.

First of all, we have a 'group of researchers' or 'team' which operates in close relationship with IM, a certain 'intellectual environment'. This bounds the research which must be carried out within a certain system of 'ideals, preferences or tastes' for certain undertakings or preferably choosing the transmission of priority concepts. Here we can see part of the 'affective warp' in operation, in which we can observe 'identity' (in the Lichtenstein-Kilian sense of the word), this being the 'transmision of patterns' or 'intellectual priorities'. IM also provides 'intellectual resources', that is, ways of thinking, logic, mathematics and so on.

The research group adopts a certain 'strategy' which governs the research process. This is applied to a sector of reality, which we shall call R. Thus, a 'knowledge system' is produced on this sector of reality. The results are communicated to the 'affected parties'. . . . Between these two elements, we have Colleagues A who specialize in the same

Figure 17.2 Scientific endeavour, according to Radnitzky and Törnebohm

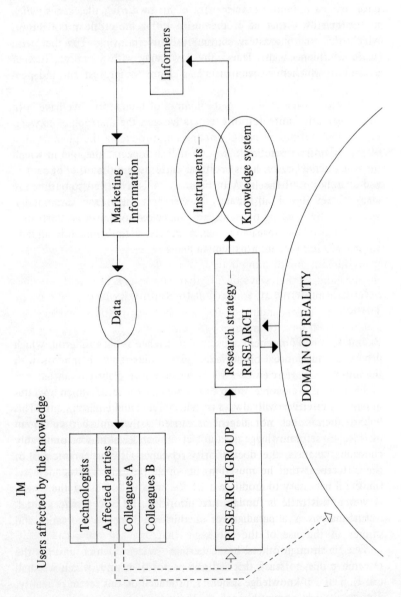

field as the researchers and Colleagues B who work in associated branches. In addition, there are intellectuals who, using the new knowledge acquired, improve or modify their 'image of the world'. One important area is that of T, the technologists, who apply the knowledge for a better mastery of reality. This reality may be modified by these technologies. Thus, physicists may 'create' new particles in their laboratories or sociologists may change society.

Dialectics and complementarity

Following normal practice, a psychoanalyst does not only get to know more about the person he is analysing but he also increases the knowledge he has of himself. According to the metascientists, this rule generally pertains in all human sciences. This thesis is fundamentally central to the thinking of Habermas. The world of meanings inherited by tradition is only revealed to the interpreter inasmuch as, when interpreting another person, a patient or another culture, he simultaneously opens himself up to himself or to the culture itself. It is only after understanding 'other ways of life' that we can imagine other 'possible ways of living'. This all forms a dialectic process which operates not only in our understanding of the past, but also in the study of other societies. Both serve to improve our own focus on the future.

This is a good moment to stop for a while and consider how it is that, while in classical or 'academic psychology' or in normal medical anamnesis the 'interview' between the doctor or psychologist is only thought of as a possible 'source of error', psychoanalytic or psychosomatic interviews will always produce (or should always produce, if the method has not degenerated into a mechanical process) an increase in self-knowledge in the person investigating or asking the questions, that is, the doctor or psychologist. In order for this to occur, I repeat that he must have an open, receptive attitude. Here I think it is necessary to modify a little the thinking of Gerard Radnitzky. However, this little is fundamental. In his desire to demonstrate that psychoanalysis is a paradigm of the dialectic 'feedback' that he enshrines in the use of the apothegm that one can only attain self-knowledge through others, he neglects the thing which is fundamental to achieve this, to reach this attitude or position, since it is not only a question of self-knowledge acquired by analysis, first personal and then didactic, which no psychoanalyst can escape, but of something more. What is essential is a 'mistrust' of anything which, in a personal interpretation, may be an 'installation' of the psychotherapist, in the interpretative schema and, on a deeper level, a mistrust of the 'destruction' of truth, which is implicit in any feverish urgency to expound. It is interesting to note how, in recent years and in widely varying fields of psychoanalysis, full importance is beginning to be given to this actively waiting attitude which has been individually discovered by such specialists with different backgrounds and ways of thinking as K. R. Eissler, Wolfgang Loch and W. R. Bion. Before dealing with this question (which, for me, is most radical, since it coincides, as we shall see later, with ideas which I have been expounding for a long time now and which, as time goes on, have been receiving ample confirmation), let us see how this 'psychoanalysis as a model' is applied by Radnitzky to shed light on the 'dialectic complementarity' between natural sciences and human sciences.

In reality, seen from our own point of view, Freud's fundamental achievement, his revolution in psychology, is based on reestablishing the disturbed dialogue between doctor and patient, between psychiatrist and neurotic or psychotic, what Alfonso de Waelhems has called the 're-establishment of the inter-subjective discourse'. In restoring this dialogue, we obtain a new image of the man.

Essential to this new image of the man is, as we saw, his 'identity', that is, the nucleus which constitutes him during the first inter-human relationship and in which we can stress the transmission aspect of tradition, or the 'tendency towards independence facet', the emancipating facet. If we only pay attention to the first of these, then we will see a picture of man alienated by society and we will conclude that by changing this society in a revolutionary manner, will we be able to (in theory) liberate him. However, man *is* the living record of his dialectic alternation between the patterns which shape the world which has been passed down to him and his *own* emancipatory powers. It is in this way that we will be better able to understand what makes a 'true psychotherapeutic dialogue'. If man were to totally conceal his subconscious, with no volition for revelation, which stems from the same emancipatory longing that, as a child, made him explore the world and withdraw from his mother, that is to say that it stems from the liberating facet of the affective warp, there would be no possibility of emancipation.

In order to understand how knowledge of the psychoanalytic situation is constantly growing, Radnitzky, using Apel's 'model' in order to apply it to the connection of natural sciences to human sciences, resorts to the principle of complementarity, introduced into the science by Bohr. According to Radnitzky, the application of the dialectic method to metascience as well as to the historiography of science is a fruitful process. In his view, dialecticians consider that 'Bohr's principle of complementarity' is the classical model with which the application of the dialectic method to the study of the growth of scientific knowledge begins. As is well known, this principle of Bohr's put an end to the conflict in microphysics that set the corpuscular theory of light against the wave theory. Following this principle, these theories are not mutually exclusive; all that happens is that they cannot be applied at the same time. This principle has been compared to what happens with a mountain; we cannot see both faces simultaneously because one hides the other. Or, we have the example of a man whose face cannot be simultaneously seen from the front and in profile. Perhaps the best image comes from psychosomatic pathology and was coined, many years ago, by Victor von Weizsäcker who talked of the 'revolving door principle'. As we pass through the door, we cannot see, at the same time, what is happening in the street and what is going on in the hotel foyer.

Now, while Bohr's 'complementarity' refers to the 'alternative ways' of describing a relationship between theories about physics, of which we can apply one as much as the other but not both at the same time, Törnebohm and Radnitzky (1970), the two pioneers of metascience, developed a more refined conceptual apparatus, for which the type of knowledge we observe in the psychoanalytic situation will serve as an accurate model.

In the classic examples of complementarity, that of the appearance as a wave or the appearance as a particle, each one complements the other, just as a face seen from the front is complemented by the appearance of this face when seen in profile. In conjunction with the idea of 'dialectic mediation' or 'complementarity', Radnitzky talks of 'polarity'. The description of a face seen from the front is 'polarly counterposed' to the description of a face in profile, and the description of a physical phenomenon in the form of particles is polarly counterposed to a description of this phenomenon in wave form. Is this really so? In reality, he adds, everything depends on the framework in which the question is considered. Within the framework of classical physics, there is 'polarity'. One explanation excludes the other. However, within the framework of the quantum theory, these explanations are not mutually exclusive. That is to say, there is no polarity. The example quoted by Radnitzky is that of the classical optics of Newton and Huyghens. Both of these concerned themselves with 'light', not different aspects of it. In this sense they were 'polar' and mutually exclusive. Nevertheless, this is so only if we move within the physics of Huyghens or Newton. Today, as our knowledge increases, we can say that they both complement each other. Polarity may become complementarity as science grows. Radnitzky deduces from all this that the impression of polarity given by the two theories stems from the totality of them both: that is to say, the pretension of each theory that it gives the only possible explanation of the phenomenon.

Let us apply this to medicine. Scientifico-natural medicine claims that there is no other explanation of the phenomenon of man or the 'reality' of the persona than that given by itself, using its own particular methods. It therefore rejects, as being polarly counterposed, any psychoanalytical or psychodynamic explanation of an illness. Let us look at another example, the one preferred by Radnitzky, that of the Marxist theory. Marx explained the totality of historic reality by means of a sole variable which he made absolute. This variable, economics, is considered as the total reality. Also, in certain schools of psychoanalytic thought, the libidinal impulse is made an absolute. The impression of polarity is not concerned with knowledge in itself, but with the tacit, implied pretension of each school of science to represent the totality of knowledge. Now, as soon as knowledge increases, that is, as soon as we know better, this polarity diminishes. Then, tension in the scientific field, the struggle which, in practice, means scorn and contempt or 'not wanting to know', disappears and changes into complementarity.

This process has been described on many occasions and I, myself, have dealt with it in my books, *Medicina y actividad creadora, El hombre como encuentro*, and *Biología y psicoanálisis*. Generally, stress is not placed on nor light shed upon the role that time plays in the acquisition of this new way of seeing things. It must be supposed that our installation of a way of seeing things (for example, the refusal to accept the psychosomatic point of view and the tendency to value only the physico-chemical explanation of reality) undergoes, with experience, hidden impacts, subconscious shocks, shakings of intimate convictions which do not cross the consciousness threshold. The same thing happens in psychoanalysis, when a reality which we have repeatedly rejected, which we have been unable to see, suddenly produces a great 'Ah' of understanding as it is revealed, in all its clarity, before our very eyes. In *El hombre como encuentro* I say:

> It is as though *something*, in an underground or secret fashion, *had been organizing itself* within ourselves, behind our back, so as

to speak, as though this something had been producing a new
restructuring of our perceptive systems. . .

And, in *Biología y psicoanálisis*, I add:

> This *active structure* (I am referring to what Merton M.
> Gill calls *functional structure*) is what allows us, in conjunction with this
> knowledge, to understand, in a simple and economic way, a much
> wider field of knowledge which *becomes internally integrated* and
> which can be explained by its internal interconnections. We have
> created a *new level of knowledge*, a knowledge which one might
> say is more structured, wider and more integrated, with more
> 'negative entropy'. This 'creative assimilation' allows us to under-
> stand not just *one* thing, but *many* things . . .

Merton M. Gill's functional structure is comparable to Piaget's cognitive assimilation (based, in turn, on the embryological model of
genetic assimilation evolved by Waddington) since 'it implies the
integration of existing structures which may remain substantially
unchanged and simply accommodate themselves to the new situation
and are used to prepare new knowledge'. In their turn, both ideas are
connected with Pribram's concept of cerebral competence (that is, the
competence of the brain to organize the stimuli it receives) and which,
according to this neurophysiologist, is essential for all learning processes.

Pribram chose the term 'competence', basing himself on embryological models. The embryonic outline of a tissue becomes competent
in order to organize a new structure, the eye, for example. It is not
enough for it to be 'pluripotent' or to possess a 'capacity for learning',
but it must also be 'prepared, ready to respond to an inductor'. I myself said (*Biología y psicoanálisis*, p. 373, 1st edn):

> to be competent is to be in a position to be able to respond to an
> inductor, in the same way as a student will only learn when he is
> prepared to actively assimilate what he is taught and a patient will
> only assimilate the psychoanalyst's 'interpretation' when he is
> 'competent' to do so. . .

'Configuration' or 'gestalt' psychology argues that in this growth of
knowledge which is the learning process, what happens is that a new
gestalt, a richer, more sense-laden configuration with wider horizons is

formed. However, this explanation does not allow us to see what there is of a creative act in the new context. From the neurophysiological point of view, it is more explanatory to think that a new 'perception organizer' has been created. Let us consider the case of a painter who, in order to obtain a better appreciation of his work, stepping back one or two paces, closes his eyes, not looking at the painting for a while, in order to see it as it really is. Thus, he tries to cut himself off, free himself, emancipate himself from his normal, routine way of looking at things. Pribram says that stimuli (which, for the behavioural physiologist, determine complex associations by 'conditioned reflexes') are not things which are associated by mere proximity, but are neurologically determined phenomena which are gathered and brought together by means of a previously established cerebral competence. This cerebral competence or 'neuronic structure' is determined by a *necessary*, previous preparatory experience. In man, however, there is another, often latent, contrasting tendency which often gets out of the control of this tyrannous organizer of the world and then there arises in him an imperative need to see the world in a different way, from a viewpoint that, since it is set further back, because it is more primitive, going back to before the one he now uses as thought, being a pre-thought or an attitude preceding that of thinking,[1] will allow him to free himself from these chains or habits which shape his world of thought and perception in accordance with traditional rules. This is when the emancipating component of the constitutive affective warp, its liberating aspect, reappears, indissolubly united and interwoven, as I have said so often, with the support aspect.

In order to achieve this, man has to overcome his strong tendency towards installation in a world schema, his mental inertia. What happens is that growth takes place, not, however, through any effort to know more or better, but through a certain difficult passivity which, paradoxically, is born from a suppression of effort. Eissler, in his book *Talent and Genius*, in trying to explain the ultimate key to the genius of his master, Freud, resorts to Goethe's phrase in *Faust: Es irrt der Mensch, so lange er strebt* (Man goes wrong as long as he strives) and comments: 'This is a profound truth.'

Notes

1 V. Chung-Yuan Chang, 'Reflections', in *Erinnerung an Martin Heidegger*, Pfullingeu, Neske, 1977, p. 65.

References

Bion, W. R. (1970), *Attention and Interpretation*, London, Tavistock.
Bowlby, J. (1970, 1973), *Attachment and Loss*: vol. I. *Attachment*; vol. II *Anxiety and Anger*; London, Hogarth Press.
Boszormenyi-Nagy, I., and Framo, James L. (1965), *Intensive Family Therapy*, New York, Harper & Row.
Chang Chung-yuan (1975), *Tao: A New Way of Thinking*, New York, London, Harper & Row.
Eissler, K. E. (1971), *Talent and Genius. The fictitious case of Tausk contra Freud*, New York, Quadrangle Books.
Foulkes, S. H. (1964), *Therapeutic Group Analysis*, London, Allen & Unwin.
Gill, M. M. (1963), *Topography and Systems in Psychoanalytic Theory*, Psychological Issues Monograph 10, New York, Int. Univ. Press.
Habermas, J. (1963), *Theorie und Praxis*, Frankfurt, Suhrkamp.
Habermas, J. (1969), *Erkenntnis und Interesse*, Frankfurt, Suhrkamp.
Habermas, J., and Niklas Luhmann (1971), *Theorie der Gesellschaft oder Sozialtechnologie*, Frankfurt, Suhrkamp.
Killian, H. (1971), *Das enteignete Bewusstsein*, Neuwied, Luchterhand.
Lichtenstein, H. (1961), 'Identity and Sexuality', *Journ. Amer. Psychoanal. Assoc.* 9, pp. 179-260.
Loch, W. (1965), *Voraussetzungen, Mechanismen und Grenzen des psychoanalytischen Prozesses*, Bern and Stuttgart, Hans Huber.
Loch, W. (1972), *Zur Theorie, Technik und Therapie der Psychoanalyse*, Frankfurt, Fischer.
Loch, W. (1974), 'Der Analytiker: Gesetzgeber und Lehrer', *Psyche*, 28.
Piaget, J. (1967), *Biologie et connaissance*, Paris, Gallimard.
Pribbram, K. H. (1971), *Languages of the Brain*, Englewood, N. J., Prentice-Hall.
Quintana, P. de la (1975), 'Medicina social, sociología médica y sociología de la Salud', *Historia Universal de la Medicina*, ed. P. Lain Entralgo, vol. VII, Madrid, Salvat.
Radnitzky, G. (1968), *Contemporary Schools of Metascience*, Göteborg, Akademiförlaget.
Rof-Carballo, J. (1960), 'Constitution, Transference and Co-existence', *Acta Psychotherap. et Psychosom.*, 8, 400.
Rof-Carballo, J. (1961), *Urdimbre afectiva y enfermedad. Introducción a una Medicina dialógica*, Barcelona, Labor.
Rof-Carballo, J. (1962), 'La dimensión personal del conocimiento científico', *Archivo Iberoamericano de Historia de la Medicina y Antropología Médica*, 14.
Rof-Carballo, J. (1964), *Medicina y actividad creadora*, Madrid, Revista de Occidente.
Rof-Carballo, J. (1972), *Biología y psicoanálisis*, Bilbao, Desclée de Brouwer.
Rof-Carballo, J. (1973), *El hombre como encuentro*, Madrid, Alfaguara.
Rof-Carballo, J. (1975), *Fronteras vivas del psicoanálisis*, Madrid, Karpos.

Törnebohm, H., and Radnitzky, C. (1969-70), 'Forschungsstrategie', *Seitschrift fur Allgem. Wissenschaftstheorie.*

Waddington, C. H. (1960), *The Ethical Animal*, London, Allen & Unwin.

Waelhens, A. (1961), *La philosophie et les experiences naturelles*, The Hague, Nijhoff.

Weizsäcker, V. von (1940), *Der Gestaltkreis*, Leipzig, Thieme.

Chapter 18
Philosophers, ideologies and outcomes in group psychotherapy

Max Rosenbaum

This volume is dedicated to the memory and contributions of S. H. Foulkes. His pioneer work did not arise out of a vacuum. He was a thoroughly trained and sophisticated psychoanalyst by the time he arrived in England.

He served as first director of the Frankfurt Psychoanalytic Clinic and was there from 1931 to 1933, just before he came to England. He had worked closely with W. Gelb, the gestalt psychologist, and for two years as assistant to Kurt Goldstein, the neurologist who formulated the organismic approach to human behaviour, a holistic approach that significantly influenced Abraham Maslow, an early figure in the human potential movement.

In 1940 B. F. Skinner reviewed Goldstein's book, *The Organism*,[1] which had been translated by 1939 to English from the original German. Skinner commented: 'To understand the essential nature of the organism (Goldstein's desire) would be avoided like the plague by most contemporary scientists.' Goldstein had stated in his book, 'The closer we stand in our relations to a living being, the sooner we may expect to arrive at a correct judgment regarding its essential nature.' Skinner, eager to formulate a technological view of man, and convinced that technology would solve all of man's problems, was astute enough to note the basic difference in philosophy between his approach and that of Goldstein, who was a marked influence upon S. H. Foulkes. The point is that Foulkes was aware in his own work of the importance of the group as based on his work with Gelb and Goldstein.

Yet there was another important philosophical view that Foulkes was exposed to and yet did not talk about or at least write about. In discussions with me, he noted that he was aware of the work of the sociologists and behavioural scientists at the University of Frankfurt who had organized themselves into what they called an Institute for

Social Research. They were attempting to offer a general theory of the modern capitalist society. What has been called the Frankfurt School was stimulated by the work of Max Horkheimer and Theodor W. Adorno and they in turn heavily influenced Erich Fromm who, while training in psychoanalysis, was also exposed to the Institute for Social Research. Among other people at this Institute was Herbert Marcuse.

The Frankfurt Group's greater relevance on Foulkes's development was their concern about a central problem — the leader and the group. They phrased it differently, in sociological terms. Beginning around 1930, the Frankfurt Group was concerned as to whether the workers of Germany, who were members of the Social Democratic Party, would resist the Nazi movement of Hitler. They postulated the hypothesis that many workers would accept dictatorship, despite differences in political ideology, because they had 'authoritarian personalities'. This personality type was derived from a psychoanalytic model of the ego; the sado-masochistic character Fromm elaborated upon in his book, *Escape From Freedom*.[2] The studies of the 'authoritarian personality' were later extended in research carried out at the University of California during and after the Second World War.

When Foulkes came to England he found himself in a culture which had not been exposed to systematic inquiry by behavioural scientists who combined Marxism, psychoanalysis and sociological study of the integration of a group. It is almost as if he put this Frankfurt exposure to rest while he worked with intrapsychic phenomena, only to come back to larger issues as he moved towards work with groups and a desire to help larger groups of patients.

I shall elaborate upon this type of shift, which seems sudden until one studies the total forces at work in the approach of a behavioural scientist.

David Berlinski, a professional philosopher, has taken a serious look at a current and influential practice in the social and behavioural sciences. The inquiry had its origins in the post-Second World War years when the computer began to be seen as the paradigm of behaviour — human, social, economic, and animal. One of the early contributors to this paradigm was Ludwig von Bertalanffy, a biologist. His research led him away from reductionism and toward studies of the organism as a whole. Von Bertalanffy postulated a new discipline — general systems theory — 'a logico-mathematical field whose task is the formulation and derivation of the general principles that are applicable to "systems" in general'. Others moved along similar lines — some following Bertalanffy's path: Herbert A. Simon, a psychologist who worked on the creation of a field called artificial intelligence; Anatol Rapaport, a mathematician and behavioural scientist who worked at the Research Center for Mental Health at the University of Michigan and later in Canada; also Erwin Lazlo who has written at length on the philosophy of systems. Berlinski, in his book *On Systems Analysis*,[3] points out the danger of taking over a word from natural language with all its vagueness and ambiguity and assigning it a mathematical meaning. This is something that any competent linguist knows and something that Jean Piaget has studied for years and that Noam Chomsky has noted again and again. In short, we cannot use a word in both its mathematical and colloquial meaning. Berlinski criticizes von Bertalanffy, Lazlo, Simon and Rapaport for their sloppy use of terms. Von Bertalanffy used the word 'model' very loosely. Rapaport was quite casual about the term 'isomorphism'. Lazlo and Simon obscured the concepts of 'system' and 'hierarchy'.

All of these people may be forgiven. They were trying to capture ideas with somewhat inadequate means. Their followers have continued to distort the original casualness. This is all of importance to the professional mathematician but what is of serious importance to behavioural scientists is the fact that since we cannot use the paradigms of the physical sciences, we decide to use the machinery of the mathematician — mathematical systems theory, graph theory, set theory, information theory, etc. But mathematics won't help us determine the usefulness of a theory. We have to have the ideas and then breathe life into the model. It is we who have to find the valid insights about psychological or sociological regularities.

Muzafer Sherif in a recent article[4] notes the explosion of research in social psychology and points out the scanty yield. Paul Hare's compilation of bibliographies on research in the small-group area, as reported by Sherif, amounts to a huge harvest that doesn't add up to much. McGrath and Altman stated in 1966,[5] 'The small group field is so segmented — in the form of idiosyncratic variables, tasks and measures peculiar to the individual investigators — that no one has a common base from which to argue' (p. 80).

Steiner, in the first annual Katz-Newcomb lecture delivered at the University of Michigan stated:[6]

By the 1960's social psychology has become much more individualistic. Interest in the group had waned and research was generally on intra-individual events or processes that mediate responses to social situations (p. 94).

By the late 50's, social psychology had turned inward. It had
centered its attention on internal state and processes: dissonance,
attitudes, attributions. Whatever happened to the group, and why?
(p. 98).

The fundamental problem that I have covered albeit rather sketchily
is this: Are the phenomena of social psychology verifiable by accepted
canons of science and indeed are the phenomena of group psychotherapy verifiable by canons of science? What attracted many psychologists to Kurt Lewin was his early German papers where he stated that
psychology was lawful.[7] By lawful, Lewin mean that even if emotions
and intentions are fluid, as long as a specific instance of an event could
be studied, psychology was lawful. In order to be clear as to what we
are examining, it is necessary to contrast the two traditions: Kant vs.
Locke and Hume. The Kantian tradition goes on to Maxwell's work in
physics, to gestalt psychology (see Max Wertheimer), to Piaget,
Chomsky and Riegel. The other tradition, from the great British philosophers Locke and Hume, goes to Isaac Newton, Comte, the Vienna
Circle with its logical positivism and the behaviourist tradition. Kant in
his emphasis on 'categories of understanding' assumes that each person
has an active intellect which is capable of constructing and ordering the
world. The patterns of relationships are fundamental. Piaget in his
studies of human behaviour is concerned about concepts such as
'reversibility' and he is clearly in the area of dynamic process. Interestingly enough, Piaget came from a background of mathematics. The
tradition of John Locke stresses a science that emphasizes the small,
detailed and specific. The Lockean would look to external rather
than internal causes. The Lockean tradition moves from the specific
to the *higher* concepts – which are of course much more abstract. The
whole concept of goals or intentions, which are internal in nature,
would appear inappropriate to the Lockean tradition. This very basic
difference in traditions, the Kantian and Lockean, serves to plague
behavioural scientists as they move forward into the area of psychotherapy and psychotherapy research.

An illustration of the Lockean tradition would be the following
case report.[8] The patient, a married female in her late twenties, complained of a sexual phobia. The treatment consisted of relaxation
training, desensitization, communication and the negotiation of behavioural contracts. The woman complained of anxiety during sexual
intercourse and was advised to eat macadamia nuts during sexual
intercourse as a counter conditioning agent. The therapists reported

that they saw the married couple together and over 7.5 months the couple moved from no sexual intercourse to orgasmic intercourse. The improvement was maintained in a follow-up eight months later.

In the same tradition, two authors report on the effectiveness of group reciprocity counselling with married couples. In this study[9] seven couples participated in an eight-week workshop. There was a pre-workshop marital counselling inventory administered during the course of the eight sessions. The participants also completed daily marital happiness ratings. The therapists found commitment to and optimism about marriage as they used their reciprocity procedure. The authors state:[9]

> In order to develop reciprocal exchanges, couples needed to identify experiences that each perceived as satisfying, agree upon a fair exchange, and specify when these exchanges would occur. An example of such an exchange was a husband who did the evening dishes twice during a week in exchange for his wife's companionship on a Sunday morning walk in the park. Another example was a wife who agreed to more frequent sexual intercourse in exchange for her husband's assistance in getting the children ready for bed (p. 79).

The two clinical experiences that have been described, can be completely restructured in the Kantian tradition. The woman who was anxious during sexual intercourse would be asked to explore what she was afraid of and what sexual intercourse represented to her. We are now in Kant's 'categories of understanding'. The married couples described in the second study, in the Kantian tradition, would be asked to understand the possible resentment that the wife experienced as she performed the menial task of washing dishes. The wife who was irritable as she sensed her husband's lack of cooperation in the responsibilities of child rearing, would be asked to look at this resentment and the displacement of her resentment into her sex life.

I am not referring to the unconscious or psychodynamic inquiry as I summarize the clinical examples. I am referring to Kant's belief that all minds are fundamentally alike and that knowledge is universal. He also believed that since all minds are of the same general nature, all people think very much alike.

I have no simple answer for the woman who suffered from a sexual phobia and who was encouraged to eat macadamia nuts during sexual intercourse. I was reminded when I read the clinical report of a former president of the United States of America who was the butt of many jokes. One of the jokes was: 'He cannot walk and chew gum at the same time.' Perhaps the nut chewing led to her treating sexual intercourse as a mechanical experience. This is the current description of what occurs in 'sex clubs' where there is complete 'sexual freedom'. Some sex therapists advocate rape fantasies as a way to a woman achieving orgasm.

Now we must examine the orientation of the people we turn to as seminal thinkers in the study of group process. Kurt Lewin was a medical student in Germany. He moved on to the study of biology and later became interested in psychology after a professor told him that he didn't really understand a particular issue in psychology and should study it further. Psychology was part of the philosophy faculty – not unlike the situation in the USA until very recently. Therefore Lewin came to psychology through the natural science of biology and in 1922 published a monograph on the concept of *identity* in physics, biology and developmental theory. Lewin was very opposed to 'reducing' psychology to physiology or physics. He believed that unique events could be lawful in nature. In the United States the emphasis on statistical regularity is what is called lawful. Lewin would stress the importance of the genotypical concept. The genotype in biology and zoology means a type determined by the genetic characters common to a group; hence, a group of organisms of such a type.[10] Lewin, following in the Kantian tradition – opposed to the Lockean positivism of the USA – stated that *genotypes* are real. He was questioning how we look at things and in many ways he predated Thomas Kuhn.

The most generally held view of science is the positivist view that stems from the Vienna Circle. This view holds that science is a strictly logical process. Theories are proposed on the basis of inductive logic, and these theories are refuted or confirmed by experimental test of predictions *deductively* derived from the theory. If an old theory fails, new theories are proposed because they seem to do a better job of explanation, and science progresses to the truth. This view – called logical empiricism – deliberately ignores the historical context of science as well as the psychological factors, such as imagination and intuition.

There are some who disagree with the approach and describe science itself as an ideology. These historians and philosophers of science take human factors into account as well as logical structures. The force behind this change of views about science was a book written by Thomas Kuhn in which he pointed out that non-rational procedures heavily influence science.[11] His thesis, in brief, is that science is not the steady accumulation of knowledge that we have been led to believe; rather it is a series of peaceful times interrupted by intellectually violent revolutions where scientists develop new theories, standards and methods. Kuhn calls this the 'paradigm'. The paradigm is basic to research — it defines which problems are interesting and worthy of study. The paradigm that is applied to the natural sciences pays off much more quickly since the natural sciences cannot be explored at random; the paradigm for the researcher in the natural sciences is an exploration plan which points both to puzzles and guarantees that they are soluble. The social sciences — and we can fairly place the behavioural sciences in that area — are in a pre-paradigm stage.

What happens is that when behavioural scientists try to extend the paradigm, they find to their dismay that there are puzzles that cannot be solved. Now a crisis arises, a crisis in the sense of the Greek 'krisis', or turning-point. So the scientist turns from the solving of puzzles to the fundamentals. Some may propose a new paradigm but that doesn't mean that the defenders of the old paradigm will simply fold up their tents and go away. Indeed, Kuhn notes: 'The competition between paradigms is not the sort of battle that can be resolved by proofs.' Kuhn describes the transfer from one paradigm to another as a 'conversion experience that cannot be forced'. What 'converts' a scientist is rarely logic but instead arguments that 'appeal to the individual's sense of the appropriate or the aesthetic'. I will add to this the matter of faith — faith that the new paradigm will resolve the irregularities that precipitated the crisis.

Kuhn asks why it is that logic cannot resolve the competition between the two paradigms. His answer is straightforward: *The two paradigms are logically not reducible to the same measure.* Two paradigms may seem to use the same words and concepts, but the words and concepts are logically different. Competing paradigms are bound to talk past one another rather than to one another because their points of reference are not comparable. A new paradigm does not build on the preceding paradigm — indeed it supplants the paradigm. I don't want to continue on Kuhn's controversial and exciting thesis other than to note again that Kuhn stresses the essentially human aspect of research in science. Kuhn is not denying logic or stressing the irrational but he wants to stress the creative quality of scientific research. Kuhn notes that social science is in the pre-paradigmatic stage. This means to me that researchers in human behaviour may find it easier to look for natural science paradigms to make their tasks easier. It doesn't mean that they have found a quicker way to the truth, but it is certainly a less anxious way.

Somewhat earlier, I noted that Lewin predated Kuhn since Lewin believed that an event is real if it has effects. He was also very aware of the problem of values. Henle noted:[12]

> Gestalt psychology arose in Germany around 1910 out of what was called the Crisis of Science. Not only science, but academic knowledge in general was losing the confidence of more and more people, intellectuals included . . . since it could not deal with major human concerns, indeed seemed uninterested in them, in . . . such problems as value, for example, or meaning.

Henle further noted that some researchers were in favor of abandoning scientific explanation to be replaced by 'understanding' – all of this was a precursor to the humanistic tradition that is stressed today.[12]

> In psychology, in opposition to the traditional experimental psychology, there arose a speculative psychology whose goal was to understand rather than to explain. Let the experimental psychologists find causal laws in their narrow domain, so the argument went. The really central human issues must be dealt with outside the natural science tradition, in the tradition called *Geisteswissenschaft* – a word for which we have no contemporary English counterpart [The word has been translated as 'the humanities.], although it is itself a translation of John Stuart Mill's expression, the mental and moral sciences. Gestalt psychologists did not accept this split within their discipline. They believed that the shortcomings of the traditional psychology arose, not because it was scientific, but because it misconceived science. . . . Using physical field theory as their model, they worked to develop a nonatomistic psychology within the tradition of natural science. . . . Gestalt psychology is clearly an explanatory natural science.

In my own writings I have noted the influence of Otto Gross, a psychiatrist, who around the early 1900s became interested in psychoanalysis and formed an erotic approach to therapy that was influential in the thinking of many leaders of art and science in Germany and Europe. He also wanted to abandon scientific inquiry.

It is conceivable that the conflict between Lockean and Kantian approaches was relevant to the controversy that finally led to the rupture of Freud and Jung's friendship. It is not relevant to this paper to discuss the 'father-son' relationship that entered into Freud and Jung's contact. But I want to note another aspect of what occurred between them. Jung was very much the religious-mystic and he cultivated that leaning. Freud, the child of science, was very distrustful of Jung's interest in religion, the occult and astrology. Freud was having enough difficulty in working with the unconscious and did not want his rational approach to be clouded. He almost consciously avoided the existential dilemma and Jung's emphasis on the collective unconscious was perceived by Freud as an evasion of the issue of sexuality. Freud also seemed to be caught somewhere between Locke and Kant – at times following one philosophy and at other times following another. In his early professional years (1876-77), Freud translated John Stuart Mill's writings into German. Mill, the English philosopher, based his entire logical theory upon the laws of association. Through the process of inferences one passed from the known to the unknown. His theory of induction is based upon collecting data through experience from which one draws certain conclusions. He followed in the line of philosophers such as Comte who believed that only knowledge which could be used was worth while.

The controversy between Freud and Adler may relate to the same issue that I have brought up. At times Adler seems to be following one philosophy and then shifts to another. When the confusion about which philosophical approach is compounded by the group experience, the task becomes even more frustrating for the psychotherapist and the researcher in psychotherapy. This may account for some of the confusion that I sense in Foulkes's approach as he moved from the practice of individual psychoanalysis with fewer variables, to work in the group with its myriad variables. Also, Foulkes's exposure to Gelb, the gestalt psychologist and then Goldstein, the organismic-holistic psychiatrist and then the move to the English scene, where Locke, Hume and Mill were philosophical leaders, may have trapped Foulkes as he attempted to find a balance.

The Lockean positivistic tradition looks to external causation as the answer. The tradition of Kant considers concepts, described by some as subjective, such as goal, self, hope and aspirations. One of the early workers with groups, Kurt Lewin, attempted to quantify both the direction – goals and intentions – as well as the magnitude. He turned to mathematics to help him in this venture, and was unsuccessful. His emphasis on this approach frustrated him and was a great disappointment. In his work he saw quite a way down the road. Of course, many years ago he spotted the weaknesses and limitations in the mathematical model, something that Berlinski (referred to earlier) has criticized in his arguments against systems theory. But to those of us who are attempting a serious evaluation of psychotherapy, there must be clarity as to what tradition we are following – the Lockean positivistic tradition, which dominates much of American thinking, or the Kantian tradition. If this is clarified, we may have a clearer dialogue as to the outcome of psychotherapy and specifically group psychotherapy.

Finally, there must be more careful attention paid to the literature in the field of psychotherapy.

In a review of one of my books, *The Intensive Group Experience*,[13] the reviewer[14] notes: 'The report by Malan and associates on the results of group psychotherapy conducted along psychoanalytic lines confirms the clinical impression that such treatment may not be beneficial to any great number of patients.' However, a careful analysis of the research report cited,[15] indicates that the basic problem in the limited efficacy of group psychotherapy with many patients is that there was very little individual preparation and no real effort to establish the positive transference that is so important as we move patients from individual to group treatment – the bridge that the patients need as they cross over to intensive group psychotherapy from one-to-one individual psychotherapy. This is a point that I stressed almost twenty years ago in the group psychotherapy text I co-authored and a point stressed again in the revised edition.[16] There must be careful preparation for the group.

So, we are back to basics again. We must spell out the philosophy behind the treatment approach and not make vague statements which are testimonial in nature. Then, we shall have a clearer picture as to what we are engaged in as we practice intensive group psychotherapy.

Consider the following. A. R. Luria, the great Russian neuropsychologist, pointed out in a survey of research in the Soviet Union[17] that there is support for the thesis that the structure of human cognitive processes differs according to the ways in which social groups live out their realities. Please note the word 'realities'.

What are the *realities* we are dealing with as we work with behavioural disorder? Currently, mental health professionals speak of a third revolution in mental health care. Hart *et al.*[18] describe a new form of psychotherapy in which patients become therapists and psychotherapists become patients. According to this *new* psychotherapy, since feelings work for or against an individual, and since those who live with unacknowledged feelings are defined as insane, the answer is simple. The way to get these feelings is to assert them and this experience leads to new levels of positive functioning.

What these authors of a new approach (and I find it to be naive) miss, is that their approach appeals to the populist quality in American life, which challenges mental health professionals and traditional theory, a populist approach with the emphasis on help yourself and help others. There is a religious quality to this type of psychotherapy and it is really not debatable since it is testimonial in nature.[19] Probably the best analysis of the craze in self-help groups has been written by Back and Taylor.[20] They note the relationship of self-help groups to social movements, using the five-stage social movement development model proposed by Blumer, the sociologist, in 1969.[21] First, there is dissatisfaction among a group of people because their needs are not met. Second, a group is formed to meet these needs. Third, morale is developed on a group and individual level. Fourth, an ideology is developed. Fifth, there is the final meeting of needs.

As we look across the American landscape, we will find more and more groups are formed in accordance with the model Blumer proposed. This applies to religious orders as well as Alcoholics Anonymous or Overeaters Anonymous. All of these groups are distrustful of the status quo. They generally express distrust of professionals and show a desire for community. They generally reject the purely rational which they identify with science. In short, they are searching for human values.

None of this can be ignored as we assess psychotherapy and what is called the 'curative factor'. That is why I have taken you earlier in this presentation through Kant and Locke. Unless we are clear as to the ideology behind individual or group treatment, we are in no position to evaluate outcome and are really not in a position to discuss coherently what is disturbed and what is culturally patterned behaviour.

References

1 Goldstein, K. (1939), *The Organism*, New York, American Book Co.
2 Fromm, E. (1941), *Escape From Freedom*, New York, Farrar & Rinehart.
3 Berlinski, D. (1976), *On Systems Analysis*, Cambridge, Mass., MIT Press.
4 Sherif, M. (1977), 'Crisis in social psychology: some remarks toward breaking through the crisis', *Personality and Social*

Psychology Bulletin, 3, pp. 368-82.
5 McGrath, J., and Altman, I. (1966), *Small Group Research: A Synthesis and Critique of the Field*, New York, Holt.
6 Steiner, I. D. (1972), 'Whatever happened to the group in social psychology?', *Jl of Experimental Social Psychology*, 8, pp. 86-96.
7 Lewin, M. A. (1977), 'Kurt Lewin's view of social psychology: the crisis of 1977 and the crisis of 1927', *Personality and Social Psychology Bulletin*, 3, pp. 159-72.
8 Tarler-Benlolo, L., and Love, W. A. (1977), 'A sexual phobia treated with macadamia nuts', *Jl of Behavior Therapy and Experimental Psychiatry*, 8, pp. 113-14.
9 Dixon, D. N., and Sciara, A. D. (1977), 'Effectiveness of group reciprocity counseling with married couples', *Jl of Marriage and Family Counseling*, 3, pp. 77-83.
10 Webster, N. (1945), *Webster's Collegiate Dictionary, 5th Edition*. Springfield, Mass.: G. & C. Marriam Co.
11 Kuhn, T. (1970), *The Structure of Scientific Revolutions*, Chicago, University of Chicago Press, 2nd edn.
12 Henle, M. (1975), 'Gestalt psychology and gestalt therapy', Paper presented at the annual conference of the American psychological Association, Chicago. Also *Jl. of the History of the Behavioural Sciences*, 1978.
13 Rosenbaum, J., and Snadowsky, A. (1976), *The Intensive Group Experience*, New York, Free Press-Macmillan.
14 Friedman, H. J. (1977), Book review, *Amer. J. Psychiatry*, 134, p. 7.
15 Malan, D., Balfour, F., and Hood, V. (1976), 'Group psychotherapy: a long-term follow-up study', *Arch. Gen. Psychiatry*, 33, pp. 1303-15.
16 Mullan, H., and Rosenbaum, M. (1962), *Group Psychotherapy: Theory and Practice*, New York, Free Press-Macmillan, rev. edn 1978.
17 Luria, A. R. (1976), *Cognitive Development: Its Cultural and Social Foundations*, Cambridge, Mass., Harvard University Press.
18 Hart, J., Corriere, R., and Binder, J. (1976), *Going Sane: An Introduction to Feeling Therapy*, New York, Dell.
19 Hurvitz, N. (1976), 'The origins of the peer self-help psychotherapy group movement', *Jl. Applied Behavioral Science*, 12, pp. 283-94.
20 Back, K. W., and Taylor, R. C. (1976), 'Self-help groups: tool or symbol?' *Jl. of Applied Behavioral Science*, 12, pp. 295-309.
21 Blumer, H. (1969), 'Social movements', in B. McLaughlin, *Studies in Social Movements: A Social Psychological Perspective*, New York, Free Press.

Additional reference for reading:
Simon, H. A. (1957), *Models of Man*, New York, Wiley.

Chapter 19
Individual and group psychology — are they opposed?

Saul Scheidlinger

The recent decline in prestige experienced by psychoanalysis has been due, in part at least, to the failure of its explanatory concepts to deal with the major societal issues of the day. For these issues fall generally into the realm of *group* rather than *individual* manifestations.

Much of this could have been avoided had psychoanalytic workers, in addition to their preoccupation with individual psychology, also followed a path of inquiry into the behaviour of groups which Freud had initiated as early as 1921. In a little volume entitled *Group Psychology and the Analysis of the Ego* he formulated some hypotheses regarding group formation with particular reference to leadership and to the behaviour of individuals within the regressive pull of a group's emotionality. Considering the state of social psychology of his time, Freud was considerably ahead of his contemporaries in explicitly denying any real dichotomy between individual and group psychology. To quote him: 'each individual is a component part of numerous groups, he is bound by ties of identifications in many directions, and he has built up his ego ideal upon the most various models' (Freud, 1955, p. 101). More recently Astley (1974) wished, as I do, that in addition to concerns that relate consistently to the individual and the intrapsychic, analysts would have 'simultaneously also interested themselves in the groups of which that individual is inevitably a member'.

Not only did psychoanalysts, including Anna Freud, generally fail to pursue the subject of Freud's group psychology, but even those few American workers who began using groups as a means of therapy in the late 1930s and early 1940s paid scant attention to issues of group dynamics. The only exceptions were Schilder, Redl, and Ackerman. The other group therapists concentrated on the individual patients, with the group itself being viewed as a kind of immobile backdrop. Among the factors responsible for this lag in awareness of group processes was the relative newness of group therapy as a treatment approach; the fact that analytic practitioners were mostly clinicians lacking familiarity with social psychologic theory or research; the therapists' preoccupation with concepts of individual personality and psychopathology; the limited range and clarity of the existing psycho-analytic concepts of group behaviour; the relatively late interest within Freudian theory generally in problems of ego psychology, especially the individual's conscious ego patterns oriented towards the environ-ment.

While the psychoanalytic literature during the 1950s continued to be generally steeped in themes of individual psychology and psycho-pathology, the growing field of group psychotherapy, however, became the arena where issues of the 'here-and-now' interpersonal context and of group dynamics began to be accorded increasing attention. Not only were the relevant conceptualizations of Freud and his co-workers brought out of mothballs; there was in addition a considerable theor-etical expansion stimulated by the writings of the so-called 'British School' of analytic group therapists examplified by Bion, Ezriel and Foulkes. Some of these, especially Bion (1959), a student of Melanie Klein, were highly critical of Freud's group psychology, maintaining that it was both not 'deep' enough as well as unduly tied to concepts of individual behaviour. In Bion's approach the group as an entity, rather than individual patients, was the focus of study and therapy. He maintained that the therapist's task resided essentially in con-fronting the group as a group with its powerful unconscious strivings and offering appropriate interpretations which were expected to lead to insight and improved behaviour.

A similar theoretical trend has emerged in the mushrooming field of family therapy. Here too there are an increasing number of writings which pay exclusive attention to the family as a unit or system, with related neglect of the behaviour and dynamics of the individual family members, including the designated patient. It is my belief that these theoretical positions, directed as they are against our field's earlier overly rigid preoccupation with concepts of the individual psyche, represent an unduly extreme reaction.

A justified and much-needed emphasis on groups as social systems does not require a simultaneous abandonment of the fundamentals of individual psychology in its dynamic and genetic context. In fact, at this time of unprecedented changes in service models within the mental health field – some had referred to these changes as a 'Third Mental Health Revolution' – conceptual breadth and clarity are of the greatest urgency. This need is compounded in our own field of small-group processes – a field already beset by professional role conflicts and confused terminology encompassing such labels as group therapy, group analysis, group education, T-groups, encounter groups, organizational development and the like. The question, 'who does what to whom in what kind of group and why' is well worth asking at every step – for the protection of the client as well as of the helper.

In my view, as may have become clear by now, not only are individual and group psychology inseparable but, in addition, their conceptual integration is essential, if we are to understand the complex phenomena inherent in our clinical practice, in the human services generally, as well as in the unprecedented social changes in the community. This move towards a conceptual integration has been much hampered by the one-sidedness of the prevalent empirical and theoretical orientations. There are thus still today some authorities within the field of group psychotherapy, for example, who persist in an exclusive orientation to individual dynamics – luckily, their number is declining (Parloff, 1967). On the other hand there are those who following the earlier noted 'British School' of group therapists, favour a central role for group-as-a-whole manifestations with a consequent neglect of individual behaviour.

As I have noted elsewhere (Scheidlinger, 1951), what we need to begin with is a recognition that in any small-group and social system, there is a continuous interplay between individual and group psychological processes. To put it differently, every item of such group behaviour could be viewed as the behaviour of individual personalities in a special process of social and emotional interaction. There are thus two interrelated sets of factors: (a) individual personalities with their genetic and dynamic properties, their motivational and defensive-adaptive patterns, some conscious and some unconscious; and (b) group dynamic elements such as climate, goals, structure, code or shared themes, and, above all, a collective awareness of the group's identity, which emerge as the product of the interactions within the group. Such interactions can occur on conscious as well as on unconscious levels. Social psychological contributions have tended to stress the conscious, overt levels of these elements, while Freud's and group psychoanalytic concepts are focused almost exclusively on the unconscious, covert level. A given group's functioning can at any point be affected primarily by the individual, or by the group dynamic set of factors, or, as happens most frequently, by a mixture of both.

In order to illustrate the organic connection between individual and group psychology, I would like to expand again (Scheidlinger, 1964) on a major psychoanalytic concept, namely identification – a concept anchored in the realm of individual development and functioning as well as in that of group development and functioning.

Identification, a process which plays a crucial role in group psychology, had originally been utilized in diverse ways in the psychoanalytic theory of individual behaviour and psychopathology. There is Freud's initial depiction of the processes of 'primary' and 'secondary' identification in child development, together with later attempts by others to distinguish between super-ego and ego identifications; also, Anna Freud's subsequent important differentiation between identification as a kind of emotional tie between people and identification as a defence mechanism, i.e., 'identification with the aggressor' or 'altruistic surrender'.

There is in addition a relatively neglected kind of identification in group life which pertains to the individual's relationship to the group as a whole. It is my impression that this kind of identification has major relevance not only to the planful use of small groups for purposes of education or therapy, but also to the broader issue of identity formation and mental health maintenance.

For the purposes of this discussion I will view identification as an endopsychic process calling for a degree of individual involvement with a perceived object or its symbolic representation. In line with Alice Balint's notions, the individual's emotional involvement in identification is not yet genital love and constitutes in a way the assimilation of an aspect of the external world as well as an extension of the ego. In terms of ego psychology, identification brings into play such functions as adaptation to reality, reality testing, sense of reality, the self-concept (with its self and object representations) and the capacity to form object relationships.

This kind of an identification does not necessarily involve a pathological engulfment of the personality by another object or a regressive replacement of an earlier object cathexis. It would rather fall under Freud's broader category, enunciated in his *Group Psychology and the Analysis of the Ego* (1955), of shared qualities, interests or ideals being capable of precipitating identifications with others, or under Anna Freud's later concept of identification as an emotional tie between people.

Let me hypothesize now about some processes which are likely to be at work when an individual is a part of a meaningful small group, a therapy group for example: I would assume that he or she brings to the situation a complex patterning of conscious and unconscious attitudes towards himself, towards other people, and towards group experiences in general – he is likely to carry with him certain images of family and of peer groupings as a Gestalt. Attitudes towards concurrent or antecedent group experiences are likely to be revived. In addition, under the impact of the tensions inherent in all group involvement, especially in its beginning phase – deeper and forgotten attitudes and levels of perceiving are reactivated as well. These revived attitudes and perceptions are likely to pertain to the leader (perhaps as a parent), to the other group members (perhaps as siblings), and to the group-as-a-whole. According to Freudian psychoanalysis, the unconscious content here includes object and self representations, hidden wishes, fantasies and affects, as well as defences. As for the attitudes and perceptions towards the group as a collective entity, these emerge on two major levels – a *contemporary-dynamic level* and a *genetic-regressive level*.

The hypothesized contemporary-dynamic level pertains to the more readily observed momentary expressions of conscious needs and ego-adaptive patterns, the group roles, the network of attractions and repulsions, as well as the group structure. The behaviour here is primarily reactive to realistic group situational factors bringing into play the more external aspects of personality. The genetic-regressive level, in contrast, refers to unconscious and preconscious motivations, to defensive patterns and conflicts, to phenomena such as transference, resistance, identification, and projection. The genetic-regressive type of phenomena are apt to emerge in situations in which the personality restraints (ego defences) have been loosened (regression), with consequent freer expression of repressed emotionality. (Regression is defined here in ego-psychological terms as the re-emergence of earlier modes of individual functioning with its *temporal* aspects and *topographical* aspects.)

On the contemporary-dynamic level, the group as a whole is likely to be viewed by the individual as an instrument for conscious need satisfaction. The range here is broad, including needs of an educational or ideological nature or 'to get therapy'. Group associations are also sought to gratify less readily articulated needs for belonging, for emotional support, for protection, for sexual or aggressive expression, for the assuaging of guilt, for self-help, and most recently to counter alienation and insensitivity to others as well as one's own body.

I have speculated in another context (Scheidlinger, 1974) that on the deeper, genetic-regressive level the group entity can become for the individual the symbolic representation of a nurturing mother. Terms such as 'mother earth' and 'motherland' or even Alma Mater which are used popularly, are of relevance here. In a broader sense the hypothesis can be advanced that the universal human need to belong, to establish a state of psychological unity with others, represents a covert wish for restoring an earlier state of unconflicted well-being inherent in the exclusive union with mother. It may well refer specifically to a yearning for a return to the child's purely positive 'need gratifying' relationship which Anna Freud had postulated as occurring developmentally between the phases of primary narcissism and that of object constancy. In this connection, in the group treatment of people who have experienced marked early deprivations with resultant ego and identity disturbances, we have observed that perceptions of the group-as-a-whole in a supportive and benign vein tend to be especially marked and fundamental. Might this element be a factor in the generally acknowledged greater accessibility of patients with severe character disorders to group therapy?

Anthony's (1967) comparative outline of development phases for dyadic and group psychotherapy is of interest in this connection. He found the first phase of both treatment modalities to be quite similar, characterized by an anaclitic type of child-parent relationship and abounding in identification, empathy and imitation. The theme of dependency and wish for exclusive possession of the parent-therapist was predominant. He concluded that groups comprising patients with pre-genital syndromes, character disorders, borderline disturbances, and early deprivation, rarely go beyond the first phase.

It is noteworthy, here, that the late S. H. Foulkes (1964) also viewed what he termed the Matrix as both the group's total web of communications and relationships as well as a universal mother symbol.

As for identification with the group as a whole, the process can perhaps be best explored within the framework of the individual group member's perception, for at any moment of his group membership each individual can be said to perceive not only selected aspects of an existing social situation (i.e., interacting group members and a 'central person' or 'central persons'), but also the Gestalt of this social situation. These perceptions occur on various 'depth' levels. They will vary, on the one hand, in line with individual personality factors such as the individual's ego organization and his ability to deal with the inevitable stress involved in joining and interacting in a group. On the other hand, there is the matter of the nature of the specific group, which can range from a rational, structured assemblage to a highly volatile grouping with a seeming absence of structure. Identification with a group entity goes beyond the mere perception of it and the investing of it with some emotional meaning, for identification in this sense also contains an element of responding, or, more specifically, an element of individual commitment. To belong to or to feel part of a group (some people have used the term 'ego involved') also implies a more or less transient giving up of some aspect of the individual's self (or self-schema) to the group as a group. To quote Murphy (1947), 'One literally "loses" oneself in the group – not just in the crowd, but in the disciplined, highly integrated military or industrial, or religious, or artistic, or scientific unit.'

The role of the individual's self in group behaviour calls for much further investigation. It has caused no end of confusion in psychoanalytic group psychology. To begin with, Freud's attempt to explain mob phenomena in terms of the individual's susceptibility to emotional contagion by substituting the crowd leader's super-ego for his own, was taken by some writers as an explanatory model for all groups. In all groups, then, there was to be found a labile emotionality, a pathological regression coupled with a loss of individual identity and a heightened suggestibility. In this vein the earlier-mentioned British psychoanalyst, Bion, has expounded a group psychological theory which postulates a group regression of greater depth than that assumed by Freud and his followers such as Redl (1942). Bion's concepts are related to Melanie Klein's ideas of depersonalization of 'part-object relationships' and of what she termed 'psychotic' anxiety from early infancy. In fact, Bion views the primary motivation in all group belonging as being related to the personality's search for defences against loss of individual distinctiveness as well as against 'psychotic' anxieties. In brief, Bion overemphasizes primary process manifestations at the expense of the well-known reality-favouring and growth-promoting elements in groups. He makes insufficient allowance for the possible non-conflictual, ego-autonomous aspects of individual belonging in a group. He also does not seem to recognize ego functions as intervening between the emerging impulsive derivatives and actual behaviour. Similarly no attention is given to individual differences in autonomy and separateness and hence to susceptibility to the regressive pull of the group, in line with personality and situational factors.

It is noteworthy that Deutsch (1967), in a contribution on adolescence, took a similarly narrow view of the dynamics of contemporary adolescent groupings. According to her, in every adolescent's group belonging there is a complete repudiation of individuality in favour of a 'conforming we'. Furthermore, to quote Deutsch: 'whether they are primitive or sophisticated in character, irrational or highly motivated . . . *all* adolescent groups have two main goals: as a vehicle for rebellion, and as a sort of counterphobic refuge from anxiety'. Contrary to Bion's and Helene Deutsch's position, in my view, individual group belonging can only under special circumstances be characterized by such pathological, regressive processes that involve the massive relinquishing of personal identity and independence or the 'introjection' of a leader's super-ego qualities. Groups with autocratic leadership, mob-like situations, and perhaps early T-group sessions or groups which comprise a membership with marked ego disorganization can approach this model; on the other hand, this is rarely the case in task-oriented groups or in groups with a 'democratic' climate where there is a balance between permissiveness and control, for example, analytically oriented therapy groups.

The phenomenon of an individual's identification with a group entity refers primarily to an ego and not to a super-ego manifestation. In so far as it can occur on various 'depth' levels, it can assume a *regressive or integrative-adaptive* character. We must remember, too, that in line with the concept of 'regression in the service of the ego', regression is no longer necessarily synonymous with pathology. Thus, Schafer (1958) defined regression in the service of the ego as a 'partial, temporary, controlled lowering of the level of psychic functioning to promote adaptation'. In this process the individual's access to preconscious and unconscious stimuli is increased without any major threat to the ego functioning. As an end result, inner balance, interpersonal relations and work are enhanced.

In trying to elaborate on the connection between the role of the individual's self-schema or self-representation and his group identification, Erikson's related concepts of an individual and of a group identity can be helpful. Erikson (1959) spoke of ego identity as 'a sense that the ego is learning effective steps toward a tangible collective future, that it is developing into a defined ego within a social reality. The sense of an ego identity is based on the common perception of an individual's self-sameness and continuity. In other words, such basic human concerns as, 'Who am I? ', 'Where have I been'? , and 'Where am I going'? are deeply ensconced in the individual's group experiences from the family on and out. Erikson insisted that healthy ego development called for a synchronization of the stages in child development with a group identity. This group identity refers to the group as a social collective with a sense of shared human qualities, a communality with others, an ideology, goals, and in a broader sense to the group's basic ways of organizing experience. While Erikson devoted a minimum of attention to the concept of group identity *per se*, he viewed ego identity as 'a subjective experience, a dynamic fact and a group psychological phenomenon'. In the last-named connotation, ego identity refers to the 'maintenance of one's inner solidarity with a group's ideals and identity'. In this sense it approximates quite closely to my earlier description of the dynamic-contemporary aspect of identification with the group as a whole. There is an element of investing varying aspects of the self in the collectivity, as illustrated in the individual's sense of belonging, in his feeling at one with the perceived group entity, to the point that it is theoretically not possible to speak of an ego identity apart from a group identity. George Klein (1976) similarly affirmed the inseparability of the 'autonomous' and the 'relatedness' aspects in our individual identity. He went on to state that 'if we can be punitive to our own ego, we can also hate the group to which we feel bound; conversely, we can be as narcissistically committed to our "we-ness" as to our "I-ness" '. The result of an individual's group identification is that he reacts to the attributes of the group as if these attributes were also his. A striking illustration is offered in the way an individual reacts to a criticism or slight of his group as though he himself had been criticized or slighted. Needless to say, in addition to this kind of an unconscious identification with one's group or organization, conscious moral elements such as sharing a system's values and goals, as well as utilitarian ones, i.e., 'a good day's work for a good day's pay', are also relevant here. In some recent work involving the use of small groups for purposes of training of group practitioners, I was struck by the almost inevitable tendency on the part of group members in the early phases to try to strengthen the group's supportive and nurturant aspects and deny and counteract the negative and disruptive aspects. Not infrequently the leader's behaviour, be it active or non-directive, becomes the avowed obstacle to the achievement of this kind of state of conflictless, unconditioned pre-Oedipal love. My co-workers and I hypothesized that we were dealing here, on the covert level, with the group members' wish to maintain the 'mother-group' in a series of unconflicted, all-giving existence. This kind of symbolic perception of the 'mother-group' has interestingly received increasing attention recently in the group therapy and T-group literature, following rare references to it in the early 1950s (Scheidlinger, 1974).

In regard to the earlier-noted strong human need for restoring the original state of unconflicted well-being represented by the tie to mother, Muensterberger (1955) asserted that 'separation anxiety is one of the fundamental elements of our being human, of our being social and cooperative creatures. . . . We do not dare to give up our inborn need for maternal gratification. Wè cling to each other as if we were mothers to each other.' This is not unlike Rochlin's (1959) assumption that 'it is a lifelong human condition to experience loss as well as to attempt restitution'.

A study by Fried (1963) revealed some fascinating findings in this connection. He reported continued marked feelings of painful loss, including manifestations of mourning and of depression, in a considerable proportion of resettled inhabitants of a slum neighbourhood in the city of Boston. It was as if this slum neighbourhood, no matter how dilapidated and inferior when compared to these peoples' new domiciles, had somehow come to stand for a treasured maternal object. The reactions of mourning were almost identical to those manifested at the loss of a close human object. This study suggests that not only one's group in a strict sense, but also one's home or neighbourhood can come to represent, on the deepest levels, a maternal image. This is especially likely with a population which has already experienced considerable traumatization in childhood, as well as emotional and social deprivation throughout their lives. On another plane, these reactions of grief can be explained in terms of a kind of identity crisis in Erikson's terms. In the old neighbourhood, each individual and family had a clear identity. Everyone knew who they were, whence they came, and where they were going. When they moved, the few social ties, no matter how tenuous, with storekeepers, peddlers, or neighbours were broken. Uprooted themselves, there was uprooted with them their sense of ego and group identity. It takes a flexible and well developed ego and considerable resiliency to restore readily these kinds of relationships with complete strangers in a strange locale.

Freud's rarely-noted speculation regarding the archaic unconscious memory, wherein the primordial horde of brothers, following the murder of the tribal father who controlled all the women, became the beginning of group psychology, received some support from writers on so-called 'self-analytic groups' such as Slater (1966), as well as from Neumann's study of *The Great Mother – An Analysis of the Archetype* (1955). The latter asserted that in early human culture the 'group psyche was dominant' and that the archetype of the Great Mother with its positive and negative attributes can also be shown to be present as a symbolic motif in all mythology and in the collective human unconscious. Groupness and the need and yearning for the 'good' mother are accordingly believed to reside in the very core of our being.

I have come in recent years to share Freud's conviction that the greatest value of psychoanalysis to society will accrue in the long run not so much from its role as a therapeutic endeavour but rather from what it can offer as a general psychology to education, to child-rearing, to primary prevention in its broadest sense as promotion of a state of individual and societal well-being.

In this connection, I have become increasingly impressed by a view impinging upon us simultaneously from psychological, sociological, psychiatric and psychosomatic sources that *all* disease, mental and physical, appears to represent the failure of the organism to adapt to the environmental stresses upon it, whether these stresses are primarily biological, psychological or social in nature (Rabkin and Struening, 1976). The major aims of primary prevention become, accordingly, (a) to increase man's tolerance for stress; and (b) to reduce the stress-inducing factors in the community.

Following on the earlier discussion of the deeper meanings in an individual's group belonging, it is not surprising that in such primary prevention, people's natural 'support systems' of family, peer-groupings, of 'kith and kin', assume major roles in offering tangible assistance, emotional support and an enhanced sense of personal identity. The many 'self-help' groups which appear to have been rediscovered in our current mental health literature − whether they aim at behavioural change or control (i.e. Alcoholics Anonymous); at learning to cope with stress (i.e. Parents Without Partners); at societal survival (i.e. Gay Liberation); or at self-actualization (i.e. sensitivity training) − appear to be an understandable part of this picture.

When I reviewed the literature on Freudian group psychology over twenty-five years ago (Scheidlinger, 1951), I was convinced, in my youthful enthusiasm, that we would soon learn all there is to know regarding 'what makes groups tick'. Today, being older and hopefully somewhat wiser, all I can see in the face of our voluminous literature is some progress in the clarification of specific concepts of group psychology, many more objective observations of manageable units of group therapy practice, as well as a good beginning in research. We appear to be still a long time away, however, from a satisfactory global theory of group psychology and group therapy, perhaps because our current concepts and research do not begin to reflect the intricate processes at work in this field.

In summary, I have suggested that had psychoanalysis as a body of knowledge maintained its short-lived early interest in group psychology, it would have been better equipped to help us understand some of today's unprecedented social changes.

I also noted a regettable 'backlash' type of reaction within some parts of the mental health field against concepts of individual personality in their dynamic and genetic context. I reaffirmed the inseparability of individual and group psychology in psychotherapeutic theory and practice. I used the concepts of ego identity and of identification with the group entity as an example of how one might go about advancing the much-needed yet very complex theoretical integration of individual and group psychology, on different depth levels.

In a more general sense, I have tried to re-emphasize man's need for finding self-esteem and coherence through stable group formations in this day of unprecedented readjustments with accompanying dissolutions of primary-group ties. Current developments in the helping professions as well as in the broader field of community mental health suggest that this need is receiving increasing attention.

(This chapter is based on a lecture delivered at the Washington Square Institute for Psychotherapy and Mental Health, New York, in May 1977.)

References

Anthony, J. (1967), 'The generic elements in dyadic and in group psychotherapy', *International Journal of Group Psychotherapy* 17, pp. 57-70.
Astley, R. (1974), 'Psychoanalysis: the future', *Journal of the American Psychoanalytic Association*, 22, pp. 83-96.
Bion, W. R. (1959), *Experiences in Groups*, New York, Basic Books.
Deutsch, H. (1967), *Selected Problems of Adolescence*, New York, International Universities Press.
Erikson, E. (1959), *Identity and the Life Cycle*, New York, International Universities Press.
Foulkes, S. H. (1964), *Therapeutic Group Analysis*, New York, International Universities Press.
Freud, S. (1955), *Group Psychology and the Analysis of the Ego*, London, Hogarth Press.
Fried, M. (1963), 'Grieving for a lost home', in *The Urban Condition*, ed. L. Duhl, New York, Basic Books.
Klein, G. (1976), *Psychoanalytic Theory: An Exploration of Essentials*, New York, International Universities Press.
Muensterberger, W. (1955), 'On the biopsychological determinants of social life', in *Psychoanalysis and the Social Sciences*, ed. W. Muen-

sterberger and S. Axelrod, New York, International Universities Press.

Murphy, G. (1947), *Personality*, New York, Harper.

Neumann, E. (1955), *The Great Mother*, New York, Pantheon.

Parloff, M. B. (1967), 'Advances in analytic group psychotherapy', in *Frontiers of Psychoanalysis*, ed. J. Marmor, New York, Basic Books.

Rabkin, J. G. and Struening, E. L. (1976), 'Life events, stress and illness', *Science*, 194, pp. 1013-20.

Redl, F. (1942), 'Group emotion and leadership', *Psychiatry*, 5, pp. 573-96.

Rochlin, G. (1959), 'The love complex', *Journal of the American Psychoanalytic Association*, 7, pp. 299-316.

Schaefer, R. (1958), 'Regression in the service of the ego', in *Assessment of Human Motives*, ed. G. Lindzey, New York, Rinehart.

Scheidlinger, S. (1951), *Psychoanalysis and Group Behavior*, New York, Norton.

Scheidlinger, S. (1964), 'Identification, the sense of belonging and of identity in small groups', *International Journal of Group Psychotherapy*, 14, pp. 291-306.

Scheidlinger, S. (1968), 'The concept of regression in group psychotherapy', *International Journal of Group Psychotherapy*, 18, pp. 3-20.

Scheidlinger, S. (1974), 'On the concept of the mother-group', *International Journal of Group Psychotherapy*, 19, pp. 417-28.

Slater, P. E. (1966), *Microcosm*, New York, Wiley.

Chapter 20
Group analysis and family therapy

A.C. Robin Skynner

'Offer a donkey a salad and he will ask you what kind of a thistle it is' — ancient Sufi proverb, quoted by Idries Shah in *The Way of the Sufi*.

It is a matter of very great sorrow that my need to postpone this lecture on the relationship between 'conventional' small-group work and conjoint family techniques has prevented me from putting forward the ideas that follow in the presence of S. H. Foulkes, whose death casts a shadow upon us all corresponding to the illumination he provided to our understanding. My own work owes so much to him, in a far more fundamental way than just the reception of facts and skills from a teacher, that I would have liked him to see what I had made from some of the materials he gave me. Moreover, his advancing years never seemed to diminish his capacity for an open, unbiased and respectful attentiveness even to the newest student, and for unexpected, original and stimulating comments which always took one's thought further than one had been able to go oneself. So, although he did not do a great deal in the direction of work with natural groups, being drawn more to the study of the 'stranger group', or the 'proxy group' as he preferred to call it, even his choice of that name — indicating immediately that the artificially-constituted groups we work with are automatically used by patients to reproduce, gain insight into, and change, the patterns learnt in their original family constellations ('root groups' as he called them) demonstrated his deep interest in both the fields we are considering — indeed, his perception that they make sense only when seen as a whole, in relationship to one another.

To begin my presentation, I should say at once that it has the wrong title, though I have left it as it is because so many seem to make this division between 'group analysis' on the one hand, and 'family therapy' on the other. But it is wrong because it is a confusion of categories, like comparing worms with vertebrates or mammals with plants. Group analysis is defined in the constitution of the Institute of Group Analysis as 'group-analytic psychotherapy'. It does not specify that this must be carried out with proxy groups rather than natural groups, and in fact I utilise group-analytic techniques with both, as Foulkes did himself; almost his last communication to his colleagues before he died was to affirm that group analysis could be applied to either situation. Of course one can compare the group-analytic approach, as used in either proxy groups or natural groups with, for example, behavioural approaches to these two kinds of group situation; or one can compare, in a general way, the different issues involved in treating proxy groups, and of treating natural groups, whatever type of theoretical orientation one is bringing to them.

Those who have read my book on family and marital psychotherapy[1] will have noticed that though I started from, and am still most firmly rooted in, the group-analytic approach to both proxy and natural groups, I was obliged to expand my field of view, embracing ideas and techniques I had previously seen as conflicting rather than compatible with group analysis, in order to make sense of the phenomena I was observing in studies of families and marriages. Tonight, I would like to widen the field of view still further, and instead of comparing work with natural groups and proxy groups, try to see if there is some simple and meaningful developmental relationship between the psychotherapies as a whole, of the kind I have hopefully discovered through studies of the family. If we look at psychoanalysis and its derivative individual psychotherapies; at psychotherapy based on behaviour modification; at family therapies as a whole; and at the range of stranger or proxy-group therapies (whether these group therapies are based more on analytic or on behavioural concepts and techniques) can we find some order and meaning in their relationship, even some deeper meaning and consequent order in the very fact that they are often presented by their exponents as in conflict and incompatible? I believe we can, if we are open to the possibility that we are involved here in a *developmental* process, involving an increase in complexity over time, and if we search for the vital clue within the structure of the family itself.

You will notice that I have listed the approaches in a way you may not have expected, and which may seem inappropriate. I have begun with individual psychoanalysis, moved next to behaviour modification approaches (which also began as an individual psychotherapy, and still finds great difficulty in moving out of the dyadic mould), and put family therapies third, leaving stranger groups till last. This conflicts with the order in which these approaches have developed, but it was not until I rearranged the order in this way that I found my ideas began to crystallise into a clear and simple pattern. Beforehand, I had tended to assume, because professionals had actually tried systematically to work with proxy groups many years in advance of serious attempts with natural groups, that adequate theories regarding the treatment of proxy groups (what we generally call 'group psychotherapy' or here call 'group analysis') had been developed before adequate theories about the treatment of natural groups (generally called 'family therapy'). I now see that this is not the case. Attempts to treat families and couples together have indeed been more delayed, but since such work began progress in construction of theory and refinement of technique has been astonishingly swift and successful, engaging its practitioners, despite the wide range of orientations and concepts with which they began, in a constructive and fundamentally cooperative joint activity that has been lacking in all other fields of psychotherapy. By contrast, I have begun to see (not least since trying to formulate this presentation) that the field of proxy-group psychotherapy, despite the fact that experimentation began much earlier, is still in a much more primitive, confused, conflicted, vague and ill-defined state even where attempts have been made to map some of the territory involved, containing, moreover, much disagreement and contention between its different practitioners. I believe now that this is the case because the theory and practice required for really effective proxy-group psychotherapy (that is, of a level we can attain with natural-group psychotherapy) is *most complex of all*, and that the rearrangement of the order of the psychotherapies I have already mentioned, placing proxy-group psychotherapy as the last item, correctly reflects this difficulty and complexity. Though discouraging at first sight, I personally found this realisation a great relief. It explained, in a way that is stimulating rather than a cause for despondency, why I am able to give what seems to me quite a clear, logical account of the work I do with families and couples, while I find myself unable to give a similarly coherent and intellectually satisfactory description of what I do with proxy-groups, although I have been working with them twice as long, spend three times as much time on them even today, and believe that I am quite skilful at working with them.

Now this is not to detract from the excellent work that has been done in the study of proxy groups, or to suggest that there is not already information sufficient to enable one to *use psycho-analytic techniques in groups*, to *employ behavioural techniques in a group situation*, and so on. All these are useful, rewarding, and will contribute towards an eventual adequate understanding, but they no more constitute a systematic theory of proxy-group psychotherapy than conventional child-guidance techniques, where one or both parents are involved in the treatment situation but the child is seen as the 'patient', constitutes family therapy as we now understand it.

Let us move on to consider how my rearrangement of the sequence in terms of *order of complexity*, rather than simple *order of appearance over time*, at once suggests a simple and elegant understanding of the situation. Because of considerations of space and time, I will not burden you with the ideas that were considered and discarded before this simple solution finally appeared. As is always the case, many years of struggle to reconcile seeming contradictions and discrepancies, seemingly requiring a theory of ever-increasing complexity, led suddenly and unexpectedly to a perception of a simple pattern. Though it made sense to me of all the problems, the pattern was too simple to see as long as one was standing too close to it, requiring one to step back and take a wider view before it could be registered. A pattern so simple, too, that one is inclined to reject it at first, as perhaps you will reject it. (You will notice the similarity here to my description of a family interview – an increasing mass of unrelated data, leading to growing confusion and fear that it is incomprehensible, resolving suddenly to perception of a simple pattern that unifies the whole.[2] Here perhaps is another simple 'systems' principle, which may be applicable to all levels of function.)

So here I shall put forward the unifying idea first, and then apply it to the facts, although of course things actually happen the other way around.

The basic integrating principle is well known to you all, forming as it does the essence of Freud's developmental scheme: that of oral, anal and genital phases. Of course he employed it in a particular way, elaborating this central three-stage process in terms of the physics of his day and producing his ideas about a libidinal energy being attached successively to different bodily zones. These details are today rejected by many, and certainly I do not find them a useful way of thinking myself, but the central concept seems to have astonishingly wide relevance, on many levels. Here I am indebted to Helen Durkin – whose book *The Group in Depth*[3] is still to my mind the best introduction and overview to the proxy-group field – for chapter 4 in that volume ('Recent developments in group dynamics') in which she relates this three-phase developmental sequence of Freud's to a similar three-phase pattern in the theories of other workers: Shutz's 'inclusion, control and affection', for example, or Bion's 'dependency, fight-flight and pairing', and Bennis's 'submissiveness, rebellion and independence' and related 'identification, self-identity and inter-dependence'. I have tried to work out some clinical applications of this phasic sequence of challenge and response in my recent book, though I realise that I did not give sufficient credit to the influence that Helen Durkin had on my thinking there, her ideas having become so much a part of my own thought that I had forgotten their origin.

My own modest contribution to these concepts, for good or ill, is the further idea that certain social situations form *challenges* to which the phases are *responses*, in the sequence *mother, father* and *couple*. Of course, this is in many ways stating the obvious. I imagine there will be little disagreement that in the first, oral phase, the mother is the central figure (or perhaps one should say today that the functions traditionally associated with mothering are essential to the child's requirements). Nor would those influenced by Freudian concepts, I imagine, disagree that the third, genital or oedipal phase is concerned with the relationship of the parents as *a couple*, particularly a *sexual* couple, rather than with their separate personalities as individuals. If I have made any contribution it is only to emphasise that the second or anal stage is concerned particularly with the issue of social control and the development of self-control, with independence and autonomy, with achieving compromises between the demands of society and of the instincts, and that this phase centres particulaily on the father (or rather the functions that are traditionally associated with the fathering role). This seems so obvious, once stated, that I feel rather foolish at mentioning it again. At the same time, it does seem to me that this obvious fact has somehow been subject to a curious neglect, or even avoidance, in recent years, perhaps because we have been passing through an era in which there has been great emphasis on mothering, a time too when the female role has been making up much lost ground as it ceases to be subordinate and devalued and comes to be appreciated as complementary and of equal importance to that of the male.

If we now look again at our series of psychotherapeutic modalities in the light of this phasic developmental sequence, I hope, you may share some of my excitement at the correspondences which at once appear. Though all the psychotherapies are concerned with facilitating maturation towards more responsible adulthood, there do seem to be rather different emphases in concept and method. It seems to me that psychoanalysis has certain traditionally *maternal* virtues as part of its core of philosophy and technique — such ideas as complete acceptance, of understanding both cognitively and in the sense of sympathy and capacity to identify with another. It provides a protective environment with secure boundaries within which it is believed that spontaneous growth will occur if harmful influences restricting it are removed. The patient is confronted with reality, to be sure, but in a graded fashion at the pace he can manage, where the very nature of the analytic session shields him from many pressures. Beyond this, the analyst does not make demands upon him for achievement and seeks to avoid as far as possible imposing his own values. Much of this corresponds to the relationship of a mother with a young baby in the oral phase of development, when patient care and nurturance provide a situation where growth occurs spontaneously, in a period before demands for socialisation and self-control are appropriate. Here, also, we see the gulf between the patient and therapist at its most extreme. In theory, at least, attention is directed entirely to the patient's needs, not those of the analyst, just as a mother in the earlier stages expects to give without return (though perhaps psychoanalysts, like mothers, can make hidden demands they do not recognise?). In no form of psychotherapy is the psychological distance greater, further from mutuality. Even the relative postures emphasise this, the patient prone upon a couch, the analyst upright, attentive but relatively passive. It is scarcely surprising that psychoanalysis, and the individual psychotherapies based upon it, are indispensable in the treatment of profound disturbances originating in the first year of a child's life.

If we move to behavioural types of psychotherapy, based upon learning theory, we see a very striking difference. We see less concern with understanding in the sense of total acceptance and empathy (though of course the cognitive aspect of understanding is there in a more specific, goal-directed fashion). The therapist's values are more openly involved, and he is much more likely to function as an educator seeking to change the patient so that he may learn to adapt more effectively to society's values. He sets standards, makes aims for the patient, and exerts pressure of one kind or another to help him attain them, whether by painful punishment (like electric shocks in the treatment of some perversions) or through support, encouragement and rewards.

The gap between patient and therapist is also less, though this is at first perhaps not so apparent. There is a clear hierarchy, it is true. The behavioural therapist functions as an expert who knows best what will benefit the patient, but they are in the relationship of teacher and pupil and the gap is less than in the analytic situation where, theoretically at least, there is no possibility of ordinary human contact or showing of the therapist's needs at all. In my book I give a quotation from A. H. Maslow and R. Días-Guerrero,[4] in which they put forward definitions of maternal and paternal roles in the following clear if somewhat extreme and stereotyped way:

> We postulate that the major task of the mother, *qua* mother, is to love unconditionally, to gratify, to heal and comfort and smooth over; and that the major task of a father, *qua* father, is to support and protect, to mediate between the family and reality (the world), and to prepare his children to live in the extra-familial world by discipline, toughening, instruction, reward and punishment, judging, differential valuing, reason and logic (rather than by unconditioned love), and by being able to say 'No' when necessary.

If there is any truth in this, it would certainly seem that behavioural psychotherapy is based on traditional paternal (rather than maternal) functioning, and that it is perhaps particularly appropriate where this influence has been lacking.

I wonder if this begins to explain the curious, implacable hostility between psychoanalysis and behaviour modification psychotherapists? 'Hostility' is perhaps the wrong word, for it does at least imply sufficient relationship for disagreement and conflict to exist, while what one observes is almost complete non-comprehension, non-communication, based on a strange inability of each to see things from the other's point of view. This has always mystified me, for even as a trainee at the Maudsley, when I was studying under Foulkes and Hoffer, I had a lively interest in the work of Wolpe, which was just then becoming known, avidly discussing these new techniques with the psychologists there and treating several cases myself using behavioural techniques. But if one's choice between the different types of approach is in fact based on a predominantly paternal or maternal identification, or perhaps a defence against the opposite one, the intensity of the resistance each type of psychotherapist shows to the theories of the other, and the resulting incapacity of each to look at things from the other's point of view, begins to make sense.

At least, it makes sense if one supposes one further condition: an inherent difficulty in the two sexes getting together in a mutual, complementary way in which each respects and acknowledges the special qualities and advantages of the other, without giving up their own, and recognising that the very differences and difficulties of communication which cause the problems, are a source of rich potentialities. In other words, there needs to be a perception, on both sides, that the whole purpose of the differences is the creative act of sexual intercourse, not a battle of the sexes.

It seems to me that this extraordinary phenomenon begins to be understandable, and indeed to fit meaningfully into the developmental sequence I am proposing, if we remember a central tenet of Freudian theory — the oedipal conflict and the jealousies and inhibitions regarding parental sexual intercourse associated with it, and if we assume that this dynamic can be reflected in systems at different levels — in this case in the system of the 'helping professions' as a whole.

If this were true, then we might anticipate that the development of conjoint family and marital therapy would have to involve a very remarkable leap forward, not only in concepts and techniques but also in the demands it would make upon its practitioners for a personal growth and for change in their relationship to colleagues; and we might anticipate too that it would take some time for the jump to be made.

When we look at the development of family therapy, we see a number of striking features which do begin to seem meaningful, at least to me, in this context. Conjoint work has indeed been slow to develop, and the early approaches to it have manifested continued splitting, separative processes, even if these have gradually become less extreme. Thus treatment facilities for adults and children have in general been kept separate and it has continued to be the custom for professionals to learn to work with one or the other, rather than both. Even in Child Guidance Clinics, where the family has been viewed more as a unit, adults and children have usually been seen separately, and provided with separate therapists. These clinics in turn have not usually been very interested in, or developed adequate skills at, the therapy of marriages, particularly sexual problems; while the latter problems have similarly been split off and dealt with in Institutes of Marital Studies or by Marriage Guidance Counselling, where the associated family and children's problems are not usually studied and treated simultaneously. If one wanted to keep the parental sexuality as far as possible from that of the children, and to deny the vital role of sexuality in the family, one could hardly conceive more effective arrangements for doing so.

But with the development of conjoint family therapy we see a kind of quantum jump in which we have at last begun to 'get it together'. Of course, family therapy has and will continue to have, like every other profession, its 'lunatic fringe' — extremists who need to polarise the world so that everything they cannot cope with in their own psyche is projected into an opposite camp and then attacked, to keep it from getting back inside themselves. But what is striking — indeed quite startling to anyone who has watched the development of psychological and therapeutic theory — is the astonishing degree of openness and willingness to share and integrate knowledge within this field between hitherto competing doctrines. Not only do different schools of dynamic psychotherapy find a common meeting-ground within it, but even dynamic and behavioural orientations are becoming integrated, as my book demonstrates, and I hope takes a little further. Ethology, communication theory, genetics, social studies, and other disciplines have found it a uniquely productive meeting-ground.

At the same time, such work demands not only a greater openness to different concepts and theoretical frameworks, but also presents a more forthright challenge to the therapist as a person, both from patients and colleagues. Working with families and marriages, it seems more difficult, and less effective, to work with a limited, professional part of oneself. We seem to find ourselves in question the whole time, obliged to put ourselves into the therapeutic equation, to change and grow at the same time as those we treat if the full capacities of the process are to be exploited; our own needs and values cannot be hidden if we are to be effective. The overall 'distance' between patient and therapist is also here further diminished, with control, challenge, and stimulation operating in both directions, though at the same time the *range* of psychological distance is in many ways greater as the therapist seeks to identify with the mother, the father, an adolescent, a baby, a teacher, a policeman, by turns.

This change to a more open-system orientation has not only removed some barriers maintaining the dualisms of intellect and emotion, of verbal and non-verbal, of conscious and unconscious, and of 'self' and 'other'. It seems also to help the therapist towards a different relationship to his own family. Although so much of our work in individual dynamic psychotherapy and psychoanalysis seems directed towards family dynamics, one often has the impression that the family is rather like a prison camp from which an escape is being organised, and that the family dynamics remain a shameful secret, still hidden from the world, even though the analysand gains some measure of freedom from it. By contrast, the move towards conjoint work has encouraged a reconciliation with the real family and its internalised representation, and indeed, in the work of Bowen[5] and Paul[6] a physical, geographical return to the family of origin to explore it more deeply. Though I was at first doubtful what the value such direct exploration of one's family might be, experience during a visit of the Nathan Ackerman Institute team from New York in 1973 was a great liberation. Revealing my family pathology openly, I began to discover that all the other professionals had the same, or very similar, families; then I began to see that there was only one family – the human family – within which variations of certain parameters – failures to present and cope with certain challenges – provided all the variety we encounter. Now, seeing that I need not flee from my family, they are allies in the therapeutic task.

Another corresponding change has been the tendency to work in pairs, as co-therapists, and in teams. Whether or not one believes that this is more effective therapeutically, it is surely a very big move away from the possessiveness so characteristic of physicians and psychotherapists, and the tendency to talk of 'my' patient. There are of course theoretical indications for making use of co-therapy – for example, where patients have not been provided with satisfactory gender role-models by their own parents, or where psychotic confusion and destructiveness is so intense that two therapists, as it were 'roped together', can undertake a perilous descent not possible for one therapist alone. But I think the tendency to work in pairs and teams is as much influenced by the realisation of therapists that, if the capacity to *share* underlies all satisfactory marriage and family life, they may need more practice at it themselves if they are to become more effective teachers. For example, the Family and Marital Course I set up within the Institute of Group Analysis (which later became the basis of the Institute of Family Therapy), a joint exercise was held each week with two of the small groups and their leaders, joined by my wife and me in which the express object was to oblige us, and the small group leaders, and the two groups, to face and struggle with our problems of sharing. Everyone found it immensely difficult, and the worst arguments that my wife and I ever had took place on the way home after these sessions.

If, then, psychoanalysis seems to make central some of those qualites that are most important in a mother as she succours her infant, and if behaviour modification techniques base themselves upon activities which are more the responsibility of the father towards the older child, then it seems as if the whole pattern and purpose of conjoint treatment of the marriage and family group makes central those issues and problems which are involved in satisfactory sexual intercourse, in the sharing and reciprocity of the marital relationship in general, and of the whole range of activities involved in bringing up the family that results from the liaison. From this point of view, the very striking differences in theory, practice, professional relationship and personal development within the family therapy movement, though at first rather surprising and puzzling, fall naturally into place.

If we now turn to the field of proxy-group psychotherapy as a whole, in the same way as we have just looked at the field of family therapies, we at once encounter a very different situation. I certainly find myself at sea, with no firm ground to stand on and with no clear and agreed landmarks. I find I do not know how to begin to organise the subject, or where to start in trying to make order and sense of it, for myself and my students. And I feel personally relieved, if not professionally reassured, to find from the literature, or from discussions with colleagues, that everyone else is in the same case and unable to help me, since I see that the whole field is still at a far more primitive stage of development than that of family therapy. It is characterised by competing schools, ignoring each other's work or conflicting with each other when they are forced to take notice at all, each striving to make sense and order of the field by oversimplifying, and ignoring or attacking those aspects of reality which fail to fit the preferred theory, rather than attempting the much more complex but infinitely more promising task of trying to see how the whole thing fits together. The theories range from extensions of individual analysis, with the 'psychoanalysis-in-groups' of Alexander and Wolff at one extreme; through Slavson, still based on individual analysis while also rejecting group-process ideas, though at least acknowledging the educational value of the group; through Bion who at least attempts to look at the group as a whole, even if he reduces it in the process to an essentially dyadic situation again; to Foulkes and Durkin who come closer than any others to recognising the full potentialities of the *group*, though still (until recently in the case of Durkin) within an essentially psycho-analytic framework. Then we have the explicit use of learning theory and behavioural approaches, by therapists like Robert Liberman, utilising much more fully and systematically the educational possibilities of the group. The encounter movement, psychodrama and Est are also much more open to the educational aspects of groups, the transmission of experience by *modelling*, giving much more importance to non-verbal communication. Then we have different types of groups for children, for adolescents and for adults, all emphasising rather different aspects of the group process; and we have small groups, large groups, and therapeutic communities where there is ongoing contact between the sessions and the situation is somewhere between the 'proxy' group and the 'natural' group dynamic.

All these, in my experience, have great usefulness and seem to me to complement each other. Yet we see a strange separation between them, and a failure to examine actively the possibilities of integration. In the United States there has been, as you know, a very deep split between those who saw value in the psychodramatic approaches of Moreno and others who preferred, like Slavson, to stay close to the psychoanalytic model. Similarly, one sees articles on Bion's work, both in this country and in the US, from which one would never learn that Foulkes existed, though I think the acknowledgment is a little fairer the other way round. There has also been a fierce opposition between the analytic group therapists and the encounter group leaders in the United States, and though I have personally found patients undergoing group analysis to make more rapid progress if they attend occasional encounter marathons, I am puzzled that I have not made a more systematic attempt to bring these two modes together rather than leave the possibility of the combination to chance and the patients' initiative. It is true that we have tried to combine these methods in the family and marital training, and that many do so in their family practice as well. My colleague Malcolm Pines has also been notably open in this respect, and while maintaining his basic position as a psychoanalyst and group analyst has been spent much time obtaining a thorough training in psychodramatic principles too.

Similarly, though the fact that patients learn from each other is recognised in most theories, analytic as well as behavioural, somehow it seems to be 'something extra', something left to chance, something not fully developed and integrated within the theory of group management. Moreover, the importance of the therapist's input (other than the provision of insight and analysis of resistance), while recognised in encounter methods and in family approaches, seems neglected in analytic theories even though everyone knows that it is a vital factor — indeed that perhaps the learning and modelling that goes on between therapist and patient, and between patient and patient, may be producing far more beneficial change than the accompanying analytic interventions, vital though the latter may be in periods of resistance and blockage of learning through projective processes. I realise that there are exceptions to these rather sweeping statements. For example, Helen Durkin, who has always seemed the most open of all the leading figures to new ideas and fresh techniques, says in a recent paper about the therapist's task:[7]

> (1) He must be vigilant in bringing such misplaced and maladaptive resistances to attention. Yet (2) he is reminded that resistance analysis is not an end in itself but merely an essential prerequisite to restoring normal input and optimal spontaneity. To accomplish this dual goal his own boundaries must be firm and flexible. *He can then exert his realistic authority in exercising his control function and employ his own creativity in stimulating spontaneous exchanges which lead to growth* [my italics].

Not surprisingly, this statement occurs in one of her papers attempting to integrate analytic ideas with systems concepts.

The more we survey the situation, the more we see that this apparent backwardness of the subject is more apparent than real, and due to the fact that the problems and possibilities involved in this kind of therapy are very much greater than in the others. In other words, proxy-group psychotherapy has potentially far more power and possibility than the forms we have considered already and it is not surprising, therefore, that we should find it a far more difficult continent to conquer. Let us just look at some of the factors involved. First of all, group psychotherapy (at least in the form Foulkes taught us to use) can have many of the advantages of individual psychoanalysis – indeed we do a brisk trade in, and are relatively successful with, some patients who have had ten or fifteen years' psychoanalysis without much movement. In a proxy group, the individual is not limited in his progress by the family defences and the common family goals. He can regress profoundly, especially in large groups, to a degree often avoided in individual analysis, and can work out many problems at very primitive levels, if the group is run properly. He has a wide range of objects to work with in examining his transference responses. Indeed the group is ideal for studying projective processes, since the anxieties which inevitably arise in the individual situation from the fact that the therapist is not only victim but also prosecutor, judge and jury, are reduced in a situation where any projective process can be scrutinised by people who are not involved in it, whether it takes place onto the therapist or onto another patient.

Similarly, as far as learning processes are concerned the group offers unrivalled opportunities. Much of this takes place by direct interaction, but as Foulkes has pointed out a great deal also occurs through vicarious learning by 'mirror reaction'. My own experience suggests that this is enhanced in large groups, where people can learn through watching the interaction of others, remaining safely concealed themselves until they feel more ready to venture out into the fray. The group also can reproduce the family, giving a second chance to re-examine and relearn patterns first acquired in an unhealthy early situation. It also goes further than this since it is not an actual family, but more a microcosm of social life. As Foulkes has emphasised, provided selection is reasonably careful the group as a whole is far more normal than the individuals contained within it, forming a consensus which is a reliable guide to the outside world and thus permitting constant resocialisation and re-education in more healthy and helpful values and forms of interaction. Moreover, the proxy group does not share (again given careful selection) the coherent defensive system that is such a feature of the individual or of the family group and marital couple. Both the analytic and re-educative work are carried on much more by the group itself, in contrast to the natural group or individual situation where the therapist has to take the main responsibility for change.

Most important of all (and most fully utilised in the group-analytic technique), the proxy group has one further invaluable advantage. If the therapist can learn to listen to the group-as-a-whole, and to understand and decode and express in ordinary language, the communications he receives, a vast additional potential is tapped for the therapeutic work. The group becomes a computer, producing answers to the questions being fed into it in the form of the individual patient's problems, going far beyond anything that the individuals themselves, or the therapist — no matter what his skill — could achieve alone. In this the large group has special possibilities quite apart from the profound regression which it encourages and supports. Moreover, the large group, if it is managed by a group of leaders who share the task and interact in an open and non-defensive way, takes the advantages of co-therapy, employed so usefully with families, a stage further. The rate and depth of change in group functioning, and in the personal growth of those participants one had information about, in the course of the six to eight weekly sessions of the large-group experience on our General Course (where these principles are operative even though the focus is more on training than therapy) was startling every time I saw it.

Now, if psychotherapy by proxy-group methods has potentially at its disposal all these different modes of change and technique, many of which will be operating no matter what method is made central, and if the ideal technique would take account of them all, the task of producing an adequate and comprehensive theory is obviously very difficult indeed. To put all this together within a unified set of concepts and principles requires a degree of effort, and a conceptual leap beyond what has already been achieved in the field of family and marital therapy, to the same extent that the systems ideas developed to cope with the treatment of families have required a leap in our thinking far beyond the individual-centred dyadic theories which sufficed for individual psychoanalysis and for behaviour modification based on learning theory. Once this was borne in upon me, in the course of preparing this talk, I found myself beginning to feel much easier about the difficulty I have experienced in clearly explaining even to myself what it is I do in proxy-group psychotherapy. At the same time a certain feeling of frustration and inadequacy was replaced by a more positive feeling of challenge, even a certain excitement, which I hope others may share with me.

Why has it taken me twenty years of practice and thought to come to this conclusion – that I don't really understand very clearly what I am doing in this chosen work which occupies the greater part of my time? Partly, perhaps, it is due to the fortunate fact that the forces of repair and healing, and the motivation towards growth and change in our patients, are very strong, so that good results occur despite our own limitations and mistakes. The 'good enough' therapist, like Winnicott's 'good enough mother', does not have to be very good, luckily for the patients as for babies. But I believe there was another, more harmful cause: an 'Emperor's clothes' phenomenon whereby we have all somehow believed that an adequate theory of group psychotherapy existed, even if we ourselves had never quite been able to grasp it clearly. There is no point in going shopping if one thinks the larder is full, and we have therefore had no motivation to look at the whole matter afresh and try to remedy the deficiency. Instead, when pressed to be more specific about what we actually do in groups we tend, like the donkey with the salad, to retreat to simpler concepts which have been more clearly worked out and with which we are familiar. Very often I find that those colleagues whose training has been through individual psychoanalysis tend, when pressed, to retreat to psychoanalytic explanations; while I, happier with the concepts of the family system, tend to lay more emphasis on the recapitulation and correction in proxy groups of disturbed family patterns. All this is certainly an enormous burden on our students, who in my experience tend to feel their lack of clarity about group functioning, and about the way to intervene therapeutically, is due to some deficiency in themselves. Often it is not. It is due to the fact that, in addition to not having a clear and comprehensive theory to teach them, we are behaving as if we have.

This is not to say, of course, that we do not have the *beginning* of a theory, fragments which, like pieces of a jigsaw in the early stages of its assembly, form isolated parts of a picture of which we cannot yet see the whole. In particular, Foulkes in this country has directed our attention towards the whole, has made us aware of it, interested in it, attentive to it, often able to use it even if only in an intuitive way we cannot explain. In the United States Helen Durkin did much, in 'The Group in Depth' and her subsequent papers, towards the integrated theory we all need, and she and James Durkin, her son, have done much to develop the concepts of systems theory, so vital in the family field, in relation to the proxy group where the idea of the 'system' so obviously corresponds to Foulkes's 'group matrix'.[8]

Since I was a student I always enjoyed teasing Foulkes a bit, and though he would get rather ruffled and on his dignity he seemed in a curious way to enjoy it too, so that it became for me an important feature of a very warm and rewarding relationship I had with him, which I greatly valued. At this point in this lecture I was quite looking forward to the probability that he would have become a little pink and upset, having realised that I was saying that *he* was the Emperor in the imaginery finery everyone was applauding, and that I was saying that he really had nothing on at all, or at least that his apparel was rather threadbare.[9] All great men have their weaknesses, and he was no exception. He prided himself on an ability for conceptualisation which in fact was not one of his strong points, not only in my opinion but according to the reaction of practically every audience of which I was a member, or in which I chaired his presentation. I can say that now he is not here, and I think it should be said, if only for the sake of the future of his own work.

What I was looking forward to even more, however, was the prospect of turning to him at this point, and saying that an Emperor, surely, was not an Emperor by virtue of his *clothes*. Anyone can wear fine clothes. An Emperor is a particular person; he is an Emperor by virtue of who and what he *is*.

Recognising this, I am able to see why I feel so rich in knowledge, and confident in skills, in relation to my proxy-group work even though I still find myself so hopelessly inadequate when I try to formulate it.

From the beginning I was attracted to what Foulkes *was* rather than to his ideas alone and I see that, without putting it into words, or perhaps without even recognising it in theoretical terms, he demonstrated in his own person and way of relating an actual integration of a variety of the fundamental modes of influence I have already spoken about, combining many of those now recognised and utilised explicitly in family therapy, as well as in psychoanalysis and other theories. His openness, his ability to be completely human and natural without losing his objectivity and therapeutic stance, his absence of defensiveness and easy communication about his personal experience – including his past life and the family with which he had such a good relationship, his ability to learn from others at the same time as he taught, and to listen with equal respect to the most senior colleague and a new student, his ability in particular to learn from the group itself and to see psychotherapy as in some measure a shared exploration – all these things developed later as striking features of the family therapy movement. Even though he may not have succeeded in conceptualising it adequately, he *was* to a very considerable degree a living actualisation of the integration we are speaking about, and of course the ability to be, and to do, is the aim of therapy, to which the theories and techniques are only incidental. As those who have read my book on family therapy will know, I find the concept of 'modelling' of very great and central importance, and think it plays more part than we realise in all forms of treatment. Those of us who have had contact with Foulkes, like myself, have received vast amounts of knowledge through this modelling process, absorbing information by a kind of osmosis, without recognising it. This I think is the explanation of the profound change which often occurred in anyone who had personal contact with him even for a short time, and why his writings have not given him the degree of recognition he deserves.

It is our task, then, to take this knowledge he has given us, which we have absorbed and made part of us as food becomes part of our bodies, and together try to conceptualise it, to put it into a form which can be communicated more adequately across space and time, through the written word. It is our task to fashion for the Emperor the clothes that he deserves.

References

1 Skynner, A. C. R. (1976), *One Flesh, Separate Persons: Principles*

of Family and Marital Psychotherapy, London, Constable. American edition entitled *Systems of Family and Marital Psychotherapy*, New York, Brunner/Mazel, 1976.

2 Skynner, A. C. R. (1981), 'An open-systems, group-analytic approach to family therapy', in Gurman, A. and Kniskern, D., *The Handbook of Family Therapy*, New York, Brunner/Mazel.

3 Durkin, H. E. (1964), *The Group in Depth*, New York, International Universities Press.

4 Maslow, A. H., and Días-Guerrero, R. (1973), 'Adolescence and juvenile delinquency in two different cultures' in Maslow, A. H., *The Farther Reaches of Human Nature*, Harmondsworth, Penguin, (p. 390).

5 Bowen, M. (1978), *Family Therapy in Clinical Practice*, New York, Jason Aronson.

6 Paul, N. L., and Paul, B. B. (1975), *A Marital Puzzle*, New York, W. W. Norton.

7 Durkin, H. E. (1975), 'General systems theory and analytic group therapy: resistance', unpublished lecture to American Group Psychotherapy Association – personal communication.

8 Durkin, J. E. (1981), *Living Groups: Group Psychotherapy and General System Theory*, New York, Brunner/Mazel.

9 Foulkes's death occurred while this lecture was in preparation.

Chapter 21
The group process in Chekhov's plays

Sheila Thompson

Shortly before he died, Dr Foulkes lent me a biography of Chekhov.
We were considering the wider implications of his concept of 'network', and he thought that a study of the way in which dramatists
have depicted interpersonal relationships might be useful for the
development and enrichment of his own theories. But there was no
time left; and when I came to see the relevance of Chekhov's work,
it was no longer possible for us to discuss it. The views put forward
here, therefore, are my own.

To summarise, a major innovation in Chekhov's last four plays[1]
was the shift in focus from the individual to the group, anticipating
developments in dynamic psychology and other behavioural sciences
which were not to take place for another half century. In these last
plays, Chekhov was attempting to do something extremely difficult
and quite without precedent; he was trying to give direct dramatic
expression to transpersonal processes taking place within a group.
It is because of a failure to recognise this, leading to successive attempts
to place his plays within existing conventions, that they have been so
frequently misinterpreted and misunderstood. On the other hand, it
is because of his success in conveying transpersonal processes, and in
drawing his audiences in to share in group experiences, that so many
people have found his plays very moving, even though they may have
often been at a loss to say why; so that, in reading about Chekhov,
one finds repeated references to his 'magic', to a mysterious and indefinable quality which cannot be put into words.

It is perhaps worth recording here that one of Dr Foulkes's early
memories was of an encounter with Chekhov in a German hotel. It
must have been at Badenweiler, in 1904, in the last month of Chekhov's
life, when he was dying of tuberculosis. Dr Foulkes retained a vivid
memory of the great interest taken by all the adults in a sickly

figure wrapped in rugs, attended by a solicitous wife.

Interest in the work of playwrights from the point of view of dynamic psychology is nothing new, and can take a number of different forms.

A play can be treated as if it were the equivalent of real life, as if the characters were real people, and the families real families, with a past and a future and a psychopathology to be examined. Thus, for example, Freud treated Ibsen's Rebecca West. Sometimes individual characters become the embodiment of some general human condition, as when Oedipus is translated into Everyman. Another approach extends the boundaries of the area under examination to include the playwright, and the characters are seen in relation to their creator, the direct or indirect representations of people, situations, or themes, important in his life.

At another level a play contains a communication about the nature of man and his position in the world, which reflects contemporary awareness, but which also may play a part in extending this awareness into new areas.

A major part of man's consciousness of himself in relation to the world around him has been concerned with the nature of the limitations on human freedom. Thus the classical Greek writers, caught up in that first great upthrusting of the individual within the group, tried to explore the situation of the hero in his new pride who dared to challenge super-personal forces and was duly punished for his presumption.

Chekhov's immediate precursor, Ibsen, was also concerned with the exceptional individual, now the product of late nineteenth-century liberalism and a potentially free man (or woman) capable of working out his own destiny. Ibsen's hero tries to demonstrate this new freedom, pits himself against the forces restraining him, struggles heroically, but ultimately goes down in defeat. Great innovator that Ibsen was, changing the conventions in order to introduce a naturalistic form of drama which could be a vehicle for the portrayal and dissection of contemporary problems, his heroes are still recognisably the tragic heroes of a long unbroken tradition, defined by their separateness and set up against events.

In Chekhov's four last plays, on the contrary, there are no heroes. Chekhov, who followed closely upon Ibsen's heels, and recorded his debt to him, carried on with the new naturalistic form of drama which Ibsen had pioneered. But it is the ways in which Chekhov departed from the tradition which Ibsen had continued which are of particular interest in our context.

It is revealing to compare the different ways in which the plays of the two writers were received. After the first performances of *Ghosts* and of *Hedda Gabler*,[2] Ibsen was hysterically abused, principally for the nature of his themes and the pessimism of his conclusions. His critics hated his plays, but they seemed to know what they were about. When it came to Chekhov, the critics were baffled and exasperated by their inability to make out what was supposed to be going on. And these critics included some of the ablest and most discerning literary men of the day. William Archer, who did so much to introduce Ibsen to British audiences, found Chekhov's plays formless and time-wasting. Tolstoy, who loved and admired Chekhov, could not bring himself to read to the end of *The Three Sisters*, and demanded to know where it was all leading. 'Where are you going with your heroines?' he asked. 'From the sofa to the privy, and from the privy back to the sofa?' Nothing happened in the plays, it was said. There was no hero or heroine: the characters did not communicate with each other in any meaningful way: no one could decide whether they were comedies or tragedies. When *The Three Sisters* was first read to the experienced company of the Moscow Art Theatre, it was received in a baffled silence.

But when his plays did come to be staged, the audience, sitting together in the auditorium, often responded as to a direct and very moving personal experience. It is the recognition of the special nature of this experience which has led people to speak of Chekhov having a mysterious and indefinable magic, 'the precise operation of which', says Allardyce Nichol, 'baffles our intelligence'.[3]

But even among his contemporaries there were a few who felt able to define what Chekhov was doing. George Calderon, who translated and produced the first Chekhov play to be presented in Great Britain (*The Seagull*, in 1909) wrote, in the introduction to his published translation, that Chekhov was a pioneer in both recognising and portraying on the stage 'the fact that our experiences and our impulses are very little private to ourselves, almost always shared with a group of other people'.[4]

This comment of Calderon's seems to come from a different level of perception to the more generally accepted view, still put forward today, that the main purpose of the plays was the portrayal of the tragic isolation of man's existence, in which 'each one speaks for himself and there is no one to listen'.[3]

There are other contradictions to be found in any examination of the reactions to Chekhov's plays. There is the question of deciding whether they are tragedies or comedies. Stanislavsky, their first producer at the Moscow Art Theatre, described them as 'great tragedies of Russian life', and seems to have stayed with this opinion despite Chekhov's own explicit denials, despite his insistence that *The Three Sisters* was a drama, and *The Cherry Orchard* 'funny, very funny . . . a comedy . . . in places even a farce'. 'You say that you have wept over my plays?' he told a fellow writer. 'Yes, and not you alone. But I did not write them for this purpose. It is Alekseev [Stanislavsky] who has made such cry babies of them.'[5] And Stanislavsky, struggling to stage Chekhov's plays within the conventions of his time, was castigated again and again by Chekhov for having distorted and misrepresented them.

Turning to those four last plays, *The Seagull*, *Uncle Vanya*, *The Three Sisters*, and *The Cherry Orchard*, it can be seen that they all share a common underlying structure and form which is different from the structure and form found in the traditional drama of that day; and which seems to indicate an alteration in purpose, a shift in interest, in fact, from the individual to the group. In each of these four plays there are no exceptional people who stand out from the rest, but a number of characters to whom a more or less equal degree of emphasis is accorded. They are collected together at the beginning of the first act, and they remain together until they disperse at the end of the play. No new characters are introduced, so that the action takes place as within a closed group. There is one location, isolated from, and at times contrasted with, the rest of the world. Problems, both individual and collective, are revealed, but there is no resolution and no solution is offered at the end. There is no clear plot or story line: there is an impression of a lack of incident. The characters tend, at some point in the plays, to be brought together in a situation in which defences are lowered as a result of exhaustion, or excitement, or anxiety; because of a fire, a storm, or a late-night vigil; and they discuss their feelings with a freedom not always found elsewhere. They share a dissatisfaction with their current lives, and a yearning for something better, but little seems to be achieved: the action seems to drift and stagnate while they deal ineffectively and repetitively with their problems. At the end of the play it seems that very little change has taken place.

It was not only Tolstoy who was exasperated at the behaviour of the three sisters. The one thing that most people recollect about this play is that it concerns three girls who long to go back to Moscow but who never manage to get there, although the reason for their failure is not very clear. The sisters and their brother Andrey, are attractive, intelligent, and well educated young people, marooned in a dull provincial town since the death of their father, a general, the year before. They are excitedly planning their return to Moscow, and, apart from the fact that Masha is married, none too happily, to a local schoolmaster, there seems no reason why they should not leave. There are a number of army officers still in attendance: the elderly doctor, Chebutikin, who once loved their mother; the indecisive little Baron Tuzenbach; Lieutenant-Colonel Vershinin tied to a sick wife; the hostile Soleni.

Although the sisters might, at the beginning of the play, be thought to have many personal advantages on their side, nothing goes right for them. Their brother marries the gauche girl they despise, and abandons an academic career in order to become a minor civil servant. Their sister-in-law turns out to be a self-centred schemer who gradually assumes complete control of the household. The work to which they turn with such idealistic hopes is found to be monotonous drudgery, bringing exhaustion and headaches, draining away youth and vitality. Masha has a hopeless love affair with Vershinin, knowing that he will have to leave her in the end. Irina, when she finally gives up hope of ever going to Moscow, where her imaginary lover awaits her, agrees to marry the Baron who is a good man but who does not attract her, only to have him killed in a duel by his rival Soleni.

Yet with all this, the play ends on a note of exaltation and triumph. The sisters, with all their former hopes and expectations blighted, together, in harmonious accord, look forward to the happy life which lies ahead, even though they do not expect it to come in their lifetime.

It was this ending that some of the critics at the play's first night found so intolerable, a false note, unrelated to what had gone before. Their additional complaint that nothing happened may seem paradoxical when even a cursory glance at the text reveals adultery, attempted suicide, a disastrous fire, and a fatal duel. Yet the impression of nothing happening remains. Chekhov is reported to have said 'a pistol shot is not a drama, it is an event'. The drama lies elsewhere.

To go back to the beginning, at the start of the play, Chekhov communicates with the members of his audience over the heads of his characters, alerting them to the existence of another level of meaning which they are in a position to discover, if they will link all the events together into one whole.

It is Irina's name day, and the sisters are together in a gay and hopeful mood. At the back of the stage, apparently engrossed in conversation, is a small group of army officers. Every now and then a remark made by one of the officers becomes audible above the sisters' conversation. When Olga speaks of her happiness, and her passionate longing to go home, two officers are heard saying 'Will you take a bet on it', and 'Oh, nonsense!', and a little later comes mocking laughter, and 'I'm tired of listening to the rot you talk'. Through this device, rather more artificial and contrived than is usual in Chekhov's work, he indicates that all is not as it seems, and that what the sisters are saying is not to be taken at its face value, or in isolation from the whole.

Scepticism about the reality of the sisters' plans is further strengthened with the arrival of Vershinin, an acquaintance from the distant past. He comes from Moscow, and he indicates that Moscow is not as the sisters remember it, or imagine it to be. His own personal life is a disaster, about which he feels able to do nothing. His escape from it is through philosophical flights of fancy, in which he expounds ideas which seem grandiose and banal; discarding the idea of a personal happiness to be sought in the present in favour of an abstract concept of a remote future happiness which will come inevitably for all.

The sisters are very conscious of their own distinction, their superior education and sensitivity. It is this which draws them together as it distinguishes them from others, and they must not put it at risk. Though they so yearn for a better and a fuller life, they dare not engage in any struggle to achieve it. There is something in Vershinin's ideas of a better life to come for everybody, in his insistence that they can contribute to this better life simply by being their special selves in a dull, provincial town, which makes an immediate and powerful appeal to them. Masha, who had been about to leave, takes off her hat again; and they invite him to stay for lunch.

This solution, proposed by Vershinin, is gradually expanded and shared among the sisters and their immediate circle; and their tendency to withdraw from any direct confrontation is reinforced. As their actual situation becomes worse and worse, and as it becomes less and less possible to do anything active about it, so the abstract ideal of happiness becomes more and more compelling; but it is placed in a future which becomes ever more remote.

It is the working out of this process in the group which Chekhov is trying to reveal, and which forms the central focus of the play. He depicts the group gradually defining its own reality, establishing a consensus at the expense of independent action. A strength is created which enables the sisters to survive all their misfortunes and still retain confidence in their chosen solution.

These misfortunes need to be seen as part of the total process, despite all the attempts which have been made to treat Natasha as intrinsically wicked, 'diabolical'. 'Nowhere else', writes David Magarshack,[6] 'has Chekhov created a more terrifyingly convincing figure of evil.' Such external references do not do justice to the completeness of Chekhov's conception. The behaviour of Natasha can be explained with reference to the behaviour of the sisters, who from the beginning make no secret of the way they feel about her, and treat her as something alien to themselves. For most of the play, when she is living in the same house and married to their brother, they manage to behave as if she were not there; and her destructive behaviour seems to start as a desperate attempt to attract some attention to herself. Her adultery with Protopopov is ignored by everyone until even the old doctor, who by then has his own reasons for trying to shake them out of their preoccupations, is moved to protest: 'Natasha is having a disgusting affair with Protopopov and you don't see it. You are just sitting here and don't see anything, while Natasha is having her disgusting affair with Protopopov.' But it has no effect; they continue as if they hadn't heard him.

At the end of the play, when they have weakly allowed her to gain possession of the family home, when she announces provocatively that the first thing she will do is to have the avenue of trees cut down, she only gets an unresponsive silence. It seems small wonder that a moment later she is screaming with rage at a helpless servant.

The other destructive character, Soleni, is not admitted into the sisters' inner circle either. He is a self-centred poseur, preoccupied with his disordered perception of his own body, who conceals his insecurity behind his ludicrous posturings. Despite his hostile behaviour, he is tolerated, mocked, protected, and not taken very seriously. His one positive act, and bid for acceptance, is his profession of love for Irina; and his reaction to his rejection is an announcement that he will kill any more favoured rival. This turns out to be the Baron, the person who has shown him most kindness. So Soleni, like Natasha, when unable to enter the charmed circle, reacts by trying to break and destroy it.

There is an inevitable quality about the duel although, logically, it seems so unnecessary. One word might prevent it, yet none of the characters seems able to speak. Like the scheming and the adultery of Natasha, the growing threat of a duel between the Baron and Soleni is simply ignored. The engagement between Irina and the Baron has been entered into with little hope of happiness, but it could all the same be a way out of the impasse for Irina. But it is not to be allowed to take place. 'Somehow or other, all this doesn't seem at all serious,' says Kulinin when Irina is telling him of her marriage plans, 'as if it was all ideas and nothing really serious.' When the fact that the duel has been arranged is being hinted, Irina make a half-hearted attempt to find out what is going on, but allows herself to be discouraged, although she seems to be anticipating some tragedy. By this time the group has defined its reality; and events are to take their course, happiness is something which is not to be sought in the present if that beautiful dream of happiness to come is to be preserved intact.

And at the end, the dream is still intact. It is expressed by Andrey:

The present is beastly, but when I think of the future how good it is! I feel so light, so free; there is a light in the distance, I see freedom. I see myself and my children freeing ourselves from vanities, from kvass, from goose baked with cabbage, from after-dinner naps, from base idleness.

It is expressed by the sisters, but more abstractly:

There will come a time when everybody will know why, for what purpose, there is all this suffering, and there will be no more mysteries. . .

our sufferings will turn into joy for those who will live after us, happiness and peace will reign on earth, and people will remember with kindly words, and bless those who are living now. Oh dear sisters, our life is not yet at an end. Let us live.

The sisters' reserves of strength, which they draw from being together, are most apparent at the beginning and at the very end of the play; and their final triumphant mood seems to derive from their feeling of being part of an even greater whole, all suffering humanity including the generations yet to come. Yet the consolation itself hardly seems adequate; and throughout the play up to now, it is when they have been most in accord that they have been deceiving themselves most.

The final comment is made by the old doctor, who has dissociated himself from life since the moment in the last act when he began to doubt even the reality of his love for their dead mother. He sings a trivial song, 'Tara . . . ra-boom-deay. . . . It is my washing day. . . . It's all the same. It's all the same.'

Chekhov might have had an easier task if he had chosen a novel rather than a play for this exploration of multipersonal relationships. In a novel the author is able to step outside the action in order to draw the attention of the reader to what is going on, and offer analysis and interpretation. The reader can follow the author's ideas at his own speed, taking time off to pause and ponder and re-read. In a play every communication is condensed, precise and explicit, the dialogue itself has to carry all the necessary information, and the audience has to grasp immediately the significance of what it is seeing and hearing.

But since he did choose a play, and boldly experimented with new forms of dramatic expression, it is of particular interest in the study of group processes to consider how the dialogue in his plays is constructed. Contained within what the characters are saying to each other, and what they are not saying, are their covert emotional preoccupations; and these preoccupations act upon each other and lead to the formation of group preoccupations. Just as every speech in the play has its place, and cannot be fully understood except in relation to the whole, so is every individual happening rooted in the group.

There are a number of different levels of meaning in Chekhov's dialogue, and the idea that he was concerned with depicting the 'tragic isolation' of human existence comes from the recognition of only one level. Rather than depicting non-communication alone, Chekhov was interested in exploring the process of communication itself in all its aspects. Communications are proffered, and either ignored or else responded to in various ways. They may be taken up and expanded, or they may elicit some more oblique response, as each hears selectively and responds selectively to what other people are saying. There may also be sudden fusions in which preoccupations merge and some new state emerges.

At one extreme, there is a total failure in communication in the farcical scene in which Soleni and Chebutikin argue about the meaning of a word, Chebutikin insisting that *chehertma* means roast mutton, and Soleni arguing that on the contrary *cheremsha* is a plant like an onion, and neither attending to the other sufficiently to notice that they are speaking of different words. This scene is surely not introduced merely for its comic effect, or even to define the two separate characters involved: its purpose is to indicate the theme, and contrast with other scenes in which the characters do manage to communicate with each other in different degrees.

There are also passages in which what is being said contains a meaning which is at variance, which is sometimes the direct opposite, of the literal meaning of the words used. In these passages an attempt is being made to fill the gap between what is being felt and what can be said. For example, there is the speech in which Andrey harangues his sisters on the night of the fire.

> Natasha is a beautiful and honest creature, straight and honourable — that's my opinion. I love and respect my wife; understand it, I respect her, and I insist that others should respect her too. I repeat, she's an honest and honourable person . . .

It is so important to treat this play as a whole; and each speech derives so much of its significance from preceding events, and from its position in the whole, that it is impossible to find short illustrative quotations which do not lose a lot of their meaning when taken out of context. 'The moon', as Chekhov wrote in one of his letters, 'can only be understood if the stars too are intelligible.'[7]

The following extract may indicate the fragmented and inconsequential nature of the dialogue, which is broken up and unpredictable, the contributions following tangentially rather than in any logical order. In order to convey the inner action, the dialogue does not have to be coherent. Indeed, it is because of the lack of logical structure that the communicational network linking all the different contributions can be revealed.

Vershinin. What a wind!

Masha. Yes. I'm tired of winter. I've already forgotten what summer's like.

Irina [*playing patience*]. It's coming out, I see. We're going to Moscow.

Fedotik. No, it won't come out. Look, the eight was on the two of spades. [*Laughs*] That means you won't go to Moscow.

Chebutikin [*reading paper*]. Tsitsigar. Smallpox is raging there.

Anfisa. Masha, have some tea, little mother. Please have some. Sir . . . excuse me, but I've forgotten your name.

Masha. Bring some here, nurse. I shan't go over there.

Irina. Nurse!

Anfisa. Coming, coming!

Natasha. Children at the breast understand perfectly. I said 'Good morning, Bobby; good morning, dear!' And he looked at me in quite an unusual way. You think it's only the mother in me that is speaking: I assure you that it isn't so! He's a wonderful child.

In this passage Masha, who has been married for seven years to a dull husband she does not love, shows that she feels her youth is over, indeed it is as if it had never been. Irina, however, is not ready to give up her dreams of Moscow, and romance, although it seems that she is deceiving herself about this as she is deceiving herself about her cards. Then comes the interjection about Tsitsigar, from the old doctor who is now reduced to culling scraps of medical information from the news-papers. David Magarshack[6] informs us that Tsitsigar is an exotic place, even more remote and unattainable than Moscow, and yet it is full of pestilence. Masha then declines to fetch her own tea from the table where Natasha is serving it. Natasha's immediate reaction is to draw attention to her motherhood, something which she often does when at points of conflict with her (childless) sisters-in-law.

There are also passages in which there is nothing disjointed about the dialogue; in which, on the contrary, the sisters seem to be sharing one thought, as if they were the same person. In these passages, which usually occur when they are defining their attitudes towards certain critical situations, the accord between them is their most character-istic feature.

One final passage from *The Three Sisters* is worth examining here because of the different levels it contains and because it has been quoted by Chekhov scholars to support very different opinions about the play: to show the way in which the isolated characters fail to under-stand each other; and to show how they all contribute to, and share in, a prevailing group emotion.

> *Tuzenbach.* Not only after two or three centuries, but in a million
> years, life will still be as it was; life does not change, it remains
> for ever, following its own laws which do not concern us, or
> which, at any rate, you will never find out. Migrant birds,
> cranes for example, fly and fly, and whatever thoughts, high or
> low, enter their heads, they will still fly and nor know why or
> where. They fly and will continue to fly whatever philosophers
> come to life among them; they may philosophise as much as they
> like, only they will fly . . .
> *Masha.* Still, is there a meaning?
> *Tuzenbach.* A meaning? . . . Now the snow is falling. What meaning?
> *Masha.* It seems to me that a man must have faith, or must search for
> a faith, or his life will be empty, empty. . . . To live and not to
> know why the cranes fly, why babies are born, why there are
> stars in the sky. . . . Either you must know why you live, or

everything is trivial, not worth a straw. [*A pause*]
Vershinin. Still, I am sorry that my youth has gone.
Masha. Gogol says: life in this world is a dull matter, my masters!
Tuzenbach. And I say it's difficult to argue with you, my masters!
Hang it all.
Chebutikin [*reading*]. Balzac was married at Berdichev. That's worth
making a note of. Balzac was married at Berdichev.
Irina [*thoughtfully*]. Balzac was married at Berdichev.

We are told that Berdichev is a town renowned in Russia for its
dullness,[6] and so contemporary audiences, to whom Balzac would be a
vital and respected figure, would have recognised an incongruity here.
All the characters, musing on the purpose of life in this passage, must
have had in their minds the sexual happiness which they each were
longing for but could not obtain; yet Balzac had found it in Berdichev. Their mood is resigned, defeated, passive; no vigorous activity
is to be expected from them.

Raymond Williams,[8] in a study of the development of successive
conventions in the theatre, transcribes this passage as if it were one
single speech, without attributing it to different speakers. He does this
so that the underlying mood can be more clearly recognised. 'An
unfamiliar rhythm is developed,' he writes, 'in which what is being said,
essentially, is not said by any one of the characters, but, as it were,
inadvertently, by the group.'

One might set alongside this a quotation from *Therapeutic Group
Analysis*:[9] 'The group as it were avails itself now of one speaker, now of
another, but it is always the transpersonal network which is sensiti-
vised and gives utterance or responds.'

There is only time to mention very briefly one more of Chekhov's
plays, and it must be *The Cherry Orchard*, his last work. This is a play
that contains virtually no unsympathetic characters at all, and there is
even less action than in *The Three Sisters*. The focus is placed squarely
upon the group as a whole, and it is a group which is struggling to dis-
band. They have all been drawn together, have come back or have been
fetched back, because they are about to lose the cherry orchard. It is
a unique and beautiful orchard which used to be so fruitful and productive, but is so no longer since they have now lost the secret recipe
for preserving the cherries. It is variously seen as something lovely and
bountiful; as containing something oppressive and tyrannical; or as
being something which they have wasted and betrayed. As each of the
characters defines his or her attitude towards the orchard which they

are about to lose, it is used to represent other primary ties as well.

Madame Ranevsky, that lovely mother figure who never fulfils the expectations they all have of her, who so neglects her own children, seems to represent in her own person much of the common conflict. It is she who expresses most clearly what the orchard represents.

> *Ranevsky.* Look, there's my dead mother going in the orchard . . .
> dressed in white! [*laughs for joy*] That's she.
> *Gaev.* Where?
> *Varya.* God bless you, little mother.
> *Ranevsky.* There's nobody there; I thought I saw somebody. On the
> right at the turning by the summer house, a white little tree bent
> down looking like a woman.

She is not the only person who sees the cherry orchard as alive. The revolutionary student, Trofimov, fears it because to him it is full of human faces and voices and long memories going back into the past. Madame Ranevsky's young daughter, on the other hand, who is absorbed in her growing friendship with Trofimov, is surprised to find that she does not love the cherry orchard as she used to do.

Memories of their childhood come crowding back as they contemplate the orchard; they want to escape from it, and they want to preserve it and recreate it as it used to be. The ambivalence which makes it impossible for them either to hold on to the orchard and to each other, or to let go, pervades the play. When at the end of the play the group does break up, the family disperses, the orchard is cut down, it happens by default; no one is able to take any positive action to prevent it or to derive any benefit from it. Even then, when all the goodbyes have been said, and the first cherry tree is falling under the speculator's axe, they cannot leave completely. By a final outrageous act of negligence the old dying servant, Firs, is left behind, locked up in the deserted house.

This ending has been found distasteful; it has even been suggested that it should be omitted on the stage. But it could be seen as a final indication of the nature of the problem, and of the fact that it has not been solved.

Stanislavsky's opinion that *The Cherry Orchard* was a social tragedy depicting the passing of the old aristocratic way of life, which has been so influential, seems largely irrelevant. They are not tragic people, and neither is their situation exceptional nor tragic. They gather in the first act in a room which, according to the stage directions 'is still called the nursery', and as they leave the same room at the end of the last act, Madame Ranevsky remembers that 'My dead mother used to like to walk about this room'. Gaev responds 'My sister, my sister', and Anya's voice is heard off stage calling 'Mother'. All the emphasis is upon the primary relationships, and the attempts to recreate them in the present. In the words of the eccentric German governess, who sometimes plays the part of a Shakespearean fool, expressing their unspoken feelings, 'I don't know how old I am and I think I'm young.'

The final level of communication with which we are concerned is that between dramatist and audience. The final product is not the play upon the stage, but the play that is fashioned in the mind of the spectator.

No one made greater demands upon his audiences than Chekhov. They are required to participate in the creative process, to recognise the clues and make the connections in the apparently unconnected dialogue, to find the transpersonal level at which all the happenings are related, and fill in the gap between the individuals and the group. 'By tuning to his key, one finds a world opening up . . .',[10] and tuning to his key seems to require a readiness of perception which has something in common with that of the group or family therapist. It seems to be a question of looking beyond separate characters and separate actions, keeping in mind the parts and the whole, not identifying exclusively with any one character, at times disregarding individual speakers in order to respond to an underlying group theme. Generations of playgoers seem to have been able to do this, without knowing what they were doing.

Chekhov seems to have been unable to define it himself, although he could react immediately and forcefully when producer or actors misunderstood his intentions. 'Why don't you read my play,' was his answer to questions. 'It's all there.'

What he did reiterate again and again was his conviction that a writer's only duty was to tell the absolute and honest truth, to formulate problems correctly and leave it to someone else to provide the solutions.

> I only wished to tell people honestly: Look at yourselves, see how badly and boringly you live. The principal thing is that people should understand this, and when they do, they will surely create for themselves another and a better life.

References

1   Chekhov, A. (1960), *Six Famous Plays*, London, Duckworth.
2   Ibsen, H. (1950), *Hedda Gabler and Other Plays*, Harmondsworth, Penguin.
3   Nichol, Allardyce (1949), *World Drama*, London, Harrap.
4   Pitcher, Harvey (1973), *The Chekhov Play*, London, Chatto & Windus.
5   Simmons, Ernest J. (1962), *Chekhov*, Chicago, University of Chicago Press.
6   Magarshack, David (1972), *The Real Chekhov*, London, Allen & Unwin.
7   Chekhov, A. (1973), *Letters*, London, Bodley Head.
8   Williams, Raymond (1968), *Drama from Ibsen to Brecht*, London, Chatto & Windus.
9   Foulkes, S. H. (1964), *Therapeutic Group Analysis*, London, Allen & Unwin.
10 Gottlieb, Nora (1960), Introduction to *Chekhov's Early Stories*, London, Bodley Head.

Chapter 22

On the Diogenes search: outlining a dialectic-systemic approach concerning the functioning of Anthropos and his suprasystems

George A. Vassiliou and Vasso G. Vassiliou

A criterion to establish if the sciences of Anthropos are for Anthropos

In the sciences of Anthropos (= the human being, both male and female, in Greek; a noun whose linguistic etymological origin remains debatable), the so-called social and behavioural sciences, for more than a decade now we have kept relentlessly repeating, while speaking or writing, a common-sense view: it is nonsensical to boast that our technological era will go down in history as the 'nuclear era'. By doing that we simply ignore the fact that if we do not make it the 'anthropological era' there will be, after a nuclear holocaust, no human era to record. Our very effort to develop technology and reach the physical world in which we live, increases the necessity of reaching our world, the world of Anthropos, to the point of being able to arrange it more syntonically to our needs as imposed by the very principles guiding the living systems. This effort, when it receives the impetus and the proportions which are imposed by the present historical circumstances, will open the 'anthropological era'. It is obvious that we talk about the era which will study and assist operationally the real Anthropos and not the idealistic distortions which have been the fictional 'Anthropos' of so many sociophilosophical systems. Needless to say, a bird's-eye view of historical developments is enough to convince any observer with no vested interests to distort his judgment, that idealistic distortions of the conceptualization of Anthropos have not led to any humanistic results, that is, to any results serving the interests of Anthropos and the systems he forms (families, groups, communities, societies).

Quite to the contrary, they have led to historically recorded dehumanizing results of proportions that would often make Mr

Cromagnon – the paleolithic man – blush. The reason is, of course, that Mr Cromagnon was humanized enough to kill only to the extent imposed by his survival needs. He was still so systemically related to the principles guiding the living systems that he had not manufactured the rationalizations – religious, sociopolitical, economic – which would make it 'highly social-patriotic-religious' to eliminate thousands and then millions (and then millions of millions?) of his fellow men.

It is frightening, though, to observe how every theoretical conceptualization or applied technique in the sciences of Anthropos is distorted, often with 'masterful' sophistry and seemingly convincing rationalizations, in such a way as to serve entrenched, vested interests alien and opposite, of course, to the real benefit of Anthropos and his societal, increasingly complex, suprasystems.

Most fortunately, however, there is one infallible criterion which we call the 'Diogenes criterion' in clarifying whether theories and applications in the social sciences are in favour of Anthropos. This criterion could enable everybody to understand the distortions. As everything which has been decisive for humanity's progress, this is also simple:

> If theoretical conceptualizations about Anthropos and the systems he forms for living socially, or if any application or technique stemming from such views, lead to antagonistic-exploitative relations they have at some point of their scientific development diverted from the principles which are operational for the function of living systems.

> If these scientific conceptualizations and the techniques-applications stemming from them have not deviated from these principles, they have to inevitably lead to cooperative-collective relations.

If we follow this principle in the sciences of Anthropos, we will find out that a real dance of stereotypes is taking place. Theories and techniques used in one sociopolitical context are discarded by another, different one, in a 'blanket manner'. However, if one examines these matters on the basis of the above-mentioned criterion, one discovers that it is a matter of developing theories and techniques in a way syntonic to the principles of living systems.

There is no doubt, of course, that theories and techniques based on mechanistic, cause and effect models have to be excluded a priori. The reason is that they are characterized by reductionism and antidialectic analytism, things that totally contradict the systemic nature of

Anthropos and the societal suprasystems he successfully forms (family, groups, communities, societies). Therefore, such theories and techniques serve the *real* Anthropos. They come to supposedly serve a fictionalized Anthropos. But, in actual practice they serve the invested, non-humanitarian, of course, interests that necessitated, in the first place, the fictionalization of the concept of 'Anthropos'.

We call this criterion the 'Diogenes Criterion' because it leads to the Anthropos he was searching for, a fact which he symbolized so dramatically with his famous act: one Attica noon when temples, amphitheatres, statues and olive trees were shimmering under the sun, Diogenes came out in the Agora with a lighted oil lamp! And the startled Athenians — the citizens who considered all outsiders as non-civilised — received the biggest slap in their history, 'for an Anthropos I search', he told them, meaning of course that he was looking for the process which is spiralling to an increasingly organized complexity and which is expressed with the Greek noun, Anthropos.

In this chapter for a 'Memorial volume to S. H. Foulkes' we want to stress the fact that this is also the most essential part of our dearest Michael's legacy to our field, a legacy summarized by his well-known principle that it does not matter what the therapist says or does; what really matters is what he is.

A very hopeful fact for the development of the sciences of Anthropos will be obvious to the reader of this chapter who is already adequately familiar with S. H. Foulkes's conceptualizations.

The approach we describe was developed quite independently in Chicago between 1958 and 1961, at a time when, exposed to systemic conceptualizations, we were totally unfamiliar with group analysis. We knew it only as 'S. H. Foulkes's approach'. This is evidence that the current convergence of views concerning Anthropos is created by no other factor but the very nature of the living process itself.

The approach described, to the extent that it is related to the conceptualizations of S. H. Foulkes, and to a large extent is related to them, has sprung from the same basic assumption, namely, that phenomena can be understood only if viewed as processes — the assumption of the ancient Hellenic philosophy.

Therefore we are bound to present views quite reminiscent of a number of key aspects of group analysis.

To mention a few:

— viewing 'Mental processes' as interacting in the group-as-a-whole (Foulkes, 1974, 1964).

— viewing the primary group of Anthropos (his nuclear family) as 'imbuing and impregnating the individual from his earlier phase of life and even before birth, with the total value system of the culture of which this family is a part', and seeing family relations as reflecting a microculture specific to each family.
— viewing intervention as optimally planned on the basis of this primary group.
— actualizing in group therapy the processes of communication and the communion of 'the commonly held ground'.
— the actualizing of the fact that 'it is impossible to neglect either individual or group'.
— arranging group therapy in full recognition of the fact that the group itself 'enforces' decisive changes in experience and of behaviour in the individual members and brings his defences and reaction formation to the fore.
— the role of the therapist as an agent 'for liberation', the emphasis of his role for value reorientation, novel ways of informationassimilation and problem-solving.
— the concepts of 'foundation matrix', 'dynamic matrix' and 'transpersonal processes during group therapy'.
— viewing analytic activity as a process in the service of the group's communication, 'in the service of the process from symptom to problem and the problem's possible solution', in other words in the service of anotropy (negentropy).
— conceptualizing the 'conductor' as not so much concerned with interpretation but with the uncovering of the unconscious in the here-and-now of the therapeutic situation.

The ground has now been prepared for the presentation of the approach we have developed and apply at the Athenian Institute of Anthropos.

Conceptualizing phenomena in terms of processes

From a wide variety of sciences there is a convergence of views which lead to a conceptual synthesis concerning Anthropos and the context in which he lives (Ashby, 1956, 1960; Bertalanffy, 1968; Buckley, 1967; Gray *et al.*, 1969; Grinker, 1956; Miller, 1965; Spiegel, 1971; Sutherland, 1973). They are views which the sciences of Anthropos are called to actualize, drawing implications for applications. They lead to the conclusion that natural phenomena in general and, more specifically, those related to Anthropos and the context in which he lives cannot be studied, comprehended and lead to operational applications except when they are conceived not statically-mechanistically, but dynamically, as *processes*.

This means that scientific models based on mechanistic, reductionistic theories, models based on linear, cause-and-effect relations, characterized by an antidialectic analytism, are being overcome.

The term 'mechanistic theory' applies to the case of viewing a whole as 'nothing else' but the summation of its parts, as a machine is nothing else but the summation of its parts. This reduction of a whole as to nothing else but the summation of its parts leads to the characterization of this tendency as reductionism. The principle though that characterizes natural developments is that every whole is something more than the mere summation of its parts. This 'something more' has a simple natural explanation. It is a result of (a) varying in each case the arrangement of the parts in the time-space continuum, and (b) the special relations which are developed among them at each instance.

The large number of possible combinations results in the large number of different wholes which could be the outcome of the different combinations of the same parts. We wrote above that the mechanistic-reductionistic viewing of phenomena is characterized by an antidialectic analytism. The reason we used this characterization is because it overlooks the fact that between the elements comprising a whole, multilateral, two-way relations develop that render it impossible for the observer to single out cause or effect.

The mechanistic-reductionistic viewing of phenomena has been replaced by a theoretical stand perceiving them as processes.

A process is a sequence of events which develop continuously in the space-time continuum. If the observer artificially stops the process in order to study the phenomena developing at the time, 'x', then what he observes is not the process of course, but an artefact due to his own intervention. For example: with the projection of a film we observe a sequence of events. In this sense, the film's projection and its viewing becomes to the observer a process. If he stops the camera in order to study statically a certain picture which he has taken at time, 'x', he will observe all the details of that picture but he would lose the process, the dynamic development of the sequence of events which he was following during the projection of the film.

A number of processes, 'dynamic entities', which are interrelated, interdependent and transacting comprise a whole which is termed 'system', characterized by what is called 'organized complexity' (see Figure 22.1 below). The term 'transaction' means that A is in process with B altering it at the same time that it is altered by it.

The simplest model of a system is the following:

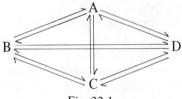

Fig. 22.1

In the above schema, the transacting entities are four. The channels of the multilateral transaction among them are twelve. When the transacting entities are multiples, the channels of transaction among them are multiplied according to the simple formula $CT=E^2-E$, where CT represent the channels of an infinite number of transactions and E the transacting entities. Consequently, the increase in the number of transacting entities is bound to result in an increase of the channels of transactions, multilaterally. This increases the organized complexity of the system. As long as the system is functioning, the transacting entities become differentiated. As a result, additional channels of transaction are established among them, so the system spirals to an increasingly organized complexity, and as a result it undergoes a more synthetic structuring.

This is what is called the process of morphogenesis (= structuring) which proceeds endlessly according to the universal law of anamorphosis (= structuring towards increasingly organized complexity). Thus the system establishes relations characterized by organized complexity within the boundaries of the suprasystem. In this case, the system is functioning, within the boundaries of its suprasystem, and enters into an interrelationship, interdependence and transaction with other systems.

Anthropos as a biopsychosocial system

Consistent with the above is the viewing of Anthropos as a biopsychosocial system. This means that the system Anthropos consists of processes. One could group them, for a general categorization, according to the order in which their organized complexity increases, in biological,

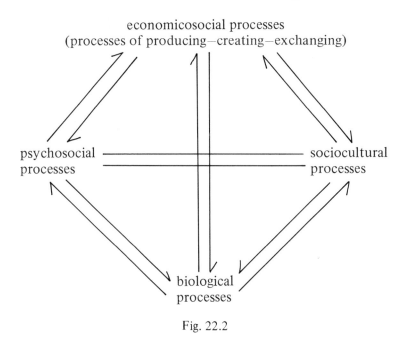

economicosocial processes
(processes of producing–creating–exchanging)

psychosocial processes ——— sociocultural processes

biological processes

Fig. 22.2

psychosocial, sociocultural processes – and the processes with the highest complexity, the economicosocial (see Figure 22.2).

The economicosocial processes within the human context concern the following: on the one hand the prevailing modalities applied by Anthropos for producing and creating, and on the other hand the complex interrelational network which Anthropos is structuring by following these modalities. This interrelational network is necessary for the transactions needed for the sociocultural and economicosocial exchanging of the output of producing and creating. It follows that these economicosocial processes at any point of the time-space continuum play a fundamental role in maintaining, differentiating and morphogenetically developing the increasingly complex suprasystems of Anthropos (groups, communities, societies). Given their fundamental role, if the economicosocial processes remain antagonistic-exploitative, they will induce analogous characteristics in all the other processes of the system with all the consequences leading to malfunctioning.

When, and to the extent that processes are differentiated, that is multiplied, additional channels of transaction are established and maintained. This increases the organized complexity of the system and its overall differentiation.

The psychosocial process is integral in its oneness. The intra- or interpersonal aspects which it occasionally presents are created by the fact that the observer chooses to observe phenomena from different points of the time-space continuum. It is in this manner that the dichotomy between 'intrapersonal' or 'interpersonal' has been quite artificially created. Although this dichotomy does not exist for the process Anthropos it still exists in the minds of many theoreticians dealing with Anthropos.

The fact that the psychosocial process is integral in its oneness makes obvious that 'Anthropos' and 'group member' are two aspects of the same process, that the human being is social and society is human.

The conclusion emerges that there is one condition for differentiation and the spiralling of Anthropos to increasingly organized complexity: to remain inseparably a member of a group which he thus makes his suprasystem. This is due to the fact that differentiation in his cognitive and emotional processes and in his patterns of transaction cannot take place in a vacuum. Equally obvious is that a number of people, by participating in group transaction, render their group a system. They make it their suprasystem, that is, their group, an increasingly organized complexity and differentiation. In other words, humanization is a process which could be accomplished only within the context of a group; by being more humanized they render their groups increasingly humanized. Thus, becoming Anthropos is becoming a group member and vice versa. This renders the notorious 'dilemma' of sacrificing part of one's 'independence' in order to secure some 'belongingness' a sheer absurdity.

The distinction between the psychosocial and sociocultural processes is made for descriptive needs. In essence, both aspects are intrinsically related. Aspects referred to as psychosocial do have, of course, sociocultural dimensions, when examined from another point of view.

Obviously, in order to conceptualize Anthropos, operationally, and to develop the applications needed for his multilateral development, we have to start from the principle that Anthropos, in his psychosocial aspects is a complex dynamic field comprised by the totality of his social relations.

At this point one becomes aware of a consequence: of suprasystems characterized by antagonistic-exploitative relationships. By making the grouping process impossible, they induce the therapist to overlook the fundamental character for Anthropos of the grouping process and to use either individual therapy or to treat a number of people as individuals even in a group, thus overlooking all significant aspects of the grouping process.

By doing this therapists run the risk of leading malfunctioning members of their society towards a conformity to the pattern of social relations characteristic of the social suprasystem.

Conceptualizing operational 'therapy'[1]

At this point the authors feel obliged to note the way in which they conceptualize therapy (therapy = 'service' in Greek). This conceptualization is applied in milieu-specific ways, that is, in ways specific to the perception of social environment (subjective culture) which prevails in the Greek milieu.

But let us first clarify that in antagonistic-exploitative frames, the conformist is doomed to perpetual exploitation. An ex-conformist, turned rebel, is bound to destroy the existing antagonism and exploitation, but he will be unprepared, that is unskilled, for the cooperation which necessarily should follow. Consequently, simply to rebel is not enough and will necessarily lead to entropic processes. On the other hand, in cooperative-collective frames, the conformist becomes a passive recipient, that is, an inactive bystander of team efforts which are task-oriented and problem-solving. For this reason, the authors define the aim of therapy as the development of a creative attitude, an attitude which will enable people to detect and synthetically resolve their own contradictions and the contradictions in their family, in the groups in which they live and work and in their social context.

This requires, of course, the activation of the self-leading processes of people. With their operation, people can form their own values, attitudes, opinions, in short, a personal ideology; a process of structuring an ideology which in their transaction is going to foster, within the boundaries of their collectives, syntonic ideological structuring. This, of course, is bound to enrich the collective elaboration which will ensue. In this way personal and collective aspects of ideological structuring are bound to transact with an increasing differentiation. At this point we should stress as strongly as possible that without forming and following the values which are imposed on Anthropos and his systems by nothing else but the very principles governing their function, no personal or collective-societal functioning can ever be achieved. It is only in this way that anotropic morphogenesis can be secured and safeguarded. Otherwise, entropic developments are bound to permeate Anthropos and his suprasystems. In addition, one should add here that in traditional pre-industrial milieux, whenever the collective, which was the basic unit of that particular society, was confronted with a problem, its members, systematically, interdependent within its boundaries, were obliged, through trial and error attempts, to find a successful solution to the problem. Repeated success would reinforce this solution and would lead to its adaptation as the way to respond in such a situation. The way of acting would gradually become justified (rationalized) and appear as an answer to 'Why do we act in this way?' in the form of traditions-customs expressed in proverbs, myths, stories, fairy-tales, religious systems, etc. The point is, though, that in certain industrialized technologically developed milieux, where the economico-social processes are maintaining an exploitative-antagonistic direction, such abstractions are used in all the Anthropos suprasystems to justify dehumanizing situations in society and in all its subsystems. Lofty ideological constructs are used 'to do the right thing for the wrong reason'. The 'wrong reason' is kept, of course, by a number of manipulating agents and institutions, including mass media, out of the awareness of people. Obviously the creative process mentioned before has to be developed in people living under such conditions. In order to do this, the therapist is called on to undertake a consistent and persistent effort of *demystification* and *demythologization*. Anthropos malfunctions when the structuring of his boundaries, processes which will be discussed below, is interfered with by the influence of a number of idealistic constructs of his social context, which, as we said, do not serve self-leading purposes, but increases his other-directedness.

For instance, in certain malfunctioning families what is meant by 'parental love' and 'care' is a series of transactional patterns covering psychosocial, sociocultural and economicosocial exploitation and antagonism. The therapist, in order to demythologize such patterns, cannot proceed on the basis of metapsychological theories. He cannot simply fight one myth with another. He has to undertake this effort in syntonic ways, compatible and in accordance with the very principles of the living process which determine the functioning of Anthropos.

Systeming versus summing

Concerning the psychosocial process of Anthropos, a creative, constructive in synthesizing the detected contradictions attitude means, of course, an unceasing effort to render both individual and group functioning more differentiated. This is naturally bound to lead people and groups to further systeming. By systeming we mean the process which opens the way for the multi-level dialogue that is required for the unhindered development of the living process within the Anthropos systems (family, group, community, society), based on (1) trust, (2) mutual acceptance and (3) the absence of any tendency to exploit others; this dialogue will proceed through the formation of a clear thesis by one of the participants. This will be followed by the formulation of an antithesis from another. In this way the possibility will be created for other group members to form a synthesis.

This synthesizing eventually is formed by those members of the group who are functioning at any given moment as the motivated nucleus. This synthesis just formulated could be actualized as a more differentiated complex thesis. Thus, other members of the group are stimulated to develop on the basis of it a second antithesis. Through this process group members are naturally led to a process of further differentiation and consequently spiral to levels of more organized complexity. One should keep in mind that the above described process of systeming is the *only* operational outcome of the grouping process. By systeming, group members are trained in the cognitive-emotional and behavioural patterns required by the cooperative, collective, egalitarian patterns of transaction on which the democratic process could finally be developed.

If, on the other hand, the members of the group restrict their dialogue to a mere summing, the above outcome of group transaction cannot possibly occur. In other words, during this summing process each member formulates his own opinion. There is no attempt to consider and evaluate the information offered by the others, in order to assimilate and synthesize it with his own views.

The development of the process of systeming presupposes that each group member enters into the group transaction in a way which will permit him to receive and assimilate information offered by other group members. This requires that the group member, by remaining aware of his emotional and cognitive processes, increases gradually his self-understanding. In this way he learns to define and pursue goals. The most practical result though, is that in this way the group member learns to act on his own initiative and according to behavioural patterns which enhance his relations with others.

With this development, Anthropos could maintain his identity while remaining open to the others for receiving new information. Anthropos has to be selective as to which information he needs to assimilate at every moment in order to achieve further differentiation. The criterion for this selective process is, of course, that the information selected be instrumental to the achievement of his goals. These goals must necessarily remain syntonic to the collective goals of the group if the psychosocial process of Anthropos is not going to be artificially fragmented, thus leading to malfunctioning.

One should clarify here that in the context of the conceptualizations which were presented up to now, the terms 'functioning' and 'malfunctioning' have to be operationally defined. They do not imply any value judgment or any idealistic construct of a 'fictionalized Anthropos'. They simply represent what is operational according to the very principles of living systems. According to these principles, whatever mode of transaction of processes leads each living system, and consequently Anthropos, to an increasingly organized complexity and, therefore, further differentiation, is 'functioning'. It leads to anotropy (negentropy). Similarly, whatever mode of transaction leads a living system to disorganized complexity, reverses its differentiation and therefore introduces entropic developments, 'malfunctioning'. Conclusion: 'functioning' and 'malfunctioning' do not represent, in this sense, any labels of idealistic constructs. They simply represent a positive or negative direction of the process of living.

On the grouping process

The group member who has succeeded in formulating a thesis which he could contribute to the group, can expect with certainty that he will be accepted by the group. The group, in turn, by offering the antithesis will eventually proceed to further differentiation. Obviously, the process of systeming is also the essential aspect of the therapeutic process. When systeming is not developed, the alternative is summing. Expressed in different terms, during summing, people do not transact, that is, they are not in process with each other. Each one of them forms a thesis independently of the other. They may develop it further but they do not modify or alter it on account of the other's thesis. Essentially one is confronted here with two monologues. Mutual exchange and differentiation are inhibited. People proceed in a fragmented, dystonic manner. Malfunctioning starts in both individual and group levels.

During systeming, group members, starting from their original overlapping, will soon develop a central collective theme, the Group

Theme. Group members may have diverse personal views about the theme. They will be able to enter into the dialectic process which enables them to detect, clarify and comprehend these individual variations. From the moment that the central theme and the individual variations are detected, clarified and comprehended, a transaction starts in relation to the central theme and its variations (Figure 22.3). Their dialectic transformation and their spiralling to an increased differentiation will proceed further. In this way an overlapping and a transaction of individual and group goals is established and the sense of *genuine belonging* is established.

Since the group plays such a crucial role within the social suprasystem, two aspects of its function should be examined in more detail given their practical implications.

The first concerns the catalytic-regulatory processes which are required to provide the unhindered development of the grouping process. By leading to an increased cognitive, emotional and behavioural differentiation, this process provides further morphogenesis for all involved. With further morphogenesis, group members develop new modalities of relating and transacting which are more syntonic to the achievement of the goals that they themselves have set for group transactions.

To summarize, group transaction acquires a form which enables the group to increasingly actualize the overt or covert *potential* of its members.

At this point it should be stressed that it is a linguistic trap to talk about the 'group leader'. It is the usual trap of using a noun instead of a verb. What the grouping process requires is, of course, the process of leading. This process is personified and initiated by the syntonizer, the therapist. He is freely selected by the group members. He is thus given a mandate which authorizes him to Catalyze and Regulate (Ca-Re) the group transaction. In order to fulfil his role as the Ca-Re system, he is expected to prevent, arrest or even intervene to actualize negative injunctions and enhance the positive. As can be expected, if he successfully fulfils his role, he might be accused of oppressing those group members who introduce negative injunctions. If he fails, then he might be accused of 'letting down' the positively motivated members. The transaction, which is initiated by the syntonizer, should be such as to include all the other group members who are positively motivated at any given moment. This leads to the conclusion that the leading effectiveness of the syntonizer is directly related to his ability to reactivate the self-leading processes of his group members. In this way every group

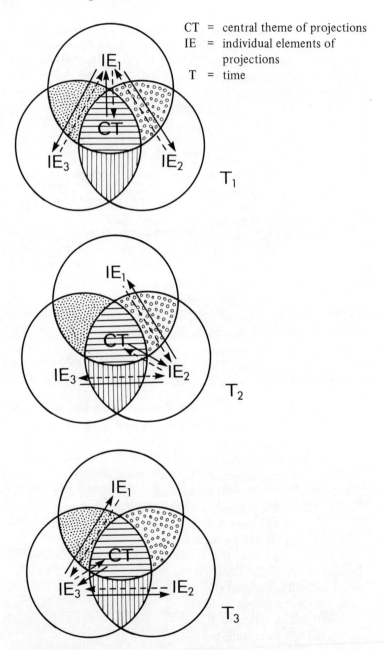

CT = central theme of projections
IE = individual elements of
        projections
T   = time

Figure 22.3 Focus alternation and feedbacks in group transaction

member is trained in developing his catalytic-regulatory processes, to form his identity, set his personal goals in a way syntonic to his collective, thus become a creative synthesizer of contradictions and an effective group participant in his life.

Another crucial aspect for the effective functioning of the group is the existence of clear and well defined operational goals (Vassiliou, 1973). Thus, one of the main tasks of the syntonizer is to initiate the catalytic-regulatory interventions which will be conducive to the formation of these operational goals.

During group transaction, processes transact through the members' boundaries, which have interpersonal and intrapersonal aspects. Consequently their transaction will be regulated or even disturbed by the functional condition of the boundaries.

Concerning the psychosocial aspects of Anthropos, his boundary is conceptual in both its social-interpersonal and intrapersonal aspects of the processes involved in its functioning. The input from inside and outside is perceived and categorized according to the stereotypes, the value orientation, the norms and the roles that the individual maintains. The filtering varies, of course, from member to member. Consequently he will experience his subjective needs, wishes, feelings and recollections, real or imaginary. They are irrational and infantile: therefore they are asocial. They will vary and will create what we are going to describe later as the individual variations of the group theme. The boundary is in a constant flux, it cannot be clearly demarcated in the space-time continuum.

Anthropos in his psychosocial aspects is the outcome of the transacting of a tremendously increased number of processes, transacting in various patterns, in the time-space continuum; consequently the boundary becomes conceptual. Therefore the psychosocial aspects of the boundaries of Anthropos become a function of the total outcome of all the transacting processes involved. The more differentiated these processes are, at any given moment, the more the morphogenesis, the structuring, they provide for the boundaries.

Needless to say, then, that malfunctioning will affect human performance at all levels. Consequently therapy which could be operationally defined as the most effective and fast restoration of functioning, should enable Anthropos to resume the best possible operational role for himself and his collective. It is self-evident, then, that group therapy presents the best therapeutic potential.

In view of the above-described systemic-dialectic conceptualization of Anthropos, his malfunctioning and the restoration of functioning depends on the possibility of the restoration and maintenance of the balance which is vital for the function of the system Anthropos, as for all other living systems: the maintenance of 'openness in organization' and 'organization in openness'. By doing that, while he remains open to receive and process new information, he achieves more differentiated emotions, cognitions and patterns of transaction. If boundary openness, however, prevails disproportionately over boundary organization, entropic processes are bound to develop and Anthropos will enter into psychosocial malfunctioning. If, on the other hand, organization prevails disproportionately, the ensuing rigidity will again introduce entropic processes with the same end result.

Implications for application in group techniques

On the role of the therapist

The 'therapeutic group' is a number of malfunctioning people who, during the group session, are interrelated, interdependent and transacting – in process with each other. Consequently the group is the suprasystem of its members and the group process is the outcome of their transaction.

This systemic nature of the group eliminates the artificial dichotomies and either/or issues, which have been created (a) by linear cause and effect models, and (b) by the circular interaction models which are equally inadequate to describe the total group transaction. To mention a few: dealing with the intrapersonal versus the interpersonal; treating the group vs. treating people in the group; dealing with the 'here-and-now' vs. the 'there-and-then'; focusing on emotional processes vs. cognitive processes; fostering 'insight' vs. 'interaction', etc. Naturally, all aspects of the grouping process have to be dealt with.

The therapist is supposed to collect, with the therapeutic contract – both individual and collective – the real needs of the members as clarified by them with his assistance, their needs concerning problem-solving and differentiation. They want him to clarify, with their help, how this interfered with their lives. Thus, the goals of the group transaction are collectively set. With this accomplished, the therapist is given a mandate by the group members. He is expected (a) to assist them in remaining aware of their goals and of the fact that their wishes are not always compatible with their needs; (b) to become a catalytic-regulatory system, the 'decider system', which will keep their transaction always syntonic to their aims and goals. In order to fulfil the mandate they give him, the therapist has to evaluate the input at each moment as it compares with the achievement of the goals set by the group.

In case, according to the therapist's expertise, this input is not conducive to the fulfilment of their goals at the moment, they expect him to generate indirectly or directly the negative or positive feedbacks indicated for their goal fulfilment.

They expect him to personify and model for them the aspects of their own selves which are aspiring to further differentiation and functioning. In other words, they assign to him this catalytic-regulatory leading role in order to be able to model after him and develop self-leading. Consequently, as we wrote, the leadership effectiveness of the therapist will be directly related to his ability to reactivate their self-leading processes. His role is clearly a self-eliminating one. The more his effectiveness, the less his interventions will be needed, time-, content-, and intensity-wise. The therapist is never alone in his efforts. Different members at different times join in to form with him a positively motivated nucleus which functions in a catalytic-regulatory way. These are members who have developed the cognitive-emotional integration needed or they are only emotionally syntonic and strengthen the Ca-Re system by remaining emotionally tuned with it. What is required of the therapist is to follow consistently the principle of the 'optimal-to-therapy activity'. Be 'active' or 'passive', 'direct' or 'indirect', as indicated, keeping intervention multifocal (from member to member) or multilevel (from individual to group to conceptual systems).

The above make obvious that the therapist should be himself a system spiralling, as uneventfully as possible, to levels of more organized complexity, maintaining the optimum equilibrium of openness in organization and organization in openness concerning the structuring of his boundaries: in short, the therapist who will fulfil the Foulkes axiom we mentioned in the beginning. Only such a therapist would be capable of having an adequate grasp of the directions which the group follows, the development of its morphogenesis, detect the directions which group members want to pursue and/or avoid, judge effectively the required positive or negative feedbacks, time- and content-wise, which the group transaction requires, in order to reach the simultaneously wanted and avoided, that is, the needed. Such a therapist would have the value orientation operational for living and so he would be able to actualize and regulate the self-leading processes of his group members and eventually help them to develop themselves the creative attitude which will enable them to overcome contradictions.

The therapist has to apply predominantly negative feedbacks if group members deviate detrimentally from the group theme and predominantly positive feedbacks if group members tend to stagnate in a narrow area of it. In both cases the therapist's interventions will aim to alter the individual boundaries of each member and consequently of the group as a whole. At times he will have to arrest the development of entropic processes and bring the discussion of a given member or the group-as-a-whole back into the limits of the group theme being discussed. At times he will provoke or challenge the rigid perceptions and assumptions of an individual. The various techniques used provide, of course, various means of doing the above.

Regulating boundaries

During each session the developing processes transact through boundaries that are at times real and at times conceptual. They have interpersonal and intrapersonal aspects. Therefore the transaction of processes will be regulated by the functional condition of the boundaries which are in a constant change in the space-time continuum.

The more differentiated the transacting processes at the moment, the more the structuring of the boundaries. Under the circumstances the growth of the system or its deterioration remains always an open possibility. What will finally determine the one or the other is the maintenance of the balance which is vital for the functioning of all living systems, including the Anthropos systems: namely, to maintain openness in organization and organization in openness.

The members of the group, the therapist included of course, need to maintain their organization while remaining open systems in order to receive new information. At the same time, while open, they have to maintain the organization they need in order to assimilate the acquired new information, proceed to a more differentiated structuring (morphogenesis) and function more effectively. The therapist needs an unchanged agent, a catalyst, in order to maintain, as a psychosocial system, organization in openness and openness in organization. This is his value system which should be operational for creating, producing and transacting. This will help him to remain psychosocially an open system, an agent of progress and synthesis for both science and society. At the same time, it will help him to maintain the organization he needs in order to be an effective therapist. The boundaries of individual members have to be kept optimally open in order to enable him to participate syntonically in the group transaction. Consequently the boundaries of their suprasystem, the group, undergo, at that particular cross-section of time, a structuring which is most conducive to the therapeutic aims and goals of all involved. This constant regulation of boundaries, at all levels, is a function of the Ca-Re system.

Rigidity or chaotic disorganization of boundaries are the two extremes which group members could manifest. All the time though, they are structuring their boundaries in a subjective way, which disturbs the whole process of receiving information. The appraisal of incoming information becomes heavily coloured by self-perception, by static assumptions concerning reality-possibilities and values, by the person's needs and wishes. At the same time, the appraisal of incoming information is distorted by an interfered sense of reality. Therefore the boundaries of the group members do not represent the flux that the boundaries of the functioning person present. However, the therapist has to keep in mind that malfunctioning individuals do not necessarily comprise a malfunctioning group. Then, he has to operate on the realization that whatever improves the functioning of one group member, by enabling him to 'system' with the other members, improves the functioning of the whole group; that is, it increases the organization of the suprasystem's complexity. This in turn increases the organized complexity of each individual member.

Group theme-individual variations-focus alternation-disequilibrium

During group transaction, as we wrote, a group theme is formed in ways which vary according to the technique used by the therapist and which is in our case the synallactic collective image technique (Vassiliou, 1968, 1973, 1974, 1975, 1976, 1977, 1981).

Upon the formation of the group theme the boundaries of the group as a whole and of each of its members enter into a process of structuring. To the extent of the overlapping that is achieved by group members concerning the formation of the group theme, a communality of problems to be solved emerges. To the extent, though, that besides the overlapping, individual variations of the group theme also emerge, the therapist is provided with opportunities to illuminate the individual variations of the group theme by alternating from member to member, as indicated, the focus of group transaction (Figure 22.3). This manoeuvre of 'focus alternation' illustrates aspects of the group theme which have a personal meaning for each member (Vassiliou, G.,

1973; Vassilou, G., and Vassiliou, V. G., 1976).

In this way, all members are helped to achieve further boundary differentiation. Focus alternation offers to the Ca-Re system all the needed concrete means to proceed in an optimal structuring of individual and group boundaries.

The therapist is called to be alert in differentiating homeostatic periods of transaction from periods of detrimental stasis which will inevitably lead to group and individual malfunctioning. Group members need, for a period of time, to maintain homeostatically the level of their transaction between certain limits, limits that are, for them, the most conducive to processing and assimilating the accumulated input. Otherwise they cannot achieve further cognitive and emotional differentiation of the through-put and develop more operational patterns of transaction.

This therapeutic actualization of such a homeostatic period is arrested at times and transaction deteriorates into a stasis. A decline of group and individual functioning follows. Stasis occurs when members realize the non-operational character of their patterns of transaction and the self-defeating vicious circles they initiate by acting on distorted self-assumptions and other perceptions dissonant with the existing reality. Then they develop aimless time-wasting and attention-distracting attempts. The therapist is expected at such times to keep group members aware of the therapeutic contract they have concluded and the mandate they have given him. This is necessary because a decisive intervention is needed. The therapist, in order to preserve the further development of the grouping processes, has to introduce disequilibrium (Vassiliou and Vassiliou, 1976). This is a potent manoeuvre which could prove to be the most therapeutic or quite detrimental. If applied as indicated, this manoeuvre will reactivate self-leading processes, foster further differentiation and promote structuring of the group. The transaction will proceed along the lines of more refined patterns with more differentiated emotions and cognitions. The final outcome is of course the development of more operational goals, norms and attitudes. But, if not, it will result in an increased closedness of both members and group. The therapist, given the above, needs to be aware of what the observable signs are which may guide him. Different techniques provide different signs, of course.

Therapeutic manoeuvres, such as role-playing, confrontations with previously expressed assumptions, stereotypes, role perception, values, etc. could lead this member to experiment with novel ways in his everyday life, due to increased differentiation. Increased differentiation concerning the above will render, of course, the boundaries of this individual more functional and capable of maintaining openness in organization and organization in openness.

Needless to say that during group transaction whatever happens between the therapist and one member influences all other members who are at the moment open to process and assimilate this newly emerged information. The individual variations, that the subject discussed has for them, are bound to illuminate matters when they are cross-explored and examined in a parallel and comparative way. During all this process, the boundaries of individual members remain optimally open. This means that members are able to participate syntonically in group transaction.

A natural consequence of the above is that the boundaries of the group as a suprasystem are led by the Ca-Re system into a structuring which is at that particular time most conducive to the therapeutic aims and goals of both therapist and group members.

Notes

1   In the present chapter we can only present theoretical views in a highly condensed form. The necessary clinical illustrations, if abbreviated, would have resulted in misunderstandings and if adequately extensive, would have largely violated the allocated space. However, they are available in Vassiliou, 1968, 1973, 1975, 1977, 1980, and Vassiliou and Vassiliou, 1974, 1975, 1976, 1981.

References

Ashby, W. R., (1956), *Introduction to Cybernetics*, New York, Wiley.
Ashby, W. R. (1960), *Design for a Brain*, New York.
Bertalanffy, L. V. (1968), *General Systems Theory: Foundation, Development, Applications*, New York, Braziller.
Buckley, W. (1967), *Sociology and Modern Systems Theory*, Englewood Cliffs, N.J., Prentice-Hall.
Foulkes, S. H. (1964), *Therapeutic Group Analysis*, London, Allen & Unwin.
Foulkes, S. H. (1974), *Group Analytic Psychotherapy, Method and Principles*, London, Gordon and Breach.
Gray, W., Duhl F., and Rizzo, N. (1969), *General Systems Theory and Psychiatry*, Boston, Little, Brown.
Grinker, R. (1956), *Towards a Unified Theory of Human Behaviour*, New York Basic Books.
Miller, G. J. (1965), 'Living Systems: Basic Concepts', *Behavioral*

Sciences, vol. 10, no. 3, July.

Spiegel, J. (1971), *Transactions*, New York, Science House.

Sutherland, J. W. (1973), *A General Systems Philosophy for the Social Sciences*, New York, Braziller.

Vassiliou, G. (1968), 'An Introduction to Transactional Group Image Therapy', in *New Directions in Mental Health*, ed. B. F. Riess, Grune and Straton.

Vassiliou, G. (1973), 'Introducing Operational Goals in Group Therapy', in the *World Biennial of Psychiatry and Psychotherapy*, vol. 2, ed. S. Arieti, New York, Basic Books.

Vassiliou, G. (1975), 'Introduction of the Symposium Catalysing-Regulating Processes', in *Group Therapy and Social Environment*, ed. A. Uchtenhagen, R. Battegay and A. Friedmann, Bern, Hans Huber.

Vassiliou, G. (1977), 'Outlining the Synallactic Collective Image Technique as used within a Systemic-Dialectic Approach', AIA *Technical Report XXIV*.

Vassiliou, G. (1980), 'Overcoming Barriers to Communication in Group Therapy with Total Strangers', in *Group and Family Therapy, 1980*, ed. L. Wolberg and M. Aronson, New York, Brunner/Mazel.

Vassiliou, G., and Vassiliou, V. G. (1974), 'On the Synallactic Aspects of the Grouping Process', in *Group Therapy, 1974*, ed. L. Wolberg and M. Aronson, New York, Stratton Intercontinental.

Vassiliou, G. and Vassiliou, V. G. (1975), 'On Methodological Procedures Enhancing the Catalytic-Regulatory Role of the Therapist', in Vassiliou (1975).

Vassiliou, G. and Vassiliou, V. G. (1976), 'Introducing Disequilibrium in Group Therapy', in *Group Therapy, 1976*, ed. L. Wolberg and M. Aronson, New York, Stratton Intercontinental.

Vassiliou, G. and Vassiliou, V. G. (1981), 'Outlining the Synallactic Collective Image Technique as used within a Systemic, Dialectic Approach', in *Living Groups*, ed. James E. Durkin, Brunner/Mazel.

Index

Abercrombie, M.L.A., 1, 7, 9
Abse, W., 3, 23
'acting out', 103-4, 133
Adler, Alfred, 29, 258, 309
adolescents, 2, 319; 'acting out',
    103-4, basic assumption
    groups, 99; dependency
    groups, 99; group therapy for,
    98, 105, 107; lack of persis-
    tence, 100-1; modifying tech-
    niques for, 99, 101; play and,
    99, 100, 102-3, 105-6; refusal
    to attend therapy, 103;
    therapist and, 101, 102, 105,
    107; work versus play, 101-2,
    106
Adorno, Theodor W., 221, 302
aggression, 236, 272
Althusser, I., 255
Altman, I., 303
American Group Psychotherapy
    Association (AGPA), 29, 31,
    76; Task Force, 82, 83-4,
    91, 92
Anthoney, T.R., 235
Anthony, E.J., 61, 207, 318;
    and child analysis, 42, 48,
    52-3; and Michael Foulkes,
    29-33, 44, 53
'anthropological era', 359
anthropological problems, 34
anthropomorphism, 80
Anthropos, 359-61, 369-70;
    biopsychosocial system, 364-7;

boundary openness, 374;
    catalytic-regulatory (Ca-Re)
    processes, 371, 373,
    375, 377, 378, 379; conceptual
    synthesis concerning, 262-3;
    conceptualizing therapy,
    367-8; conceptualization,
    366, 370; 'Diogenes criterion',
    360-1; disequilibrium, 378;
    economicosocial processes,
    365; 'focus alternation', 377-8;
    'group member', 366, 369,
    370-4, 376; group theme,
    370-1, 377; group transactions,
    372, 373, 377, 379; mal-
    functioning, 370, 373, 374;
    morphogenesis, 375, 376;
    processes, 361-3; psychosocial
    process, 366, 368-9, 373,
    376; regulating boundaries,
    376-7; role of therapist, 366-7,
    368, 374-6, 377-8; summing,
    369; suprasystems, 361, 366,
    368; systeming process, 368-70
Anzieu, D., 175
archaeology, 233; architecture,
    241-2; Aryan tribes, 240;
    Cenozoic era, 238; culture,
    244; Denmark, 241-2; Egypt,
    241, 256; evolution of Homo
    Sapiens Sapiens, 237-40;
    Gravettian culture, 239;
    H. Habilis, 238; H.Erectus,
    238; life of early humans,

381

Resolution, 62; follow-up questionnaires, 64, 68-70; group contract, 58; group setting and structure, 61-2; initial interview parameters, 64-5; negative change after, 67, 68, 69; patients' comments, 70-1; patients' life changes, 72; patients' relationship changes, 72; patients' self-selection, 58; positive change, 69-70; post-group ratings, 66; pre-group ratings, 66; prior treatment, 56, 73; recording of sessions, 62; relationships within, 62-3; results of 73-4; selection for, 56, 57-9, 73; symptoms of patients, 59, 60; task of groups, 55-6; termination procedure, 63-4; Tuckerman model of group sequence, 63; unchanged patients, 68; use of Foulkes's model, 62
Group Analytic Society, 2, 4
group association, 269-70
group discussion, 8, 9, 10-11, 13, 14, 15
group dynamics, 85, 270-1
group dynamics movement, 76
group formations: primates, 236-7
group reciprocity counselling, 305
group structure, 237
group teaching, 4-13
groups: abstraction, 162-3, 166; activity, 154, 165; bureaucratic organisation, 160, 161, 162; Carnap language system, 154-5; Chomsky, 155; casuality, 151, 152, 153, 160, 163, 165; communication, 151-2, 154, 156, 158, 160, 161, 162, 163, 165; conscious communication, 155; conventional information theory, 152; creativity, 157-8; depressives, 159, 162, 165; 'entropy', 153-4, 166; formal semantics,

154; free association, 155; genetic information transmission, 152; group as an integrated system, 156; group as a super-organism, 156, 165; group behaviour, 156-7, 158-9; group formation, 160; hierarchy, 160; imagination, 161-2; information, 152, 153, 154, 155, 160-1, 165; informational level structure, 155-6, 159, 160, 161, 162, 165, 166; integration, 157, 159, 160, 165; internal/external reality, 161, 162; learning, 155; meta-level, 154, 155; Model of Man, 156, 161; moral code, 164-5, 166; organisations, 153; physical systems theory, 152; related to scientific theories, 163; schizoid behaviour, 159, 162, 165; symbolism, 163, 166; therapeutic group, 157, 158, 165; unconscious communication, 155; use of model, 165-6
guilt feelings, 19, 23, 24
Guntrip, H., 258

Habermas, J., 293
Haley, Jay, 82
Hamilton anxiety rating scale, 59
Hare, Paul, 303
Hargreaves, Ronald, 203
Harris, Armstrong, 207
Harrison, A., 250
Hart, J., 310
Hartmann, H., 34, 39
Hawkes, J., 234, 241
healing groups, 22
Hegel, Georg, 172
Heigl, F., 124
Henle, M., 308
'here and now' transactions, 38, 117, 179, 183, 186, 278, 314
Herrnstein, R.J., 234, 237, 243, 245
Heyerdahl, Thor, 241
higher education, 3